AP® PSYCHOLOGY PREMIUM PREP

22nd Edition

The Staff of The Princeton Review

PrincetonReview.com

The Princeton Review
110 East 42nd St, 7th Floor
New York, NY 10017

Published in the United States by Penguin Random House LLC,
New York.

ISBN: 978-0-593-51772-7
eBook ISBN: 978-0-593-51773-4
ISSN: 2690-652X

AP is a trademark registered and owned by the College Board,
which is not affiliated with, and does not endorse this product.

The Princeton Review is not affiliated with Princeton University.

The material in this book is up-to-date at the time of publication.
However, changes may have been instituted by the testing body in
the test after this book was published.

If there are any important late-breaking developments, changes, or
corrections to the materials in this book, we will post that information online in the Student Tools. Register your book and check your
Student Tools to see whether there are any updates posted there.

Editor: Aaron Riccio
Production Editors: Sarah Litt and Emily Epstein White
Production Artist: Jennifer Chapman
Content Contributors: Sarah Kass, Anthony Krupp, Christine
            Lindwall, Toni Scorsese

22nd Edition

The Princeton Review Publishing Team
Rob Franek, Editor-in-Chief
David Soto, Senior Director, Data Operations
Stephen Koch, Senior Manager, Data Operations
Deborah Weber, Director of Production
Jason Ullmeyer, Production Design Manager
Jennifer Chapman, Senior Production Artist
Selena Coppock, Director of Editorial
Aaron Riccio, Director, Editorial Admissions Content
Orion McBean, Senior Editor
Meave Shelton, Senior Editor
Chris Chimera, Editor
Patricia Murphy, Editor
Laura Rose, Editor
Isabelle Appleton, Editorial Assistant

Penguin Random House Publishing Team
Tom Russell, VP, Publisher
Alison Stoltzfus, Senior Director, Publishing
Emily Hoffman, Associate Managing Editor
Patty Collins, Executive Director of Production
Mary Ellen Owens, Assistant Director of Production
Alice Rahaeuser, Associate Production Manager
Maggie Gibson, Associate Production Manager
Suzanne Lee, Senior Designer
Eugenia Lo, Publishing Assistant

For customer service, please contact
editorialsupport@review.com,
and be sure to include:

- full title of the book

- ISBN

- page number

Acknowledgments

The Princeton Review would like to give special thanks to Sarah Kass, Anthony Krupp, Christine Lindwall, and Toni Scorsese for their valuable contributions to the latest edition of this book.

Additionally, thank you to Sarah Litt and Emily Epstein White for their time and attention to each page.

Contents

Get More (**Free**) Content
at **PrincetonReview.com/prep**

As easy as 1·2·3

1 Go to PrincetonReview.com/prep or scan the **QR code** and enter the following ISBN for your book: **9780593517727**

2 Answer a few simple questions to set up an exclusive Princeton Review account. *(If you already have one, you can just log in.)*

3 Enjoy access to your **FREE** content!

Once you've registered, you can...

- Access your third, full-length practice AP Psychology Exam, plus an answer key and detailed explanations

- Get our take on any recent or pending updates to the AP Psychology Exam

- Take a full-length practice SAT and/or ACT

- Get valuable advice about the college application process, including tips for writing a great essay and where to apply for financial aid

- If you're still choosing between colleges, use our searchable rankings of *The Best 390 Colleges* to find out more information about your dream school

- Access comprehensive study guides and a variety of printable resources, including: Key Terms lists, score conversion tables for the Practice Tests, and bubble sheets

- Check to see whether there have been any corrections or updates to this edition

---

Need to report a potential **content** issue?

Contact **EditorialSupport@review.com** and include:

- full title of the book
- ISBN
- page number

Need to report a **technical** issue?

Contact **TPRStudentTech@review.com** and provide:

- your full name
- email address used to register the book
- full book title and ISBN
- Operating system (Mac/PC) and browser (Chrome, Firefox, Safari, etc.)

Look For These Icons Throughout The Book

 ONLINE ARTICLES

 PROVEN TECHNIQUES

 APPLIED STRATEGIES

 ONLINE PRACTICE TESTS

Part I
Using This Book to Improve Your AP Score

- Preview: Your Knowledge, Your Expectations
- Your Guide to Using This Book
- How to Begin

PREVIEW: YOUR KNOWLEDGE, YOUR EXPECTATIONS

Your route to a high score on the AP Psychology Exam depends a lot on how you plan to use this book. To help you determine your approach, respond to the following questions.

1. Rate your level of confidence about your knowledge of the content tested by the AP Psychology Exam:

    A.   Very confident—I know it all

    B.   I'm pretty confident, but there are topics for which I could use help

    C.   Not confident—I need quite a bit of support

    D.   I'm not sure

2. Circle your goal score for the AP Psychology Exam:

    5   4   3   2   1   I'm not sure yet

3. What do you expect to learn from this book? Circle all that apply to you.

    A.   A general overview of the test and what to expect

    B.   Strategies for how to approach the test

    C.   The content tested by this exam

    D.   I'm not sure yet

YOUR GUIDE TO USING THIS BOOK

This book is organized to provide as much—or as little—support as you need, so you can use this book in whatever way will be most helpful to improving your score on the AP Psychology Exam.

- The remainder of **Part I** will provide guidance on how to use this book and help you determine your strengths and weaknesses.

- **Part II** of this book contains Practice Test 1, the Diagnostic Answer Key, and answers and explanations for each question. We strongly recommend that you take this test before going any further, in order to realistically determine:

    o   your starting point right now

    o   which question types you're ready for and which you might need to practice

    o   which content topics you are familiar with and which you will want to carefully review; our Diagnostic Answer Key will assist you with this process

Looking for More Help with Your APs?
We now offer specialized AP tutoring and course packages that guarantee a 4 or 5 on the AP. To see which courses are offered and available, and to learn more about the guarantee, visit PrincetonReview.com/college/ap-test-prep.

Once you have nailed down your strengths and weaknesses with regard to this exam, you can focus your test preparation, build a study plan, and be efficient with your time.

- **Part III** of this book will:

  o provide information about the structure, scoring, and content of the AP Psychology Exam

  o help you to make a study plan

  o point you toward additional resources

- **Part IV** of this book will explore various strategies, including the following:

  o how to solve multiple-choice questions

  o how to write effective essays

  o how to manage your time to maximize the number of points available to you

- **Part V** of this book covers background content you may want to know for the AP Psychology Exam.

- **Part VI** of this book covers the content you need for the AP Psychology Exam.

- **Part VII** of this book contains Practice Test 2 and its answers and explanations. If you skipped Practice Test 1, we recommend you give yourself at least a day or two between each test so that you can compare your progress. Additionally, this will help to identify any external issues: if you answer a certain type of question wrong each time, you probably need to review it. If you answered it incorrectly only once, you may have run out of time or been distracted by something. In either case, comparing exams will allow you to focus on the factors that caused the discrepancy in scores and to be as prepared as possible on the day of the test.

Don't Forget!

To take Practice Test 3, be sure to register your book online following the instructions on pages viii–ix. You'll also gain access to a bunch of other helpful Student Tools, including study guides and a list of key terms!

You may choose to use some parts of this book over others, or you may work through the entire book. Your approach will depend on your needs and how much time you have. Let's now look at how to make this determination.

HOW TO BEGIN

1. **Take a Test**

   Before you can decide how to use this book, you need to take a practice test. Doing so will give you insight into your strengths and weaknesses, and the test will also help you make an effective study plan. If you're feeling test-phobic, remind yourself that a practice test is a tool for diagnosing yourself—it's not how well you do that matters but how you use information gleaned from your performance to guide your preparation.

So, before you read further, take Practice Test 1 starting on page 9 of this book. Be sure to do so in one sitting, following the instructions that appear before the test.

2. **Check Your Answers**

   Using the Diagnostic Answer Key on page 45, follow our three-step process to identify your strengths and weaknesses with regard to the tested topics. This will help you determine which content review chapters to prioritize when studying this book. Don't worry about the explanations for now, and don't worry about missed questions. We'll get to that soon.

3. **Reflect on the Test**

   After you take your first test, respond to the following questions:

   • How much time did you spend on the multiple-choice questions?
   • How much time did you spend on each essay?
   • How many multiple-choice questions did you miss?
   • Do you feel you had the knowledge to address the subject matter of the essays?
   • Do you feel you wrote well-organized, thoughtful essays?

4. **Read Part III of This Book and Complete the Self-Evaluation**

   Part III will provide information on how the test is structured and scored. It will also list areas of content that are tested.

As you read Part III, reevaluate your answers to the questions above. At the end of Part III, you will revisit and refine your answers to these questions. You will then be able to make a study plan, based on your needs and time available, that will allow you to use this book most effectively.

5. **Engage with Parts IV, V, and VI as Needed**

   Notice the word *engage*. You'll get more out of this book if you use it intentionally than if you read it passively, hoping for an improved score through osmosis. Strategy chapters in Part IV will help you think about your approach to the question types on this exam. This part opens with a reminder to think about how you approach questions now and then closes with a reflection section asking you to think about how/whether you will change your approach in the future.

   The content chapters in Part VI are designed to provide a review of the content tested on the AP Psychology Exam, including the level of detail you need to know and how the content is tested. You will have the opportunity to assess your proficiency of the content of each chapter through test-appropriate questions and a reflection section.

6. **Take Practice Test 2 and Assess Your Performance**

   Once you feel you have developed the strategies you need and gained the knowledge you lacked, you should take Practice Test 2, which starts on page 293 of this book. You should do so in one sitting, following the instructions at the beginning of the test.

When you are done, check your answers to the multiple-choice sections. See whether a teacher will read your essays and provide feedback.

Once you have taken the test, reflect on what areas you still need to work on, and revisit the chapters in this book that address those deficiencies. Through this type of reflection and engagement, you will continue to improve. Use the rest of your practice tests to measure your progress along the way.

7. **Keep Working**

As we'll discuss in Part III, there are other resources available to you, including a wealth of information on the section of the College Board's AP website called AP Students. You can continue to explore areas that can stand to improve and engage in those areas right up to the day of the test.

Part II
Practice Test 1

- Practice Test 1
- Practice Test 1: Diagnostic Answer Key and Explanations

Practice Test 1

AP® Psychology Exam

SECTION I: Multiple-Choice Questions

DO NOT OPEN THIS EXAM UNTIL YOU ARE TOLD TO DO SO.

DISCLAIMER: The official AP Psychology exam will be administered digitally. Instructions for the digital exam may differ from this practice test.

At a Glance

Total Time
90 minutes
Number of Questions
75
Percent of Total Grade
66.7%

Instructions

Section I of this exam contains 75 multiple-choice questions. Fill in only the ovals for numbers 1 through 75 on your answer sheet.

Indicate all of your answers to the multiple-choice questions on the answer sheet. Give only one answer to each question. If you change an answer, be sure that the previous mark is erased completely. Here is a sample question and answer.

Sample Question   Sample Answer

Omaha is a

(A) state
(B) city
(C) country
(D) continent

Use your time effectively, working as quickly as you can without losing accuracy. Do not spend too much time on any one question. Go on to other questions and come back to the ones you have not answered if you have time. It is not expected that everyone will know the answers to all of the multiple-choice questions.

GO ON TO THE NEXT PAGE.

PSYCHOLOGY
Section I
Time—90 minutes
75 Questions

Directions: Each of the questions below is followed by four answer choices. Select the one that is best in each case.

Questions 1 through 3 refer to the following.

A total of 700 adults between the ages of 55 and 90 were recruited to participate in a chronic pain management study. The pilot data collected included the level of pain participants experienced and self-report inventories on symptoms of depression, anxiety, and sleep habits, as well as social activity measures. The following pain scale was used to assess a baseline level of pain, which was compared to ratings on the self-report inventories.

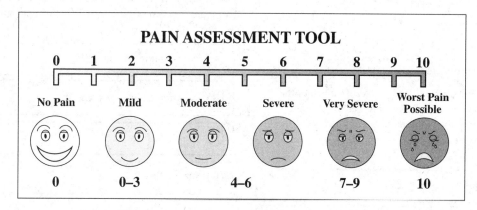

1 ☐ Mark for Review

Which of the following research methodologies was used by the pilot study?

(A) A longitudinal experiment

(B) A correlational analysis

(C) An observational study

(D) A case study

2 ☐ Mark for Review

Why was a rating scale used to gauge participants' pain levels?

(A) Because another person's pain is subjective

(B) Because it serves as an independent variable

(C) Because it serves as a control variable

(D) Because it is the best objective measure of another person's pain

3 ☐ Mark for Review

After the pilot data were collected, the researchers implemented a new pain-management program for these participants. One part of the program teaches participants how to be mindful of their breathing patterns and how to modify those patterns. Which of the following techniques describes this aspect of the program?

(A) Cognitive-behavioral therapy

(B) Rational-emotional therapy

(C) Biofeedback

(D) Hypnosis

GO ON TO THE NEXT PAGE.

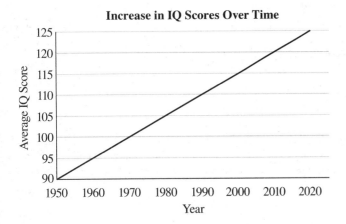

Increase in IQ Scores Over Time

4 Mark for Review

As shown in the graph above, IQ scores across much of the world have generally increased over time due to societal factors, such as higher socioeconomic status and access to better health care and nutrition. Which of the following describes this increase?

Ⓐ The serial-position effect

Ⓑ The Stroop effect

Ⓒ The Flynn effect

Ⓓ The bystander effect

5 Mark for Review

A psychologist places a mouse into a box that delivers periodic electric shocks. The mouse learns to press a lever to stop the shocks whenever they begin. Which of the following processes is responsible for the increased lever pressing behavior?

Ⓐ Positive punishment

Ⓑ Negative punishment

Ⓒ Negative reinforcement

Ⓓ Positive reinforcement

6 Mark for Review

Researchers located at the campus of a major technology company in Silicon Valley wanted to assess employees' attitudes toward the idea of increasing diversity among the company's workforce. So, one day, they stationed themselves at the entrance of the building that houses the web design department, and they selected every fifth person entering the building. The selected people were led down the hall to a private room where they could complete a survey. These subjects were assigned code numbers so that their responses would not be personally identifiable. The researchers are now using their findings to make recommendations to the company's board of directors. What is a possible flaw in this research methodology?

Ⓐ Non-random sampling

Ⓑ Non-representative sampling

Ⓒ Observer bias

Ⓓ Observer effect

7 Mark for Review

Assume that behavioral psychologists have found that there is a strong inverse relationship between the amount of alcohol that first-year college students consume and their grade point averages. Which of the following is the likeliest correlation coefficient produced by this research?

Ⓐ +1.0

Ⓑ −0.2

Ⓒ +0.1

Ⓓ −0.75

GO ON TO THE NEXT PAGE.

Alpha waves	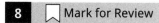
	Awake but unfocused/resting
Beta waves	
	Receiving stimuli or actively thinking
Theta waves	
	Drowsy or sleepy
Delta waves	
	Deep sleep

8 ☐ Mark for Review

Kevin participated in a sleep study for school credit. He spent the night in a laboratory and had his brain waves recorded overnight. The above image represents data from his participation. Which imaging technique was used during the study?

(A) PET

(B) MRI

(C) fMRI

(D) EEG

9 ☐ Mark for Review

A diligent AP Psychology student is attempting to memorize the different parts of the nervous system. The student uses the following strategies to assist in memorization: the method of loci, the peg-word system, and chunking. All of these are examples of which of the following?

(A) Algorithms

(B) Displacement errors

(C) Mnemonic devices

(D) Problem-solving strategies

GO ON TO THE NEXT PAGE.

Questions 10 through 12 refer to the following.

A study was conducted to examine taste preferences among different age groups. The study surveyed 200 participants divided into four age groups: 18–29, 30–44, 45–59, and 60+. Each participant was asked to indicate their preferred taste category: Sweet, Salty, Sour, or Bitter. The results of that study are presented below.

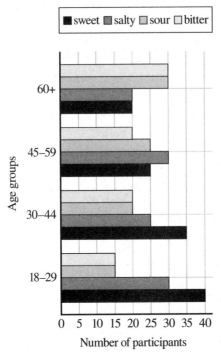

Taste Preferences by Age Group

10 ☐ Mark for Review

What research design did the study above use?

Ⓐ Longitudinal

Ⓑ Cross-sectional

Ⓒ Archival

Ⓓ Naturalistic

11 ☐ Mark for Review

Which of the following is best supported by the data above?

Ⓐ The preference for bitter flavors decreases with age.

Ⓑ The preference for salty flavors is highest among those in the 30–44 age group.

Ⓒ The preference for sweet flavors declines with age.

Ⓓ Those in the 18–29 age group have the highest preference for sour flavors.

GO ON TO THE NEXT PAGE.

12 ☐ Mark for Review

Which age group has the lowest preference for salty flavors?

(A) 18–29

(B) 30–44

(C) 45–59

(D) 60+

13 ☐ Mark for Review

Alex recently took a math and a history exam. He scored well on the math exam and attributed his grade to hard work and his own intelligence level. On the history exam, he did very poorly. Alex blamed that grade on the exam being unfairly difficult and the teacher not explaining the material clearly. What attribution error has Alex made in this example?

(A) The self-serving bias

(B) The actor-observer bias

(C) The fundamental attribution error

(D) The optimism bias

Age-adjusted percentage of adults age 18 and older who practiced yoga in the past 12 months, by sex, age group, race and Hispanic origin, and family income: United States 2022

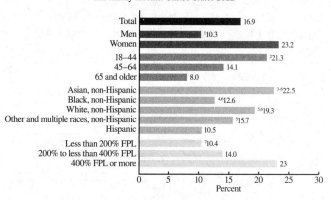

Elgaddal N, Weeks JD. Yoga among adults age 18 and older: United States, 2022. NCHS Data Brief, no 501. Hyattsville, MD: National Center for Health Statistics. 2024.

14 ☐ Mark for Review

The data in the graph represent a yes/no response to the following survey question: "During the past 12 months, did you practice yoga as part of a class or on your own?" Based on these data, which of the following is true?

(A) Women were more than twice as likely as men to practice yoga.

(B) The percentage of adults who practiced yoga increased with increasing age.

(C) Black individuals were more likely to practice yoga than Asian individuals were.

(D) Hispanic individuals were just as likely to practice yoga as white individuals were.

GO ON TO THE NEXT PAGE.

15 ☐ Mark for Review

It has been many years since Cassie first rode on a roller coaster, yet she continues to have vivid memories of that experience. The proximity of which two brain areas would explain that experience?

(A) Frontal lobes and occipital lobes

(B) Amygdala and hippocampus

(C) Broca's area and Wernicke's area

(D) Thalamus and hypothalamus

16 ☐ Mark for Review

Martin is cleaning out a closet. There was something he wanted to grab on a top shelf, but he could not reach it, and he finally gave up. It never occurred to him to use the hook end of an umbrella in the closet to reach this item. He considered the umbrella useful only for keeping rain off one's head. Which of the following cognitive process was occurring in this scenario?

(A) Functional fixedness

(B) The trial-and-error approach

(C) Algorithmic thinking

(D) The availability heuristic

17 ☐ Mark for Review

Of the reflexes found in infants, like rooting, grasping, and the Moro reflex, only the sucking reflex seems to persist beyond infancy. Why might this be the case?

(A) It helps in developing motor skills.

(B) It is essential for maintaining balance.

(C) It is crucial for feeding and nutrition.

(D) It aids in temperature regulation.

18 ☐ Mark for Review

Which of the following scenarios best illustrates the defense mechanism of displacement?

(A) After receiving a poor grade on an exam, a student decides to study harder for the next test.

(B) A woman, frustrated by an argument with her boss, comes home and yells at her children.

(C) A man refuses to acknowledge his own anger and insists he is not upset.

(D) After a stressful day at work, an individual goes for a long run to clear their mind.

GO ON TO THE NEXT PAGE.

Questions 19 through 21 refer to the following.

A researcher aims to investigate whether the color of the walls in a classroom has an impact on the rate of self-injurious behavior among children diagnosed with autism spectrum disorder (ASD). The colors red and yellow will be evaluated by exposing the same children to both classrooms. Before exposing the children to the colored classrooms, baseline data on the rate of self-injurious behavior is collected in a neutral-colored classroom (e.g., white or beige). After exposure to the red classroom, a "washout" period is implemented where the children return to the neutral-colored classroom for a week. Following the "washout" period, the children are introduced to the yellow classroom for the same duration as the red classroom.

19 ☐ Mark for Review

What is the purpose of the "washout" period in this study?

- (A) To collect additional baseline data between conditions
- (B) To allow the children to rest between conditions
- (C) To ensure observed effects are due to the color change only
- (D) To change the classroom layout between color tests

20 ☐ Mark for Review

How does using the same group of children for both the red and yellow classrooms help improve the study?

- (A) It increases the overall sample size of the study.
- (B) It controls for individual differences, ensuring behavior changes are due to the wall color.
- (C) It makes conducting the study much easier overall.
- (D) It reduces the necessity for extensive statistical analysis.

21 ☐ Mark for Review

What type of data will the researcher primarily collect in this study?

- (A) Survey responses from the parents about self-injurious behavior
- (B) Observations of the frequency and intensity of self-injurious behaviors
- (C) Academic performance scores from classroom activities
- (D) Interviews with the children about their experiences

GO ON TO THE NEXT PAGE.

22 ☐ Mark for Review

Participants in an experiment are shown images on a computer screen. Half of the images are neutral, like landscapes, and the other half are potentially fear-inducing images, like spiders or snakes. As participants view the images, researchers monitor participants' physiological responses for heightened arousal, like heart rate and skin conductance, indicating activation of the fear response. After this arousal subsides, researchers detect a return to homeostasis. Which of the following systems was responsible for this return?

(A) Sympathetic

(B) Parasympathetic

(C) Somatic

(D) Limbic

23 ☐ Mark for Review

Scientists found a young woman who had memorized a dictionary and displayed other attributes of a "super memory." They were interested in what factors may have contributed to her amazing abilities. So, they obtained permission to follow her around for a week; during that time, they looked at her daily activities: her diet, her exercise, her sleep habits, her reading habits, her hobbies, and her social and family relationships. Which of the following forms of research were these scientists performing?

(A) Correlational study

(B) Double-blind experiment

(C) Case study

(D) Longitudinal study

24 ☐ Mark for Review

Four stimuli—similar images of a hyena, wolf, fox, and dog—were presented to participants in a study about fear of animals. Participants were classically conditioned in this experiment to be afraid of hyenas. Some of them reacted with the same level of fear to pictures of the other three animals. The researchers in this study were attempting to demonstrate which of the following?

(A) Stimulus discrimination

(B) Stimulus generalization

(C) Spontaneous recovery

(D) Behavioral extinction

GO ON TO THE NEXT PAGE.

25 ☐ Mark for Review

An automobile company buys advertising during football games on television. Its research indicates that most viewers are uninterested and even, sometimes, annoyed because their game is being interrupted. According to the elaboration likelihood model, which of the following is the company's best course of action if it wants to persuade these viewers to buy its cars?

(A) It should use an attractive spokesperson, have the vehicle in an exotic location, like a beach, and play popular music in the background

(B) It should emphasize comparative prices with its competitors' models

(C) It should show its cars being driven by average people in typical, everyday situations

(D) It should explain that viewers must pay close attention because a car purchase may be an individual's next most expensive purchase after their home

26 ☐ Mark for Review

A college student is preparing for final exams. As the exam period approaches, he experiences increasing levels of stress due to the pressure to perform well. At this point, he feels anxious and tense as his body prepares to confront the stressor. As he continues to study, his physiological responses begin to stabilize, and he manages to maintain a sense of equilibrium. However, his stress levels persist for an extended period of time without relief, and he experiences burnout. Which of the following are the most likely effect(s) of chronic, long-term stress?

(A) Flashbacks and nightmares

(B) Phobias related to the stressor

(C) Development of multiple personalities

(D) Greater risk of physical illness

GO ON TO THE NEXT PAGE.

Questions 27 through 29 refer to the following.

As part of a larger study, researchers examined what deficits follow damage to the limbic system; specifically to the amygdala. The researchers asked a participant with amygdalar damage to draw six different emotions, as seen below. The researchers reported the drawing labeled *AFRAID* to be remarkable and pointed to her having neglected to draw an adult face.

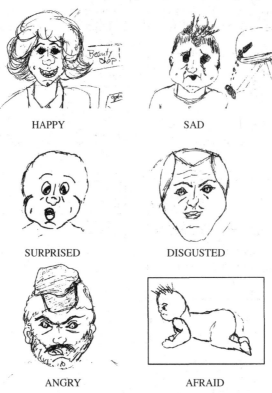

HAPPY   SAD

SURPRISED   DISGUSTED

ANGRY   AFRAID

Adolphs, R.; Tranel, D.; Damasio, H.; Damasio, AR (September 1995). Fear and the human amygdala. *Journal of Neuroscience.* © 1995 by Society for Neuroscience.

---

27 ▢ Mark for Review

In addition to processing emotion, which of the following does the amygdala also mediate?

(A) It processes musical sounds

(B) It controls salivation

(C) It is responsible for voluntary movements

(D) It aids in memory formation

---

28 ▢ Mark for Review

As compared to the other drawings, which of the following does the patient's interpretation of *AFRAID* suggest about damage to the amygdala?

(A) The patient likely no longer recognizes the expression of fear

(B) The patient is now afraid of babies

(C) The patient has difficulty drawing facial expressions

(D) The patient cannot understand certain words

GO ON TO THE NEXT PAGE.

29 ☐ Mark for Review

Emotion is adaptive. Based on the study's findings, how might damage to the amygdala be dangerous for this patient?

(A) She might be at risk for depression.

(B) She might have difficulty with activities of daily living.

(C) She might misinterpret a potential threat and fail to protect herself.

(D) She might be at higher risk for stroke.

30 ☐ Mark for Review

Arty and Joan were discussing historical events such as the Kennedy assassination in the 1960s; the *Challenger* space shuttle explosion in the 1980s; and the World Trade Center attack in 2001. Joan pointed out that each of these very important events created intense emotions. What type of memories are evoked by such events?

(A) Reconstructive memories

(B) Eidetic memories

(C) Flashbulb memories

(D) Proactive memories

31 ☐ Mark for Review

Theories of cognition hold that children develop *schemas*, concepts about objects and ideas in the world around them. They then evaluate those schemas based on information from their daily experiences. Which of the following occurs when children find that this new information could fit into the schemas they have already developed?

(A) Assimilation

(B) Accommodation

(C) Object permanence

(D) Conservation

GO ON TO THE NEXT PAGE.

Condition	Baseline State Anxiety	Follow-up State Anxiety	Baseline Neuroticism	Follow-up Neuroticism
Dosage 1	17	9*	45	43
Dosage 2	20	11*	39	39
Dosage 3	18	9*	40	40
Placebo	21	19	42	40

* signifies a significant difference

32 ☐ Mark for Review

In order to test whether a new anti-anxiety drug is effective, researchers administered different dosage levels or a placebo to 4 groups of participants. All of these participants scored low on the personality trait of emotional stability and on state anxiety at baseline. Their anxiety scores significantly improved for those in all dosage groups (as compared to placebo). What did researchers find regarding emotional stability scores and what might explain this finding?

(A) They significantly increased because personality traits are not stable over the lifespan.

(B) They significantly decreased because the anti-anxiety drug was effective.

(C) They did not change significantly because the anti-anxiety drug was ineffective.

(D) They did not change significantly because anti-anxiety drugs do not significantly alter personality traits.

33 ☐ Mark for Review

A child has difficulty with executive functioning and staying on task. Often, this child also exhibits fidgeting and impulsive behaviors. All of these symptoms and signs are indicative of which mental disorder?

(A) Social anxiety disorder

(B) Attention Deficit Hyperactivity Disorder (ADHD)

(C) Somnambulism

(D) Autism Spectrum Disorder

34 ☐ Mark for Review

Grant has sustained a stroke affecting the left side of his brain. While he can understand what is being said to him, he is unable to produce intelligible speech. What part of Grant's brain was likely damaged?

(A) Wernicke's area

(B) Broca's area

(C) auditory nerve

(D) optic chiasm

GO ON TO THE NEXT PAGE.

Questions 35 through 37 refer to the following.

Dr. Benton was trying to determine whether participants were slower at identifying words from a previously memorized word list if they were under the influence of a decaffeinated beverage as compared to a caffeinated beverage. Immediately after they were given the list of words, participants were asked to drink a beverage. Half of them were given caffeinated coffee, and half were given decaf coffee; they were unaware of which beverage they drank, but did sign a consent form. Next, they performed a distractor task (identifying common images). Finally, they were shown a new list of words and were asked to determine whether each word was old or new (30% of the words were from the previous list). Mean reaction time for both groups is shown below.

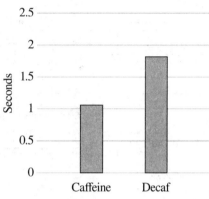

Mean Reaction Time

35 ☐ Mark for Review

What was the average reaction time for participants who drank decaf?

Ⓐ Just over two seconds

Ⓑ Just over one second

Ⓒ Just under two seconds

Ⓓ Just under one second

36 ☐ Mark for Review

What was a potential confounding variable Dr. Benton did not account for, if the only variable of interest in the above experiment was caffeine versus no caffeine?

Ⓐ Giving half the participants caffeine and the other half decaf

Ⓑ Including only 30% of old words on the new list

Ⓒ Not informing participants of which beverage they drank

Ⓓ Introducing a distractor task that might have resulted in interference

37 ☐ Mark for Review

Was it unethical for Dr. Benton to keep each participant unaware of which beverage they drank?

Ⓐ Yes, because participants should never be deceived during research.

Ⓑ No, because participants signed an informed consent form.

Ⓒ Yes, because some participants might have ill effects after ingesting caffeine.

Ⓓ No, because participants are deceived in research all the time.

GO ON TO THE NEXT PAGE.

38 ☐ Mark for Review

Jennifer is expecting a baby. She went to her doctor as soon as she found out she was pregnant and was prescribed prenatal vitamins. The doctor also recommended she avoid certain toxins, like smoking, that might harm her developing fetus. She followed doctor's orders and began taking folic acid, calcium supplements, and vitamins. The one recommendation she did not follow was to quit smoking. Which of the following categories includes nicotine?

Ⓐ A neurotransmitter

Ⓑ A teratogen

Ⓒ A dietary supplement

Ⓓ An antioxidant

39 ☐ Mark for Review

Meta-analytic studies have found qualitative similarities among patients with depression that inform treatment protocols. Commonalities in these patients include selective attention to negative information, self-criticism, rumination, and cognitive distortions. Which of the following might a therapist trained in the cognitive approach focus on?

Ⓐ Difficult events from their childhoods, usually related to sex and/or aggression

Ⓑ Medications that could affect imbalances of neurotransmitters that they were experiencing

Ⓒ Catastrophic assessments of life events and selective perceptions

Ⓓ Getting increased attention from family and friends when they had mood swings

GO ON TO THE NEXT PAGE.

Questions 40 through 42 refer to the following.

Psychology students hypothesized that younger people are more sensitive to comments made on social media than older people are. They decided to study four different age groups of students at their college. They recruited equal numbers of randomly selected participants from each of the following age groups: 18–25, 26–33, 34–41, 42–49. They planted comments, favorable or unfavorable, about the students on social media sites that they know the students followed. They administered a reliable, well-regarded mood inventory at three points in time to the participants in order to see how the participants' moods changed with the comments. The data for these students are presented in the tables below.

Table 1: Mean Sensitivity Ratings for Favorable Comments

Age Group	Measure 1	Measure 2	Measure 3
18–25	8.2	7.8	8.9
26–33	9.5	8.8	9.2
34–41	8.3	7.5	7.2
42–49	9.4	9.7	9.5

Ratings from 1–5 represent unpleasant mood;
6–10 represent pleasant mood

Table 2: Mean Sensitivity Ratings for Unfavorable Comments

Age Group	Measure 1	Measure 2	Measure 3
18–25	4.8	6.7	6.5
26–33	5.2	5.7	5.4
34–41	4.8	4.6	4.2
42–49	6.2	7.2	6.8

Ratings from 1–5 represent unpleasant mood;
6–10 represent pleasant mood

40 ▢ Mark for Review

Which of the following is age considered to be in the study?

(A) An extraneous variable

(B) A dependent variable

(C) An independent variable

(D) An operational variable

41 ▢ Mark for Review

Which of the following is the most problematic limitation of the mood inventory used by these psychology students?

(A) They are only periodically administering it

(B) The participants may fall into the social-desirability bias

(C) Construct validity is low or lacking

(D) The tool is culturally biased against the students

42 ▢ Mark for Review

Based on the descriptive data in the tables, the psychology students' hypothesis was not supported. Which age group responded with the lowest mood ratings for unfavorable comments across all three measures?

(A) 18–25

(B) 26–33

(C) 34–41

(D) 42–49

GO ON TO THE NEXT PAGE.

43 ☐ Mark for Review

The entire brain is used to make and retrieve long-term memories, but there are several deep-seated subcortical structures vital to creating new memories. By what name are these structures collectively described?

- (A) The reticular formation
- (B) The basal ganglia
- (C) The ventricles
- (D) The limbic system

44 ☐ Mark for Review

Marjorie has been struggling to keep up with work, school, and taking care of herself. She started using a day-planner to help her stay organized and keep track of tasks on her to-do list each week. What type of memory was Marjorie trying to enhance?

- (A) Prospective
- (B) Episodic
- (C) Semantic
- (D) Procedural

45 ☐ Mark for Review

Suchi is playing a video game in which visual and auditory inputs from space aliens flash onto the screen very quickly; the player must absorb this information and make immediate strategic decisions. What does this game primarily test?

- (A) Sensory adaptation
- (B) Episodic memory
- (C) Crystallized intelligence
- (D) Fluid intelligence

GO ON TO THE NEXT PAGE.

Questions 46 through 48 refer to the following.

A cognitive psychologist wants to determine how well 25 children diagnosed with ADHD can learn the labels of items when the labels are presented either visually or orally. Each child was exposed to both conditions (visual and oral presentation), with the order of presentation counterbalanced. Five common items were used in each condition. The number of trials required to master the labels in each condition was recorded, and the means were calculated. Descriptive statistics and results are presented below.

Stimulus Presentation Type Used	Sample Mean (number of trials to mastery)	$n =$
Visual	26.5	25
Oral	33.2	25

$t(24) = 4.31$, $p = 0.032$, two-tailed

---

46 ☐ Mark for Review

Why was the order of presentation of the conditions counterbalanced in this study?

(A) To ensure each child received the same treatment

(B) To control for potential order effects and reduce bias

(C) To increase the sample size of the study

(D) To simplify the data analysis process

---

47 ☐ Mark for Review

What was the dependent variable being measured in this study?

(A) The age of the children

(B) The type of items used

(C) The number of trials required to master the labels

(D) The order of the conditions presented

---

48 ☐ Mark for Review

Which of the following symptoms are the participants most likely to demonstrate?

(A) Deficits in adaptive functioning that result in failure to meet developmental and sociocultural standards for personal independence and social responsibility.

(B) Persistent deficits in social communication and social interaction across multiple contexts.

(C) A persistent pattern of inattention and/or impulsivity that interferes with functioning or development.

(D) Difficulties learning and using academic skills, such as inaccurate or slow and effortful word reading.

GO ON TO THE NEXT PAGE.

49 ☐ Mark for Review

Marcia recently suffered a traumatic brain injury. To test what areas of her brain were affected, doctors presented her with visual stimuli. Marcia could not see images presented to her left visual field. Which of the following parts of her brain was likely damaged?

(A) Right parietal lobe

(B) Left parietal lobe

(C) Right occipital lobe

(D) Left occipital lobe

50 ☐ Mark for Review

François needed to get a dozen items from the supermarket. However, when he got there, he discovered that he had left his list at home. In trying to shop from memory, he found that he remembered the items at the beginning of his list and those at the end of the list, but he had made errors on several of the items in the middle. What is the phenomenon that expresses the likelihood of this outcome?

(A) Motivated forgetting

(B) Repression

(C) Anterograde amnesia

(D) Serial position effect

51 ☐ Mark for Review

A young child is asked what he did the previous day, and his response is "I goed to the store with Mommy." Which of the following does this answer represent?

(A) Overgeneralization

(B) Intellectual disability

(C) Reconstructive memory

(D) Linguistic relativity

GO ON TO THE NEXT PAGE.

Questions 52 through 54 refer to the following.

A four-year longitudinal study examined associations between changes in stereotype threat and motivation (self-efficacy, task values, and perceived costs) among 425 undergraduates from racial/ethnic groups typically underrepresented in science, technology, engineering, and mathematics (STEM). Growth analyses indicated that students' stereotype threat and perceived cost of studying science increased during college, whereas science self-efficacy, intrinsic value, and attainment value declined. Parallel growth analyses suggested that higher initial stereotype threat related to a faster decline in attainment value and a faster increase in perceived costs throughout college. Higher initial levels and a steeper increase in stereotype threat related to lower STEM GPA. Higher initial levels and a slower decline in motivation variables related to higher STEM GPA and more completed STEM courses. These findings provide empirical evidence for the relationship between stereotype threat and motivation among underrepresented minority students during a key developmental period.

---

52 ☐ Mark for Review

Which of the following conclusions is supported by the results of the study?

(A) There appears to be a negative correlation between a steep increase in stereotype threat and academic performance.

(B) There appears to be a positive correlation between a steep increase in stereotype threat and academic performance.

(C) There appears to be a weak correlation between attainment value and perceived costs.

(D) There appears to be a strong correlation between attainment value and perceived costs.

---

53 ☐ Mark for Review

Which of the following best illustrates the concept of stereotype threat?

(A) The proctor of a math exam comments that Asian students are likely to do better on the exam than other students. An Asian student ends up with a perfect score.

(B) The proctor of a math exam comments that male students are likely to do better on the exam than other students. A female student ends up with a low score.

(C) The proctor of a math exam comments that Asian students are likely to do better on the exam than other students. A female student ends up with a perfect score.

(D) The proctor of a math exam comments that male students are likely to do better on the exam than other students. An Asian student ends up with a low score.

GO ON TO THE NEXT PAGE.

54 ☐ Mark for Review

Which of the following best illustrates the concept of self-efficacy?

(A) Albert feels good about himself because he was picked to be prom king.

(B) Barbara is confident in her ability to serve as DJ for the prom.

(C) Carlos believes that there is nothing he can do to get a prom date.

(D) Daenerys believes that Albert was just lucky to have been picked to be prom king.

55 ☐ Mark for Review

Which of the following scenarios best illustrates the use of systematic desensitization to treat a specific phobia of driving?

(A) Emily is taken to a busy highway and asked to drive continuously with her therapist in the car until her intense fear of driving diminishes.

(B) John writes his thoughts about driving in a journal in order to see how his thoughts change over time.

(C) Sarah gradually learns to drive by first practicing in a driving simulator, then driving in an empty parking lot, and finally driving on quiet roads.

(D) Mark attends a series of group therapy sessions where participants share their experiences and fears related to driving.

GO ON TO THE NEXT PAGE.

56 ☐ Mark for Review

Janet was recently diagnosed with multiple sclerosis (MS). Her symptoms include, but are not limited to, numbness in her hands and feet, extreme fatigue, and visual disturbances, like color blindness. Which alterations of her brain are likely causing these symptoms?

Ⓐ Lesions to gray matter

Ⓑ Disruptions to neural transmission

Ⓒ Enlarged ventricles

Ⓓ Constricted ventricles

57 ☐ Mark for Review

Ron was the track coach at a very diverse high school. Early on in the team's practices, Ron mentioned that, in his experience, students of Scandinavian heritage did much better in sprints than in distance events. He had students run a variety of races for time. He found that the Scandinavian students were the only group that had worse times for distance events now than they had achieved during tryouts. Which of the following concepts is most relevant to this outcome?

Ⓐ Availability heuristic

Ⓑ Stereotype threat

Ⓒ Self-serving bias

Ⓓ Representativeness heuristic

GO ON TO THE NEXT PAGE.

Questions 58 through 60 refer to the following.

A study was conducted to investigate the existence of critical periods for language development in children. Researchers recruited participants from different age groups: infants, toddlers, children, and teens who had been exposed to a new language for the first time. Each group was exposed to the same new language through immersive and interactive sessions over a period of six months. Researchers assessed the participants' proficiency in the new language using standardized tests that measured vocabulary acquisition, grammatical understanding, and pronunciation skills.

Age Group	English Speakers' Language Proficiency Score	French Speakers' Language Proficiency Score
Infants (0–2 years)	90	92
Toddlers (3–5 years)	75	73
Children (6–11 years)	60	64
Teens (12–17 years)	35	41

58 ☐ Mark for Review

Which of the following can be said of the data in the table above?

(A) Infants have the highest proficiency in learning a new language independent of their native language

(B) Toddlers have the lowest proficiency in learning a new language independent of their native language

(C) Children have the lowest proficiency in learning a new language for French speakers only

(D) Teens have the highest proficiency in learning a new language for English speakers only

59 ☐ Mark for Review

What was the main hypothesis tested in the study on language development?

(A) Language proficiency improves with age.

(B) There is an optimal window during early childhood for language acquisition.

(C) Teenagers are better at learning new languages than infants.

(D) Language development is the same across all age groups.

60 ☐ Mark for Review

The researchers in this study used a quantitative measure to test their hypothesis. Which of the following would have given the researchers qualitative data as well?

(A) Multiple-choice tests assessing participants' understanding of vocabulary, grammar, and language structure

(B) Timed reading comprehension tests evaluating the speed and accuracy with which participants read and understand passages

(C) Parent interviews and home observations of the participants using the new language

(D) Listening comprehension tests assessing participants' ability to understand spoken language through standardized listening tests

GO ON TO THE NEXT PAGE.

61 🔖 Mark for Review

Many psychological disorders tend to occur together ("comorbidity"). People who suffer from panic disorder are often unaware of what brought about their attacks; therefore, they do not know what "triggers" to avoid. This may result in comorbidity with which disorder that causes people to stay at home for fear they will create a scene in public?

(A) Schizotypal disorder

(B) Dependent personality disorder

(C) Generalized anxiety disorder

(D) Agoraphobia

62 🔖 Mark for Review

David has a large, malignant tumor at the junction of his occipital and temporal lobes. His surgeon has determined that the best course of action is to remove cortical tissue at the occipitotemporal border. Which of the following will David likely experience post-operatively?

(A) Night blindness

(B) Prosopagnosia

(C) Aphasia

(D) Ataxia

63 🔖 Mark for Review

Dr. Kotz had shrimp salad for lunch one day but felt nauseated that night. Although the nausea was due to the flu, she felt revulsion for months afterward whenever she saw any shrimp. Which of the following best explains her reaction?

(A) Habituation

(B) Sensitization

(C) Taste aversion

(D) Extinction

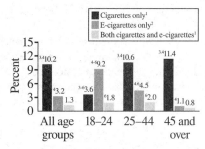

[1]Significant quadratic trend by age ($p < 0.05$).
[2]Significant linear trend by age ($p < 0.05$).

Source for research study:
Kramarow EA, Elgaddal N. Current electronic cigarette use among adults aged 18 and over: United States, 2021. NCHS Data Brief, no 475. Hyattsville, MD: National Center for Health Statistics. 2023.

64 🔖 Mark for Review

The data in the graph represent findings to the survey question: "Do you now use e-cigarettes or other electronic vaping products every day, some days, or not at all?" According to the graph, what is true of those in the 18–24 age group?

(A) They are more likely than adults 45 and over to smoke only cigarettes.

(B) They are less likely than adults between 25–44 to smoke only e-cigarettes.

(C) They are more likely than any other age group to smoke only e-cigarettes.

(D) They are less likely than any other age group to smoke both cigarettes and e-cigarettes.

65 🔖 Mark for Review

Darren has lost vision in one eye due to an accident. He has had to compensate for the loss of binocular vision but can still accurately judge depth and distance. One reason for this is experience. Which of the following is another reason Darren can accurately judge depth and distance?

(A) Retinal disparity

(B) Convergence

(C) Linear perspective

(D) Stereopsis

GO ON TO THE NEXT PAGE.

Questions 66 through 68 refer to the following.

A behavior analyst working in a business wants to study the relationship between intensity of training for its employees and the time required for employees to complete a job-related task. Two levels of employee training are used: low-intensity and high-intensity training. Sixty (60) new employees were randomly selected, and each employee was randomly assigned to one of the two training levels. After the training was complete, the time (in minutes) it took each employee to complete the task was recorded. Descriptive statistics and results are given below.

Training Type Used	Sample Mean (time to complete a job task in min)	$n =$
Low-Intensity	46.9	30
High-Intensity	38.8	30

$t(29) = 5.36$, $p = 0.011$, one-tailed

66 ⬜ Mark for Review

What is the independent variable in the above study?

(A) The number of participants assigned to each condition

(B) The number of minutes it took participants to complete the job task

(C) The intensity of the training each participant received

(D) There is no independent variable in this correlational study

68 ⬜ Mark for Review

Which of the following types of research method best describes this study?

(A) Within-subjects experiment

(B) Between-subjects experiment

(C) Naturalistic study

(D) Observational study

67 ⬜ Mark for Review

Which of the following conclusions is supported by the data?

(A) Intensity of training has no effect on how many minutes it takes employees to complete a job-related task.

(B) Low-intensity training may decrease the number of minutes it takes employees to complete a job-related task

(C) High-intensity training may increase the number of minutes it takes employees to complete a job-related task

(D) High intensity training may decrease the number of minutes it takes to complete a job-related task

GO ON TO THE NEXT PAGE.

69 ☐ Mark for Review

Dr. Klug, an AP Psych teacher, points out to her students that the middle row of standard keyboards shows the letters ASDFGH from left to right, and that these letters can help them remember the universal emotions: A for anger, S for sadness, D for disgust, F for fear, G for surprise (OMG!), and H for happiness. Which of the following concepts is most relevant to this suggestion?

(A) Eidetic memory

(B) Dual coding

(C) Chunking

(D) Mnemonic device

70 ☐ Mark for Review

Robert was involved in a serious boating accident and sustained a neck and head injury. His semicircular canals were affected. Which of the following symptoms will Robert experience as a result of this damage?

(A) A ringing in his ears and deafness

(B) Difficulty speaking

(C) Blindness

(D) Balance issues and vertigo

GO ON TO THE NEXT PAGE.

Questions 71 through 73 refer to the following.

Researchers used functional magnetic resonance imaging to investigate the neural basis of the mere exposure effect in music listening, which links previous exposure to liking. Prior to scanning, participants underwent a learning phase in which exposure to melodies was systematically varied. During scanning, participants rated their liking for each melody and, later, their recognition of them. Participants showed learning effects, better recognizing melodies heard more often. Melodies heard most often were most liked, consistent with the mere exposure effect.

71 ☐ Mark for Review

Brain scans such as the fMRI promote understanding of which of the following?

(A) How different brain waves correspond to different states of consciousness

(B) The current state of the different structures of the brain

(C) How the different structures of the brain work and how the brain functions together as a whole

(D) The level of plasticity of the brain over time

72 ☐ Mark for Review

Damage to which of the following structures would likely have interfered with valid data collection?

(A) The cochlea

(B) The retina

(C) The somatosensory cortex

(D) The olfactory bulb

73 ☐ Mark for Review

Which of the following best illustrates the concept of the mere exposure effect?

(A) Listening to a Mahler symphony, a music critic becomes more attentive upon noticing a quotation from Bach.

(B) A fan of Imogen Heap's "Hide and Seek" is excited to hear a sample from it in Jason Derullo's "Whatcha Say."

(C) A music critic is excited after a first exposure to new music by a living composer.

(D) Someone listening to Imogen Heap's "Hide and Seek" feels exposed because it speaks to them deeply.

GO ON TO THE NEXT PAGE.

74 ☐ Mark for Review

Adam referees high school basketball games. He knows that it is a difficult job and that players, coaches, and spectators are often unfairly critical of the referees. Nevertheless, when he attends his daughter's games, he often yells at the referees. During one such hostile confrontation the referee tells Adam that his behavior is strange in light of the fact that Adam is a referee himself. Adam looks uncomfortable and then says: "If people pay their money for a ticket, they have a right to say whatever they want." What does Adam's response exemplify?

Ⓐ Projection

Ⓑ Denial

Ⓒ Cognitive dissonance

Ⓓ Social facilitation

75 ☐ Mark for Review

A 26-year-old graphic designer recently moved to a vibrant city to pursue her career aspirations. She is outgoing, creative, and values deep connections with others. Despite her busy work schedule, she decides to join a local art collective, where she meets a diverse group of artists who share her passion for creativity. Which of the primary tasks for personality development is she addressing?

Ⓐ Integrity about her life experiences

Ⓑ A meaningful life, thereby avoiding stagnation

Ⓒ Trust in having her needs met by others

Ⓓ Intimate relationships with others

END OF SECTION I

Section II: Free-Response

1 ☐ Mark for Review

Article Analysis Question (AAQ)

Your response to the question should be provided in six parts: A, B, C, D, E, and F.

Write the response to each part of the question in complete sentences. Use appropriate psychological terminology in your response.

Using the source provided, respond to all parts of the question.

(A) Identify the research method used in the study.

(B) State the operational definition of a logical fallacy.

(C) Describe the meaning of the differences in the means for the concept formation task between the stimulus pairing group, the match-to-sample group, and the self-study group.

(D) Identify at least one ethical guideline applied by the researchers.

(E) Explain the extent to which the research findings may or may not be generalizable using specific and relevant evidence from the study.

(F) Explain how at least one of the research findings supports or refutes the researchers' hypothesis that type of instruction a participant is exposed to affects being able to define and identify logical fallacies.

GO ON TO THE NEXT PAGE.

Source

Introduction
Teaching logical reasoning has been of ongoing interest from college faculty. Any explicit instruction tends to occur via required writing skill courses or elective philosophy coursework using self-study materials or lecture. Such strategies, however, may be insufficient to establish critical thinking skills. In this study, researchers examined whether two different types of computer-based instruction would be superior to self-study to teach college students about logical fallacies, which are types of faulty reasoning in which assertions or statements are incorrectly assumed to be true.

Participants
Forty-two undergraduate psychology students from a small private liberal arts university served as participants. They ranged in age from 18 to 30 years. All procedures were approved by the university's institutional review board and adhered to the US Federal Policy for the Protection of Human Subjects. All participants gave their written informed consent prior to the study. Two students were excluded from participation because they achieved 75% or higher on the written pretest; this resulted in 40 participants in total.
A computer randomly assigned participants to three groups. Participants in Group 1 (Matching) received instruction via a computer in which they were required to match a logical fallacy's name to its definition and different examples of the fallacy to its definition by clicking on the words with the computer mouse. Participants in Group 2 (Pairing) received instruction via a computer in which they were required to click on a button reading YES if the fallacy's definition matched its name and whether the fallacy's definition matched different examples of the fallacy. Participants in Group 3 (control group) simply studied a textbook passage containing information about logical fallacies names, definitions, and examples. The sample size of Group 1 was 14 people, the sample size of Group 2 was 13 people, and the sample size of Group 3 was 13 people.

Method
Participants were compensated with course credit and entry into a raffle for a $250 gift card to an online store regardless of how they did in the study. Participants were required to learn four different logical fallacies: ad hominem, circular argument, faulty analogy, and slippery slope. Each fallacy consisted of the definition of the fallacy, its name, and three examples of the fallacy.
Participants in Group 1 (Matching) viewed a logical fallacy's definition at the top of the computer screen and were required to select the correct fallacy name. They also viewed a logical fallacy's definition at the top of the computer screen and were required to select the correct example of the fallacy. Participants received the feedback words "correct" or incorrect" on the screen for their response during each trial and they continued until they scored 100% correct.
Participants in Group 2 (Pairing) received similar instruction except that they selected the word YES on the screen if the fallacy's definition matched its name and YES if the fallacy's definition matched different examples of the fallacy. They selected NO on the screen if the definition and name or definition and example did not belong together.
Participants in Group 3 (control group) were given a text passage containing information about the four logical fallacies including their names, definitions, and examples. They were instructed to study the passage until they believed they had learned the fallacies. They did not receive any feedback during self-study.
Two different tasks were used to measure mastery of logical fallacies in this study: Written and computerized tests were completed before and after instruction for the three groups. The written tests, which were completed using pencil and paper, contained multiple-choice and matching questions about the four fallacies, including novel examples of the fallacies. The computerized test asked participants to match the fallacy names and definitions to novel examples of the fallacies in different combinations. Participants did not receive any feedback on their performance during the written and computer tests.

GO ON TO THE NEXT PAGE.

Results and Discussion

The results showed that both Group 1 (Matching; mean = 94%) and Group 2 (Pairing; mean = 93%) scored significantly higher during the computerized posttests than Group 3 (Self-study; mean = 77%), although there were no significant differences between Group 1 and Group 2. During the written tests, however, all three groups scored moderately (Group 1 Matching; mean = 53%; Group 2 Pairing; mean = 54%; Group 3 Self-study; mean = 48%), but there were no significant differences between the three groups. Participants responded correctly to the novel examples of logical fallacies during the computerized posttests, but they did not generalize to novel examples during the written posttests.

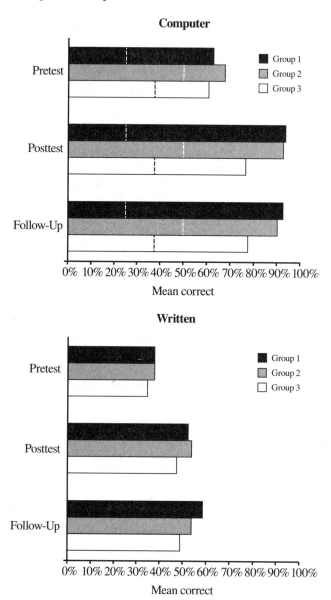

The results showed that both Matching and Stimulus Pairing training procedures were superior to self-study procedures with respect to computerized test outcomes for logical fallacies, but not written test outcomes. In addition, the effects of Matching and Stimulus Pairing were similar to one another on computerized tests and written tests. These results increase the range of procedures that may be used to establish concepts related to logical fallacies.

Adapted from *Behavioral Interventions:*

Gallant, E. E., Reeve, K. F., Reeve, S. A., Vladescu, J. C., & Kisamore, A. N. (2021). Comparing two equivalence-based instruction protocols and self-study for teaching logical fallacies to college students. *Behavioral Interventions, 36*(2), 434–456. https://doi.org/10.1002/bin.1772

GO ON TO THE NEXT PAGE.

2 🔖 Mark for Review

Evidence-Based Question (EBQ)

This question has three parts: Part A, Part B, and Part C. Use the three sources provided to answer all parts of the question.

For Part B and Part C, you must cite the source that you used to answer the question. You can do this in two different ways:

- Parenthetical Citation:
  For example: "...(Source A)"

- Embedded Citation:
  For example: "According to Source A,..."

Write the response to each part of the question in complete sentences. Use appropriate psychological terminology.

Using the sources provided, develop an explanation as to why there are inconsistent findings regarding eye contact among the studies.

(A) Identify a specific and defensible claim based in psychological science that responds to the question.

(B) (i)   Support your claim using at least one piece of specific and relevant evidence from one of the sources.

  (ii) Explain how the evidence from Part B (i) supports your claim using a psychological perspective, theory, concept, or research finding learned in AP Psychology.

(C) (i)   Support your claim using an additional piece of scientific and relevant evidence from a different source than the one that was used in Part B (i).

  (ii) Explain how the evidence from Part C (i) supports your claim using a different psychological perspective, theory, concept, or research finding learned in AP Psychology than the one that was used in Part B (ii).

GO ON TO THE NEXT PAGE.

Source A

Introduction
Attentional biases in social anxiety (SA) were investigated in a study using eye-tracking technology during a real-life social situation. Specifically, researchers wondered if three phenomena typically reported in the literature (hypervigilance, avoidance, and short scanning length of images of faces on a computer) would also be present in participants that were confronted by a real person. Based on the body of literature, the vigilance-avoidance hypothesis suggests that individuals with elevated anxiety are initially hypervigilant for threat but subsequently avoid it, although results from previous studies have varied. In this study, researchers hypothesized those with higher levels of SA would show different eye-gaze patterns than those with lower levels of SA.

Participants
Thirty college students between 18–39 years old ($M = 20.30$, $SD = 3.81$; 8 males) were recruited for the study and received course credit for their participation. Determination of sample size was based on a previous study. All of the participants had either normal vision or had corrected-to-normal vision and all were tested for levels of SA. Every participant signed an informed-consent form.

Method
The participants were each seated alone in a room, equipped with eye-tracking glasses, and were asked to complete measures of state and trait SA. They were told the study focused on visual-search tasks and that their eye movements would be recorded. However, researchers actually sought to observe their eye movements during an unexpected social interaction with a stranger. After the first visual search task ("Where's Wally"), the researcher stepped out of the room, and a male confederate (posing as another participant) entered. The confederate briefly acknowledged the participant in a neutral manner and then sat down to work on his own questionnaires, allowing the researchers to monitor the participant's eye movements in this social interaction.

Results and Discussion
While there was no relationship found between anxiety scores and total amount of time participants looked at the confederate, it was determined that all participants avoided maintained eye-contact with the stranger (similar to the phenomenon that occurs in an elevator). But those with higher SA scores did have shorter fixation times on the confederate's face. Further, those with higher levels of SA explored the environment with fewer fixations and a shorter scanning length of the overall environment, similar to earlier findings. In comparison to previous studies, these participants did not show a hypervigilance pattern in their gaze, suggesting they preferred to avoid sustained social interaction with a live person.

Adapted from *PLoS ONE.*

Konovalova I., Antolin J.V., Bolderston H., Gregory N.J. (2021). Adults with higher social anxiety show avoidant gaze behaviour in a real-world setting: A mobile eye tracking study. *PLoS ONE 16*(10): e0259007. https://doi.org/10.1371/journal.pone.0259007

GO ON TO THE NEXT PAGE.

Source B

Introduction

People with social anxiety disorder (SAD) tend to show attentional biases (e.g., hypervigilance, avoidance, and fixation on stimuli). Most studies evaluate these biases in participants by using static stimuli of different emotional valences (e.g., happy, angry, threatening, neutral). This study tracked eye movements and gaze-following behaviors with a more dynamic model using neutral stimuli.

Participants

The researchers recruited 105 participants, but excluded those that did not meet criteria for either high or low SAD traits. The final analysis included 27 people with high social anxiety traits (HSA) and 25 with low social anxiety traits (LSA). Forty-eight of the participants were females. All participants received course credit for their participation. Each participant provided signed, informed-consent form.

Method

Participants watched a video with no soundtrack while they were seated in front of an eye-tracking apparatus. They were only told to watch the video in its entirety. The two actors in the video were female. The women in the clip sat in a waiting room, maintained neutral expressions, and predominantly ignored each other while focusing on their cell phones or magazines in the room. They interacted with each other briefly on only two occasions. The actors did shift their gaze five separate times toward items their periphery, or in anticipation of an upcoming event. While participants watched, researchers measured fixation times on the actors' faces, latency to fixate, and gaze-following behavior.

Results and Discussion

During the first two seconds of the video, participants with HSA focused more on the actors than those with LSA and had shorter initial fixations on the actors' faces. This fixation was defined by the researchers as "dwell time" (Figure 1) and suggests that people with higher levels of anxiety in a social setting have an initial bias on faces while inspecting a scene. The researchers, however, found no additional differences between groups for eye movements or gaze behaviors. They also found no support for avoidance behaviors, but attribute that, in part, to the neutrality of the actors' facial expressions.

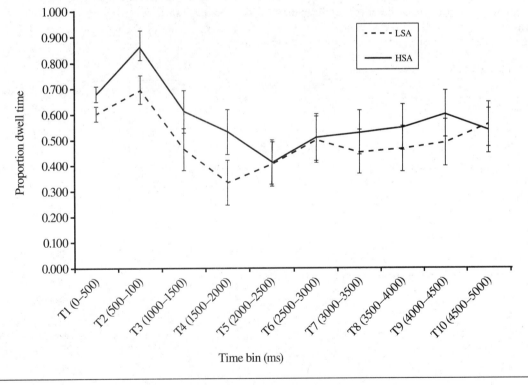

Adapted from *Cognition and Emotion*.

Gregory, N.J., Bolderston, H. & Antolin, J.V. (2018). Attention to faces and gaze-following in social anxiety: preliminary evidence from a naturalistic eye-tracking investigation, *Cognition and Emotion*, DOI: https://doi.org/10.1080/02699931.2018.1519497

GO ON TO THE NEXT PAGE.

Source C

Introduction
Research has established that people who are highly anxious tend to maintain anxious symptoms for many reasons, including enjoying less meaningful social interactions by avoiding eye contact. The current study investigated trait social and state anxiety, eye-contact avoidance, and self-perception on performance in a live conversation to determine the relationships among these.
Participants
Female undergraduate psychology students were pre-screened for their social anxiety disorder (SAD) scores to become eligible to participate in this study. Twenty women were selected for the sample (M=19.15 years of age, SD=1.35); 90% were white. The sample was evenly distributed on the SAD scale and all of them received course credit for their participation.
Method
Participants were measured on several scales of anxiety (e.g., social phobia, social anxiety, social interaction anxiety, and subjective discomfort). They were told they were contributing to a study looking at webcam interactions (i.e., how people feel & behave). They were also told they'd be conversing for four minutes with another participant via webcam, who was actually a confederate. There were 13 confederates in the study, all of whom were females.
Participants completed a pre-interaction discomfort level questionnaire, then the web interaction with the confederate began. While they were interacting with the confederate, researchers covertly took three eye movement measures, including total time of eye contact with confederate ("Lookzone"), fixation on confederate, and fixation duration. Participants were asked to assess their discomfort level again post-interaction as well as to complete a self-evaluation on their performance during the conversation.
Results and Discussion
Researchers tested two hypotheses. First, they predicted time in the Lookzone, average fixations, and duration of fixations would be negatively correlated with trait social anxiety scores. Second, they expected there would be more social anxiety and worse self-evaluation interaction performance scores associated with reduced time in the Lookzone.
Among the results, researchers found that participants with high social anxiety scores do report more discomfort in social settings. They also noted that these participants negatively evaluate their performance after an event has occurred. Both of these findings are in line with previous research. On the other hand, this study showed that eye-contact behavior is not significantly correlated with low performance self-assessment or social anxiety post interaction.

Table 1. Bivariate correlations among study measures ($n = 20$).

	1.	2.	3.	4.	5.	6.	*M*(SD)[b]
1. Trait Social Anxiety (LSAS)	1						39.25(23.04)
2. Pre-Task State Anxiety (Pre-SUDS)	.57	1					17.40(18.20)
3. Post-Task State Anxiety (Post-SUDS)	.50	.19	1				18.78(20.76)
4. Post-Task Perception of Interaction Performance (PIP)[a]	.55	.38	.54	1			24.70(10.35)
5. Average Total Time in Lookzone (seconds)	−.51	−.24	.01	−.06	1		1.05(1.38)
6. Average Number of Eye Fixations	−.56	−.26	−.003	−.13	.98	1	2.49(3.65)
7. Average Total Fixation Duration (seconds)	−.53	−.23	.01	−.09	.99	.99	0.88(1.27)

[a]*Higher scores indicate poorer self-perceived performance.*
[b]*Means and standard deviations before measures were transformed.*

Adapted from *Cognitive Behaviour Therapy.*

Howell, A.N., Zibulsky, D.A., Srivastav, A., & Weeks, J.W. (2016). Relations among social anxiety, eye contact avoidance, state anxiety, and perception of interaction performance during a live conversation. *Cognitive Behaviour Therapy, 45*(2), 111-122, DOI: http://dx.doi.org/10.1080/16506073.2015.1111932

WHEN YOU ARE FINISHED WRITING, CHECK YOUR WORK ON SECTION II IF TIME PERMITS.

STOP
END OF EXAM

Practice Test 1: Diagnostic Answer Key and Explanations

PRACTICE TEST 1: DIAGNOSTIC ANSWER KEY

Let's take a look at how you did on Practice Test 1. Follow the three-step process in the Diagnostic Answer Key below and go read the explanations for any questions you got wrong or you struggled with but got correct. Once you finish working through the answer key and the explanations, go to the next chapter to make your study plan.

STEP 1 >> **Check your answers and mark any correct answers with a ✔ in the appropriate column.**

Section I: Multiple Choice						
Q #	Ans.	✔	Unit	Q #	Ans.	✔	Unit
1	B		1, Biological Bases of Behavior (Chapter 7)	21	B		5, Mental and Physical Health (Chapter 11)
2	A		1, Biological Bases of Behavior (Chapter 7)	22	B		1, Biological Bases of Behavior (Chapter 7)
3	C		1, Biological Bases of Behavior (Chapter 7)	23	C		2, Cognition (Chapter 8)
4	C		2, Cognition (Chapter 8)	24	B		3, Development and Learning (Chapter 9)
5	C		3, Development and Learning (Chapter 9)	25	A		4, Social Psychology and Personality (Chapter 10)
6	B		4, Social Psychology and Personality (Chapter 10)	26	D		5, Mental and Physical Health (Chapter 11)
7	D		5, Mental and Physical Health (Chapter 11)	27	D		1, Biological Bases of Behavior (Chapter 7)
8	D		1, Biological Bases of Behavior (Chapter 7)	28	A		1, Biological Bases of Behavior (Chapter 7)
9	C		2, Cognition (Chapter 8)	29	C		1, Biological Bases of Behavior (Chapter 7)
10	B		3, Development and Learning (Chapter 9)	30	C		2, Cognition (Chapter 8)
11	C		3, Development and Learning (Chapter 9)	31	A		3, Development and Learning (Chapter 9)
12	D		3, Development and Learning (Chapter 9)	32	D		4, Social Psychology and Personality (Chapter 10)
13	A		4, Social Psychology and Personality (Chapter 10)	33	B		5, Mental and Physical Health (Chapter 11)
14	A		5, Mental and Physical Health (Chapter 11)	34	B		1, Biological Bases of Behavior (Chapter 7)
15	B		1, Biological Bases of Behavior (Chapter 7)	35	C		2, Cognition (Chapter 8)
16	A		2, Cognition (Chapter 8)	36	D		2, Cognition (Chapter 8)
17	C		3, Development and Learning (Chapter 9)	37	B		2, Cognition (Chapter 8)
18	B		4, Social Psychology and Personality (Chapter 10)	38	B		3, Development and Learning (Chapter 9)
19	C		5, Mental and Physical Health (Chapter 11)	39	C		5, Mental and Physical Health (Chapter 11)
20	B		5, Mental and Physical Health (Chapter 11)	40	C		4, Social Psychology and Personality (Chapter 10)

Section I: Multiple Choice (Continued)

Q #	Ans.	✔	Unit	Q #	Ans.	✔	Unit
41	B		4, Social Psychology and Personality (Chapter 10)	59	B		3, Development and Learning (Chapter 9)
42	C		4, Social Psychology and Personality (Chapter 10)	60	C		3, Development and Learning (Chapter 9)
43	D		1, Biological Bases of Behavior (Chapter 7)	61	D		5, Mental and Physical Health (Chapter 11)
44	A		2, Cognition (Chapter 8)	62	B		1, Biological Bases of Behavior (Chapter 7)
45	D		3, Development and Learning (Chapter 9)	63	C		3, Development and Learning (Chapter 9)
46	B		5, Mental and Physical Health (Chapter 11)	64	B		5, Mental and Physical Health (Chapter 11)
47	C		5, Mental and Physical Health (Chapter 11)	65	C		2, Cognition (Chapter 8)
48	C		5, Mental and Physical Health (Chapter 11)	66	C		4, Social Psychology and Personality (Chapter 10)
49	C		1, Biological Bases of Behavior (Chapter 7)	67	A		4, Social Psychology and Personality (Chapter 10)
50	D		2, Cognition (Chapter 8)	68	B		4, Social Psychology and Personality (Chapter 10)
51	A		3, Development and Learning (Chapter 9)	69	D		5, Mental and Physical Health (Chapter 11)
52	A		4, Social Psychology and Personality (Chapter 10)	70	D		1, Biological Bases of Behavior (Chapter 7)
53	B		4, Social Psychology and Personality (Chapter 10)	71	C		2, Cognition (Chapter 8)
54	B		4, Social Psychology and Personality (Chapter 10)	72	A		2, Cognition (Chapter 8)
55	C		5, Mental and Physical Health (Chapter 11)	73	B		2, Cognition (Chapter 8)
56	B		1, Biological Bases of Behavior (Chapter 7)	74	C		4, Social Psychology and Personality (Chapter 10)
57	B		2, Cognition (Chapter 8)	75	D		3, Development and Learning (Chapter 9)
58	A		3, Development and Learning (Chapter 9)				

Section II: Free Response

Q #	Ans.	✔	Unit
1	See Explanation		2, Cognition (Chapter 8)
2	See Explanation		4, Social Psychology and Personality (Chapter 10)

 **STEP 2 »** Tally your correct answers from Step 1 by unit. For each unit, write the number of correct answers in the appropriate box. Then, divide your correct answers by the number of total questions (which we've provided) to get your percent correct.

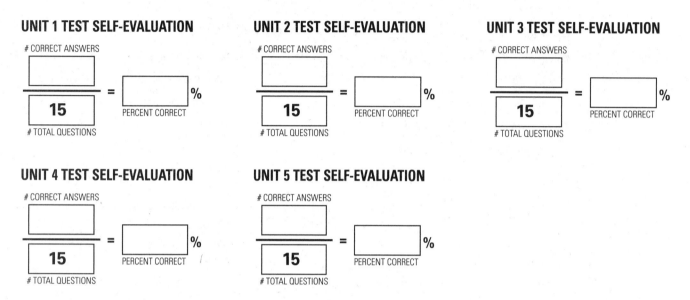

UNIT 1 TEST SELF-EVALUATION

CORRECT ANSWERS

$$\frac{}{15} = \boxed{} \%$$

TOTAL QUESTIONS   PERCENT CORRECT

UNIT 2 TEST SELF-EVALUATION

CORRECT ANSWERS

$$\frac{}{15} = \boxed{} \%$$

TOTAL QUESTIONS   PERCENT CORRECT

UNIT 3 TEST SELF-EVALUATION

CORRECT ANSWERS

$$\frac{}{15} = \boxed{} \%$$

TOTAL QUESTIONS   PERCENT CORRECT

UNIT 4 TEST SELF-EVALUATION

CORRECT ANSWERS

$$\frac{}{15} = \boxed{} \%$$

TOTAL QUESTIONS   PERCENT CORRECT

UNIT 5 TEST SELF-EVALUATION

CORRECT ANSWERS

$$\frac{}{15} = \boxed{} \%$$

TOTAL QUESTIONS   PERCENT CORRECT

 **STEP 3 »** Use the results above to customize your study plan. You may want to start with, or give more attention to, the units with the lowest percents correct.

PRACTICE TEST 1: ANSWERS AND EXPLANATIONS

Section I: Multiple Choice

1. **B** *Understand the Question/Key Words*: The key concept is to compare methodologies. *Predict the Answer*: Choice (B), correlational analysis, because baseline levels are simply being compared to the other quantitative ratings; nothing was manipulated (ruling out an experiment). Eliminate (A), which refers to a study done over time. Eliminate (C) and (D) because both of these use primarily qualitative data.

2. **A** *Understand the Question/Key Words*: The key words are *rating scale*. *Predict the Answer*: A scale is used to measure something, like pain, which is subjective, (A). That is why the participant will report their pain, as it is impossible to measure someone else's pain; eliminate (D) on this basis. Eliminate (B), because an independent variable is manipulated, not measured. Eliminate (C) because a control variable is held constant in an experiment to avoid confounds, which affect interpretation of results.

3. **C** *Understand the Question/Key Words*: The key language is that participants will attend to a physiological pattern (i.e., breathing patterns) and then adjust that pattern. This question seeks the name for such a procedure. Go ahead and use POE. Eliminate (A) and (B) because they address cognitive and emotional behaviors, not physiological ones. While hypnosis, (D), might have the same effect as biofeedback, hypnosis is performed by a practitioner, whereas biofeedback is executed by the individual. Therefore, (C) is the correct choice.

4. **C** *Understand the Question/Key Words*: The key concept provided is that increases in a variety of factors that improve quality of life seem to be related to an increase in IQ scores. Use POE to answer this question. Eliminate (A), which describes how well a person recalls words on a word list. Eliminate (B), which describes the inability to perform a neuropsychological task that requires participants to avoid the urge to read color words printed in a different color ink (e.g., the word "red" printed in green ink). Eliminate (D), which represents the phenomenon of ignoring a person in need of aid in the presence of other people. Choice (C) is correct.

5. **C** *Understand the Question/Key Words*: The key language is *learns to press a lever to stop the shocks*. *Predict the Answer*: Choice (C), negative reinforcement. You can use POE to confirm. Punishment involves producing less of a behavior; here, more of a behavior (lever pressing) is being produced, so eliminate (A) and (B). While this is reinforcement, nothing is being added for the mouse's benefit; rather, an aversive stimulus (the shock) is being removed. So, eliminate (D). Shaping involves rewarding successive approximations of a goal. Choice (C) is the correct answer.

6. **B**   *Understand the Question/Key Words:* The key words are *the building that houses the web design department* and *flaw*. *Predict the Answer*: Choice (B), non-representative sampling. Researchers are not sampling from the entire company. Web designers could have different attitudes than other employees. They may, for example, present a different gender mix than other departments. You can also use POE to find the right answer. If the flaw is not immediately apparent, consider your options. Eliminate (A) because the sampling was done randomly ("every fifth person"). Eliminate (C) because this is not an observational study and the researchers are interpreting the subjects' responses. Eliminate (D) because the subjects are not being observed as they respond to the survey.

7. **D**   *Understand the Question/Key Words*: The key words are *correlation coefficient* and *inverse*. *Predict the Answer*: Correlation coefficients range from –1.0 to 1.0, with a negative sign indicating an inverse relationship, such as the one described here. Use POE to eliminate (A) and (C) because they describe a positive relationship. Choice (B) would reflect a weak inverse relationship. Choice (D) is the correct answer.

8. **D**   *Understand the Question/Key Words*: The question is providing a visual stimulus of brain wave activity. *Predict the Answer*: Brain waves are collected by EEG, so (D) is correct. PET, MRI, and fMRI would show images or either brain activity or anatomy. Eliminate (A), (B), and (C).

9. **C**   *Understand the Question/Key Words*: The key words are the *method of loci, the peg-word system,* and *chunking*. *Predict the Answer*: Mnemonic devices, (C), are strategies designed to improve memory for information, which would assist in memorization.

10. **B**   *Understand the Question/Key Words*: The key concept presented in the passage was that four different age groups participated at the same time. *Predict the Answer:* Cross-sectional, (B), is the correct response. Choice (A) represents a study conducted over lengthy periods of time. Eliminate it. Choice (C) refers to a more complex research design (two or more groups of different ages compared over lengthy periods). Eliminate it. A retrospective study (D) is a type of observational study that uses existing data to answer clinical questions. Eliminate (D).

11. **C**   *Understand the Question/Key Words*: The key words are *best supported* and *data above*. Use the bar graph provided to do POE on this question. The only true statement was that preference for sweet flavors declines with age, (C). The preference for bitter flavors increases with age, so eliminate (A). The preference for salty flavors is not highest among the 30–44 age group, (B), nor does the 18–29 age group have the highest preference for sour flavors (D). Eliminate (B) and (D).

12. **D**   *Understand the Question/Key Words*: The key words are *lowest preference* and *salty flavors*. Again, use the bar graph to rule out the incorrect responses: (A), (B), and (C). The lowest preference for salty flavors, according to the graph, is participants 60 and older; (D) is the correct choice.

13. **A**   *Understand the Question/Key Words:* The key concepts are that Alex attributed his success to his work and intelligence, but his failure on other factors. *Predict the Answer:* The tendency to attribute our successes to internal, personal factors and our failures to external factors is referred to as the self-serving bias. Choice (A) is correct.

14. **A**   *Understand the Question/Key Words*: The bar graph provides data on yoga practices. Use POE. According to the graph, women were more than twice as likely to practice yoga than men were. Choice (A) is correct.

15. **B**   *Understand the Question/Key Words*: The key words here are *roller coaster, vivid memories, brain,* and *proximity*. The question is seeking what it is about brain structure that would make recall of an arousing event more likely. *Predict the Answer*: Anytime that you see "memory" and "brain" together you should be thinking about the hippocampus, which is found only in (B). If you didn't remember that, you can also use POE. Eliminate (C) because these areas deal with language. Eliminate (D): though the hypothalamus is part of the limbic system, it is not related to memory. Eliminate (A): though the lobes contain parts of the association cortex, and thus are related to memory, the frontal lobes are not specifically related to arousal. It is significant that the amygdala is the "fear center" of the brain.

16. **A**   *Understand the Question/Key Words*: The key language is *It never occurred to him to use the hook end of an umbrella*. *Predict the Answer*: You are looking for a barrier to effective problem-solving that involves objects. Use POE. Choices (B), (C), and (D) refer to other problem-solving strategies or issues. Only (A) refers to the barrier to effective problem-solving that involves the inability to see any but the most common possible uses for an object.

17. **C**   *Understand the Question/Key Words*: The key terms are *sucking reflex* and *persists beyond infancy*. Use POE here. Choices (A), (B), and (D) are all unrelated to the sucking reflex; eliminate all of these. Answer (C) is most relevant for feeding and nutrition.

18. **B**   *Understand the Question/Key Words:* The key words are *defense mechanism of displacement*. *Predict the Answer*: Answer (B) describes a person who redirects their emotional reaction from the rightful recipient onto another person or object.

19. **C**   *Understand the Question/Key Words*: The key words are *purpose* and *"washout" period*. *Predict the Answer*: If the "washout" color was meant to control for confounds, then it will also help researchers ensure the observed effects in behavior are due to color change only. Choice (C) is correct.

20. **B**   *Understand the Question/Key Words*: The key language indicates the study is improved by conducting a within-subjects experiment. *Predict the Answer:* Using the same group of participants for all conditions of an experiment controls for individual differences. This ensures any behavioral changes are due only to wall color; (B) is the correct response.

21. **B**   *Understand the Question/Key Words*: The concept tested is what *type of data* was collected. Go for POE here. Eliminate (A) and (D) as these both are self-report data. Choice (C) is not relevant to the research question. Choice (B) best reflects the type of data collected by the researchers.

22. **B** *Understand the Question/Key Words*: The key concepts are *fight-or-flight* and *homeostasis*. Go ahead and use POE. Choice (A) is synonymous with the fight-or-flight arousal response and thus incorrect. Choices (C) and (D) involve balance and emotion, respectively, and do not involve achieving homeostasis. Choice (B) is correct because, after sympathetic activation, it is the parasympathetic system that brings us back to homeostasis.

23. **C** *Understand the Question/Key Words*: The key language indicates that the researchers were taking an in-depth look at one unusual subject. Use POE to eliminate (A) because a correlational study would require many more subjects in order to establish a relationship between variables. Eliminate (B) because this is not an experiment. Eliminate (D) because this study was not conducted at multiple points in time. Choice (C) is correct because a case study takes a detailed look at an unusual subject or situation.

24. **B** *Understand the Question/Key Words*: The key phrases are *similar images* and *reacted with the same level of fear*. When participants respond to stimuli that are similar to the original conditioned stimulus, it is referred to as generalization (B). Eliminate (A), as this reaction is the opposite of generalization. Spontaneous recovery occurs when a response reappears after it's been extinguished; eliminate (C). Eliminate (D), as extinction is what happens when a conditioned response ceases.

25. **A** *Understand the Question/Key Words*: The key words are *most viewers are uninterested* and *elaboration likelihood model*. *Predict the Answer*: The elaboration likelihood model suggests that, if the target audience is not engaged in the subject matter, persuasion should be pursued via the peripheral route (emphasizing superficial qualities) rather than the central route (emphasizing facts and logic). Use POE. Eliminate (B), (C), and (D) because they follow the central route approach. Choice (A) contains the sort of superficial elements that are characteristic of the peripheral route.

26. **D** *Understand the Question/Key Words*: The key words are *most likely effect(s) of chronic, long-term stress*. *Predict the Answer*: Selye's general adaptation syndrome would predict exhaustion would lead to physical illness. Choice (D) looks correct, but use POE to consider the other options. Eliminate (A) because these symptoms of PTSD would likely follow a deeply traumatic event. Eliminate (B) because phobias are also not likely outcomes of prolonged, low-level stress. Eliminate (C) because multiple personalities (at least in theory) emerge in response to extremely traumatic and abusive events in childhood.

27. **D** *Understand the Question/Key Words*: The key concept is that the *amygdala* does more than one thing in the brain. You should know that the amygdala, a part of the limbic system, is also involved in making new memories (D). The temporal lobes process auditory information, eliminate (A). Eliminate (B), as the medulla controls salivation, and eliminate (C), which is describing frontal lobes.

28. **A**   *Understand the Question/Key Words*: The question is asking for a comparison between the pictured labeled *AFRAID* and the other drawings. As this rendition is vastly different from the others, it appears the patient no longer understands or recognizes what fear looks like, answer (A). It's highly unlikely the patient is afraid of babies, eliminate (B). It is clear the patient can draw many different facial expressions, so eliminate (C). Eliminate (D) because, again, the patient was able to draw the other five faces, suggesting that a comprehension of words is not the issue.

29. **C**   *Understand the Question/Key Words*: The key words are *adaptive* and *dangerous*. The study required the patient to draw an expression for each of the words presented to her. The only one she did not seem to draw accurately was "afraid," indicating she may no longer be able to recognize fear. This might then be dangerous if she encounters a threatening situation because she won't recognize it as such and won't take measures to protect herself (C). Choices (A), (B), and (D) are not relevant to the task described in the passage.

30. **C**   *Understand the Question/Key Words*: The key words are *events created intense emotions. Predict the Answer*: Events like these often produce powerful memories for people about where they were and how they learned about the event. Use POE. Eliminate (A) because it involves people changing their memories in response to later events, expectations, and other factors. Eliminate (B) because it involves the ability to recall an image from memory after seeing it only once. Eliminate (D) because it involves previously learned information interfering with retention of more recently learned information. Only (C) refers specifically to events involving high levels of arousal and emotion.

31. **A**   *Understand the Question/Key Words*: The key language here is the definition of *schema* and the fact that *new information could fit. Predict the Answer*: Assimilation and accommodation are the relevant processes, and the issue is whether children had to change the existing schema. Here, they did not, so the correct answer is (A). Accommodation, (B), is the process that would require alteration of the existing schema.

32. **D**   *Understand the Question/Key Words:* The key words are *find regarding neuroticism scores and what might explain this finding*. Use POE to interpret data in the table. Eliminate (A) and (B) because neuroticism scores did not significantly increase or decrease. Eliminate (C) because they did not remain neutral because the drug was ineffective; in all three dosage groups, it was significantly efficacious. Choice (D) is correct because personality traits, like neuroticism, are stable over the lifespan and would not be affected by the anti-anxiety drug.

33. **B**   *Understand the Question/Key Words*: The key terms are *executive functioning, staying on task, fidgeting and impulsive behaviors. Predict the Answer*: Symptoms of ADHD include difficulties in staying on task. Choice (B) is correct.

34. **B**   *Understand the Question/Key Words*: The key words are *stroke affecting the left side* and *unable to produce intelligible speech. Predict the Answer*: Choice (B), Broca's area, is responsible for the production of intelligible speech. If this were not immediately known, consider your options and use POE. Eliminate (A) because it involves comprehension of speech. Eliminate (C) because it involves hearing. Eliminate (D) because it involves vision.

35. **C**   *Understand the Question/Key Words*: The key words are *reaction time* and *decaf*. *Predict the Answer*: The bar graph clearly shows average reaction times for both groups of participants (i.e., caffeinated vs. decaf), and at just under two seconds for decaf, (C) is correct.

36. **D**   *Understand the Question/Key Words*: The question is asking which variable described in the passage might produce an alternative explanation for the findings. Choice (D) is a variable the researcher was not manipulating or measuring and could have altered the outcome of the experiment.

37. **B**   *Understand the Question/Key Words*: The question is asking if it is permissible to deceive participants about what they ingested. *Predict the Answer*: As long as participants are aware they may drink a caffeinated or decaf beverage and sign an informed-consent form, it is not only permissible to keep them unaware but necessary to answer the research question. Choice (B) is correct.

38. **B**   *Understand the Question/Key Words*: The key concept is that Jennifer did not follow all of her doctor's orders by continuing to smoke. Nicotine is a teratogen that is harmful to the fetus, (B). Eliminate (A), (C), and (D), as none of these are considered a teratogen.

39. **C**   *Understand the Question/Key Words*: The key words are *cognitive therapy* and *depression*. *Predict the Answer*: In the cognitive approach, problems would be caused by dysfunctional thinking patterns. Choice (C) looks pretty good, but you can use POE to be sure. Eliminate (A) because it references psychoanalytical factors. Eliminate (B) because the emphasis is on biology. Eliminate (D) because getting attention is reinforcing and that indicates a behavioral approach. Choice (C) is correct because these "assessments" and "perceptions" are cognitive processes.

40. **C**   *Understand the Question/Key Words:* The key words are *variable* and *age*. *Predict the Answer*: The variable researchers manipulate, or control, is the independent variable (C).

41. **B**   *Understand the Question/Key Words:* The key words are *limitation* and *mood inventory*. Use POE if you cannot predict the answer. Administering a test periodically is not necessarily a limitation. It could be a strength of a study as more than one administration provides more data; eliminate (A). Because the test is "well-regarded," you should assume it has already been tested for construct validity; eliminate (C). Eliminate (D) as there is no evidence the test is culturally biased against students. A self-inventory relies on participants providing truthful responses to survey questions, but they often lie to look more socially favorable. Choice (B) is correct.

42. **C**   *Understand the Question/Key Words:* The question wants you to determine which age group had the *lowest mood ratings for unfavorable comments across all three measures*. This requires interpretation of the data in the second table. Choice (C) is correct.

43. **D** *Understand the Question/Key Words:* The key words are *subcortical structures* and *new memories.* *Predict the Answer:* Choice (D), the limbic system. If you weren't sure about this, go for POE. Eliminate (A) because it is involved in arousal and consciousness. Eliminate (B), which is responsible for motor control. Choice (C) can be eliminated because the ventricles produce and recycle cerebrospinal fluid.

44. **A** *Understand the Question/Key Words:* The question is asking what type of memory would be assisted or improved by keeping track of day-to-day tasks. *Predict the Answer:* Choice (A), remembering to remember something, is correct, but use POE if you are unsure. Eliminate (B) and (C), which are part of long-term memories for past events. Eliminate (D), which represents automatic memories like motor skills.

45. **D** *Understand the Question/Key Words:* The key language is *visual and auditory inputs, very quickly,* and *immediate strategic decisions.* *Predict the Answer:* Focusing on the speed of responsiveness should lead to the correct answer. Use POE to go through your options. Choice (A) involves a sense organ sending fewer messages to the brain when there has been a constant stimulus over time. Eliminate it. Choice (B) involves recollection of events in one's life. Eliminate it. Choice (C) involves knowledge of facts. Eliminate it. Only (D) involves the processing of sensory inputs at speed.

46. **B** *Understand the Question/Key Words:* The key word is *counterbalanced.* *Predict the Answer:* A researcher uses counterbalancing to control the effects of confounds when the same participants are repeatedly subjected to conditions, treatments, or stimuli. Choice (B) is the correct response.

47. **C** *Understand the Question/Key Words:* The key term is *dependent variable.* *Predict the Answer:* The dependent variable is that variable measured in an experiment. In this experiment, the average number of trials required is what the researcher is measuring. Choice (C) is correct.

48. **C** *Understand the Question/Key Words:* The question requires you to recall information about AD/HD. *Predict the Answer:* AD/HD is marked by inattention and/or hyperactivity. *Use POE:* Choices (A), (B), and (D) refer respectively to Intellectual Disability, Autism Spectrum Disorder, and Specific Learning Disorder. Choose (C).

49. **C** *Understand the Question/Key Words:* The key terms are *traumatic brain injury* and *Marcia could not see images presented to her left visual field.* *Predict the Answer:* The occipital lobe is responsible for vision and the images from the left and right visual fields are contralaterally perceived, so if she cannot view images presented to the left, it must be the right occipital lobe that was damaged (C). Eliminate (A), (B), and (D).

50. **D** *Understand the Question/Key Words*: The key words are from *memory* and *errors . . . in the middle*. *Predict the Answer*: This phenomenon, with better memory for beginnings and endings of lists, is (D), serial position effect. You can also use POE to eliminate (A) because François did not want to forget this information. Eliminate (B) because repression, which involves unconsciously burying a memory because it is distressing, is not the issue here. Eliminate (C) because it involves an inability to create new memories and does not involve placement within a list.

51. **A** *Understand the Question/Key Words*: The key here is what the child said: *I goed to the store with Mommy*. *Predict the Answer*: This child is overusing the English rule for adding "-ed" to the ends of words to make them past tense and he has not yet learned exceptions to this rule. This involves grammar, so the correct choice is (A).

52. **A** *Understand the Question/Key Words*: The question asks which conclusion is supported by the results of the study. *Predict the Answer*: The data indicate that a steep increase in stereotype threat relates to a lower GPA, so look for an answer that fits this correlation. Choice (B) is the opposite; both (C) and (D) are irrelevant to the prediction. Choice (A) is correct.

53. **B** *Understand the Question/Key Words*: The question asks which of the following best illustrates the concept of stereotype threat? *Predict the Answer*: Stereotype threat involves damage to one's performance after one has been introduced to a negative stereotype. *Use POE*: Choice (A) represents stereotype boost, while choices (C) and (D) do not show a match between the stereotype and the performance. Choice (B) is correct.

54. **B** *Understand the Question/Key Words*: The question asks which of the following best illustrates the concept of self-efficacy. *Predict the Answer*: Self-efficacy involves the belief that one is good at doing something, so the correct answer should involve that idea. Choice (A) involves high self-esteem, (C) involves an external locus of control, and it isn't clear what (D) involves. Choice (B) is correct.

55. **C** *Understand the Question/Key Words*: The key words are *systematic desensitization* and *treat a specific phobia of driving*. *Predict the Answer*: Systematic desensitization is a behavioral technique that involves gradually exposing someone to an anxiety-producing object, thought, or experience whilst simultaneously performing relaxation techniques to reduce the symptoms of anxiety. Choice (C) looks correct, but use POE to be sure. Choice (A) describes a flooding approach, so eliminate it. Choice (B) describes a similar approach, but does not actually expose John to the phobic activity; eliminate it. Eliminate (D) because group therapy is not the same approach as described in the question stem.

56. **B** *Understand the Question/Key Words*: The key term is *multiple sclerosis* and *visible on MRI*. *Predict the Answer*: MS attacks myelin (white matter), which is the fatty sheath that surrounds the axon of a neuron, so the answer is (B). Eliminate (A), (C), and (D).

57. **B** *Understand the Question/Key Words*: The key language is what the coach said to students of *Scandinavian heritage* and what their results were. *Predict the Answer*: Generalizations about anticipated performance based on things like gender, race, and ethnicity can create a self-fulfilling prophecy, which is what the correct answer, (B), describes.

58. **A** *Understand the Question/Key Words:* The question requires interpretation of data presented in the table; use POE. For both English and French speakers, infants have the highest proficiency scores; (A) is correct. Eliminate (B) as toddlers do not have the lowest score. Choice (C) is wrong because children have neither the lowest scores nor is there a difference between English and French speakers. Eliminate (D) because teens have the lowest proficiency score and there is no difference in native speakers.

59. **B** *Understand the Question/Key Words:* The key concepts provided in the passage are that critical periods in childhood exist for acquisition of a new language. The only answer choice that agrees with that notion is (B). Eliminate (A) and (C), as they suggest it is easier to acquire language as a person ages. Choice (D) suggests there are no age differences in development across our lifespan; eliminate it.

60. **C** *Understand the Question/Key Words:* The key concept here is qualitative data. Use POE to identify the quantitative results and eliminate them: multiple-choice tests (A), timed reading comprehension (B), and listening comprehension tests (D). Interviews and observations are narrative in nature and are, therefore, qualitative; (C) is correct.

61. **D** *Understand the Question/Key Words*: This question is seeking the name of a "disorder" that is described in the language leading up to the question mark. *Predict the Answer*: Phobias are irrational or exaggerated fears. The "agora" was the marketplace in ancient Greece; hence, agoraphobia is a fear of being in public. Choice (D) is correct.

62. **B** *Understand the Question/Key Words*: The key words *occipital and temporal lobes* and *remove cortical tissue at the occipitotemporal border*. *Predict the Answer:* Damage to the occipitotemporal border will result in the inability to recognize faces, a special form of agnosia called prosopagnosia (B). If you are not sure, use POE. Night blindness, (A), results from damage to the retina, not the lobes of the brain. Aphasia, (C), is the inability to process language, not visual information, and ataxia, (D), describes poor muscle control that causes clumsy movements.

63. **C** *Understand the Question/Key Words*: The scenario depicts a taste aversion developed after one exposure to a stimulus. *Predict the Answer*: Taste aversion occurs when an organism develops a distaste for a food or beverage after it has been paired with an aversive stimulus. *Use POE*: Choices (A), (B), and (D) name other forms of non-associative learning and/or classical conditioning. Choice (C) is correct.

64. **B**   *Understand the Question/Key Words*: This question requires you to interpret the data presented in the bar graph. According to the graph, those who are 18–24 are less likely to smoke only e-cigarettes than those between 25-44. Choice (B) is the correct response.

65. **C**   *Understand the Question/Key Words*: The key words are *loss of binocular vision* and *accurately judge depth and distance*. Binocular vision requires two working eyes, which means that you can use POE to rule out (A), (B), and (D). Answer (C) is correct.

66. **C**   *Understand the Question/Key Words*: The key words are *independent variable*. *Predict the Answer*: The intensity of training is what the researcher is manipulating, or the independent variable. Choice (C) is correct. Choice (A) is simply the sample size; eliminate it. Choice (B) is the dependent variable, eliminate it. Choice (D) is wrong because this is not a correlational study, but an experiment.

67. **A**   *Understand the Question/Key Words*: The key concept being tested is whether intensity of training has an effect on how long it takes the employees to complete their task. Use the table provided and POE. Remember, it is always the null hypothesis that is being tested in an experiment (i.e., the experimental manipulation will have no effect on the dependent variable). Therefore, (A) is the correct answer.

68. **B**   *Understand the Question/Key Words*: The research design compared two groups of participants to each other. That is correctly described by (B), a between-subjects experiment.

69. **D**   *Understand the Question/Key Words*: The question asks which concept best relates to a teacher's suggestion to use the layout of a keyboard to remember new information. *Predict the answer*: A mnemonic device is any trick that helps one remember something. *Use POE*: choice (A) is not a mnemonic device, and choices (B) and (C) are not relevant mnemonic devices, so they can be safely eliminated. Choice (D) is correct.

70. **D**   *Understand the Question/Key Words*: The key words were *semicircular canals* and *damage*. *Predict the Answer*: Choice (D) is correct, as semicircular canals are responsible for balance and damage to them will result in dizziness. If you are unsure, use POE. A ringing in the ears and deafness will likely result from damage to the ear drum; eliminate (A). The semicircular canals are not involved in speech or vision; eliminate (B) and (C).

71. **C**   *Understand the Question/Key Words*: The question asks which of the following brain scans such as the fMRI promote understanding of. *Predict the Answer*: The fMRI provides insight into both structure and function, so look for an answer choice that involves both. *Use POE*: Choice (A) refers to the EEG, (B) refers to the MRI, and (D) refers to brain plasticity. Choice (C) is correct.

72. **A** *Understand the Question/Key Words*: The question asks which brain structure would most likely interfere with valid data collection in a study involving music. *Predict the Answer*: Something involving hearing would make sense. *Use POE*: Choice (B) relates to vision, (C) relates to sensation, and (D) relates to smell. Choice (A) is correct.

73. **B** *Understand the Question/Key Words*: The question asks which scenario best illustrates the concept of the mere exposure effect. *Predict the Answer*: According to this concept, one likes or is attracted to things or people to which one has been exposed before. *Use POE*: Choice (A) might be tempting, so keep it for now. Choices (C) and (D) merely use the word exposure but do not reflect the concept. Between (A) and (B), being more attentive is less clearly an instance of attraction than being excited, so eliminate (A). Choice (B) is correct.

74. **C** *Understand the Question/Key Words*: The key language here indicates that Adam's beliefs and actions are not in sync and that this makes him uncomfortable. Try using POE. Adam is not projecting either his thoughts or his actions onto others, so (A) should be eliminated. Neither is he denying the existence of a problem; the problem is why he is uncomfortable. Eliminate (B). The quality of Adam's performance is not affected by whether others are around, so eliminate (D). Choice (C) is correct because Adam's discomfort when providing an excuse for his behavior is evidence of the tension predicted by cognitive dissonance.

75. **D** *Understand the Question/Key Words:* The key concepts are *26-year-old* and *values deep connections with others*. *Predict the Answer*: The stage for young adults is "intimacy versus isolation," so it is about developing deep connections with others. Choice (D) is correct.

Section II: Free Response

1. Credit is awarded for responses that incorporate the following points:

   (A) Identify the research method used in the study.

   - Accurately identifies an experiment, or a mixed-groups design experiment or proposes that variables result in an interaction effect.

   (B) State the operational definition of a logical fallacy.
   - The response states that the operational definition of a logical fallacy is type of flawed reasoning where an assertion or statement is mistakenly accepted as true.

   (C) Describe the meaning of the differences in the means for the concept formation task between the stimulus pairing group, the match-to-sample group, and the self-study group.

   - Accurately describes that the means show that the stimulus pairing group and the match-to-sample group learned significantly more than the self-study group.

   (D) Identify at least one ethical guideline applied by the researchers.

   - Accurately identifies that the researchers used informed consent, or that they received approval from the university's Institutional Review Board and adhered to guidelines for the protection of human subjects.

   (E) Explain the extent to which the research findings may or may not be generalizable using specific and relevant evidence from the study.

   - References "the larger population of a population relevant to the study's participants" and notes that the study is generalizable to men and women because both were used, or only to older adults, because that was the only group used. OR that participants responded correctly to the novel examples of logical fallacies during the computerized posttests, but they did not generalize to novel examples during the written posttests.

   (F) Explain how at least one of the research findings supports or refutes the researchers' hypothesis that the type of instruction a participant is exposed to affects being able to define and identify logical fallacies and the results of the study are accurately interpreted.

   - Notes that because the score increases were only significant in the computerized posttest, the type of instruction cannot be said to have an effect on the written test. AND the response uses at least one of the research findings to accurately show how means were significantly higher for the matching and pairing groups.

2. Credit is awarded for responses that incorporate the following points.

   A.   Identify a specific and defensible claim based in psychological science that responds to the question.

   (1)   "Eye contact is measured differently across the studies."

   (2)   "Not all researchers will interpret avoidance of eye contact the same way."

   (3)   "Avoiding eye contact will vary based on stimuli used in an experiment."

   B.   (i)   Support your claim using at least one piece of specific and relevant evidence from one of the sources.

   (1)   Source B: "They found no support for avoidance behaviors, but attribute that, in part, to the neutrality of the actors' facial expressions."

   (ii)   Explain how the evidence from Part B (i) supports your claim using a psychological perspective, theory, concept, or research finding learned in AP Psychology.

   1.   "This evidence supports the claim that neutral stimuli do not elicit avoidance of eye contact because it is not threatening. Stimuli that appear unpleasant or dangerous will lead one to avert their gaze."

   C.   (i)   Support your claim using an additional piece of scientific and relevant evidence from a different source than the one that was used in Part B (i).

   (1)   Source C: "Eye-contact behavior is not significantly correlated with low performance self-assessment or social anxiety post interaction."

   (ii)   Explain how the evidence from Part C (i) supports your claim using a different psychological perspective, theory, concept, or research finding learned in AP Psychology than the one that was used in Part B (ii).

   1.   "Hypervigilance suggests the need to assess potential danger."

Part III
About the AP Psychology Exam

- The Structure of the AP Psychology Exam
- AP Psychology Exam Goes Fully Digital
- How the AP Psychology Exam Is Scored
- Overview of Content Topics
- How AP Exams Are Used
- Other Resources
- Designing Your Study Plan

THE STRUCTURE OF THE AP PSYCHOLOGY EXAM

The AP Psychology Exam is divided into two sections with the following time allotments:

→ Section I—Multiple Choice

75 questions . . . . 90 minutes

→ Section II—Free Response

2 essay questions . . . . 70 minutes

Section I

Section I of the AP Psychology Exam contains 75 multiple-choice questions. You have 90 minutes to complete the section, and your Section I score counts for two-thirds of your overall AP Psychology grade.

If you did a double-take when you saw that you are given only 90 minutes to do 75 questions, take a deep breath. Although that's little more than a minute per question, knowing certain techniques, which we will discuss in more detail in Part IV, will make this time constraint much less daunting.

Section II

Section II of the AP Psychology Exam consists of two free-response questions (aka essays). They each count for the same percentage of your grade, and you must answer both. Section II counts for one-third of your AP Psychology grade. You have 70 minutes to complete BOTH essays—again, take a deep breath. If you understand the expectations of the essay, as covered in Part IV, you will be able to respond effectively to each part for maximum credit.

The Article Analysis Question and Evidence-Based Question are brand-new for the May 2025 exam. As such, there isn't a history of sample student responses to refer back to. Consequently, the scoring tips are based largely on the College Board's rubric and The Princeton Review's experience and expectations of the AP Psychology exam.

AP PSYCHOLOGY EXAM GOES FULLY DIGITAL

Beginning with the May 2025 administration of the test, the AP Psychology Exam will be conducted digitally. To take the exam, students must have access to the College Board's Bluebook testing app, available for Windows and Mac laptop/desktops, iPads, tablets, and Chromebooks. If your computer or tablet is owned or managed by your school, then a school official will likely have to install this app for you if it is not already on it. The test cannot be taken on a smart phone.

The testing app will allow you to annotate and highlight texts, eliminate answers, and flag questions for review later. You will also have access to scratch paper to plan responses to essay questions. Unlike other digital exams like the SAT, the digital AP exam will NOT be adaptive: this means that the difficulty of questions will not change depending on how well you do on earlier sections of the test.

Although only the online test in your student tools is digital, the two printed tests in this book provide the same types of questions and strategy practice necessary to prepare you for the digital exam.

For the latest information regarding the digital AP Exams and testing accommodations, visit the College Board website at apcentral.collegeboard.org/exam-administration-ordering-scores/digital-ap-exams.

HOW THE AP PSYCHOLOGY EXAM IS SCORED

The following represents how the old 2024 version of the AP Psychology exam was scored. The College Board aims to make sure there is a smooth transition to the new 2025 implementation, but know that these scores may be slightly less predictive for this first year.

Score	2024 Percentage	Credit Recommendation	College Grade Equivalent
5	18%	Extremely Well Qualified	A
4	23%	Well Qualified	A–, B+, B
3	20%	Qualified	B–, C+, C
2	12%	Possibly Qualified	–
1	27%	No Recommendation	–

Scores from May 2024 AP administration. Data taken from the College Board website.

Preview the Digital AP Exam

View the College Board's walk-through video of what each part of the digital AP exam will look like here: https://www.youtube.com/watch?v=LfB3tyJjDqc

---

Looking for More Help with Your APs?

We now offer specialized AP tutoring and course packages that guarantee a 4 or 5 on the AP. To see which courses are offered and available, and to learn more about the guarantee, visit PrincetonReview.com/college/ap-test-prep.

If you had studied previous versions of the AP Psychology exam, the old Unit 1 on Scientific Foundations is no longer tested. The following is an estimated breakdown of how things have changed:

The new Unit 1 covers what the old Unit 2 did (Biological Bases of Behavior) as well as the first part of Unit 3 (Sensation & Perception).

The new Unit 2 covers the second part of Unit 3 (Sensation & Perception) as well as Unit 5 (Cognitive Psychology).

The new Unit 3 covers the old Unit 4 (Learning) and Unit 6 (Developmental Psychology).

The new Unit 4 covers the old Unit 7 (Motivation, Emotion, and Personality) and Unit 9 (Social Psychology).

The new Unit 5 covers the old Unit 8 (Clinical Psychology).

OVERVIEW OF CONTENT TOPICS

The new format for the AP Psychology exam evenly splits the possibility for content across each of its five newly aligned units. In short, 15–25% of Section I will be allocated to each of the five units. In practice, this means that you may have 15% coverage of one topic and 25% of another, but since there's no way to know for sure, you should aim to do your best across the board. There's no one "less-tested" unit to skip, though if you're pressed for time you may want to use Practice Test 1 as a diagnostic and then focus on improving your knowledge in the unit that you were least accurate in.

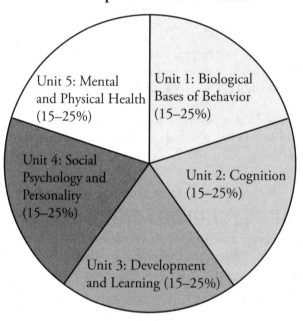

Which Topics Are Tested the Most?

Unit 5: Mental and Physical Health (15–25%)

Unit 1: Biological Bases of Behavior (15–25%)

Unit 4: Social Psychology and Personality (15–25%)

Unit 2: Cognition (15–25%)

Unit 3: Development and Learning (15–25%)

Notice that we have divided the review portion of this book (Part VI) into chapters based on those units for your convenience. We have also modified the former Unit 1, Scientific Foundations, into an optional Part V that may help to better understand the rest of the course. By focusing strictly on psychology as it's tested by the AP Exam, we'll teach you what you need to know to make the grade.

HOW AP EXAMS ARE USED

Different colleges use AP Exam scores in different ways, so it is important that you go to a particular college's website to determine how it uses those scores. The following three items represent the main ways in which AP Exam scores can be used.

- **College Credit**. Some colleges will give you college credit if you score well on an AP Exam. These credits count toward your graduation requirements, meaning that you can take fewer courses while in college. Given the cost of college, this could be quite a benefit, indeed.

- **Satisfy Requirements**. Some colleges will allow you to "place out" of certain requirements if you do well on an AP Exam, even if they do not give you actual college credits. For example, you might not need to take an introductory-level course, or perhaps you might not need to take a class in a certain discipline at all.

- **Admissions Plus**. Even if your AP Exam will not result in college credit or even allow you to place out of certain courses, most colleges will respect your decision to push yourself by taking an AP course or even an AP Exam outside of a course. A high score on an AP Exam shows proficiency of more difficult content than is taught in many high school courses, and colleges may take that into account during the admissions process.

Stay Up to Date!

For late-breaking information about test dates, exam formats, and any other changes pertaining to AP Psychology, make sure to check the College Board's website at apstudents.collegeboard.org/courses/ap-psychology.

OTHER RESOURCES

There are many resources available to help you improve your score on the AP Psychology Exam, not the least of which are your **teachers**. If you are taking an AP class, you may be able to get extra attention from your teacher, such as obtaining feedback on your essays.

Another wonderful resource is **AP Students**, the official site of the AP Exams. The scope of the information at this site is quite broad and includes:

- the course description, which provides details on what content is covered (and a handful of sample questions)

- the scoring guidelines

- access to AP Classroom if you are enrolled in a course (teacher assistance required)

- free-response prompts from previous years (though this may be less useful than usual, given the new testing format) and exam tips

- access to the Bluebook app for digital exam practice with a College Board account

The AP Students home page address is apstudents.collegeboard.org/home.

For up-to-date information about any potential changes to the AP Psychology Exam, please visit apstudents.collegeboard.org/courses/ap-psychology.

Finally, The Princeton Review offers tutoring for the AP Psychology Exam. Our expert instructors can help you refine your strategic approach and add to your content knowledge. For more information, call 1-800-2REVIEW.

DESIGNING YOUR STUDY PLAN

In Part I you identified some areas of potential improvement. Let's now delve further into your performance on Practice Test 1, with the goal of developing a study plan appropriate to your needs and time commitment.

Read the answers and explanations associated with the multiple-choice questions (starting on page 49). After you have done so, respond to the following questions:

- How many days/weeks/months away is your AP Psychology Exam?

- What time of day is your best, most focused study time?

- How much time per day/week/month will you devote to preparing for your AP Psychology Exam?

- When will you do this preparation? (Be as specific as possible: Mondays and Wednesdays from 3:00 to 4:00 P.M., for example.)

- Based on the answers above, will you focus on strategy (Part IV), content (Part VI), or both?

- What are your overall goals in using this book?

Based on your answers to these questions, you should now have a better understanding of how to study for the exam. Use your answers to build a study plan that meets your specific needs based on the amount of time you have until test day. It is important to tailor your study plan to your schedule and topics you need to further review.

Don't Forget!

Register your book online to access your AP Psychology Study Guide by following the directions on the "Get More (Free) Content" page!

Part IV
Test-Taking Strategies for the AP Psychology Exam

PREVIEW

Review your responses to the questions on page 2 of Part I and then respond to the following questions:

- How many multiple-choice questions did you miss even though you knew the answer?

- On how many multiple-choice questions did you guess randomly?

- How many multiple-choice questions did you miss after eliminating some answers and guessing based on the remaining answers?

- Did you create an outline before you wrote each essay?

- Did you find either of the essays easier/harder than the other—and, if so, why?

HOW TO USE THE CHAPTERS IN THIS PART

Before you read the following chapters, think about what you are doing now. As you read and engage in the directed practice, be sure to consider the ways you can change your approach. At the end of Part IV, you will have the opportunity to reflect on how you will change your approach.

Chapter 1
How to Approach
Multiple-Choice
Questions

OVERVIEW OF THE MULTIPLE-CHOICE SECTION

Section I of the AP Psychology Exam contains 75 multiple-choice questions that cover the 5 units of the AP Psychology course. You have 90 minutes to complete this section, and it counts for two-thirds of your overall score. This time limit gives you a little bit more than one minute to answer each question. You might ask: "How can I possibly do well on this test when I have only about 80 seconds to answer each question?"

The answer: You do *not* need to work through all of the questions to do well on Section I of the AP Psychology Exam. In fact, smart testers often do not try to attempt every question and risk careless errors. Instead, smart testers choose which questions to tackle and which questions to simply guess on. "How do I choose?" you ask. To answer that question, let's take a closer look at the way the test is set up.

Order of Difficulty

The AP Psychology exam has been newly updated for the May 2025 administration, and as such, there are still some unknowns about this first administration, especially in a digital format. It is unclear as of the print date of this book whether the College Board planned to arrange questions in order of difficulty.

Traditionally, the College Board's AP exams have followed in the steps of other exams, putting the easier questions up front so that students don't get stuck on the hardest questions first and stand a better chance of making it through the full test. That decision has yielded, more often than not, a nice bell curve where most students score somewhere around the middle as opposed to creating two distinct groups: one of high-scorers who know the material and are good test-takers, and one for everybody else.

To make sure that students are as prepared as possible for however the College Board may present its questions on the exam, the practice tests in this book have randomly ordered the questions. What this means for you is that your personal order of difficulty is more important than ever. If you encounter a question or topic that you don't feel comfortable with, consider skipping it and coming back with whatever time is left. After all, every multiple-choice question is equal in value, so if you can answer two easier questions in the time it would take to digest one harder one, that's the best way to boost your score.

No One Will Ever Know

Raw scores are not reported to you, your school, or your colleges. Only the final score, ranging from 1 to 5, is reported. In other words, no one will ever know that you got an AP Psych grade of 5 (extremely well qualified), but got only 75 percent of Section I questions correct and rocked the essays. It's the final grade that matters here, so take the test the smart way.

Tripartite Questions

Note that the new AP Psychology exam will feature some question sets, in which a passage or data will be presented, followed by three different questions. Some of these questions tend to test research methods and design as well as data interpretation, so even if you don't necessarily understand the psychological concept, you might want to skim each question in a set to see if there are some that are more approachable than others.

In Chapter 3, we'll discuss in more depth how to pace yourself to maximize your score. Now, we'll introduce you to some specific multiple-choice strategies.

SMART-TESTER STRATEGIES

Your own knowledge of psychology will be the key to doing well, but certain strategies will help you stretch your psych knowledge and crack the trickier questions. Once you've mastered some of the smart-tester strategies, we'll talk about how you can develop your personal approach to Section I.

Smart-Tester Strategy #1:
Understand the Question/Key Words

How often have you zipped through a question and picked the obvious answer, only to find that you misread the question? The most important thing you can do to increase your score on Section I is to make sure you understand what you are being asked.

After you read a question, take a second to make sure you understand it. Put the question in your own words, or circle the key words in the question. Taking this first step will eliminate the possibility of your answering the wrong thing. Try the following example:

> 1. A person's refusal to accept an accurate diagnosis of a spouse's mental illness demonstrates the use of which of the following defense mechanisms?

How would you ask this question in your own words?

When someone doesn't want to accept really bad news, they are in…

Now the answer should be obvious: *denial*. By stating this question in everyday language, the answer pops out at you. Try another example:

> 19. The failure of bystanders to respond to a stranger's cries for help is sometimes explained as an instance of

How would you ask the question?

Why don't people do anything when someone is yelling "help"?

In the case of question 19, you may not know the answer off the top of your head, but clarifying the question makes you better prepared to deal with the answer choices.

Let's look at one more:

> 22. The dependent variable in the experiment above is

In this case, you don't need to put the question into your own words. However, you want to make sure you look for the right thing when you hit the answer choices. Therefore, circle the key words *dependent variable* before you head to the answer choices.

Understand the Question/Key Words

For each of the following questions, circle the key words in the question (you can try highlighting them on the digital test). Then, if appropriate, jot down in your own words (using notes or the scrap paper on the digital exam) exactly what is being asked. Answers are in Chapter 12.

3. Angie is a scientist who is interested in the physical basis of psychological phenomena such as motivation, emotion, and stress. She is called a(n)

10. One of the primary tools of the school of structuralism was

18. Binocular cues provide important cues for depth perception because

35. Constance is presented with a list of words. When asked to recall the words, she remembers only the words from the beginning and the end of the list. This phenomenon demonstrates which of the following types of effect?

47. The recognition-by-components theory asserts that we categorize objects by breaking them down into their component parts and then

56. Veronica is competing in a regional gymnastics competition. As she waits for her turn on the mat, she ignores the sounds of the crowd and instead mentally reviews her routine. Veronica is managing an anxiety-producing situation by employing

70. Which of the following was true of Stanley Milgram's studies of obedience?

88. In their discussions of the process of development, the advocates of the importance of nurture in the nature-nurture controversy emphasize which of the following?

Question Types

On the new exam, about 65% of the questions ask you to use your knowledge of psychology to address a specific scenario. Application questions are no problem as long as you understand the question first. Just be sure to *Understand the Question/ Key Words!*

Smart-Tester Strategy #2: Predict the Answer

Once you've translated the question, you go to the answer choices, right? *Stop right there. . . .* Do you really think it's that easy? Of course not, or everyone would get all the questions right. You need to do a little work before you get mired down in the answer choices.

Beware of the Answer Choices

Answer choices are not your friends. In fact, think about what it takes for a test-writer to develop four answer choices for each question. First, she needs to write the correct answer, making sure it is accurate but not too obvious. Then, she has to put in at least one or two close second choices. Finally, she needs to fill in the remaining choices and move on to the next question.

When taking a standardized test, most students read the question and then read each answer choice. What they fail to realize is that the answer choices are riddled with tricks, traps, and distractors designed to bump them off course.

Enter: The Smart Tester

If you have an idea of the answer before you read the answer choices, you won't be tempted to pick something that is way off base. Moreover, because three of the four choices you read are wrong, it's best to assume that an answer is wrong until proven right.

After you translate the question into your own words, answer it *in your own words*. Now, that may mean actually knowing the exact answer (as in the case of *denial*), or it may mean putting yourself in the right ballpark before looking at the answer choices. Sometimes, it's actually helpful to cover the answer choices to make your best prediction of what the answer should be. Then, look at the choices and see which comes closest to your original thought. Let's look at one of the questions from your last drill:

> 3. Angie is a scientist who is interested in the physical basis of psychological phenomena such as motivation, emotion, and stress. She is called a(n)

First, how would you ask this question in your own words? Okay, now maybe you know the answer to this question, and maybe you don't. No problem. You can still answer the question before you look at the answer choices. If you can't spit out Angie's correct title immediately, answer the question by saying:

Angie is called a person who is into the physical basis of psychology.

With your answer in mind, look at each answer choice.

> (A) psychologist
> (B) physical therapist
> (C) paleontologist
> (D) biopsychologist

Now, use your answer to find the credited response:

(A) Is a *psychologist* a person who's into the physical basis of psychology? No, this person is into more than just the physical basis.

(B) Is a *physical therapist* a person who's into the physical basis of psychology? No, this person is not into the psychology part.

(C) Is a *paleontologist* a person who's into the physical basis of psychology? No idea what this person is.

(D) Is a *biopsychologist* a person who's into the physical basis of psychology? Yes.

Your answer? Choice (D), *biopsychologist*. By predicting the answer to the question before reading the answer choices, you were able to avoid getting tripped up in the first three answer choices. Plus, you realized the answer had to be (D), *biopsychologist*, without necessarily knowing anything about (C), *paleontologist* (a paleontologist studies fossils, by the way).

Smart-Tester Strategy #3: Process of Elimination (POE)

You have just learned your next big strategy: Process of Elimination (POE for short). Every time you answer a question, you will use POE, which means eliminating wrong answer choices and then choosing from what you have left. Why does it make sense to always answer questions this way? Because three of the four answer choices you read for each question are wrong. In other words, most of the answers you read on the test are wrong. Sometimes, it is much easier to identify one or two wrong answers on each question than it is to concentrate on finding the one right answer each time. By getting rid of those answer choices on each question, you can substantially increase your accuracy and your guessing power.

Let's try another example:

26. Which of the following is an example of metacognition?

Understand the Question/Key Words: Circle *metacognition*, and then define it:

Understanding cognitive (thought) processes

Predict the Answer:

Find an example of people understanding how they think and learn.

Now, use POE to get rid of wrong answers:

(A) Recognizing the faces of new in-laws after seeing them only in pictures
(B) Memorizing 100 words from the dictionary
(C) Understanding the role of various parts of the brain in perception
(D) Knowing the effectiveness of different strategies for learning statistical formulas

(A) Is *recognizing the faces* of people the same as understanding how one thinks and learns? No. Cross off this answer choice. Every time you decide an answer is not the one you want, cross it off.

(B) Is *memorizing* something the same as understanding how one thinks and learns? No. Cross it off.

(C) Is *understanding the role of various parts of the brain in perception* the same as understanding how one thinks and learns? Not sure? Keep it and read the rest.

(D) Is *knowing the effectiveness of different strategies for learning* the same as understanding how one thinks and learns? Sounds pretty close.

By using POE, you were able to easily narrow your choices down to (C) and (D). Once you have it down to two, compare your choices. Which one is closer to the answer you came up with? In this case, the answer is (D). *Understanding the role of various parts of the brain in perception* is still only knowledge of fact, not of mental processes. Notice the word *understanding* was used in (C), and not by coincidence. By using POE, you were able to escape the trap and answer the question correctly.

Meta What?

Okay, so POE is a great strategy, but what if you don't know what the key term in a question actually means? You have two choices: If this is a very hard question, which it was, you can simply skip it and come back to it if you have time. However, don't underestimate your knowledge. You may not be able to cough up the dictionary definition of *metacognition*, but you can pull the word apart. If you have spent more than a week in AP Psych class, you know that cognition has something to do with thinking. Then, recall how you have heard the prefix *meta* used. How about metaphysics? So there's physics and metaphysics, and there's thinking (cognition) and meta-thinking (metacognition). It's probably some higher level of thinking. Although this rough definition may not get you to the exact answer, it will help you cross off some answer choices and help you make an educated guess.

> ### Smart-Tester Strategy Review
>
> **Strategy #1:** Understand the Question/Key Words: Read the question and put it into your own words. Circle any key words or phrases that might point you in the right direction.
>
> **Strategy #2:** Predict the Answer: Come up with your own answer to the question (exact or ballpark).
>
> **Strategy #3:** Process of Elimination (POE): Cross off each answer that is not close to yours. Pick the best match.

More on POE

Now, let's say you read a question and don't know the answer. All is not lost. You can use your brain, the information in the question, and POE to get to the answer (or at least to a fifty-fifty chance of guessing the right answer). Look at the following example:

74. Which of the following best supports the assertion that intelligence is at least in part inherited?

 (A) Pairs of fraternal twins have a greater correlation of IQ score than do other pairs of siblings.

 (B) Pairs of twins reared together have a greater correlation of IQ score than do pairs of twins reared apart.

 (C) Pairs of identical twins have a greater correlation of IQ score than do pairs of fraternal twins.

 (D) Adopted children and their adoptive parents have a greater correlation of IQ score than do the same children and their biological parents.

Did you read the answer choices for question 74 before you answered on your own? Don't forget, wrong answers are designed to confuse, not to assist. Be sure to follow your smart strategy and *not* look at the answer choices too soon. First, let's do smart strategies for question 74.

Understand the Question/Key Words: Circle the words *intelligence* and *inherited*. Then restate the question:

Which of the answers says genetics affects smarts?

Predict the Answer: If you answered, I don't know, no problem. Simply use what you do know and POE.

Use POE for each answer choice:

(A) Does the fact that *pairs of fraternal twins have a greater correlation of IQ score than do other pairs of siblings* indicate that genetics affects smarts? Careful—are fraternal twins any different genetically from other sibling pairs? If you are unsure, leave this choice and go on.

(B) Does the fact that *pairs of twins reared together have a greater correlation of IQ score than do pairs of twins reared apart* indicate that genetics affects smarts? No, it indicates the opposite because it implies that the nongenetic factors are more significant. Cross it off.

(C) Does the fact that *pairs of identical twins have a greater correlation of IQ score than do pairs of fraternal twins* indicate that genetics affects smarts? Yes. Identical twins come from one egg, while fraternal twins come from two, making fraternal twins genetically less similar. Keep this answer choice and read on.

(D) Does the fact that *adopted children and their adoptive parents have a greater correlation of IQ score than do the same children and their biological parents* indicate that genetics affects smarts? No, it also indicates nurture over nature. Cross it off.

There's no penalty for guessing, so don't leave anything blank! Maybe you don't spend time on every question, but take an educated guess on those you work on, and choose the same letter for all those you have no idea on or don't have time for. By using the same letter when guessing randomly (what we call your Letter of the Day, or LOTD), you will most likely guarantee yourself a couple extra points!

You've at least narrowed it down to two choices without even really knowing the answer—that's pretty cool. Now look at the two choices you have not crossed off. Choice (C) very clearly shows genetics affects smarts, while (A) may or may not. What's your best guess? You got it: (C).

Even if you're left with two very hard answer choices to choose between, just choose one and move on. Don't sweat it; **there's no penalty for guessing**. And you can't score another point without moving on to another question!

HOW LONG IS 90 MINUTES?

Right about now you are probably thinking, "Nice idea, and I'll probably finish about 10 questions in 70 minutes following this strategy." Even though you don't need to work through every question on the test to do well, you do need to work efficiently and effectively.

As you know, rushing through the test and getting easy questions wrong is a bad idea. But how slow is too slow? After all, this is a timed test, and you do need to complete a significant number of the questions to do well.

Work Efficiently and Effectively

The best way for you to determine your own personal pace is to work efficiently (don't dawdle) and effectively (get right what you do answer). In other words, although you don't want to rush through and make careless errors, you don't want to spend all day on one question. Work at a pace that allows you to get questions right without dragging your heels. If you find yourself lingering for too long over a question, make a decision and move on. However, if you are doing some good, effective work on a question and have narrowed it down to two choices, don't lose the point because you "need to get to the next question."

> **Your Personal Pace**
>
> It is imperative that you choose a pace that is efficient and effective for *you*. It doesn't matter if your best friend can complete the entire section in 30 minutes. You need to work at a pace that will allow you to do as many questions as you can while maintaining accuracy. Set your own personal pace and you will do your personal best.

UNDERSTANDING DIFFICULTY

Because it is unclear whether the new AP Psychology will put its questions in order of difficulty, it is important that you have a good sense for what makes a question easier or harder. The following drill consists of content questions (for test-like questions, take the three full-length practice tests) sorted by difficulty. As you solve each set of drills, see if you can identify what makes a type of question easier or harder for yourself. This will help you decide on the test whether you want to skip a question and come back to it or if you want to solve it right away.

Easy Questions Drill

Easy questions tend to be shorter and, in general, take less time to complete. Note that the actual test will have some passages and data accompanying questions. The difficulty of that material will be consistent, so before you spend time reading this material, you might want to skim the question(s) associated with it to see if you're going to skip it for now or not. As a bonus, if you do decide to solve the problem on this first pass, you'll know what you're looking for!

Try this drill, working quickly but carefully. Before you begin, jot down your start time. Once you have finished, note your end time and check your answers for accuracy. Remember, the goal is to be efficient (work rapidly) and effective (work accurately). Dive in and test drive those smart-tester strategies.

Start Time: _____

Drill vs. Practice Questions

If you've already taken the diagnostic Practice Test, you'll notice a difference between those test-like questions and these drill questions.

These drills, including at the end of each chapter and at the end of the book, are designed simply to test your content knowledge. They have five multiple-choice questions, not the four that you'll face on the test, but you can apply the same strategies. When you're ready to practice the full thing, including the timing of the test and the new passage style.

1. Sigmund Freud is thought of as the originator of which of the following perspectives of psychology?

   (A) Biological
   (B) Psychoanalytic
   (C) Behavioral
   (D) Humanistic
   (E) Cognitive

2. A person who is attempting to overcome a heroin addiction is experiencing hallucinations, tremors, and other side effects. These painful experiences associated with the termination of an addiction are known as

   (A) denial
   (B) transduction
   (C) withdrawal
   (D) transference
   (E) psychosis

3. After several trials during which a dog is given a specific type of food each time a light is lit, there is evidence of conditioning if the dog salivates when

   (A) the food is presented and the light is not lit
   (B) the light is lit and the food is not present
   (C) the food and the light occur simultaneously
   (D) a different kind of food is presented
   (E) a tone is sounded when the food is presented

4. The basic unit of the nervous system is called the

   (A) soma
   (B) axon
   (C) cell
   (D) neuron
   (E) synapse

5. Which of the following methods of research is central to the behaviorist perspective?

   (A) Inferential statistics
   (B) Naturalistic observation
   (C) Surveying
   (D) Case study
   (E) Experimentation

End Time: _____

Right: _____

Turn to Chapter 12 to check your answers. How did you do? Remember, if you finished quickly but missed even one question, you were working too fast. Don't throw away points on the easy questions.

Medium Questions Drill

Medium difficulty questions tend to be those you sort of know, but can also be ones that you know, but which you will need to answer very carefully so you don't lose points to tricks and traps. Try the next five questions as you did on the previous drill, working more slowly but still efficiently and effectively.

> **By the Way...**
> The more psychology you have under your belt, the easier this test will be. The strategies you are learning here are designed to make the most of the psychology knowledge you possess—to keep you from missing answers to questions that you should be getting right. The strategies will also help you stretch your knowledge so you can answer questions about topics you only sort-of know. However, although they will help you make smart guesses, the strategies won't make a question on a completely unfamiliar topic easy.

Start Time: _____

33. The primary drives of hunger and thirst are, for the most part, regulated by which of the following?
    - (A) The medulla oblongata
    - (B) The thalamus
    - (C) The hypothalamus
    - (D) The kidneys
    - (E) The adrenal glands

34. Imposing order on individual details in order to view them as part of a whole is a basic principle of which of the following types of psychologists?
    - (A) Behaviorist
    - (B) Psychodynamic
    - (C) Humanistic
    - (D) Gestalt
    - (E) Cognitive socialist

35. To determine the number of students in the school who own personal computers, a school bookstore decides to survey the members of the introductory computer science class. A problem with this study is that
    - (A) the survey may not elicit the information the store is looking for
    - (B) the store is not surveying a representative sample of students
    - (C) the survey is being constructed without a hypothesis
    - (D) it is unclear as to whether the bookstore will be able to establish causation
    - (E) the survey is being given during school hours

36. When an individual looks through a window in the morning, the two regions of the cortex that are stimulated are

   (A) the temporal lobes and the occipital lobes
   (B) the parietal lobes and the frontal lobes
   (C) the frontal lobes and the temporal lobes
   (D) the temporal lobes and the parietal lobes
   (E) the occipital lobes and the parietal lobes

37. Which of the following statements is true of behaviorism?

   (A) It holds that most behaviors are the result of unconscious motives that come into conflict.
   (B) It focuses on the development of the cognitive self in regard to behavior.
   (C) It holds that development is largely a product of learning.
   (D) It emphasizes the role of nature over the impact of nurture.
   (E) It was developed to replace the cognitive and humanistic perspectives.

End Time: _____

Right: _____

Turn to Chapter 12 to check how you did this time. If you missed a question, no big deal. If you missed more than one question and were finished in less than five minutes, you were working too fast. Slow your pace and pick up your accuracy.

Should You Ever Leave a Question Blank?

Maybe you skip it for later, but make sure to select a response through POE and common sense, or use your Letter of the Day if you are completely lost.

To Skip or Not to Skip

No order of difficulty is perfect for each individual, especially on an exam that is testing each individual's knowledge of a particular subject. If you hit a topic you don't know very well, or feel that a question is too long to tackle right now, it's perfectly fine to skip it and move on to some of the other 74 questions first. Remember, this is your test—you should take it in the order that is best for you.

A Few Things to Consider for the Hardest Questions

Roughly one third of the questions on the test are likely going to be harder than the others, and if you're aiming for a 5 or even a 4 on the AP, you're going to need to get some of them right (even more, if you don't think you'll do well on the free-response section). This is where your time management to this point will pay off. The more time you have to think about these questions, the greater your chance of either outright solving it or narrowing down your choices and improving your odds with POE. Be sure to use your smart-tester strategies: Understand the Question/Key Words, Predict the Answer, and POE. If you get it down to two choices and don't know which one is correct, make a smart guess and move on. You have a fifty-fifty chance of guessing correctly, so you are a lot better off than when you started.

Smart Guessing = Common Sense. Sometimes you will be familiar with the topic of a question, but not enough to answer the question. In addition to using your usual strategy, you can also use your common sense, and the information you do have, to use POE and then take a smart guess. Look at the following example:

87. Which of the following most accurately lists the stages of Hans Selye's general adaptation syndrome?

(A) Shock, anger, self-control
(B) Appraisal, stress response, coping
(C) Alarm, resistance, exhaustion
(D) Anxiety, fighting, adapting
(E) Attack, flight, defense

Now, let's assume you have no idea what Hans Selye's general adaptation syndrome is. You can still follow the smart strategy, and use your common sense to get close to the answer.

Understand the Question/Key Words: Highlight *general adaptation syndrome*. Think about what that term might mean:

It has something to do with adapting, and it's a syndrome, which often means something negative.

Predict the Answer: Stages of adaptation that seem to characterize a kind of syndrome.

Use POE:

(A) Are *shock, anger,* and *self-control* stages of adaptation that characterize a kind of syndrome? No, a syndrome would not end up in self-control. Cross it off.

(B) Are *appraisal, stress response,* and *coping* stages of adaptation that characterize a kind of syndrome? No, they seem much more normal and positive. Cross it off.

(C) Are *alarm, resistance,* and *exhaustion* stages of adaptation that characterize a kind of syndrome? This is the most feasible choice so far. Keep it and read on.

(D) Are *anxiety, fighting,* and *adapting* stages of adaptation that characterize a kind of syndrome? Again, a syndrome would not have a last stage of adapting. Cross it off. Don't let the word *adapting* in this choice throw you off.

(E) Are *attack, flight,* and *defense* stages of adaptation that characterize a kind of syndrome? This one also has negative attributes that could constitute a syndrome.

Stay Tuned!

Given the newness of the AP Psychology exam, it's a good idea to check both your online student tools for any late-breaking announcements or changes and also to check out The Princeton Review's YouTube channel for any other tips, advice, or news: www.youtube.com/ThePrincetonReview.

You are left with (C) and (E). Take a guess, and remember that you have narrowed your choices down to a fifty-fifty shot on a question about which you had no clue. The correct answer, by the way, is (C). Given that the name of the syndrome is the "general adaptation syndrome" and not the "best way to cause a fight" syndrome, (C) is your smarter guess.

Here's another example of how your common sense can help you eliminate wrong answers:

(A) Personal conscience is innate, and all human beings develop it at the same rate.
(B) By adulthood, all people judge moral issues in terms of self-chosen principles.

Hey, wait a minute. Where's the question? We've given you these two answer choices to demonstrate how common sense can play an important role in getting rid of wrong answer choices. Let's evaluate these two answer choices. Choice (A) says that *personal conscience is innate, and all human beings develop it at the same rate.* Does that sound accurate? Even without knowing the question, it is hard to imagine that any psychologist would suggest that all human beings develop personal conscience at the same rate. You know this answer cannot be the answer to the question simply by using common sense. Cross it off.

How about (B): *By adulthood, all people judge moral issues in terms of self-chosen principles.* Again, is this statement true? Even if a lot of people judge moral issues in terms of self-chosen principles, it is rare that all people ever do anything the same way. The extreme language of this answer choice can help you determine that it is wrong. Without even knowing the question, you are able to eliminate two answer choices by using your common sense.

Be Selective. In dealing with hard questions, remember that you don't need to work through them all. You choose the difficult questions you want to do and in what order you want to do them.

CREATE YOUR PERSONAL PACING STRATEGY

The smart-tester strategies are best when you've practiced them enough that they become second nature. Once you are comfortable with your question strategy, do some timed work to help determine your personal pacing strategy. As you strengthen your test-taking skills, try to finish more and more of Section I. Determine what working *efficiently and effectively* means for you. And remember, you have an essay portion that will contribute to your final grade, as well. Emphasize your strengths to get the best grade you can. Oh yeah, and you'd better review some psychology, too!

Chapter 2
How to Approach
Free-Response
Questions

OVERVIEW OF THE FREE-RESPONSE SECTION

Section II: Free Response. It has a nice ring to it, doesn't it? That word *free* gives it a melodic sound. Well, don't be fooled. On the AP Psychology Exam, "free response" is simply a euphemism for *timed essays*. Let's review the facts about Section II.

- You are required to answer two essays.

How Do They Score Them?

Before the graders begin reading essays, they are given a checklist of points they should look for. The test makers determine exactly how many points each essay is worth by doing a count. Keep in mind that the readers are locked into that scale—they will not give you an extra point for unrelated information or anything else.

- The first is an Article Analysis Question: You will read one summarized, peer-reviewed article. You must identify elements of a research study. Additionally, you will be required to interpret basic statistics, discuss whether the study generalizes to the population, and determine if psychological concepts are supported or refuted by the article. You have 25 minutes to complete this essay (including a 10-minute reading period).

- The second is an Evidence-Based Question: You will read three related summarized, peer-reviewed articles. Using those sources and what you learned in AP Psychology, you will present an assertion about the topic. Remember to use evidence from what you read to support or refute your claim. You have 45 minutes to complete this essay (including a 15-minute reading period).

- There is no choice—two essays are presented, and you must do both.

- Each essay is worth 16.65 percent of your score.

- Each essay has a specified number of pieces of information you need to provide, usually 7.

Sound Familiar?

Often, when a student realizes he needs to write an essay under timed conditions, panic sets in. As he begins to read the question, his heart races, and he has difficulty concentrating on what the question is asking. He knows he should outline something, but he is afraid he will run out of time, so he just jumps in and starts writing. Midway through paragraph one, feeling a little light-headed, he realizes that he doesn't really understand the question. He glances back at the question but, worried that he's losing precious minutes, decides he needs to forge ahead.

Partway through paragraph two (yes, he did remember to use paragraphs), he realizes that he has skipped a big point he needs to make. Should he cross off what he has written, or do the verbal backpedal until he can work it in? "How much time is left, anyway?" he asks himself. And on it goes.

Relax: It's common for one's sympathetic nervous system to kick into gear at the mention of a timed essay. How can you effectively write not one but two essays in a limited period of time? By being a smart tester.

SMART-TESTER ESSAY WRITING

Compared to the panicked tester from the example above, the smart tester knows that she can't write an effective essay without understanding the question. She spends her first 1–2 minutes "working the question over," pulling it apart to make sure she knows exactly what she is being asked to do. Next, she sets up a chart and spends 3–5 minutes outlining the points she will make. She then counts up her points and sketches the layout of the essay.

In that first 7–10 minutes, the smart tester has done the bulk of the work for her essay without actually writing a word of it. She can then spend the next 15 minutes writing the essay, whose framework she has already created; no skipped points, no major cross-outs. She may even be able to put in some impressive vocabulary. Spending time planning the essay actually gives you more time for writing the essay.

Be the Smart Tester

Because you have read this far in the book, you must be a smart tester. We're now going to teach you all the secrets of writing a great essay (or two, for that matter) without activating your adrenal glands. To become the smart essay-writer, you first need to know what the readers—the people who will grade your essays—are looking for.

What's in an Essay

There are lots of different ways to write a quality essay. However, you have a more specific goal in mind when it comes to the AP Psychology essays—you want to get points. Therefore, you need to know what the graders want so that you can write an essay that will earn a good score.

> **Need More Help on Essays?**
> We've got just the book for that! *How to Write Essays for Standardized Tests* contains advice and examples of best practices on an assortment of AP exams, plus the ACT, and others!

According to the College Board's published materials on the AP Psychology free-response questions, you may be asked to do one of the following:

- **Describe:** Provide the relevant characteristics of a specified topic.

- **Explain:** Provide information about how or why a relationship, situation, or outcome occurs, using evidence and/or reasoning to support or qualify a claim. **Explain how** typically requires analyzing the relationship, situation, or outcome. **Explain why** typically requires analysis of motivations or reasons for the relationship, situation, or outcome.

- **Identify/State:** Indicate or provide information about a specified topic, without elaboration or explanation.

- **Propose:** Provide a claim for a specific topic using your own words.

- **Support or Refute:** Provide reasoning that explains whether a claim or evidence should be upheld or rejected.

- **Use evidence:** Provide information from a study (i.e., data, rationales, conclusions, hypotheses) that is specific and relevant to a given topic.

In each of these cases, if you want a good score, you'll benefit from making your essay as readable as possible so it's easy for the grader to give you top marks:

- Get right to the point.
- Use the correct psychology terms where appropriate.
- Define all terms.
- Support everything with an example or study, preferably from your course work (*not* an example from your own personal life).
- Clearly state the purpose of the example or study (support or contrast).
- Be clear, concise, and direct.

What Not to Do

In addition, there are a few no-nos that the College Board implies or states outright.

- Do *not* restate the question in your essay.
- Do *not* suggest anything that can be misconstrued as unethical.
- Do *not* write everything you know on the topic; stay focused on the question.
- Do *not* begin writing until you have a clue about what you are going to write.

If it helps, understand that each of your essays is only going to get about five minutes of a reader's time. That's the context you're writing toward: you don't need beautiful prose so much as you need clear answers that satisfy their rubric.

The Reading

After the AP Exams are given, the College Board and ETS get together a slew of high school teachers and college professors and stick them in a room for six days to do nothing but read essays. ETS and the Board fondly refer to this process as the Reading (always capitalized). During the Reading, the readers are typically required to read hundreds of essays.

The test-makers first create a rubric by which to grade the essays. Each part of each FRQ is assigned a number of possible points, and then depending on the specific prompts, readers are told which kinds of responses merit points and which do not. The closer you come to satisfying each question, the more likely you are to be awarded full points. Note that your essay may be read and scored by a number of readers. (You can see the current framework of the rubric by looking in the 2024 Course and Exam Description here: https://apcentral.collegeboard.org/courses/ap-psychology/revisions-2024-25/exam.)

Talkin' About Good News

This is all good news for you because it means that you can put together a high-scoring essay without panicking about time constraints and exact wording. Let's work through the smart-tester strategies for writing a high-scoring essay, and then finish up with some pointers for adding polish.

Smart-Tester Strategy #1: Work It

Imagine you are in the boxing ring of the AP Psychology Championship. You have already sustained 90 minutes of multiple-choice sparring, and now you have to take on two more big questions in 70 minutes to come out the winner. You're not hanging back, passively reading the question, hoping to understand it. If you took that approach, you'd get pummeled, and so would your score. Instead, you get in there and work it over; you pull it apart, examine each piece, and determine what the important stuff is.

Work It

The first step is reading all the prompts and sources provided. Then, start taking it apart piece by piece.

QUESTION 1: ARTICLE ANALYSIS QUESTION (AAQ)

Researchers believe that students' exposure to negative life events is a significant cause of poor school performance. To test their idea, they first analyzed the sorts of events they had in mind and assigned them point values indicating how serious an adverse effect they might have. For example, "witnessing a violent crime" was assigned 70 points; experiencing the death of a close family member, 100 points; breaking up with a boyfriend or girlfriend, 30 points; being diagnosed with a sexually transmitted disease, 85 points; and so on.

Next, researchers got permission from the school system to administer a questionnaire to students who gave, or whose parents gave (if they were minors), an informed consent to participate. As part of the questionnaire, students listed the negative life events that they had experienced in the preceding two years.

Finally, researchers added the points for each student and found that the totals fell into three clear categories that they labeled "low stress," "medium stress," and "high stress." They then looked at the students' grade point averages and found that these varied inversely with the stress groups (i.e., high stress was correlated with low GPA, etc.), thereby validating their hypothesis.

The students and parents involved first found out about these findings when the researchers published them in a professional journal.

Your response to the question should be provided in six parts: A, B, C, D, E, and F.

Write the response to each part of the question in complete sentences. Use appropriate psychological terminology in your response.

Using the source provided, respond to all parts of the question.

(A) Identify the type of research design used in this study.
(B) State the operational definition of the variable "stress."
(C) Identify results and explain how statistical significance would apply to an analysis of this study.
(D) Identify a possible ethical concern about how this research was conducted.
(E) Explain how Hans Selye's general adaptation syndrome applies to the study described above.
(F) Explain how both learned helplessness and Maslow's Hierarchy of Needs might apply to the study.

Highlight the key words—words that indicate transitions and changes in the direction of the sentence—and mark the critical terms. Make notes as needed to ensure that you understand what is written.

Here's what we did:

Researchers believe that students' exposure to negative life events is a significant cause of poor school performance. To test their idea, they first analyzed the sorts of events they had in mind and assigned them point values indicating how serious an adverse effect they might have. For example, "witnessing a violent crime" was assigned 70 points; experiencing the death of a close family member, 100 points; breaking up with a boyfriend or girlfriend, 30 points; being diagnosed with a sexually transmitted disease, 85 points; and so on.

Next, researchers got permission from the school system to administer a questionnaire to students who gave, or whose parents gave (if they were minors), an informed consent to participate. As part of the questionnaire, students listed the negative life events that they had experienced in the preceding two years.

Finally, researchers added the points for each student and found that the totals fell into three clear categories that they labeled "low stress," "medium stress," and "high stress." They then looked at the students' grade point averages and found that these varied inversely with the stress groups (i.e., high stress was correlated with low GPA, etc.), thereby validating their hypothesis.

The students and parents involved first found out about these findings when the researchers published them in a professional journal.

NOTES:

Adverse events and school performance were being compared

This was a correlational study (compares 2 variables) not experimental. A questionnaire was used, no control/randomization of variables

"Stress" is defined based on points assigned to each student (high/med/low)

Results showed inverse relationship (i.e., negative correlation)—statistic not provided

Students and parents were not informed of results; is this a problem?

Smart-Tester Strategy #2: Chart It

The first essay has six parts (A–F), and organizing your thoughts will help to address each. Look at one part at a time:

Let's work Parts A–F together.

Part (A): Identify the type of research design used in this study.

You're being instructed to *identify* the methodology used. You need to know what the graders are told about this: **Definitions alone do NOT score points!** So, no matter how well you might know some of these concepts and how expertly you may define them, without *explaining* them or *applying* these facts to the source provided, you will get no credit for your response.

From our breakdown of the source and from your notes, you know the researchers are looking for a relationship between two variables: negative life events and poor school performance. You also know they ranked the events on a scale and provided a questionnaire to participants. Let's chart accordingly to keep our thinking straight.

Parts	Instruction	Explain
(A)		
(B)		
(C)		
(D)		
(E)		
(F)		

Look at each topic to make sure that you can 1) follow the instructions in each part of the question and 2) explain it. Remember, you're trying to do only enough to earn the point and then move on so that you can hit all of the topics in the 25 minutes you have. So, your chart might look like this:

Parts	Instruction	Explain
(A) Research Design		
(B)		
(C)		
(D)		
(E)		
(F)		

So far, so good. Now, let's look at Part B. Once again, address the critical stuff: you must define and explain, but this time in regard to what the researchers did with "stress."

> Part (B): State the operational definition of the variable "stress." Your chart might look something like this:

Parts	Instruction	Explain
(A) Research Design		
(B) Operational Definition		
(C)		
(D)		
(E)		
(F)		

But Wait, There's More

You're well on your way to a great essay, but first, you need to complete your chart. And don't worry about this taking a long time; it won't after a little practice. Just jot a few notes under the Instruction/Explain columns using your notes. Let's do Parts A and B together:

For Part A, write the following in your Instruction and Explain columns:

Identify: Correlation

So, here you are identifying the construct of "correlation" in the Instruction column. In the Explain column, you will address why:

Compares 2 variables; NOT experiment (no controls)

Now, your chart might look like this:

Parts	Instruction	Explain
(A) Research Design	Identify: Correlation	Compares 2 variables; NOT experiment (no controls)
(B) Operational Definition		
(C)		
(D)		
(E)		
(F)		

For Part B, write:

Define: STRESS
How? points assigned to each student for negative events (high/med/low)

Your chart now looks something like this:

Parts	Instruction	Explain
(A) Research Design	Identify: Correlation	Compares 2 variables; NOT experiment (no controls)
(B) Operational Definition	Define: STRESS	How? points assigned to each student for negative events (high/med/low)
(C)		
(D)		
(E)		
(F)		

Avoid the tendency to try to download everything you know about the concepts in your responses. Save time and avoid overkill! Here's an example of a finished chart:

Parts	Instruction	Explain
(A) Research Design	Identify: Correlation	Compares 2 variables; NOT experiment (no controls)
(B) Operational Definition	Define: STRESS	How? points assigned to each student for negative events (high/med/low)
(C) Significance	Identify: VALIDATED	Inverse relationship, strength not mentioned, significance level not mentioned
(D) Ethical Issues	Identify: Failed to debrief students/parents; problem? Yes!	Students/parents: seek help/assist/counseling School: offer more services/accommodations
(E) Hans Selye GAS	Identify: alarm, resistance, exhaustion	Effects of prolonged stress → illness → poor academics
(F) Learned Helplessness	Identify: continued efforts make no difference	Negative events can't change → give up trying → poor grades
Maslow's Hierarchy	Identify: meet basic needs first	More motivation to meet basic needs (coping) instead of grades

Smart-Tester Strategies #1 and #2

Let's review. Smart-Tester Strategy #1: Work It—work the question over so that you know exactly what you are being asked. While you are working over the question, you will also begin to do Smart-Tester Strategy #2: Chart It—draw your chart and, if you feel comfortable, fill it in at the same time (why add another step?). You may wish to give the question a quick read-through before you begin, but you don't need to artificially separate working the question from writing your outline. This entire process should take you between five and seven minutes.

Smart-Tester Strategy #3: Count It

On the new version of the AP Psychology exam, both the EBQ and AAQ are scored on a 7-point scale. In the case of this question, that means they would assign one point per topic if you did the two things required of you: Answer the Instruction *and* Explain. So, now is a good time to go back over what you've charted out and make sure that you have all of the points covered.

Do not despair if there are one or two concepts that you do not know or are unclear about. Students have achieved overall scores of 5 in such situations. The important thing is that if you are hung up on a concept or two, and racking your brain for information that you vaguely remember from a class or from your textbook, you do NOT get bogged down by every individual part of the question and you do NOT ruin your pacing! If necessary, leave a blank for now and move on. Perhaps, during the writing process, when you look at the question with fresh eyes, it will shake something loose from your memory. If not, so be it. You can miss some things here and there and still achieve an excellent score.

One thing that you never want to do is go past 35 minutes for the first essay, "borrowing" time from the second essay. Although each question is worth the same number of points, you don't want to put yourself in a situation where you have fewer than 45 minutes to answer the EBQ, or you may end up rushing and making avoidable mistakes.

Smart-Tester Strategy #4: Sketch It

Sketch out your essay in the one minute or so before you begin to write. Often, these questions do not require either an introduction or a conclusion. Sometimes, an opening statement can be beneficial.

You are going to follow the Instruction and Explain all six parts of the question (Part F is worth 2 points, so you are going to have up to seven paragraphs, which you will indicate by drawing a box around what will be in each paragraph. But in which order should you address this first essay's seven points? If you feel relatively confident about the five concepts, address them in the order in which they are presented. This makes things easier for the grader and, if there is a paragraph whose subject you haven't been clear about, the grader is instructed to give you credit for the concept that fits in the sequence. If, however, your confidence level varies greatly among the concepts, start with the ones you feel best about and leave any that you feel shaky about to the end. This way, the grader gets a sense of your overall understanding of the material and may give you the benefit of the doubt later on. If you take this "out-of-order" approach, however, you MUST indicate clearly within each paragraph which concept you are addressing.

So, it might look like this:

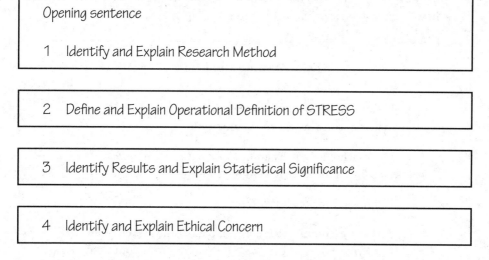

Opening sentence

1   Identify and Explain Research Method

2   Define and Explain Operational Definition of STRESS

3   Identify Results and Explain Statistical Significance

4   Identify and Explain Ethical Concern

5   Support/Explain Hans Selye's GAS

6   Support/Explain Learned Helplessness

7   Support/Explain Maslow's Hierarchy of Needs

Smart-Tester Strategy #5: Write It

Now that you have a sketch, your essay will practically write itself. You just need to piece it together in a clear, concise manner. As you write, check off each point on your sketch as you complete it. That way you'll be sure not to skip anything. Keep in mind that the readers will not grade your charts or outlines. The essay must be written in paragraph form. Be sure to write in complete sentences. Don't use symbols or bulleted lists to define or give examples. If you are running out of time, continue writing pertinent information. Your essay should take about 10 to 15 minutes to write. Then it's on to the second essay!

The Opening

Did you think we'd desert you without first guiding you through the actual writing? Never! Let's review how to get a good score according to the College Board.

> **Essay-Writing Guidelines**
>
> - If you wish to write an introductory sentence, make sure that it is not a repeat of the question.
>
> - Use psychology terms and proper names of theories, theorists, and other important concepts.
>
> - Define and mark all key terms.
>
> - Support each part with an example or study, preferably from your course work (*not* an example from your own personal life).
>
> - Clearly state the purpose of the example or study (support or contrast).
>
> - Be clear, concise, and direct.

You could simply jump into your discussion of the research method you've identified and why (or another concept you felt more confident about if you were going out of order). On the other hand, an acceptable opening sentence might be:

Many life events are negative and affect a person's well-being, socialization, and a number of other areas of daily functioning that researchers find interesting to study using various research paradigms.

Note that this sentence is not going to earn you any points on its own, which is why it is optional. However, it does indicate to the grader that you carefully read the question and that your discussion of each concept might go in a different direction than the one before or after it.

Choose Your Words Wisely

The more appropriate psychological terms you use, the better the point-value of your essay. For example, in your discussion of the research design, if you use terms like *control group* or *random assignment*, all the better. If your pacing is going along well, you might consider ending this section with the following line:

Because an experiment was not conducted, no causal inference between negative life events and academic performance can be drawn.

While this sentence isn't going to earn you additional points, it may solidify in the grader's mind that you know your stuff and resolve any benefit of the doubt in your favor. But remember that it's only going to help if you have related this new research methods topic to the content of the source.

Examples, Examples, Examples

All the College Board literature clearly states that the graders like, and often expect, to see students' points supported by appropriate examples. When inserting examples, remember the following:

1. Don't use examples from your personal life.

2. Make sure they are relevant to your point and make a clear reference to the question being asked.

3. Flag your examples with the words "for example."

A good example is something that you learned in your course, from your own reading, or from this book. A bad example is, "I always notice a drop in my own grades when I'm under stress." Enough said.

Before you give the example, make it clear whether it is supporting your point or contesting your point. This procedure ties in perfectly with the third point about examples: always flag your examples with an introductory phrase. Again, the readers are reading your essay quickly. They will pause if they see an example and will be impressed by examples that are clearly delineated. If your example supports a point you just made, flag it with "for example." If it contrasts the point, insert a sentence that introduces it:

> And while it's not the school's responsibility to address these needs, had the school system known of this connection earlier, they could have offered more services to these students, and it might have advised teachers about possible accommodations to implement for students with these issues.

Note that the phrase "And while it's not the school's responsibility…" introduces a change in the direction of the paragraph and further indicates to the grader your understanding of the concept.

Closing

As with the opening, a closing statement is not necessary and is not likely to earn you any specific points. However, if you have time and wish to sum up, make sure that your statement is consistent with the points you have already made.

Plain, Good Writing

Finally, don't add in a lot of fluff. The AP Psych essay questions are pretty meaty. Your job is to write an essay that has no additives or fillers. At the same time, it's important that your essay be complete. Don't skip over points. Your reader is counting up the 7 points you are supposed to make. If you miss one, you lose a point. That also goes for running out of time. There is no reason to run out of time on an essay, and if you do, it will hurt your score. To avoid this problem, use the plans below.

Article Analysis Question (25 Minutes Total)

Essay Smart-Tester Strategies	Total Time 7–10 minutes
#1 Work It	1–2 minutes
#2 Chart It	3–5 minutes
#3 Count It	1 minute
#4 Sketch It	1–2 minutes

Essay Smart-Tester Strategies	Total Time 10–15 minutes
#5 Write it	Keep track of your own time. Finish the essay before time is called.

Evidence Based Question (45 Minutes Total)

Essay Smart-Tester Strategies	Total Time 12–15 minutes
#1 Work It	5–7 minutes
#2 Chart It	3–5 minutes
#3 Count It	1 minute
#4 Sketch It	1–2 minutes

Essay Smart-Tester Strategies	Total Time 20–30 minutes
#5 Write it	Keep track of your own time. Finish the essay before time is called.

When you hit the 35-minute mark, wrap things up and move on to the second essay.

Finishing Touches

There are just a few more things to make sure you get all the points you can. First, when you've finished an essay, double-check that you have addressed all the points you originally counted. Second, as you move from one thought to another, use trigger words and transitional phrases. For example:

> In Selye's general adaptation syndrome, people react to stress in three phases: they respond to the stress with alarm; then they resist its effects; but then, if it goes on for a long time, they can become exhausted. This exhaustion can then lead to physical illness.

As compared with:

> In Selye's general adaptation syndrome, people in the exhaustion phase get physically sick.

Although there's nothing wrong with the second sentence, the first sentence creates better flow and more cohesion in the essay.

Also, use the highest level of vocabulary that is comfortable for you. In other words, don't use too much slang, but don't write in a way that will sound awkward or forced. Do your best to use the most concise terminology possible. Misused words stick out like sore thumbs. Err on the side of caution.

Lookin' Good

Lastly, remember that first impressions count. In the case of your essays, the better they look, the more positive a reader is likely to regard them at the outset. You won't have to worry about your handwriting on a digital test, but other factors like length, formatting, and a lack of glaring typos will work in your favor. Make sure you indent the paragraphs and proofread as you go to revise any errors.

After you finish writing this practice Article Analysis Essay, check your work against ours in Chapter 12.

> **TIME!**
> Don't rely on your proctor to keep time accurately, or to remember to give you a 35-minute warning. Wear a kind of watch that is permitted at your test site and keep your own time.

Put It All Together

Now that you have the knowledge to be a smart essay-writer, put your skills to the test on the following question. (It's a question #2, so "Evidence Based.") When you are finished, check your work against ours. You can find many more sample prompts from real tests to practice on at the College Board's AP Students website: apstudents.collegeboard.org/courses/ap-psychology/free-response-questions-by-year. Good luck and good writing!

QUESTION 2: EVIDENCE-BASED QUESTION (EBQ)

This question has three parts: Part A, Part B, and Part C. Use the three sources provided to answer all parts of the question.

For Part B and Part C, you must cite the source that you used to answer the question. You can do this in two different ways:

- Parenthetical Citation:
  For example: "...(Source A)"

- Embedded Citation:
  For example: "According to Source A,..."

Write the response to each part of the question in complete sentences. Use appropriate psychological terminology.

Using the sources provided, make a claim about the mixed findings regarding efficacy of pet ownership and attachment to animals in improving mental and/or physical health, and how such studies might better replicate generalizability.

A. Identify a specific and defensible claim based in psychological science that responds to the question.

B. (i) Support your claim using at least one piece of specific and relevant evidence from one of the sources.

(ii) Explain how the evidence from Part B (i) supports your claim using a psychological perspective, theory, concept, or research finding learned in AP Psychology.

C. (i) Support your claim using an additional piece of scientific and relevant evidence form a different source than the one that was used in Part B (i).

(ii) Explain how the evidence from Part C (i) supports your claim using a different psychological perspective, theory, concept, or research finding learned in AP Psychology than the one that was used in Part B (ii).

Source A

Introduction
Research has predominantly shown that having a pet will increase health and psychological well-being (e.g., stress reduction). Studies have looked at the effects of pet ownership on individuals, and attachment to pets (similar to that of parents with their children), but none has investigated the relationship between strength of attachment to a pet and level of reported family conflict. The current research hypothesized that deep attachment to one's pet would be associated with families reporting high levels of conflict.
Participants
Data were collected from participants that had been recruited for a longitudinal study (1968-2014). The current study used a subset of those data (from 2013), which included 1,421 people (M = 36.5 years, 83.7% women). All of these participants were primary caregivers (PCGs) of at least one child under the age of 18 and were also pet owners (79% dogs, 34% cats, 28% "other"). More than half of the sample was white (69.1%), only 25.6% were Black, 10.8% Latinx, and 5.3% were from other races. No informed consent was required.
Method
Sociodemographic data from the longitudinal study were mined for this study including gender, income, education, marital status, number of children, race, and ethnicity. Additional data from the longitudinal study the current research analyzed included three questions the PCG answered about attachment to their pet, coded on a scale from 3 (weak) to 12 (strong). These scores were based on types of interactions with the pet in their home (e.g., played with pet, sought comfort from pet, considered pet a family member).   The PCGs had also been asked two questions about family conflict: 2 (low conflict) to 10 (high conflict). The scores on this scale were derived by answers to questions about discussion style and instances of criticism in the family. Group differences were analyzed for PCGs with weak versus strong pet attachment, and then for sociodemographic and family conflict characteristics.
Results and Discussion
Taking the sociodemographic factors into account, analyses revealed that family conflict was a significant direct predictor of strength of attachment to pets. As compared to PCGs that were women (44.5%), a larger proportion of PGCs that were men (57.1%) reported higher attachment to their pets, despite that more women were PCGs in the total sample. Fewer white people reported strong pet attachment than Black people and respondents of other races. PGCs with strong attachment to their pets reported significantly higher family conflict than those with weak attachment [$t(1,419) = -2.11$, $p < 0.05$].

Adapted from *Anthrozoös.*

Applebaum, J.W., & Zsembik, B.A. (2020). Pet attachment in the context of family conflict. *Anthrozoös, 33*(3), 361-370, DOI: 10.1080/08927936.2020.1746524

Source B

Introduction
Dog ownership has been found to decrease psychological distress and, temporarily, benefit physical health, including a boost to the immune system (i.e., decreased cortisol levels, increased oxytocin), often referred to as the "pet effect." However, the literature shows mixed results because of inconsistent methodologies. To compensate for confusion in the literature, the following study took a social-context based approach to develop a more systematic paradigm. The researchers measured indices of stress after exposing participants to a demanding set of tasks during interaction with either a live dog or a stuffed teddy bear.

Participants
Researchers recruited 223 undergraduate students (M = 19.2 years old, 80% = female, 80% = Caucasian), who all received extra credit in their courses for participation. All of the participants were pre-screened for positive attitudes toward dogs (specifically large ones) and signed an informed consent form. Those with allergies to animals were excluded. Participants were admonished from participating in exercise or drinking caffeine two hours prior to their arrival.

Method
Using self-report scales (empirically normed), psychological measures like state and trait anxiety were taken, and heart rate and blood pressure were the physiological indices measured. A single dog served as the pet-live stimulus (100 lbs., male black Labrador), and, as a control for tactile stimulation, the researchers used a brown teddy bear (1/3 the size of the dog) for the pet-stuffed condition.
Each participant was given a solitary, 10-minute relaxation period in a waiting room. During this 10 minutes, they could read a magazine, but no academic materials or electronic devices, and a baseline measure of state anxiety, blood pressure, and heart rate were taken (Time 1). After this relaxation period, the participant was tasked with writing a five-minute speech on why they would make a good pet store manager. They were given five minutes to write the speech, meant to be delivered to a panel of judges in front of a video camera.
At this point, half the participants were introduced to the black Lab; half to the teddy bear. Each participant was instructed to continuously pet the dog/bear while preparing their speech. After the participant delivered the speech, they were given a series of subtraction problems to perform in front of the judges, while still stroking their "pet," and peak stress (Time 2) was measured again. Finally, the participant was returned to the waiting room, without their "pet" for 10 minutes, after which a post stress measure was taken (Time 3).

Results and Discussion
As predicted, those in the pet-live condition had lower state anxiety scores than those in the pet-stuffed condition. Additionally, participants that scored high on trait anxiety also had higher state anxiety scores than those that scored low on anxiety traits. Also, as predicted, there was a significant effect of time for both pet conditions, such that heart rate and blood pressure increased at Time 2 (peak stress), but decreased at Time 3.
Further, there was an interaction effect: Those in the pet-stuffed condition had a significantly higher state anxiety score at peak anxiety (Time 2) than pet-live, but only for participants that scored high on trait anxiety.
Below represents pet condition differences (live vs. stuffed) in average blood pressure, heart rate, and state anxiety measures at peak stress.

	Blood Pressure		Heart Rate		State Anxiety	
	High Trait	Low Trait	High Trait	Low Trait	High Trait	Low Trait
Pet-Live Condition	117	118	79	81	45	37
Pet-Stuffed Condition	124*	120	86*	79	52*	40

Peak Stress measures (Blood Pressure/ Systolic, Heart Rate/bpm)
Represents significantly higher scores

Adapted from *Society & Animals*.

Wheeler, E.A., & Faulkner, M.E. (2015). The "pet effect" physiological calming in the presence of canines. *Society & Animals 23*, 425-438, DOI: 10.1163/15685306-12341374

Source C

Introduction
Prior research has shown that having a pet is instrumental in mitigating the effects of childhood neglect (e.g., better coping mechanisms, increased oxytocin levels). An additional source of support might be found in attachment to stuffed animals. The following study examined the relationship among childhood neglect, attachment to pets, and attachment to toy, stuffed animals.
Participants
Psychology undergraduates were recruited for participation (N = 457, M = 22.7 years; 54% women). The students all received partial course credit and gave signed informed consent for their online participation.
Method
Three self-report tools were used: Pet Attachment and Life Impact Scale (PALS), Stuffed Animal Attachment Questionnaire (SAQ), and the Multidimensional Neglectful Behavior Scale. All three surveys have been tested empirically for reliability and validity. After the questionnaires were completed, participants were debriefed. Researchers were testing whether childhood neglect would be associated with attachment to companion, and/or stuffed animals and they expected a gender differential such that women would be more attached to both as compared to men.
Results and Discussion
Preliminary analyses showed that attachment to companion animals was positively related to attachment to stuffed animals and those participants that owned at least one stuffed animal had higher attachment to pets than those that had no stuffed animals. Analyses of the three hypotheses bore that childhood neglect was not significantly related to attachment to pets or to stuffed animals for the sample on the whole. However, an unexpected gender finding showed for women that self-reported neglect (as compared to women who did not), there was a positive relationship between neglect scores and attachment to companion animals only and, women were significantly more attached to both companion, and stuffed animals, than men.

Adapted from *Anthrozoös*.

Barlow, M.R., Hutchinson, C.A., Newton, K., Grover, T. & Ward, L. (2012). Childhood neglect, attachment to companion animals, and stuffed animals as attachment objects in women and men. *Anthrozoös, 25*(1), 111-119, DOI: 10.2752/175303712X13240472427159

Chapter 3
Using Time Effectively to Maximize Points

BECOMING A BETTER TEST-TAKER

Very few students stop to think about how to improve their test-taking skills. Most assume that if they study hard, they will test well, and if they do not study, they will do poorly. Most students continue to believe this even after experience teaches them otherwise. Have you ever studied really hard for an exam and then blown it on test day? Have you ever aced an exam for which you thought you weren't well prepared? Most students have had one, if not both, of these experiences. The lesson should be clear: factors other than your level of preparation influence your final test score. This chapter will provide you with some insights that will help you perform better on the AP Psychology Exam and on other exams, as well.

PACING AND TIMING

Remember, when guessing randomly, choose a letter that you will use consistently, your Letter of the Day (LOTD). If you choose the same letter, odds are that one in five random guesses will be correct.

A big part of scoring well on an exam is working at a consistent pace. The worst mistake made by inexperienced or unsavvy test-takers is that they come to a question that stumps them, and rather than just skip it, they panic and stall. Time stands still when you're working on a question you cannot answer, and it is not unusual for students to waste five minutes on a single question (especially a question involving a graph or the word EXCEPT) because they are too stubborn to cut their losses. It is important to be aware of how much time you have spent on a given question and on the section you are working. There are several ways to improve your pacing and timing for the test.

- **Know your average pace.** While you prepare for your test, try to gauge how long you take on 5, 10, or 20 questions. Knowing how long you spend, on average, per question will help you identify the number of questions you can answer effectively and how best to pace yourself for the test.

- **Have a watch or clock nearby.** You are permitted to have a watch or clock nearby to help you keep track of time. It is important to remember, however, that constantly checking the clock is in itself a waste of time and can be distracting. Devise a plan. Try checking the clock after every 15 or 30 questions to see whether you are keeping the correct pace or whether you need to speed up. This will ensure that you're cognizant of the time but will not permit you to fall into the trap of dwelling on it.

- **Know when to move on.** Because all questions are scored equally, investing appreciable amounts of time on a single question is inefficient and can potentially deprive you of the chance to answer easier questions later on. If you are able to eliminate answer choices, do so, but don't worry about picking a random answer (try picking your Letter of the Day!) and moving on if you cannot find the correct answer. Remember, tests are like marathons; you do best when you work through them at a steady pace. You can always come back to a question you don't know the answer to. When you do, very often you will find that your previous mental block is gone, and you will wonder why the question perplexed you the first time around (as you gleefully move on to the next question). Even if you still don't know the answer, you will not have wasted valuable time you could have spent on easier questions.

- **Be selective.** You don't have to do any of the questions in a given section in order. If you are stumped by an essay or multiple-choice question, skip it or choose a different one. You may not have to answer every question correctly to achieve your desired score. Select the questions or essays that you can answer, and work on them first. This will make you more efficient and give you the greatest chance of getting the most questions correct.

- **Use Process of Elimination on multiple-choice questions.** Many times, one or more answer choices can be eliminated. Every answer choice that can be eliminated increases the odds that you will answer the question correctly. Review the strategies in Chapter 1 to find these incorrect answer choices and increase your odds of getting the question correct.

Remember, when all the questions on a test are of equal value, no one question is that important, and your overall goal for pacing is to get the most questions correct. Finally, you should set a realistic goal for your final score. In the next section, we will break down how to achieve your desired score and ways of pacing yourself to do so.

GETTING THE SCORE YOU WANT

Depending on the score you need, it may be in your best interest not to try to work through every question. Check with the schools to which you are applying. Do you need a 3 to earn credit for the test? A raw score of 50 out of 75 on the multiple-choice section and a similar percentage on the essays may help you to get a 3.

AP Exams in all subjects no longer include a "guessing penalty" of a quarter of a point for every incorrect answer. Instead, students are assessed only on the total number of correct answers. If you are running out of time, make sure you fill in an answer to every remaining question (using your LOTD) so that you've at least got a chance of getting points. Even if you don't plan to spend a lot of time on every question and even if you have no idea what the correct answer is, it is to your advantage to fill something in.

TEST ANXIETY

Everybody experiences anxiety before and during an exam. To a certain extent, test anxiety can be helpful. Some people find that they perform more quickly and efficiently under stress. If you have ever pulled an all-nighter to write a paper and ended up doing good work, you know the feeling.

However, *too much* stress is definitely a bad thing. Hyperventilating during the test, for example, almost always leads to a lower score. If you find that you stress out during exams, here are a few preemptive actions you can take.

- **Take a reality check.** Evaluate your situation before the test begins. If you have studied hard, remind yourself that you are well prepared. Remember that many others taking the test are not as well prepared, and (in your classes, at least) you are being graded against them, so you have an advantage. If you didn't study, accept the fact that you will probably not ace the test. Make sure you get to every question you know something about. Don't stress out or fixate on how much you don't know. Your job is to score as high as you can by maximizing the benefits of what you do know. In either scenario, it is best to think of a test as if it were a game. How can you get the most points in the time allotted to you? Always answer questions you can answer easily and quickly before you answer those that will take more time.
- **Try to relax.** Slow, deep breathing works for almost everyone. Close your eyes, take a few slow, deep breaths, and concentrate on nothing but your inhalation and exhalation for a few seconds. This is a basic form of meditation, and it should help you to clear your mind of stress and, as a result, concentrate better on the test. If you have ever taken yoga classes, you probably know some other good relaxation techniques. Additionally, chewing gum may help relax you, and studies have suggested that chewing gum before (but not during) an exam may increase your score.
- **Eliminate as many surprises as you can.** Make sure you know where the test will be given, when it starts, what types of questions are going to be asked, and how long the test will take. You don't want to be worrying about any of these things on test day or, even worse, after the test has already begun.

The best way to avoid stress is to study both the test material and the test itself. Congratulations! By reading this book, you are taking a major step toward a stress-free AP Psychology Exam.

Chapter 4
Strategy Drills

USING THE DRILLS IN THIS CHAPTER

The drills in this chapter are designed to help you hone your test-taking skills before you begin your psychology review. Use these drills to practice the various smart-tester strategies you have learned.

DRILL 1: UNDERSTAND THE QUESTION/KEY WORDS

Before you can answer a question, you need to know what it is asking. To avoid careless errors, put the question into your own words before you try to answer it. On some questions, you may find it useful to circle the key word(s) in the question. Use the following drill questions to practice Smart-Tester Strategy #1: Understand the Question/Key Words. The answers are in Chapter 12.

7. Which of the following best summarizes the differences between the psychoanalytic and the behaviorist perspectives?

22. Louis is suffering from severe headaches and occasional moments of disorientation or even mental paralysis. His doctors are interested in examining his brain for lesions. Which of the following technologies would prove most useful in examining various regions of Louis's brain?

39. The somatosensory cortex is the primary area of the

58. In the processing of visual information, a fully integrated image does not appear until the information has reached which of the following regions of the brain?

78. If a participant does not report a stimulus when no stimulus is present in a signal-detection experimental trial, it is known as a

89. The lower the *p*-value of a study, the

DRILL 2: PREDICT THE ANSWER

Before you even think about looking at the answer choices, you need to have an idea of what the answer to the question might be; otherwise, you might be adrift in a sea of confusion, tricks, and traps. Use the following questions to practice both Understand the Question/Key Words and Predict the Answer. Speaking of answers, see Chapter 12 to check your work on these questions.

5. Thomas knows how to roast meat, cook vegetables, and prepare salad. In order for him to learn to prepare a meal for 20 people, Thomas will most likely employ which of the following learning techniques?

What does the question ask?

What's your answer?

22. The endocrine system is a collection of glands that

What does the question ask?

What's your answer?

35. What was Wilhelm Wundt's contribution to the field of psychology?

What does the question ask?

What's your answer?

45. Which of the following best explains why regeneration is essential for taste receptors?

What does the question ask?

What's your answer?

72. Which of the following technologies is most useful in the study of brain waves?

What does the question ask?

What's your answer?

DRILL 3: USING ALL THREE

Now, practice the first two smart-tester strategies (Understand the Question/Key Words and Predict the Answer) and then find the "credited response" from the choices given. If you're having trouble, use POE to get your answers into the right ballpark. Once you've crossed off what you can, take a smart guess! Answers are in Chapter 12.

15. Of the following variables, which typically requires a measurement that is more complex?

Understand the Question/Key Words.

Predict the Answer.

        (A) Categorical
        (B) Continuous
        (C) Extraneous
        (D) Independent
        (E) Dependent

35. Which of the following most accurately states the role of the iris?

Understand the Question/Key Words.

Predict the Answer.

    (A) To provide adaptive trait distinctions (eye color) within a species
    (B) To dilate or constrict the pupil in order to regulate the amount of light that enters the eye
    (C) To refract light that enters the eye, projecting it onto the retina
    (D) To house the aqueous humor and supply the eye with oxygen and nutrients
    (E) To transduce visual sensations into visual perceptions of color

42. The nature-nurture controversy concerns

Understand the Question/Key Words.

Predict the Answer.

    (A) the question of determinism versus free will
    (B) the degree to which the kinesthetic prowess of an individual overrides other aspects of intelligence
    (C) the degree to which inborn processes versus environmental factors determine behavior
    (D) the natural tendency of humans to nurture their young
    (E) the role of unconscious processes as a determinant of behavior

66. Prior to the fall of the Berlin Wall, East Berlin schools de-emphasized the individuality of the student. As a result, many of the children from those schools tend to have a(n)

Understand the Question/Key Words.

Predict the Answer.

    (A) optimistic explanatory style
    (B) pessimistic explanatory style
    (C) internal locus of control
    (D) external locus of control
    (E) indiscriminate set of expectancies

85. A prototypic example of a category is called a(n)

Understand the Question/Key Words.

Predict the Answer.

    (A) expectancy
    (B) defining feature
    (C) concept
    (D) phenotype
    (E) exemplar

DRILL 4: POE

You are going to read an awful lot of wrong answer choices while working on Section I of the AP Psychology Exam. And, believe it or not, a lot of those choices are not only wrong, but also just plain silly. Using your knowledge of psychology, plus the information in the question itself, examine each of the following sets of answer choices to determine which is the best answer to the question. Remember, if it's silly, extreme, or fallacious, it cannot be the answer to any question. Check your POE smarts in Chapter 12 when you're finished.

4. Blah, Blah, Blah?

   (A) Obese people have fewer but larger fat cells than average-weight people.
   (B) Obese people have many more fat cells than average-weight people.

27. Connectionist approaches blah, blah

   (A) are carried out by individual segments of the brain
   (B) occur simultaneously through the action of multiple networks

47. Blah, blah, chunking?

   (A) Christina remembers two new phone numbers by recognizing that each has a familiar exchange and that the second half of each represents a familiar date in history.
   (B) Chelsea learns her times tables by methodically practicing one set each night and then reviewing with flashcards.

85. Blah, blah, person-centered psychotherapy blah

   (A) suppresses negative feelings that arise within the client
   (B) uses a didactic approach to teach the client to correct maladaptive behavior
   (C) accepts the client unconditionally so that their desire for healing will grow

92. Blah, blah, blah, blah, blah

   (A) repressing the client's deviant feelings
   (B) slowly altering the contingencies of reinforcement for the client
   (C) removing the underlying causes of a client's problems for the client

REFLECT

Think about what you've learned in Part IV, and respond to the following questions:

- How will you change your approach to multiple-choice questions?

- What is your multiple-choice guessing strategy? On which part of the test should you be most willing to guess?

- What will you do before you begin writing an essay?

- How will you change your approach to the essays, now that you know that graders are usually looking for 7 pieces of information on which to judge your essay?

- Will you seek further help, outside of this book (such as from a teacher, Princeton Review tutor, or AP Students), on how to approach multiple-choice questions, the essay, or a pacing strategy?

Part V
Background Information for Psychology

Chapter 5
Foundations:
History

PRE-HISTORY AND HISTORY OF PSYCHOLOGY

Psychology is the study of behavior and the mind. **Behavior**, a natural process subject to natural laws, refers to the observable actions of a person or an animal. The **mind** refers to the sensations, memories, motives, emotions, thoughts, and other subjective phenomena particular to an individual or animal that are not readily observed.

Psychology today is a science because it uses systematic observation and the collection of data to try to answer questions about the mind, behavior, and their interactions. Psychology seeks to describe, predict, and explain behavior and the mental processes underlying behavior. In psychology, as in science in general, people tend to accept one theory and proceed under the assumptions of that theory until sufficient data inconsistent with the theory is collected. At this point, the prevailing theory is replaced by another theory. Many theories are simply elaborations or revisions of previous ones. As you read over the history of psychology, pay attention to how theories relate to and influence one another.

The ancient Greeks' speculations on the nature of the mind heavily influenced the pre-history of psychology as a science. Socrates and his student, Plato, argued that humans possess innate knowledge that is not obtainable simply by observing the physical world. Aristotle, by contrast, believed that we derive truth from the physical world. Aristotle's application of logic and systematic observation of the world laid the basis for an empirical, scientific method.

The questions raised by the early Greeks pertain to the concept of **dualism**. Dualism divides the world and all things in it into two parts: body and spirit. Dualism is a theme that recurs often in early psychology, but the distinction between body and spirit prefigures current debates around the difference between the **brain** (that is, the command center of the central nervous system) and the **mind** (that is, the sensations, memories, emotions, thoughts, and other subjective experiences of a particular individual).

After the heyday of the Greek philosophers, there was a long period of time during which relatively little systematic investigation of psychological issues was conducted. This dearth of investigation was due, in part, to religious beliefs that said that the "spirit" portion of human nature could not be studied scientifically. These same prevailing theological views indicated that studying the natural world was only useful for what it demonstrated about God. These views changed with the advent of the scientific revolution (c. 1600–1700) when great discoveries were being made in biology, astronomy, and other sciences. These discoveries, along with corresponding movements in philosophy and art, made it clear that human nature was indeed subject to scientific inquiry.

René Descartes (1596–1650), an early modern philosopher, continued the dualist view of the human being. He believed that the physical world and all of the creatures in it are like machines, in that they behave in observable, predictable ways. However, Descartes believed that humans were the exception to this rule because they possess minds. The mind, according to Descartes, is not observable and is not subject to natural laws. Descartes hypothesized that the mind and body interact, and the mind controls the body while the body provides the mind with sensory input for it to decipher.

John Locke (1632–1704), another philosopher, extended Descartes's application of natural laws to all things, believing that even the mind is under the control of such laws. Locke's school of thought is known as **empiricism**—the acquisition of truth through observations and experiences. In his book, *Essay Concerning Human Understanding,* Locke proposed that humans are born knowing nothing; Locke used the term **tabula rasa** (Latin for "blank slate") to describe the mind of an infant. Almost all knowledge we have must be learned; almost nothing is innate. Locke felt that all knowledge must derive from experience. Like the future psychologist B.F. Skinner, Locke emphasized nurture over nature as the greater influence on development.

Thomas Hobbes (1588–1679) believed that the idea of a soul or spirit, or even of a mind, is meaningless. Hobbes's philosophy is known as **materialism**, which is the belief that the only things that exist are matter and energy. What we experience as consciousness is simply a by-product of the machinery of the brain. In addition to Locke, Hobbes greatly influenced behaviorism, which will be discussed later.

The 19th century was a time of great discovery in biology and medicine. One new theory, in particular, revolutionized science—the theory of natural selection. In *On the Origin of Species* (1859), **Charles Darwin** (1809–1882) proposed a theory of **natural selection**, according to which all creatures have evolved into their present states over long periods of time. This evolution occurs because there exists naturally occurring variation among individuals in a species, and the individuals that are best adapted to the environment are more likely to survive and then reproduce—and are likely to produce more successful offspring. Their offspring, in turn, will probably have some of the traits that made their predecessors more likely to survive. Over time, this process "selects" physical and behavioral characteristics that promote survival in a particular environment. **Evolutionary theory** affected psychology by providing a way to explain differences between species and justifying the use of animals as a means to study the roots of human behavior.

> **Darwin in a Nutshell**
> Behavior evolves just like physiology: both function to help individuals survive.

Many credit **Wilhelm Wundt** (1832–1920) as the founder of the science of psychology. In 1879 in Leipzig, Germany, Wundt opened a laboratory to study consciousness. Wundt was trained in physiology and hoped to apply the methods that he used to study the body to the study of the mind. **Edward Titchener** (1867–1927) was a student in Wundt's laboratory and was one of the first to bring the science of psychology to the United States. Titchener sought to identify the smallest possible elements of the mind, theorizing that understanding all of the parts would lead to the understanding of the greater structure of the mind. This theory, known as **structuralism**, entails looking for patterns in thought, which are illuminated through interviews with a subject describing their conscious experience. This interview process is known as **introspection**. For example, the experimenter could present stimuli to subjects, ask them to describe their conscious experience, and then work to identify commonalities among various participants' conscious descriptions.

William James (1842–1910), an American psychologist, opposed the structuralist approach. Instead, he argued that what is important is the function of the mind, such as how it solves a complex problem. James, heavily influenced by Darwin, believed that the important thing to understand is how the mind fulfills its purpose. This function-oriented approach is appropriately called **functionalism**.

A number of major historical figures in psychology are discussed in the following chapters, as their work informs the units of study in AP Psychology. But other figures also play an important role in the history of psychology, due to both their individual accomplishments as well as the light they shed on the gender biases that affected their careers in particular and the field as a whole.

Dorothea Dix was crucial in advocating for the rights of mentally ill poor people, and she was instrumental in founding the first public mental hospital in the United States. **Mary Whiton Calkins** was the first female graduate student in psychology, although she was denied a PhD because of her gender. (She outscored all of the male students in her qualifying exams.) **Margaret Floy Washburn** was not only the first female PhD in psychology, she also served as the second female president of the American Psychological Association (APA), an organization formed in 1892. (**G. Stanley Hall** was its first president.) Although Washburn's thesis was the first foreign study published by Wilhelm Wundt, she was not allowed to join the official organization of experimental psychologists because of her gender.

Today, about two-thirds of doctorates in psychology are held by women, and about half of the presidents of the Association for Psychological Science have been women.

APPROACHES

The theories discussed above laid the groundwork for modern psychology as a science. This next section will deal with nine of the most prominent approaches to modern psychology. The roots of these approaches are in the theoretical perspectives we discussed above.

Approach 1: Biological

Biological psychology is the field of psychology that seeks to understand the interactions between anatomy and physiology (particularly, the physiology of the nervous system) and behavior. This approach is practiced by directly applying biological experimentation to psychological problems: for example, in determining which portion of the brain is involved in a particular behavioral process. To accomplish this, researchers might use CAT scans, MRIs, EEGs, or PET scans.

Approach 2: Behavioral Genetics

Behavioral genetics is the field of psychology that explores how particular behaviors may be attributed to specific, genetically based psychological characteristics. This perspective takes into account biological predispositions as well as the extent of influence that the environment had on the manifestation of that trait. For example, a person studying behavioral genetics might investigate to what extent risk-taking behavior in adolescents is attributable to genetics.

Approach 3: Behaviorist

Behaviorism posits that psychology is the study of observable behavior. The mind or mental events are unimportant, as they cannot be observed. **Classical conditioning**, first identified by Ivan Pavlov (1849–1936), was one of the behaviorists' most important early findings. Classical conditioning is defined as a basic form of learning in which a behavior comes to be elicited by a formerly neutral stimulus. **John Watson** (1878–1958) and his assistant Rosalie Rayner applied classical conditioning to humans in the famed Little Albert experiment: they made loud sounds behind a 9-month-old whenever he would touch something white and furry, and voilà: he was afraid of everything white and furry afterwards. **B.F. Skinner** (1904–1990), through the development of his Skinner Box, described **operant conditioning**, in which a subject learns to associate a behavior with an environmental outcome. Although behaviorism is no longer the prevailing approach in psychology, many behavioral principles are still used in **behavior modification**—a set of techniques in which psychological problems are considered to be the product of learned habits, which can be unlearned by the application of behavioral methods.

Approach 4: Cognitive

Cognitive psychology is an approach rooted in the idea that to understand people's behavior, we must first understand how they construe their environment—in other words, how they think. Cognitive psychology focuses much of its attention on learning, memory, problem solving, decision-making, language, and intelligence. This approach combines both the structuralist approach of looking at the subcomponents of thought and the functionalist approach of understanding the purpose of thought. The cognitive approach, sometimes called the cognitive-behavioral approach, largely replaced the purely behavioral approach as the predominant psychological method used in the United States.

Approach 5: Humanistic

The **humanistic approach** is rooted in the philosophical tradition of studying the roles of consciousness, free will, and awareness of the human condition. This is a holistic study of personality that developed in response to a general dissatisfaction with behaviorism's inattention to the mind and its function and psychoanalysis's focus on unconscious conflicts and drives. Humanistic psychologists emphasize personal values and goals and how they influence behavior, rather than attempting to divide personality into smaller components. **Abraham Maslow** (1908–1970) proposed the idea of self-actualization, the need for individuals to reach their full potential in a creative way. Attaining **self-actualization** means accepting yourself and your nature while knowing your limits and strengths. **Carl Rogers** (1902–1987) stressed the role of **unconditional positive regard** in interactions and the need for a positive self-concept as critical factors in attaining self-actualization.

Approach 6: Psychoanalytic/Psychodynamic

While laboratory psychology was passing through its various theories, **Sigmund Freud** (1856–1939) developed a theory of human behavior known as **psychoanalytic theory**. Freud was concerned with individuals and their mental problems. Freud drew a distinction between the **conscious mind**—a mental state of awareness that we have ready access to—and the **unconscious mind**—those mental processes that we do not normally have access to but that still influence our behaviors, thoughts, and feelings. Psychoanalytic theory stresses the importance of early childhood experiences and a child's relationship with their parents to the development of personality. The psychoanalytic approach to therapy focuses on the resolution of unconscious conflicts through uncovering information that has been **repressed**, or buried in the unconscious.

Approach 7: Sociocultural

Those subscribing to the **sociocultural approach** believe that the environment a person lives in has a great deal to do with how the person behaves and how others perceive that behavior. According to this approach, cultural values vary from society to society and must be taken into account if one wishes to understand, predict, or control behavior. Additionally, this approach considers the role of sociological factors such as socioeconomic status, education, occupation, and demographics in understanding a person's psychological health.

Approach 8: Evolutionary

The **evolutionary approach** draws upon the theories of Darwin. Behavior can best be explained in terms of how adaptive that behavior is to our survival. For example, fear is an adaptive evolutionary response; without fear, our survival would be jeopardized.

Approach 9: Biopsychosocial

As the name implies, the **biopsychosocial approach** emphasizes the need to investigate the interaction of biological, psychological, and social factors as contributing to a behavior or a mental process.

Approach	Question	Cause of Behavior	Methods
Biological	How is the physiology of high risk-takers different from that of non-risk-takers?	Physiology	Brain scans
Behavioral genetics	Which genes contribute to the development of risk-taking?	Genes	Genetic analysis
Behavioral	How does rewarding or punishing a risk-taker affect their behavior?	Learning and reflexes	Behavior modification
Cognitive	How do risk-takers think and solve problems?	Thoughts	Computer models of memory networks
Humanistic	How does the adolescent's self-esteem encourage or discourage risk-taking behavior?	Self-concept	Talk therapy
Psychoanalytic/ Psychodynamic	How might a child's early experiences affect risk-taking in adolescence?	Unconscious mind	Dream analysis, talk therapy

Sociocultural	How might an adolescent's culture lead to risk-taking?	Cultural environment	Cross-cultural studies
Evolutionary	Is risk-taking an evolutionarily adaptive trait?	Natural selection	Species comparison
Biopsychosocial	What factors predict risk-taking?	Interaction of biology with individual psychological and social factors	Combination of the above

DOMAINS

Broad areas of psychological research are also known as domains. A question that concerns the effect of drugs on behavior refers to the **biological domain**, but a question that deals with relationships between drug users and their families refers to the **social** domain, and a question that considers treatment options for someone addicted to drugs deals with the **clinical** domain.

Other domains include: **cognitive** (What thoughts might someone entertain to justify their drug use?), **counseling** (How might a school counselor talk to a student about drugs?), **developmental** (At what ages might someone be more susceptible to peer pressure?), and **educational** (How effective are school-based programs?).

Yet other domains include: **experimental** (dealing with experiments, as discussed in the next chapter), **industrial-organizational** (dealing with workplaces), **personality** (dealing with—you guessed it!—personality), **psychometric** (dealing with how to measure things in psychology), and the **positive domain** (which focuses on positive aspects and strengths of human behavior).

KEY TERMS

History

psychology
behavior
mind and brain
René Descartes and dualism
John Locke and empiricism
tabula rasa
Thomas Hobbes and materialism
Charles Darwin and evolutionary theory
natural selection
Wilhelm Wundt and structuralism
Edward Titchener and introspection
William James and functionalism
Dorothea Dix
Mary Whiton Calkins
Margaret Floy Washburn
G. Stanley Hall

Approaches

biological psychology
behavioral genetics
behaviorism
    John Watson and classical conditioning
    B.F. Skinner and operant conditioning
    behavior modification
cognitive psychology
humanistic approach
    Abraham Maslow and self-actualization
    Carl Rogers and unconditional positive regard
psychodynamic/psychoanalytic approach
    Sigmund Freud and psychoanalytic theory
    conscious mind vs. unconscious mind
    repressed
sociocultural approach
evolutionary approach
biopsychosocial approach

Domains

biological
social
clinical
cognitive
counseling
developmental
educational
experimental
industrial-organizational
personality
psychometric
positive

Chapter 5 Drill

See Chapter 12 for answers and explanations.

1. A cognitive psychologist would likely be most interested in

    (A) concentration of neural transmitters in the spinal cord
    (B) unconditional positive regard in the therapeutic setting
    (C) token economies in prisons
    (D) perceptual speed on word-association tests
    (E) development of fine motor skills in toddlers

2. The concept of *tabula rasa*, or "blank slate" (the idea that human beings come into the world knowing nothing, and thereafter acquire all of their knowledge through experience) is most closely associated with

    (A) David Hume
    (B) Charles Darwin
    (C) John Locke
    (D) Sigmund Freud
    (E) Erich Fromm

3. The concept of dualism refers to the division of all things in the world into

    (A) thought and action
    (B) body and spirit
    (C) structural and functional
    (D) theoretical and practical
    (E) dependent and independent

4. The humanistic approach to psychology emphasizes the importance of

    (A) childhood experiences
    (B) biological predispositions
    (C) maladaptive thoughts
    (D) free will and conscious awareness
    (E) cultural experiences

5. Psychologists who emphasize the importance of repressed memories and childhood experiences subscribe to which of the following perspectives?

    (A) Cognitive
    (B) Behavioral
    (C) Psychodynamic
    (D) Sociocultural
    (E) Medical/biological

6. Psychologists who believe behaviors are learned most likely ascribe to the philosophy of

    (A) Abraham Maslow
    (B) B.F. Skinner
    (C) Carl Rogers
    (D) Sigmund Freud
    (E) Wilhelm Wundt

7. According to the psychoanalytic perspective, a person who does not remember a painful event experiences which defense mechanism?

    (A) Denial
    (B) Self-actualization
    (C) Projection
    (D) Consciousness
    (E) Repression

8. Carl Rogers is most closely associated with which psychological approach?

    (A) Unconditional positive regard
    (B) Cognitive psychology
    (C) Humanistic
    (D) Sociocultural
    (E) Behaviorism

9. According to Abraham Maslow's hierarchy of needs, the most basic of human needs is

    (A) self-actualization
    (B) esteem
    (C) belonging
    (D) safety
    (E) physiological

10. Which approach would most likely involve the study of identical twins separated at birth?

    (A) Biological
    (B) Behavioral genetics
    (C) Humanistic
    (D) Sociocultural
    (E) Biopsychosocial

Chapter 6
Foundations:
Methods and
Approaches

EXPERIMENTAL, CORRELATIONAL, AND CLINICAL RESEARCH

Three major types of research in psychology include: experimental, correlational, and clinical. An **experiment** is an investigation seeking to understand relations of cause and effect. The experimenter changes a variable (cause) and measures how it, in turn, changes another variable (effect). At the same time, the investigator tries to hold all other variables constant so she can attribute any changes to the manipulation. The manipulated variable is called the **independent variable**. The **dependent variable** is what is measured. For example, an experiment is designed to determine whether watching violence on television causes aggression in its viewers. Two groups of children are randomly placed in front of either violent or nonviolent television programs for one hour. The program type is the independent variable because it can be manipulated by the experimenter. Afterward, a large doll may be placed in front of each child for one hour while the experimenter records the number of times that child hits, kicks, or punches the doll. This behavior is the dependent variable because it is the variable that is measured. The presence of the doll in both groups is the **control variable**, because it is constant in both groups.

Also Remember...

Other terms to remember include the following: the group receiving or reacting to the independent variable is the **experimental group;** the **control group** does not receive the independent variable but should be kept identical in all other respects. Using two groups allows for a comparison to be made and causation to be determined.

In order to draw conclusions about the result of the controlled experiment, it is important that certain other conditions are met. The researcher identifies a specific **population,** or group of interest, to be studied. Because the population may be too large to study effectively, a **representative sample** of the population may be drawn. **Representativeness** is the degree to which a sample reflects the diverse characteristics of the population that is being studied. **Random sampling** is a way of ensuring maximum representativeness. Once sampling has been addressed, subjects are **randomly assigned** into both the experimental and control groups. Random assignment is done to ensure that each group has minimal differences.

Sampling Bias

A classic example of unintentional sampling bias occurred during the 1948 U.S. Presidential Election: a survey was conducted by randomly calling households and asking them whom they intended to vote for: Harry Truman or Thomas Dewey. Based on this phone survey, Dewey was projected to win. The results of the election proved otherwise, as Truman was re-elected. What could have possibly gone wrong? In 1948, having a telephone was not such a common thing, and households that had them were generally wealthier. As a result, the "random" selection of telephone numbers was not a representative sample because many people (a large proportion of whom voted for Truman) did not have telephone numbers. A more recent example occurred in the 1990s and early 2000s when telephone polls were found to have undercounted young voters because all of the calls were being made over landlines, while younger people were relying exclusively on cell phones. Here are some need-to-know sampling **biases**:

- The **bias of selection** from a specific real area occurs when people are selected in a physical space. For example, if you wanted to survey college students on whether or not they like their football team, you could stand on the quad and survey the first 100 people that walk by. However, this would not be completely random because people who don't have an upcoming class at that time are unlikely to be represented.

- **Self-selection bias** occurs when the people being studied have some control over whether or not to participate. A participant's decision to participate may affect the results. For example, an Internet survey might elicit responses only from people who are highly opinionated and motivated to complete the survey.

- **Pre-screening** or **advertising bias** occurs often in medical research; how volunteers are screened or where advertising is placed might skew the sample. For example, if a researcher wanted to prove that a certain treatment helps people to stop smoking, the mere act of advertising for people who "want to quit smoking" might provide only a sample of people who are already highly motivated to quit and might have done so without the treatment.

- **Healthy user bias** occurs when the study population tends to be in better shape than the general population. As with the bias of selection from a specific real area, this is an instance in which those subjects might not accurately represent the true diversity of the target population.

To avoid inadvertently influencing the results, as in the previous examples, researchers use a **single-** or **double-blind design**. Single-blind design means that the subjects do not know whether they are in the control or experimental group. In a double-blind design, neither the subjects nor the researcher knows who is in the two groups. Double-blind studies are designed so that the experimenter does not inadvertently change the responses of the subject, such as by using a different tone of voice with members of the control group than with the experimental group. Obviously, a third party has the appropriate records so that the data can be analyzed later. In some double-blind experiments, the control group is given a **placebo**, a seemingly therapeutic object or procedure, which causes the control group to believe they could be in the experimental group but actually contains none of the tested material.

Correlational research involves assessing the degree of association between two or more variables or characteristics of interest that occur naturally. It is important to note that, in this type of design, researchers do not directly manipulate variables but rather observe naturally occurring differences. If the characteristics under consideration are related, they are correlated. It is important to note that *correlation does not prove causation;* correlation simply shows the strength of the relationship among variables. For example, poor school performance may be correlated with lack of sleep. However, we do not know whether lack of sleep caused the poor performance, or whether the poor school performance caused the lack of sleep, or whether some other unidentified factor influenced them both. If an unknown factor is playing a role, it is known as a **confounding variable**, a **third variable**, or an **extraneous variable**.

Types of Research

Two specific types of research that can be set up as correlational or experimental designs are **longitudinal studies** and **cross-sectional studies**. Longitudinal studies happen over long periods of time with the same subjects (e.g., studying the long-term effects of diet and exercise on heart disease), and cross-sectional studies are designed to test a wide array of subjects from different backgrounds to increase generalizability.

One way to gather information for correlational studies is through **surveys**. Using either questionnaires or interviews, one can accumulate a tremendous amount of data and study relationships among variables. Such techniques are often used to assess voter characteristics, teen alcohol and drug use, and criminal behavior. For example, survey studies might examine the relationship between socioeconomic status and educational levels.

Correlational studies can be preferred to experiments because they are less expensive, not as time consuming, and easier to conduct. In addition, some relationships cannot be ethically studied in experiments. For example, you may want to study how child abuse affects self-efficacy in adulthood, but no one will allow you to randomly assign half of your baby participants to the child-abuse condition. One danger in surveys that researchers need to take into account is that some responders may not be completely honest in their answers, especially when asked about controversial subjects. They may respond with what they think is socially correct or what the questioner wants to hear. This is referred to as social desirability bias, or courtesy bias.

Clinical research often takes the form of case studies. **Case studies** are intensive psychological studies of single individuals. These studies are conducted under the assumption that an in-depth understanding of single cases will allow for general conclusions about other similar cases. Case studies have also been used to investigate the circumstances of the lives of notable figures in history. Frequently, multiple case studies on similar cases are combined to draw inferences about issues. Researchers must be careful, though, because case studies, like correlational ones, cannot lead to conclusions regarding causality. Sigmund Freud and Carl Rogers used numerous case studies to draw their conclusions about psychology. The danger of generalizing from the outcomes of case studies is that the individuals studied may be atypical of the larger population. This is why researchers try to ensure that their studies are **generalizable**—that is, applicable to similar circumstances because of the predictable outcomes of repeated tests.

Experimental Design

Two important features of studies are the **conceptual definition** and the **operational definition**. Whereas the conceptual definition is the theory or issue being studied, the operational definition refers to the way in which that theory or issue will be directly observed or measured in the study. For example, in a study on the effects of adolescent substance abuse, the way in which taking drugs affects adolescent behavior is the conceptual definition, while the number of recorded days the student is absent from school due to excessive use of substances is the operational definition.

Operational definitions have to be internally and externally valid. **Internal validity** is the certainty with which the results of an experiment can be attributed to the manipulation of the independent variable rather than to some other, confounding variable. **External validity** is the extent to which the findings of a study can be generalized to other contexts in the real world. The principal threats to internal validity are confounding variables, variables that haven't been adequately controlled by the experimenter. The principal threat to the external validity of an experiment is the often-artificial nature of the experimental environment. A laboratory may not resemble the real world very much, making it difficult to generalize results to the real world. It is also important that the study have **reliability**, which means that the same results appear if the experiment is repeated under similar conditions. A related concept is **inter-rater reliability**, the degree to which different raters agree on their observations of the same data.

OTHER TYPES OF RESEARCH

In addition to organizing experiments inside of a lab, researchers can observe behavior outside of the lab; such naturalistic observation has enriched our knowledge of psychology. The advantage of **naturalistic observation** is that it allows the study of authentic real-world behaviors; however, its disadvantage is the difficulty of controlling for the numerous extraneous variables present in real-world environments, which can limit the reliability of findings. Psychology also uses **qualitative research**, which provides detailed descriptions of experience rather than the numerical data of quantitative methods. Types of qualitative research include case studies, phenomenological studies, ethnographic studies, narrative studies, and grounded theory.

STATISTICS

Psychologists and other scientists collect data. This data is then subjected to statistical analysis. Statistical methods can be divided into descriptive and inferential statistics. **Descriptive statistics** summarize data, whereas **inferential statistics** allow researchers to test hypotheses about data and determine how confident they can be in their inferences about the data.

Descriptive Statistics

Descriptive statistics do just what their name implies—they describe data. They do not allow for conclusions to be made about anything other than the particular set of numbers they describe. Commonly used descriptive statistics are the mean, the mode, and the median. These descriptive statistics are measures of **central tendency**—that is, they characterize the typical value in a set of data.

> **MMM MM!**
> The Mean, Mode, and Median Measure the Middle!

The **mean** is the arithmetic average of a set of numbers. The **mode** is the most frequently occurring value in the data set. (If two numbers both appear with the greatest frequency, the distribution is called **bimodal**.) The **median** is the number that falls exactly in the middle of a distribution of numbers. These statistics can be represented by a **normal curve.** In a perfectly normal distribution, the mean, median, and mode are identical. The **range** is simply the largest number minus the smallest number.

Although the mean, the mode, and the median give approximations of the central tendency of a group of numbers, they do not tell us much about the variability in that set of numbers. **Variability** refers to how much the numbers in the set differ from one another. The **standard deviation** measures a function of the average dispersion of numbers around the mean and is a commonly used measure of variability. For example, say you have a set of numbers that has a mean of 100. If most of those numbers are close to 100, say, ranging from 95 to 105, then the standard deviation will be small. However, if the mean of 100 comes from a set of numbers ranging from 50 to 150, then the standard deviation will be large.

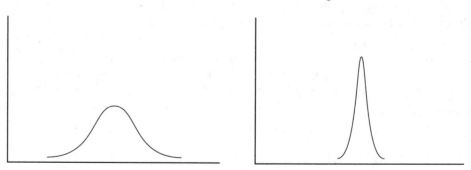

The curve on the left is shorter and wider than the curve on the right, because the curve on the left has a greater standard deviation.

The graph of a normal distribution depends on two factors—the mean and the standard deviation. The mean of the distribution determines the location of the center of the graph, and the standard deviation determines the height and width of the graph. When the standard deviation is large, the curve is short and wide; when the standard deviation is small, the curve is tall and narrow. All normal distributions look like a symmetric, bell-shaped curve, as shown below.

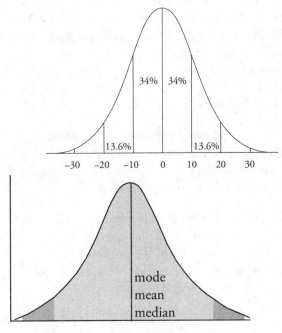

Perfect Normal Curve

In a typical distribution of numbers, about 68 percent of all scores are within one standard deviation above or below the mean, and about 95 percent of all scores are within two standard deviations above or below the mean. So, for example, IQ is typically said to have a mean of 100 and a standard deviation of 15, so a person with a score of 115 is one standard deviation above the mean.

Q: What is standard deviation?

Answer on page 134.

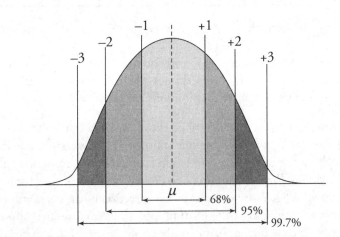

It's unlikely that there will be any questions that actually exercise your math skills, but you should be able to read and interpret a graph and understand what the standard deviation represents in a study. For example, suppose that 1,000 subjects participate in a study on reaction time and that the reaction times of the subjects are normally distributed with a mean of 1.3 seconds and a standard deviation of 0.2 second. In this particular instance, participants with reaction times between 1.1 and 1.5 seconds represent the group between one standard deviation below the mean and one standard deviation above it, which, as we've established, is generally around 68 percent of the population. Therefore, roughly 680 of 1,000 people would have reaction times within this range. Meanwhile, a reaction time of more than 1.9 seconds would be extremely rare—more than three standard deviations above the mean. It's likely that only 0.3 percent of the data would fall into the category of three standard deviations above or below the mean. Thus, only 0.15 percent would be that far above the mean, or about 1.5 (1 or 2, in real-world terms) of the 1,000 subjects.

Another common descriptive statistic is the **percentile**. This statistic is used frequently when reporting scores on standardized tests. Percentiles express the standing of one score relative to all other scores in a set of data. For example, if your SAT score is in the 85th percentile, then you scored higher than 85 percent of the other test-takers.

In skewed distributions, the median is a better indicator of central tendency than the mean. A **positive skew** means that most values are on the lower end, but there are some exceptionally large values. This creates a "tail" or skew toward the positive end. A **negative skew** means the opposite: most values are on the higher end, but there are some exceptionally small values. This creates a "tail" or skew toward the negative end.

> **A:** Standard deviation measures the average distribution of numbers around the mean.

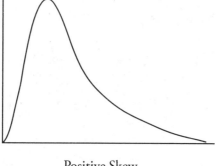 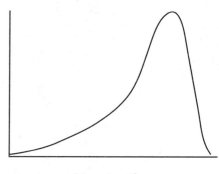

Positive Skew   Negative Skew

On the new format of the AP Psychology exam, you may see one or two math questions about distributions. Because skewed distributions do not all share the same mathematical properties, questions about percentages and these distributions are often trick questions.

When looking at correlational data, as described above, we need statistical techniques to describe how the attributes we are studying relate to one another. The **correlation coefficient** is a statistic that will give us such information. The correlation coefficient is a numerical value that indicates the degree and direction of the relationship between two variables. Correlation coefficients range from +1.00 to −1.00. The sign (+ or −) indicates the direction of the correlation, and the number (0 to 1.00) indicates the strength of the relationship. The **Pearson correlation coefficient** is a specific type of correlation coefficient that describes how close to linear the relationship between two attributes is. A correlation of 1 indicates a perfect positive correlation. This means that as attribute X increases, attribute Y always increases proportionally. A correlation of −1 is a perfect negative correlation: as the value of attribute X increases, the value of attribute Y always decreases proportionally. A correlation of 0 indicates that the attributes are not related.

Positive Correlation (As years of education increase, income increases.)

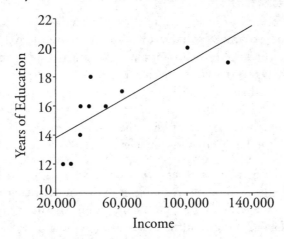

Negative Correlation (As absences for math lessons increase, math score decreases.)

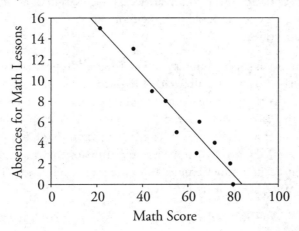

To use another example, take the following study, which assessed 200 male children from ages 1 to 12. A standardized questionnaire was given to the parents of the children and used to check the children's "agreeableness" on a scale from 0 to 5. Additionally, psychologists took standard measures of the behavioral problems exhibited by the children. After the incidents were totaled for each subject, the psychologists found a correlation between child agreeableness and later behavioral problems of −0.6.

You don't need any math here either, but you do have to understand that this is an inverse correlation between the scores: as the child's agreeableness increases, behavioral problems decrease. Don't forget, however, what we stressed earlier in this chapter: *correlation does not imply causation*.

Correlation and Causation

A famous example of the tricky relationship between correlation and causation can be taken from an observation once made about New York City: that the murder rate is directly correlated to the sale of ice cream (as ice cream sales increase, so do the number of murders). Does this mean that buying ice cream is definitively the cause of the increase in murders? Of course not! When two variables are correlated (especially two variables that are as complex as the measures of human behavior studied in the example above), there are always a number of other factors that could be influencing either correlated variable. In the ice cream/murder example, one such potential confounding variable might be temperature; as the temperature rises, more crimes are committed, but people also tend to eat more cold foods, such as ice cream.

Inferential Statistics

Inferential statistics are used to determine our level of confidence in claiming that a given set of results would be extremely unlikely to occur if the result were only up to chance. When experiments are conducted, they are typically conducted using small groups of people. However, psychologists typically want to be able to generalize the results of the experiments to larger groups of people, perhaps even to all people. The small group of people in an experiment constitutes the sample, and the large group to whom the psychologist is trying to generalize is called the population. It is important that the sample reflects the characteristics of the population as a whole. If it does, then the sample is referred to as being representative.

Sample size refers to the number of observations or individuals measured. The sample size is typically denoted by N (the total number of subjects in the sample being studied) or n (the total number of subjects in a subgroup of the sample being studied). The sample size used in a study is typically determined based on convenience, expense, and the need to have sufficient statistical power (the likelihood that your sample includes a sufficient number of subjects to conclude that the hypothesis being evaluated is true within an acceptable margin of error). Larger sample sizes are always better—the larger the sample size, the more likely it is that the inferences about the broader population are correct.

Inferential statistics are tools for hypothesis testing. The **null hypothesis** states that a treatment had no effect in an experiment. The **alternative hypothesis** is that the treatment did have an effect. Inferential statistics allow us the possibility of rejecting the null hypothesis with a known level of confidence—that is, of saying that our data would be extremely unlikely to have occurred were the null hypothesis true. Tests such as these are statistically significant because they enable us to examine whether effects are likely to be a result of treatment or are likely to be simply the normal variations that occur among samples from the same population. If a result is found to be statistically significant, then that result may be generalized with some level of confidence to the population.

Alpha is the accepted probability that the result of an experiment can be attributed to chance rather than the manipulation of the independent variable. Given that there is always the possibility that an experiment's outcome can happen by chance, psychologists usually set alpha at 0.05, which means that an experiment's results will be considered statistically significant if the probability of the results happening by chance is less than 5 percent.

Two primary types of errors can occur when testing a hypothesis. A **Type I error** refers to the conclusion that a difference exists when, in fact, this difference does not exist. A **Type II error** refers to the conclusion that there is no difference when, in fact, there is a difference. Psychologists pay particularly close attention to Type I errors because they want to be conservative in their inferences: they do not want to conclude that a difference exists if, in fact, it does not. A good analogy for Type I and Type II errors is that a Type I error is a "false positive," and a Type II error is a "false negative." The probability of making a Type I error is called the **_p_-value**. A p-value indicates that the results are statistically significant (not due only to chance). If $p = 0.05$, we have only a 5 percent chance of making a Type I error. In other words, a difference as extreme as what was obtained would be found only 5 percent of the time if the null hypothesis were correct.

Reality

		The null is True	The null is False
Your Statistical Decision	Fail to reject the null	Correct decision	**Type II error**
	Reject the null	**Type I error**	Correct decision

Statistical Decision-Making: The Four Possible Outcomes

ETHICS IN RESEARCH

Occasionally, psychological experiments involve **deception**, which may be used if informing participants of the nature of the experiment might bias results. This deception is typically small, but in rare instances it can be extreme. For example, in the 1970s, **Stanley Milgram** conducted obedience experiments in which he convinced participants that they were administering painful electric shocks to other participants, when, in fact, no shocks were given. The shocked "participants" were in fact **confederates**; that is, they were aware of the true nature of the experiment but pretended to be participants. Those giving the shocks were the real participants. Many people felt that this study was unethical because the participants were not aware of the nature of the study and could have believed that they had done serious harm to other people. Since this time, ethical standards have been set forth by the American Psychological Association (APA) to ensure the proper treatment of animal and human subjects. **Institutional Review Boards (IRBs)** assess research plans before the research is approved to ensure that it meets all ethical standards. Additionally, participants must give **informed consent**; in other words, they agree to participate in the study only after they have been told what their participation entails. Participants are also allowed to leave the experimental situation if they become uncomfortable about their participation. After the experiment is concluded, participants must receive a **debriefing,** in which they are told the exact purpose of their participation in the research and of any deception that may have been used in the process of experimentation.

> **Painless Experiments**
>
> Pain, both physiological and psychological, is also an issue in experiments. In the past, shock was an acceptable technique with human participants. However, physical pain is infrequently used in experiments today. Psychological stress is also minimized.

Confidentiality is another area of concern for psychology. Many experiments involve collecting sensitive information about participants that the participants might not want to be revealed. For this reason, most psychological data is collected anonymously, with the participants' names not attached to the collected data. If such anonymity is not possible, it is the researcher's ethical obligation to ensure that names and sensitive information about participants are not revealed.

The use of animals in psychological experiments is a topic of controversy. According to animal-rights activists, animals often endure both physiological and psychological stress in experiments. Often, the animals are euthanized at the end of the research. Psychologists counter that many lifesaving drugs could not be tested were it not for tests with animals. Moreover, animal models afford a level of experimental control that is not attainable with human participants. Of course, no ethical researcher wants to cause unnecessary pain or discomfort to any subject—animal or human.

KEY TERMS

Experimental, Correlational, and Clinical Research

experiment
independent variable
dependent variable
control variable
population
representative sample
representativeness
experimental group
control group
random sampling
randomly assigned
biases
    bias of selection
    self-selection bias
    pre-screening/advertising bias
    healthy user bias
single-/double-blind design
placebo
correlational research
confounding/third/extraneous variable
surveys
longitudinal studies
cross-sectional studies
clinical research
case studies
generalizable
conceptual definition
operational definition
internal validity
external validity
reliability
inter-rater reliability
naturalistic observation
qualitative research

Statistics

descriptive statistics
inferential statistics
central tendency
mean
mode
bimodal
median
normal curve

range
variability
standard deviation
percentile
positive skew
negative skew
correlation coefficient
Pearson correlation coefficient
positive correlation
negative correlation
sample size
null hypothesis
alternative hypothesis
alpha
Type I error
Type II error
p-value

Ethics in Research

deception
Stanley Milgram
confederates
Institutional Review Boards (IRBs)
informed consent
debriefing
confidentiality

Chapter 6 Drill

See Chapter 12 for answers and explanations.

1. In a double-blind experimental design, which of the following would be true?

   (A) The experimental subjects know whether they are in an experimental group or in a control group, but the researchers do not.
   (B) The researchers know whether particular subjects have been assigned to an experimental group or a control group, but the experimental subjects do not.
   (C) Both the researchers and the experimental subjects know whether the latter have been assigned to an experimental group or a control group.
   (D) Neither the researchers nor the experimental subjects know whether the latter have been assigned to an experimental group or a control group.
   (E) The observers are unable to see the responses or behaviors of the experimental group during the course of the experimental manipulation.

2. In a normal distribution of scores, approximately what percentage of all scores will occur within one standard deviation from the mean?

   (A) 34
   (B) 68
   (C) 95
   (D) 97.5
   (E) 100

3. A Type II error involves

   (A) concluding a difference between groups exists after the experimental manipulation when, in fact, a difference does not exist
   (B) concluding a difference between groups does not exist after the experimental manipulation when, in fact, a difference does exist
   (C) concluding a score is two standard deviations above the mean when, in fact, it is two standard deviations below the mean
   (D) concluding a score is two standard deviations below the mean when, in fact, it is two standard deviations above the mean
   (E) rejecting the null hypothesis when, in fact, it should have been accepted

4. Which of the following would NOT be considered essential for a proposed research design to meet the requirements for ethicality?

   (A) Research subjects must consent to participate in the project, and a full description of what their participation consists of must be spelled out before they are asked to give consent.
   (B) Participants must be allowed to withdraw from the project at any time.
   (C) Both the subjects and the researchers must know which of the subjects will be part of the experimental group.
   (D) If deception is involved, a full debriefing of the subjects must occur soon after the completion of the project.
   (E) In keeping with protecting the privacy and confidentiality of the subjects, data should be obtained as anonymously as possible.

5. The correlation between two observed variables is −0.84. From this, it can be concluded that

   (A) as one variable increases, the other is likely to increase, showing a direct relationship
   (B) as one variable increases, the other is likely to decrease, showing an inverse relationship
   (C) the two variables are unrelated
   (D) one variable causes the other variable to occur
   (E) one variable causes the other variable not to occur

6. A study seeks to find the effects of video games on violent behavior. The researcher creates an experimental design in which 100 random participants play violent video games and another 100 play non-violent video games for one hour. The researcher then records and observes the behavior of the subjects. The behavior of the subjects is known as the

   (A) control variable
   (B) independent variable
   (C) dependent variable
   (D) confounding variable
   (E) categorical variable

7. Which of the following is concerned with the real-life applicability of a study?

   (A) Test-retest reliability
   (B) Inter-rater reliability
   (C) Construct validity
   (D) External validity
   (E) Internal validity

8. A study that analyzes the effects of heart disease across different regions of the country and socio-economic statuses is called a

   (A) longitudinal study
   (B) experimental design
   (C) double-blind study
   (D) cross-sectional design
   (E) case study

9. A researcher seeks to study the effects of a weight-loss supplement and decides to place an advertisement on buses and subways in New York City to attract subjects. All could happen with this type of subject selection EXCEPT

   (A) pre-screening bias
   (B) self-selection bias
   (C) selection bias
   (D) healthy user bias
   (E) courtesy bias

10. When graphing the distribution of a study, a researcher notices that a disproportionate number of subjects scored low on their test, shifting the peak of the bell curve she was expecting. This is called a

   (A) positive skew
   (B) negative skew
   (C) normal curve
   (D) positive correlation
   (E) negative correlation

Part VI
Content Review for the AP Psychology Exam

Chapter 7
Unit 1:
Biological Bases
of Behavior

INTRODUCTION TO BIOLOGY AND BEHAVIOR

Physiological psychology is the study of behavior as influenced by biology. It draws its techniques and research methods from biology and medicine to examine psychological phenomena.

HEREDITY AND ENVIRONMENT: BEHAVIORAL GENETICS

Behavioral genetics is the application of the principles of evolutionary theory to the study of behavior. **Traits** are distinctive characteristics or behavior patterns that are determined by genetics. Genes are the basic biological elements responsible for carrying information about traits between successive generations. The **evolutionary perspective** on psychology talks about how the principles of evolution, including survival of the fittest and natural selection, apply to psychology. For instance, an evolutionary perspective on a behavior will try to understand why that behavior has endured over millennia when other behaviors may have died out. Eugenics refers to a branch of science that has been discredited where evolutionary theory has been misused to discriminate, stating that some genes are superior to others. The behavioral-genetics approach examines the ways in which we are different from one another. The term **heritability** is used here to discuss the degree of variance among individuals that can be attributed to genetic variations. Many physical and psychological characteristics are inherited. However, genes do not determine everything about us. **Environmentality** is the degree to which a trait's expression is caused by the environment in which an organism lives. Psychology has long been concerned with the relative influences of genetics and environment. This controversy is known as the **nature versus nurture debate**. Today, the common view is that nature and nurture work together; our psychological makeup is largely the result of the interaction of these two forces.

Twin studies, family studies, and adoption studies are the primary methods of research in behavioral genetics. Twin studies compare monozygotic twins to dizygotic twins. Family studies look at the prevalence of certain traits in biological families. Adoption studies look at the intersection between genetics and the environment—i.e., how would monozygotic twins raised in different environments differ from one another. Some disorders are the result of genetic abnormalities. **Down syndrome** occurs when there are three copies of the 21st chromosome, which generally causes some degree of intellectual disability. **Huntington's chorea** is a genetic disorder that results in muscle impairment that does not typically occur until after age 40. It is caused by the degeneration of the structure of the brain known as the basal ganglia, and it is fatal. Because of the late onset of the disease, it is frequently passed down to the next generation before its symptoms are manifested. New genetic mapping techniques are revealing other relationships between specific genes and disorders, and scientists are trying to address ways to correct genetic flaws and provide genetic counseling.

OVERVIEW OF THE NERVOUS SYSTEM

The **nervous system** can be divided into two distinct subsystems: the **central nervous system (CNS)**—comprising the brain and the spinal cord—and the **peripheral nervous system (PNS)**—comprising all other nerves in the body.

The brain is located in the skull and is the central processing center for behavior, thoughts, motivations, and emotions. The brain, as well as the rest of the nervous system, is made up of **neurons**, or nerve cells. The neurons form a network that extends to the spinal cord, which is encased in the protective bones of the spine, or the vertebrae. Both the brain and the spinal cord are bathed in a protective liquid called cerebrospinal fluid. In the spinal cord, the neurons are bundled into strands of interconnected neurons known as nerves. The nerves of the spine are responsible for conveying information to and from the brain and the PNS. Nerves sending information to the brain are **sensory** (or **afferent**) **neurons**; those conveying information from the brain are **motor** (or **efferent**) **neurons**. Although most movements are controlled by the brain, a certain small subset of movements are controlled by direct transmission from afferent to efferent cells at the level of the spinal cord. These responses, known as **reflexes**, are quick and involuntary responses to environmental stimuli. The path of a reflex arc goes from sensory neurons to motor neurons. Three types of neurons in the spinal cord create the reflex arc: sensory neurons, motor neurons, and **interneurons**.

> **Test Tip**
> A memory tip for *afferent* and *efferent* is that **a**fferent connections are **a**rriving to the brain and **e**fferent are **e**xiting the brain.

The PNS comprises all of the nerve cells in the body with the exception of those in the CNS (the brain and spinal cord). The PNS can be subdivided into the **somatic nervous system** and the **autonomic nervous system**. The somatic nervous system is responsible for voluntary movement of large skeletal muscles. The autonomic nervous system controls the nonskeletal or smooth muscles, such as those of the heart and digestive tract. These muscles are typically not under voluntary control. (Think *autonomic = automatic*.) The autonomic nervous system can be further divided into the sympathetic and parasympathetic nervous systems.

The **sympathetic nervous system** is associated with processes that burn energy. The **parasympathetic nervous system** is the complementary system responsible for conserving energy. When the sympathetic system is aroused in a fight, for example, digestion ceases, blood transfers to skeletal muscle, and heart rate increases. When the fight ends, however, the parasympathetic system becomes active, sending blood to the stomach for digestion, slowing the heart rate, and conserving energy. This returns the body to homeostasis.

> **Mnemonic Tip!**
> The *sympathetic* system is *sympathetic* to you while you deal with a problem. The *parasympathetic* system helps you come down afterwards, like a *parachute*.

NEURAL TRANSMISSION

Much of our discussion has involved the idea of information or stimulation being passed along nerves. **Nerves** are bundles of **neurons**, the basic unit of the nervous system. Neurons are cells with a clearly defined, nucleated cell body, or **soma**. Branching out from the soma are **dendrites**, which receive input from other neurons through receptors on their surface. The **axon** is a long, tubelike structure that responds to input from the dendrites and soma. The axon transmits a neural message down its length and then passes its information on to other cells. Some neurons have a fatty coating known as a **myelin sheath** surrounding the axon. Myelin serves as insulation for axons and also speeds up the rate at which electrical information travels down them. The better insulated the myelin sheath, the faster and more efficient the sending of action potentials. The myelin looks like beads on a string; the small gaps between the "beads" are known as the **nodes of Ranvier**. These nodes help speed up neural transmission. The axon ends in **terminal buttons**, knobs on the branched end of the axon. The terminal buttons come very close to the cell bodies and dendrites of other neurons, but they do not touch. The gap between them is known as a **synapse**. A terminal button releases **neurotransmitters**, chemical messengers, across the synapse, where they bind with receptors on subsequent dendrites. Also in the nervous system are **glial cells**, which are non-neuronal cells that provide support, both physical and chemical, to the neurons.

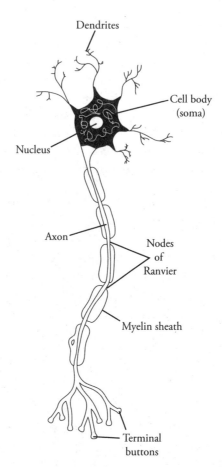

Neuronal communication occurs both within and between cells. Communication within cells is electrochemical. An electric potential across the plasma membrane of approximately –70 millivolts (mV), known as the **resting membrane potential**, exists, in which the interior of the cell is negatively charged with respect to the exterior of the cell. Thus, the cells can be described as polarized: negative on the inside and positive on the outside. An **action potential**, also referred to as a **nerve impulse**, is a disturbance in this membrane potential.

It can be thought of as a wave of depolarization of the plasma membrane that travels along an axon. (Depolarization is a change in the membrane potential from the resting membrane potential to a less negative, or even positive, potential.) The change in membrane potential during passage of an action potential is caused by movement of ions into and out of the neuron through ion channels, leading to the eventual release of the neurotransmitter. After depolarization, repolarization returns the membrane potential to normal.

Action potentials are "all or none," meaning that they are either generated or not, with nothing in between. They are always of a fixed strength, never weaker or stronger. After a neuron fires, it passes through an absolute refractory phase, during which no amount of stimulation can cause the neuron to fire again. The absolute refractory phase is followed by the relative refractory phase, in which the neuron needs much more stimulation than usual to fire again.

Communication between cells happens via neurotransmitters, which bind to receptors on the dendrites of the adjacent neurons. **Excitatory** neurotransmitters serve to excite the cell or cause the neuron to fire. **Inhibitory** neurotransmitters inhibit (or stop) cell firing. After a neurotransmitter is released and has conducted the impulse to the next cell or cells, it is either broken down by **enzymes** or is absorbed back into the cell that released it in a process called **reuptake**. A helpful metaphor for the process of cell communication is thinking of neurotransmitters as keys that open the locks on the postsynaptic cell.

The following are a few key neurotransmitters:

- **Acetylcholine**, which affects memory function, as well as muscle contraction, particularly in the heart

- **Serotonin**, which is related to arousal, sleep, pain sensitivity, and mood and hunger regulation

- **Dopamine**, which is associated with movement, attention, and reward; dopamine imbalances may play a role in Parkinson's disease and in schizophrenia

- **GABA**, or *gamma*-Aminobutyric acid, which is an inhibitory neurotransmitter

- **Glutamate**, which is an excitatory neurotransmitter and the all-purpose counterpart to GABA

- **Norepinephrine**, which affects levels of alertness; a lack of norepinephrine is implicated in depression

- **Endorphins**, which are the body's natural painkillers

- **Substance P**, which appears to be linked to pain, mood, vasodilation, and learning.

Study Tip

Some textbooks and test questions have used the category of antidepressants known as SSRI's (e.g. Prozac, Paxil, Zoloft) as a way to illustrate neuron transmission. See whether you can explain why these drugs are "selective serotonin reuptake inhibitors" and why the effects of these medications might help someone with depression.

ENDOCRINE SYSTEM

The **endocrine system** provides another way by which various parts of our bodies relay information to one another. This system works through groups of cells known as glands, which release substances called **hormones.** Hormones affect cell growth and proliferation. The primary gland is the **pituitary gland**, which is also known as the master gland. The pituitary releases hormones that, in turn, control hormonal release by many other glands. Hormones are different from neurotransmitters in many ways. Neurotransmitters are released locally in the synapses of neurons, while hormones are released into the bloodstream and travel throughout the body. Hormones coordinate a wide range of responses, while neurotransmitters trigger highly localized and specific reactions. Hormones also affect the body for long periods of time compared with neurotransmitters.

The pituitary is located just under the part of the brain that controls it—the hypothalamus. Stressful situations cause the pituitary to release **adrenocorticotropic hormone (ACTH)**, which stimulates the **adrenal glands**, resulting in fight-or-flight reactions. The adrenal glands secrete **epinephrine** (adrenaline) and **norepinephrine** (noradrenaline). **Leptin** is a hormone involved in regulating hunger and energy, and resistance to leptin is implicated in obesity. **Ghrelin** tells your brain it is hungry. **Melatonin** is involved with sleep and is controlled by the level of light. Melatonin production increases when it is dark and is inhibited when it is light. **Oxytocin** is involved with sexual arousal, romantic attachment, and parental bonding. It is also important in the process of childbirth.

PSYCHOACTIVE DRUG EFFECTS

Psychoactive drugs can change how a person acts, thinks, or feels. There are different types of psychoactive drugs, categorized by their effect on the body, notably depressants, opioids, hallucinogens, and stimulants. Some drugs are classified as **agonist**, meaning they increase the effect of the neurotransmitter at the synapse. Others are **antagonists**, meaning they decrease the effect of the neurotransmitter at the synapse. Some of the common psychoactive drugs and their effects are:

Q: Why are narcotics effective?

Answer on page 151.

Drug	Effect on CNS	Effects on the Brain and Body	Effects on Behavior
Alcohol	Depressant	Decreases dopamine levels	Dizziness, slurred speech, impaired judgment High doses can result in respiratory depression and death.
Barbiturates Examples: Seconal, Nembutal	Depressant	Inhibit neural arousal centers	Decrease anxiety; increase relaxation High doses can result in respiratory depression and death. Can be very addictive and dangerous when mixed with other depressants or alcohol
Tranquilizers Examples: Xanax, Valium, Librium	Depressant	Inhibit neural arousal centers	Reduce anxiety without inducing sleep
Caffeine	Stimulant	Accelerates heart rate; constricts blood vessels Reduces levels of adenosine, a neurochemical regulator of norepinephrine release	Can lead to irritability, anxiety, insomnia
Amphetamines Examples: diet pills, Adderall	Stimulant	Increase body temperature and heart rate Increase production of dopamine and norepinephrine	Can be addictive Produce feelings of euphoria High doses can lead to motor dysfunction.

Drug	Effect on CNS	Effects on the Brain and Body	Effects on Behavior
Cocaine	Stimulant	Stimulates heart rate and blood pressure Increases dopamine, serotonin, and norepinephrine release	Users feel as though they have increased mental abilities and social ability. Can be highly addictive
Nicotine	Stimulant	Stimulates acetylcholine transmission Increases heart rate	Has depressant behavioral effects such as decreasing appetite while increasing heart rate and respiration Can sometimes cause euphoria and dizziness Highly addictive
Opioids Example: Oxycodone, Heroin	Depressant	Activate receptors for endogenous endorphins	Induce relaxation and euphoria; can relieve pain May cause impaired cognitive ability, sweating, nausea, and respiratory depression Highly addictive and available only by prescription or through illicit means
Hallucinogens Examples: LSD and marijuana	Distort sensory perceptions	May increase serotonin levels	May induce sensory synesthesia, in which stimuli from one sense, such as hearing, produce sensory effects in other modalities, such as vision Occasionally, the perceptual alterations are extremely unpleasant and terrifying. This state may also be accompanied by paranoia.

In discussing psychoactive drugs, it is important to distinguish among dependence, tolerance, and withdrawal. **Dependence** occurs when an individual continues using a drug despite overarching negative consequences in order to avoid unpleasant physical and/or psychological feelings associated with not taking it. (This term has generally replaced the term *addiction* in psychological and health circles.) Like physical dependence, psychological dependence is biologically based. Enjoyable behaviors produce activity in dopamine circuits in the brainstem, most notably in the nucleus accumbens, the "pleasure center" of the brain. This dopaminergic pathway naturally leads to feelings of reward and pleasure. Many addictive drugs share the characteristic of stimulating the release of dopamine in the nucleus accumbens.

> **A:** They are effective because they bear a striking resemblance to the endogenous endorphins, neurochemicals responsible for pain relief and implicated in pleasant feelings and euphoria.

A person has developed **tolerance** to a drug when increasingly larger doses are needed in order for the same effect to occur. It is possible to develop tolerance without being dependent. **Withdrawal** refers to the process of weaning off a drug one has become dependent upon; this often involves physical and psychological symptoms of a highly unpleasant nature.

NEUROANATOMY

The brain is divided into two distinct regions that have evolved over time. These are the **hindbrain** and the **forebrain** (limbic system and cerebral cortex).

The Hindbrain

- The oldest part of the brain to develop, in evolutionary terms

- Composed of the cerebellum, medulla oblongata, reticular activating system (RAS), and pons

- **Cerebellum**—controls muscle tone and balance, coordination of movement, and some procedural learning

- **Brain Stem** (which includes the **Medulla oblongata**)—controls involuntary actions, such as breathing, digestion, heart rate, and swallowing (basic life functions)

- **Reticular activating system (RAS) and the brain's reward system**—controls arousal (wakefulness and alertness). This is also known as the reticular formation. Also controls some voluntary movement and eye movement. Additionally, it plays a role in learning, emotion, and cognition.

- **Pons**—Latin for "bridge," the pons is a way station, passing neural information from one brain region to another. The pons is also implicated in REM sleep.

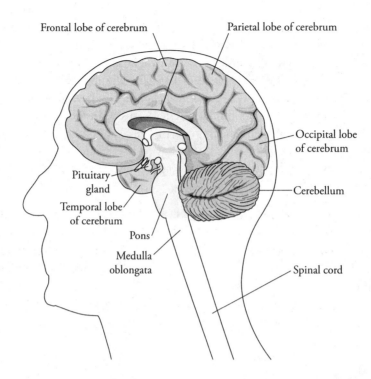

Frontal lobe of cerebrum

Parietal lobe of cerebrum

Occipital lobe of cerebrum

Cerebellum

Pituitary gland

Temporal lobe of cerebrum

Pons

Medulla oblongata

Spinal cord

The Forebrain

- Contains the **limbic system**, or emotional center of the brain

  - The limbic system is composed of the thalamus, hippocampus, amygdala, and hypothalamus

  - **Thalamus**—relays sensory information; receives and directs sensory information from visual and auditory systems

  - **Hippocampus**—involved in processing and integrating memories. Damage to the hippocampus does not eliminate existing memories, because memories are stored in the neocortex, but rather it prevents the formation of new memories. This condition is known as **anterograde amnesia.**

  - **Amygdala**—implicated in the expression of anger, frustration, and fear

  - **Hypothalamus**—controls the temperature and water balance of the body; controls hunger and sex drives; orchestrates the activation of the sympathetic nervous system and the endocrine system; and it can be divided into the **lateral hypothalamus** and **ventromedial hypothalamus**, the combination of which regulates eating behaviors and body weight. The lateral hypothalamus is the "on switch" for eating, while the ventromedial hypothalamus is the "off switch." A lesion to the ventromedial part would cause obesity and even death from overeating, while a lesion to the lateral part would lead to a decreased hunger drive and even self-starvation.

Q: What parts of the brain make up the limbic system?

Answer on page 153.

Mnemonic Tip!
Ventromedial lesion ⟹ Give me **V**ery much food!

Lateral lesion ⟹ Give me **L**ess food!.

- Also contains the **cerebral cortex**, or the wrinkled outer layer of the brain

  - The cortex is involved in higher cognitive functions such as thinking, planning, language use, and fine motor control.

  - This area receives sensory input (**sensory cortex**) and sends out motor information (**motor cortex**).

  - The cortex covers two symmetrical-looking sides of the brain known as the **left and right cerebral hemispheres**. These hemispheres are joined together by a band of connective nerve fibers called the **corpus callosum**.

  - The left hemisphere is typically specialized for language processing, as first noticed by Paul Broca, who observed that brain damage to the left hemisphere in stroke patients resulted in **expressive aphasia**, or loss of the ability to speak. This area of the brain is known as **Broca's area**. Another researcher, Carl Wernicke, discovered an area in the left temporal lobe that, when damaged in stroke patients, resulted in **receptive aphasia**, or the inability to comprehend speech. This is called **Wernicke's area**.

  - Others have noted that the right hemisphere processes certain kinds of visual and spatial information. Roger Sperry demonstrated that the two hemispheres of the brain can operate independently of each other. He did this by performing experiments on **split-brain patients** who had their corpora callosa severed to control their epileptic seizures. Split-brain patients can describe objects without deficit if presented in the right visual field (processed on the left, more verbal side of the brain), but they have great difficulty drawing the image; whereas, if the image is presented in the left visual field (and processed in the more visual right side of the brain), the person can draw or choose the object but cannot explain it verbally. Thus, split-brain patients demonstrate a lack of **contralateral processing**—the ability of (non-split) brains to use both hemispheres and integrate information between them via the corpus callosum.

Cortex Components

- The cortex can be divided into four distinct lobes: the frontal, the parietal, the temporal, and the occipital.

  - The **frontal lobe** is responsible for higher-level thought and reasoning. That includes accessing working memory, paying attention, solving problems, making plans, forming judgments, and performing movements. The frontal lobe is located at the front of the brain.

  - The **parietal lobe** handles somatosensory information and is the home of the primary somatosensory cortex. This area receives information about temperature, pressure, texture, and pain. The parietal lobe is located at the top of the brain, moving towards the back of the brain.

  - The **temporal lobe** handles auditory input and is critical for processing speech and appreciating music. The temporal lobe is located at the side of the brain near the ears.

  - Finally, the **occipital lobe** processes visual input. This information crosses the **optic chiasm**. The occipital lobe is located at the back of the brain.

A: The limbic system is home to the thalamus, hippocampus, amygdala, and hypothalamus.

- Much of the cerebral cortex is composed of **association areas**, which are responsible for associating information in the sensory and motor cortices (this is the plural of *cortex*!). Damage to these association areas can lead to a variety of dysfunctions, including **apraxia**, the inability to organize movement; **agnosia**, a difficulty processing sensory input; **alexia**, the inability to read; and **agraphia**, the inability to write.

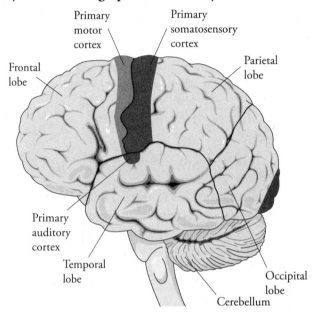

It is important to note that the brain can reorganize itself by forming or severing neural connections throughout one's life. This important ability, called **neuroplasticity**, allows the brain to compensate for injury or disease in order to continue responding adaptably to the environment.

IMAGING TECHNIQUES

Many different techniques are used to examine the interrelationship between the brain and behavior. **Imaging techniques** allow researchers to map the structure and/or activity of the brain and correlate this data with behavior. An **EEG (electroencephalogram)** measures subtle changes in brain electrical activity through electrodes placed on the head. This data can be filtered mathematically to yield evoked potentials, which allow psychologists to get an electrical picture of brain activity during various cognitive states or tasks. EEG is especially useful in sleep studies, since different brain wave patterns are indicative of different stages of sleep.

Computerized axial tomography scans, better known as **CAT scans**, generate cross-sectional images of the brain using a series of X-ray pictures taken from different angles. **MRI (magnetic resonance imaging)** uses extremely powerful electromagnets and radio waves to get 3D structural information from the brain. These techniques capture only "snapshots" of the brain. They do not allow observation of the brain in action over time. **Functional MRI (fMRI)** and **PET scans (positron emission tomography)** do allow scientists to view the brain as it is working. Functional MRI provides such viewing by rapid sequencing of MRI images; PET scans provide images via diffusion of radioactive glucose in the brain. Glucose is the primary "fuel" of brain cells; the more glucose being used in a given brain area, the more that area is in active use. This procedure allows psychologists to observe what brain areas are at work during various tasks and psychological events.

CONSCIOUSNESS

Consciousness is defined as the awareness that we have of ourselves, our internal states, and the environment. A **state of consciousness** enables us to evaluate the environment and to filter information from the environment through the mind, while being aware of the occurrence of this complex process. One state of consciousness is that of being alert. **Alertness** and the associated state of **arousal** involve the ability to remain attentive to our surroundings. It is something that we often take for granted; however, many patients who arrive in an emergency room are not alert for various reasons, arriving in a so-called **altered state of consciousness**. This can be due to head injuries, toxins, or other medical conditions. The ability to be alert is impaired in a variety of disorders, including narcolepsy, attention-deficit disorder, depression, and chronic fatigue syndrome. Even without these disorders, it is not possible to maintain a heightened state of alertness indefinitely, and alertness varies over a 24-hour cycle. Alertness and arousal are controlled by structures within the brainstem. These structures are known as the reticular formation (also known as the reticular activating system, or RAS).

Philosophers and psychologists have debated the nature of consciousness for centuries. William James spoke of a **stream of consciousness**. The cognitive psychologist Robert Sternberg refers to consciousness as a **mental reality** that we create in order to adapt to the world. The **unconscious** level commonly refers to automatic processes, such as breathing or the beating of the heart. These occur because the brain tells them to occur, but they do not happen as a result of conscious intervention. Sigmund Freud referred to the unconscious as an area of mental life that has a huge impact on our thoughts, feelings, and behaviors, but which is only indirectly accessible through symptoms, slips of the tongue or physical accidents, and dreams, for example.

Consciousness serves two important functions. First, consciousness is responsible for keeping track of ourselves, our environment, and our relationship with the environment. Additionally, consciousness serves a controlling role, planning our responses to the information gathered by this monitoring. We typically think of ourselves as fully conscious, but there are lower levels of consciousness, specifically the **preconscious** and unconscious levels.

Consciousness exists on a continuum—starting from **controlled processing**, in which we are very aware of what we are doing, and moving on to **automatic processing**, in which we perform tasks mechanically, such as brushing our teeth. The continuum proceeds through daydreaming, a state in which we can regain consciousness in a moment, and meditation. Next comes sleep and dreaming and, at the far end of the spectrum, coma and unconsciousness.

SLEEP AND DREAMING

Sleep is an altered state of consciousness. Interestingly, scientists still do not precisely understand the function of sleep. One theory holds that sleep is necessary for restorative processes. If this theory is correct, then some chemical in the body should be associated with sleep. Researchers have discovered some neurochemicals, notably **melatonin**, that play a role in sleep, yet a definitive cause-and-effect relationship between a brain chemical and the control of sleep has not been demonstrated.

In addition to conducting chemical investigations of sleep, psychologists investigate the functions of sleep by depriving animals or humans of it. It is difficult to deprive organisms of sleep, as the need for sleep is very strong. One 24-hour cycle without sleep is tolerable (although we will see diminished cognitive and physical functioning akin to driving under the influence of alcohol), but the second such cycle is considerably more difficult. By the third 24-hour cycle, **hallucinations** can begin, as well as **delusions.** Four 24-hour cycles of sleep deprivation can lead to paranoia and other psychological disturbances. All of the symptoms of sleep deprivation disappear when the deprived person is allowed to sleep again.

circa = around

dia = day

circadian = around the day

Another approach to the study of sleep is to investigate the pattern of sleeping. Sleeping generally occurs in humans during the time their area of the world is in darkness—that is, at night. People who live in extreme northern or southern exposures, where it may be light for close to 24 hours, generally try to create conditions of darkness in order to sleep. Our body temperature and other physiological markers follow a day-to-night pattern, known as a **circadian rhythm.** Body temperature rises as the morning approaches, peaks during the day, dips in early afternoon, and then begins to drop again before sleep at night. Although this is a general description of the flow of alertness throughout the day, the pattern varies by individual, and circadian rhythms also vary with age. Newborns can spend two-thirds of a day asleep. Older adults tend to peak in the morning and decline as the day progresses, while adolescents and young adults tend to be more energetic in the mid- to late evening.

Light, both natural and artificial, also influences the biological clock by activating light-sensitive photoreceptors in the retina. Photoreceptors send signals to the brain's **pineal gland**, which is the region responsible for the production of melatonin. Because of the nature of the relationship of the Earth and the Sun, this natural day-night rhythm is a 24-hour one. Our circadian rhythms generally match this pattern. However, if all time cues (such as sunlight, clocks, and television) are removed, then we tend to follow roughly a 25-hour rhythm, called free-running rhythm.

External stimuli are important to setting our circadian rhythms. Rapidly changing these stimuli, such as in the case of traveling across time zones, can disturb circadian rhythms. In this example, the result can be the unpleasant feelings associated with **jet lag**.

Sleep itself is not a uniform process. Rather, sleep can be divided into stages based on brain-wave patterns. Brain waves are usually measured with **electroencephalograms (EEGs)**, which provide a picture of the electrical activity of the brain. When we are awake and focused, **beta wave** activity is happening. While still awake but more relaxed, we drift into **alpha waves**. Then, when we drift off to sleep, **theta wave** activity takes over. This is stage NREM 1—the first stage of Non-Rapid Eye Movement sleep. In stage NREM 2 sleep, a pattern of waves known as **sleep spindles** appear. These spindles are occasionally broken up by **K complexes**, which are large, slow waves. The skeletal muscles relax during this portion of sleep. In stage NREM 3, **delta waves** are most common—this is the deepest stage of sleep. The last stage of sleep is called REM (rapid eye movement) sleep. Researchers Eugene Aserinsky and Nathaniel Kleitman discovered that the eyes move vigorously during the REM stage. This stage of sleep is typically associated with dreaming. In REM sleep, our brain waves resemble beta waves. REM sleep is also known as **paradoxical sleep** because the voluntary muscles are essentially paralyzed during this stage so that you are not acting out your dreams. **Hypnagogic sensations** refer to some of what a person feels in the transitional space between sleep and wakefulness. A person may experience muscle jerks, lucid dreams, or sleep paralysis during hypnagogia.

> ## Study Tip
> Questions about the paradoxical nature of REM sleep are common, so make sure that you can describe brain activity, the status of the autonomic nervous system, and muscle tone during REM.

Each sleep cycle is approximately 90–110 minutes long. Over the course of the night, assuming a person sleeps on average for about eight hours, a person cycles multiple times from NREM 1 to NREM 3 and then into REM sleep.

As the period of sleep progresses, stage NREM 3 diminishes and eventually disappears. Meanwhile, the REM or dream sleep gets longer until near morning, when the dreams are approximately one hour long. Because of their proximity to an awakened state and their length, dreams occurring toward the end of sleep are more easily remembered. Psychologists note that the big difference in sleep is between REM and non-REM.

Sleep researcher William Dement studied the effects of the deprivation of REM sleep. When participants were deprived of REM sleep (waking them every time they entered a REM period) and then allowed to sleep normally after the experimental period, participants' REM periods increased from the normal 90 minutes of REM per night to 120 minutes of REM sleep in the period immediately following the deprivation. This is known as **REM rebound**, and it helps reinforce the idea that we need to sleep.

Researchers currently believe that the purpose of dreaming is for memory consolidation and restoration. The **problem-solving theory of dreaming** holds that dreams provide a chance for the mind to work out issues that occupy its attention during waking hours. Neural repair, consolidation of memories, and protein synthesis seem to occur during dreams. The **activation-synthesis hypothesis of dreaming** postulates that dreams are the product of our awareness of neural activity due to sensory input while we are sleeping. Thus, if it starts raining while you are sleeping, you may dream of a waterfall. A **nightmare** is an elaborate dream sequence that produces a high level of anxiety or fear for the dreamer. The dreamer may experience a sense of physical danger to himself or his loved ones or a strong sense of embarrassment about doing something unacceptable. These dreams are vivid and can often be elaborately described by the dreamer upon awakening; they generally occur during REM sleep.

Given that sleep is such an important factor in our lives, it is not surprising that psychologists are interested in disorders of sleep. **Dyssomnias** are abnormalities in the amount, quality, or timing of sleep, and they include insomnia, narcolepsy, and sleep apnea. **Insomnia** is the most common of the sleep disorders and represents the inability to fall asleep or to maintain sleep. Chronic stress can cause temporary insomnia, as can the use of alcohol or stimulants such as caffeine.

Narcolepsy is the inability to stay awake. A narcoleptic has irresistible and persistent urges to sleep throughout the day and at inappropriate times, such as when driving. Interestingly, when narcoleptics fall asleep, it is typically only for a few minutes, and the sleep is almost all REM sleep. Although narcolepsy can be treated, the cause of the disorder is unknown. However, recent research suggests that the cause of narcolepsy is a dysfunction in the region of the hypothalamus that produces the neurotransmitter hypocretin (also called orexin).

Sleep apnea is a disorder in which a person repeatedly stops breathing while sleeping, which results in awakening after a minute or so without air. This disorder can occur hundreds of times in a night, leaving the sufferer exhausted during the day. Sleep apnea is associated with obesity and also may be linked to alcohol consumption. **Sudden infant death syndrome (SIDS)** may also be linked to sleep apnea.

Parasomnias involve abnormalities of movement during deep sleep; they include sleepwalking (or **somnambulism**) and **night terrors.** Sleepwalking occurs when an individual walks around, and sometimes even talks, while sleeping. Scientists have shown that sleepwalking is not simply acting out dreams, as it occurs during stage 3 and 4 sleep, rather than during REM. Night terrors involve actual behaviors such as screaming, crying, and jerking/lunging movements while asleep. A person suffering a night terror may also be quite mobile, going through all the motions of being attacked by some horror and yet be fully asleep. Nevertheless, there is usually no memory of these actions later on.

Rapid eye movement (REM) sleep behavior disorder is when a person physically acts out vivid, often unpleasant dreams. Behaviors may include vocalizing and/or sudden, often violent, arm and leg movements during REM sleep. This is sometimes called dream-enacting behavior.

> Sensation **EN**codes information.
>
> Perception **DE**codes information.

INTRODUCTION TO SENSATION

To study **sensation** is to study the relationship between physical stimulation and its psychological effects. Sensation is the process of taking in information from the environment.

THRESHOLDS

In **psychophysics**, the branch of psychology that deals with the effects of physical stimuli on sensory response, researchers determine the smallest amount of sound, pressure, taste, or other stimuli that an individual can detect. Psychologists conducting this type of experiment are attempting to determine the **absolute threshold**—the minimum amount of stimulation needed to detect a stimulus. "Detection" means that the stimulus is correctly identified as either present or absent at least 50% of the time. This number is important, because it is the point at which you are no longer guessing. Imagine you are looking five miles down the road at someone with a flashlight; you are likely not detecting whether it is in one of two states: on or off. If asked to report on the flashlight's status, you'll only be right about 50% of the time. But as you get closer to that person, at some point, you will start answering more accurately. That point, where your eyes can begin to detect the light, exceeds the absolute threshold.

Gustav Fechner (1801–1887), the founder of psychophysics, determined that the perceived brightness of a visual sensation and the perceived loudness of an auditory sensation are both proportional to the logarithm of their actual intensity.

In a typical absolute-threshold experiment, an experimenter plays a series of tones of varying volume to determine at exactly what volume the participant first reports that she can hear the tone. Another approach to measuring **detection thresholds** involves **signal detection theory (SDT)**. This theory takes into consideration that there are four possible outcomes for each trial in a detection experiment: the signal (stimulus) is either present or it is not, and the participants respond that they can detect a signal or they cannot. Therefore, we have the following four possibilities:

- **Hit**—the signal was present, and the participant reported sensing it.

- **Miss**—the signal was present, but the participant did not sense it.

- **False alarm**—the signal was absent, but the participant reported sensing it.

- **Correct rejection**—the signal was absent, and the participant did not report sensing it.

For example, if you are sick and the doctor confirms this, that's a hit. If you are sick and the doctor says "You're fine! Go take that vacation," then, unfortunately, that's a miss. If you are healthy, but the doctor says "you are sick," you will definitely be alarmed for a reason that was false. And if you're healthy, and the doctor says "you're fine!," then this is a correct rejection. SDT takes into account response bias, moods, feelings, and decision-making strategies that affect our likelihood of having a given response.

Another type of threshold is the **discrimination threshold**, which is the point at which one can first distinguish the difference between two stimuli. The minimum amount of distance between two stimuli that can be detected as distinct is called the **just noticeable difference (JND)** or **difference threshold**.

In this case, the experiment might involve playing pairs of tones of varying volumes. The participants would try to determine whether the volumes of those tones were the same or different.

Weber's Law

Ernst Weber (1795–1878) noticed that at low weights, say one ounce, participants in a study found it easy to notice half-ounce increases or decreases in weight; however, at high weights, say 32 ounces, participants were not well able to judge half-ounce differences. The observation that the JND is a proportion of stimulus intensity is called **Weber's law**. Simply put, this law states that the greater the magnitude of the stimulus, the larger the differences must be to be noticed.

Sensory interaction refers to how the different sensory processes work together and how they influence each other.

Synesthesia is a neurological condition in which stimulation of one sense leads to automatic activation of another sense; for example, one might "hear" colors.

RECEPTOR PROCESSES

Sensory organs have specialized cells, known as **receptor cells**, which are designed to detect specific types of energy. For example, the visual system has specialized receptor cells for detecting light waves. The area from which our receptor cells receive input is the **receptive field**. Incoming forms of energy to which our receptors are sensitive include mechanical (such as in touch), electromagnetic (such as in vision), and chemical (such as in taste and smell). No matter what the form of the input at the level of the receptor, it must first be converted into the electrochemical form of communication used by the nervous system. Through a process called **transduction**, the receptors convert the input, or stimulus, into neural impulses, which are sent to the brain. For example, in order for us to hear something, tiny receptor cells in the inner ear convert vibrations coming from the outer and then middle ear into electrochemical signals. These signals are then carried by neurons to the brain. Transduction takes place at the level of the receptor cells, and then the neural message is passed to the nervous system. The incoming information from all of our senses (except for that of smell) travels to the sensory neurons of the thalamus. The thalamus, as you may recall from the neuroanatomy section, redirects this information to various sensory cortices in the cerebral cortex, where it is processed. The thalamus may also filter out some sensory inputs; this is an adaptive mechanism for humans because it means that they will not be overwhelmed by incoming sensory information. It is at the level of the thalamus that the **contralateral shift** occurs, in which much of the sensory input from one side of the body travels to the opposite side of the brain. Olfaction, or the sense of smell, travels in a more direct path to the cerebral cortex, without stopping at or being relayed by the thalamus.

SENSORY MECHANISMS

Sensory receptors deal with a wide range of stimuli, and we experience a wide variety of input within each given sensory dimension. Imagine, for example, the gamut of colors and intensities that the eye can sense and relate to the brain. **Sensory coding** is the process by which receptors convey such a range of information to the brain. Every stimulus has two dimensions: what it is (its **qualitative dimension**) and how much of it there is (its **quantitative dimension**). The qualitative dimension is coded and expressed by which neurons are firing. For example, neurons firing in the occipital lobe would indicate that the sensory information is light, and neurons firing in the temporal lobe might indicate that the sensory stimulus is sound. In contrast, the quantitative information is coded by the number of cells firing. Bright lights and loud noises involve the excitation of more neurons than those brought on by dim lights and quiet noises. The wavelengths of light and frequency of sound are perceived as hue and pitch, respectively. The physical characteristic of amplitude is perceived as brightness for light and loudness for sound. The complexity of light is called saturation, and the complexity of sound is called timbre. Sensory neurons

Talk about a complex sound: "timbre" is pronounced "tamber," not "timber"!

respond to differing environmental stimuli by altering their firing rate and the regularity of their firing pattern. **Single-cell recording** is a technique by which the firing rate and pattern of a single receptor cell can be measured in response to varying sensory input.

SENSORY ADAPTATION

Our sensory systems need to do more than simply detect the presence and absence of stimulation. They also need to do more than detect the intensity or quality of stimuli. A key feature of our sensory systems is that they are dynamic: that is, they detect changes in stimulus intensity and quality. Two processes are used in responding to changing stimuli: adaptation and habituation.

Adaptation is an unconscious, temporary change in response to environmental stimuli. An example of this process is our adaptation to being in darkness. At first, it is difficult to see, but our visual system soon adapts to the lack of light. Sensory adaptation to differing stimuli leaves our sensory systems at various adaptation levels. The adaptation level is the new reference standard of stimulation against which new stimuli are judged. A familiar example is that of the swimming pool. If you enter a 75-degree swimming pool directly from an air-conditioned room, it will feel warm, as your adaptation level is set for the cold room. If, however, you are on a hot beach and then enter the same pool, it will feel cold, as your adaptation level is set for the heat of the beach.

VISUAL MECHANISMS

Visual sensation occurs when the eye receives light input from the outside world. Note that the object as it exists in the environment is known as the **distal stimulus**, whereas the image of that object on the retina is called the **proximal stimulus**. Because of the shape of the retina and the positions of the cornea and the lens, the proximal stimulus is inverted. The brain, through perceptual processes, is then capable of interpreting this image correctly.

Visual sensation is a complex process. First, light passes through the **cornea**, a protective layer on the outside of the eye. Just under the cornea is the **lens**. The curvature of the lens changes to accommodate for distance. These changes are called, logically, **accommodations**. The **retina** is at the back of the eye and serves as the screen onto which the proximal stimulus is projected. The retina is covered with receptors known as **rods** and **cones**. Rods, located on the periphery of the retina, are sensitive to low light. Cones, concentrated in the center of the retina, or **fovea**, are sensitive to bright light and color vision. After light stimulates the receptors, this information passes through horizontal cells to **bipolar** and **amacrine cells**. Some low-level information processing may occur here. The stimulation then travels to the **ganglion cells** of the **optic nerves.** Where the optic nerve exits the retina, humans have a **blind spot** because there are no photoreceptors there. We rarely notice the blind spot for two reasons: first, our two eyes are set a few inches apart, so they individually have different blind spots. Second, due to Gestalt principles (see pages 174–176), our brains "fill in" the gaps in the visual field without us even recognizing that this is happening. The optic nerves cross at the **optic chiasm**, sending half of the information from each visual field to the opposite side of the brain. Each visual field includes information from both the left and the right eye. From here,

> **Tip!**
> Think C for cones and C for color.

information travels to the primary visual cortex areas for processing. The brain processes the information received from vision—color, movement, depth, and form—in parallel, not serial, fashion. **Serial processing** occurs when the brain computes information step-by-step in a methodical and linear matter, while **parallel processing** happens when the brain computes multiple pieces of information simultaneously. In other words, the brain is simultaneously identifying the patterns of what is seen. Over time and through practice, serial processes can turn into parallel processes, just as riding a bike initially requires a person to consider each decision, but later is done seemingly automatically. **Feature detector** neurons "see" different parts of the pattern, such as a line set at a specific angle to the background. Like pieces of a jigsaw puzzle, these parts are amalgamated to produce a perception of the pattern in the environment. This process starts at the back of the occipital lobe and moves forward. As the information moves forward, it becomes more complex and integrated. This process, by which information becomes more complex as it travels through the sensory system, is known as **convergence** and occurs across all sensory systems. Once lines and colors have been sensed, the information travels through two pathways: the dorsal stream and the ventral stream. The ventral stream is the "what" pathway that connects to the prefrontal cortex, allowing a person to recognize an object. The dorsal stream is the "where" pathway that integrates visual information with the other senses through a connection to the somatosensory cortex at the top of the brain. Through experiments with cats, it was determined that mammals, including humans, will develop normal vision along these lines so long as any impairments are corrected during the **critical period,** the first months after birth.

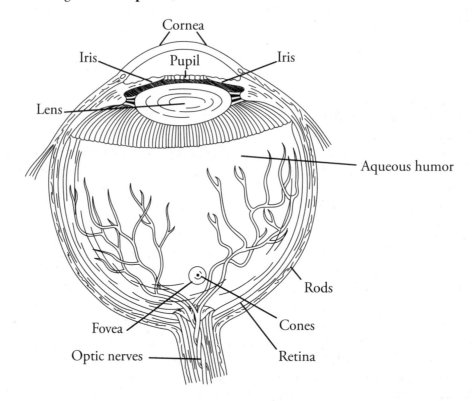

Two different processes contribute to our ability to see in color. The first is based on the **Young-Helmholtz** or **trichromatic theory**. According to this theory, the cones in the retina of the eye are activated by light waves associated with blue, red, and green. We see all colors by mixing these three, much as a television does. However, this does not tell the whole story. Another theory, known as **opponent process theory**, contends that cells within the thalamus respond to opponent pairs of receptor sets—namely, black/white, red/green, and blue/yellow. If one color of the set is activated, the other is essentially turned off. For example, when you stare at a red dot on a page and then you turn away to a blank piece of white paper, you will see a green dot on the blank piece of paper because the red receptors have become fatigued and, in comparison, the green receptors are now more active. This is known as an **afterimage**. **Color blindness** (also known as Color Vision Deficiency) responds to this theory, as well. Most color blindness occurs in males, which provides strong evidence that this is a sex-linked genetic condition. **Dichromats** are people who cannot distinguish along the red/green or blue/yellow continuums. **Monochromats** see only in shades of black and white (this is much more rare). Most color blindness is genetic.

Prosopagnosia refers to a disorder where a person cannot perceive faces. People who have prosopagnosia often do not recognize members of their own family based on facial features but are forced to rely upon other cues such as voice or hair or style of dress. **Blindsight** is a phenomenon where a person can respond to visual stimuli (for instance, making a facial expression) despite damage to the occipital lobe, which has rendered them unable to see in the traditional sense.

AUDITORY MECHANISMS

Auditory input, in the form of sound waves, enters the ear by passing through the outer ear, the part of the ear that is on the outside of your head, and into the ear canal. The wavelength (also known as frequency) determines one's perception of pitch. Longer sound waves have lower frequency and produce a lower pitch, while shorter waves have higher frequency and a higher pitch. The amplitude, or height of the sound wave, determines the perception of sound volume. Larger waves are perceived as louder.

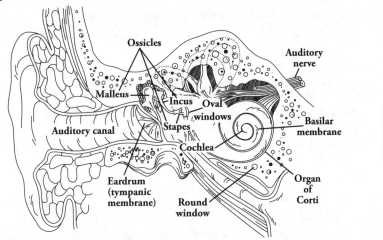

Q: What are the ossicles?

Answer on page 164.

The outer ear collects and magnifies sound waves. The vibrations then enter the middle ear, first vibrating the **tympanic membrane**. This membrane abuts the **ossicles**, the three tiny bones that comprise the middle ear. Vibration of the tympanic membrane vibrates the ossicles. These three bones are called the **malleus**, **incus**, and **stapes**, the last of which vibrates against the oval window. The oval window is the beginning of the inner ear. The vibrations further jiggle the **cochlea**. Within the cochlea are receptor cells, known as hair cells, so named for their hair-like cilia, which move in response to the vibrations. The hair cells line a structure in the cochlea called the basilar membrane. From the cochlea, sound energy is transferred to the auditory nerve and then to the temporal lobe of the auditory cortex. The inner ear is also responsible for balance and contains **vestibular sacs**, as well as the **semicircular canals**: both structures that give information about bodily position in space.

Various theories have been suggested for how hearing occurs. Current thinking relies on the work of Georg von Békésy, which asserts that a traveling wave energizes the basilar membrane. As frequencies get higher, so do the peaks of the traveling wave, increasing the stimulation of the receptors for hearing. This accounts for recognition of sound above 150 Hz. However, humans can hear from 20 to 20,000 Hz. The volley principle—which states that receptor cells fire alternatively, increasing their firing capacity—appears to account for the reception of sound in the lower ranges.

Place theory asserts that sound waves generate activity at different places along the basilar membrane. **Frequency theory** in hearing states that we sense pitch because the rate of neural impulses is equal to the frequency of a particular sound. **Deafness** can occur from damage to the ear structure or the neural pathway. **Conductive deafness** refers to injury to the outer or middle ear structures, such as the eardrum. Impairment of some structure or structures from the cochlea to the auditory cortex results in **sensorineural**, or nerve, **deafness.** Conductive deafness and milder forms of sensorineural deafness may be addressed successfully with hearing aids. However, profound sensorineural hearing loss may not be recoverable without a cochlear implant, which stimulates the auditory nerve directly.

> ## Study Tip
> Of all the individual parts of the visual and auditory system, the most likely to show up on exam questions are the retina and the cochlea. This is because that is where transduction takes place. So, make sure that you understand this process and how it takes place in each.

OTHER SENSORY MECHANISMS

A: The ossicles are three tiny bones in the middle ear, called the malleus, incus, and stapes, that connect the eardrum to the oval window.

Olfaction (smell) is a chemical sense. Scent molecules reach the olfactory epithelium, deep in the nasal cavity. The scent molecules contact receptor cells at this location. Axons from these receptors project directly to the olfactory bulbs of the brain. From there, information travels to the olfactory cortex and the limbic system. Because the amygdala and hippocampus connect to olfactory nerves, it is easy to understand why certain smells trigger memories. **Pheromones** are chemical substances produced and released into the environment that impact the behavior or physiology of others of its species. Mammals and insects are particularly responsive to pheromones.

Gustation (taste) is also a chemical sense. The tongue is coated with small protrusions known as papillae. Located on the papillae are the taste buds, the receptors for gustatory information. There are five basic tastes: sweet, salty, bitter, sour, and umami (savory). These five tastes may have evolved for specific reasons. For example, sweetness, which we tend to like, is often accompanied by calories. Most poisonous plants, in contrast, taste bitter, a taste we generally do not like. Information from the taste buds travels to the medulla oblongata and then to the pons and the thalamus. This information is then relayed to the gustatory areas of the cerebral cortex, as well as the hypothalamus and limbic system. Structures in the mouth, tongue, and brain interact to process taste, and the number of taste receptors determines how sensitive people are to different tastes. There are three types of tasters: supertasters, medium tasters, and nontasters.

The two chemical senses interact—problems with smell can change the way things taste. Think about how hard it is to taste food when one has a stuffed-up nose.

The skin has **cutaneous** and **tactile receptors** that provide information about pressure, pain, and temperature. The receptor cells sensitive to pressure and movement are fast-conducting myelinated neurons, which send information to the spinal cord. From here, the information goes to the medulla oblongata, the thalamus, and finally, to the somatosensory cortex. Pain information is sent via two types of neurons; C fibers are unmyelinated and responsible for the throbbing sense of chronic pain, while myelinated A-delta fibers send information about acute pain. The pain signal first reaches the spinal cord and triggers the release of "substance P" (a neuropeptide, or chemical signal similar to a neurotransmitter, that alerts the spinal cord to the presence of a painful stimulus). The signal then travels to the thalamus and to the cingulate cortex, which is responsible for attention. Once pain is perceived, the brain begins to reduce the intensity of the signal through a process known as "pain-gating." As described by the **gate theory of pain**, a signal is sent from the brain to opiate receptors in the spinal cord, which reduces the sensation of pain. This information projects to the limbic system and then to the somatosensory cortex. The receptor cells for temperature can be divided into **cold fibers**, which fire in response to cold stimuli, and **warm fibers**, which are sensitive to warm stimuli. **Phantom limb sensation** refers to the feeling that there is real pain, which can be severe, or other sensations in a limb that has been amputated.

Other senses include the **vestibular sense**, which involves the sensation of balance. This sense is located in the semicircular canals of the inner ear. **Kinesthesis** refers to one's sense of the body's location and motion; this sense is supported by sensors in the joints and ligaments.

Use this table to compare and contrast different sensory systems.

Sensory System	Receptor Cells Location	Type of Energy	Transduction	Processing Center Location
Visual	Eye	Light	Rods and cones in the retina	Occipital lobe
Auditory	Ear	Sound	Cochlea	Temporal lobe
Tactile	Tactile and cutaneous cells on the skin	Pressure	Tactile cells	Somatosensory cortex
Olfaction (smell)	Nose	Chemical	Olfactory receptor cells	Olfactory bulb
Gustation (taste)	Tongue	Chemical	Taste buds	Cerebral cortex

KEY TERMS

physiological psychology

Heredity and Environment: Behavioral Genetics

traits
evolutionary perspective
heritability
environmentality
nature versus nurture debate
Down syndrome
Huntington's chorea

Overview of the Nervous System

nervous system
central nervous system (CNS)
peripheral nervous system (PNS)
neurons
sensory (afferent) neurons
motor (efferent) neurons
reflexes
interneurons
somatic nervous system
autonomic nervous system
sympathetic nervous system
parasympathetic nervous system

Neural Transmission

nerves
neurons
soma
dendrites
axon
myelin sheath
nodes of Ranvier
terminal buttons
synapse
neurotransmitters
glial cells
resting membrane potential
nerve impulse (action potential)
excitatory
inhibitory
(neurotransmitters, continued)
  acetylcholine
  serotonin
  dopamine
  GABA
  glutamate

norepinephrine
endorphins
substance P

Endocrine System

hormones
pituitary gland
adrenocorticotropic hormone (ACTH)
adrenal glands
epinephrine
norepinephrine
leptin
ghrelin
melatonin
oxytocin

Psychoactive Drug Effects

agonist
antagonist
drugs
  alcohol
  barbiturates
  tranquilizers
  caffeine
  amphetamines
  cocaine
  nicotine
  opioids
  hallucinogens
effects
  dependence
  tolerance
  withdrawal

Neuroanatomy

hindbrain
  cerebellum
  brain stem
  Medulla oblongata
  reticular activating system (RAS)
  brain's reward system
  pons
forebrain
  limbic system
    thalamus
    hippocampus
    anterograde amnesia
    amygdala

hypothalamus
  lateral hypothalamus
  ventromedial hypothalamus
cerebral cortex
  sensory cortex
  motor cortex
  left and right cerebral hemispheres
  corpus callosum
  expressive aphasia (Broca's area)
  receptive aphasia (Wernicke's area)
  split-brain patients
  contralateral processing
    cortex components
      frontal lobe
      parietal lobe
      temporal lobe
      occipital lobe
      optic chiasm
  association areas
    apraxia
    agnosia
    alexia
    agraphia
  neuroplasticity

Imaging Techniques

EEG (electroencephalogram)
CAT (computerized axial tomography) scans
MRI (magnetic resonance imaging)
fMRI (functional MRI)
PET (positron emission tomography) scans

Consciousness

state of consciousness
alertness
arousal
altered state of consciousness
stream of consciousness
mental reality
unconscious
preconscious
controlled processing
automatic processing

Sleep and Dreaming

sleep
melatonin
hallucinations
delusions
circadian rhythm
pineal gland
jet lag
electroencephalograms (EEGs)
beta waves
alpha waves
theta waves
sleep spindles
K complexes
delta waves
paradoxical sleep
hypnagogic sensations
REM rebound
problem-solving theory of
   dreaming
activation-synthesis hypothesis
   of dreaming
nightmare
dyssomnias
   insomnia
   narcolepsy
   sleep apnea
   sudden infant death
   syndrome (SIDS)
parasomnias
   somnambulism
   night terrors

Introduction to Sensation

sensation

Thresholds

psychophysics
absolute threshold
detection thresholds
signal detection theory (SDT)
   hit
   miss
   false alarm
   correct rejection
discrimination threshold
just noticeable difference
   (JND) (difference threshold)
Weber's law
sensory interaction
synesthesia

Receptor Processes

receptor cells
receptive field
transduction
contralateral shift

Sensory Mechanisms

sensory coding
qualitative dimension
quantitative dimension
single-cell recording

Sensory Adaptation

adaptation

Visual Mechanisms

visual sensation
distal stimulus
proximal stimulus
cornea
lens
accommodations
retina
rods
cones
fovea
bipolar
amacrine cells
ganglion cells
optic nerves
blind spot
optic chiasm
serial processing
parallel processing
feature detector
convergence
critical period
Young-Helmholtz theory
   (trichromatic theory)
opponent process theory
afterimage
color blindness (color vision
   deficiency)
dichromats
monochromats
prosopagnosia
blindsight

Auditory Mechanisms

auditory input
tympanic membrane
ossicles
malleus
incus
stapes
cochlea
vestibular sacs
semicircular canals
place theory
frequency theory
deafness
conductive deafness
sensorineural deafness

Other Sensory Mechanisms

olfaction
pheromones
gustation (taste)
cutaneous receptors
tactile receptors
gate theory of pain
cold fibers
warm fibers
phantom limb sensation
vestibular sense
kinesthesis

Unit 1 Drill

See Chapter 12 for answers and explanations.

1. Damage to Broca's area in the left cerebral hemisphere of the brain would likely result in which of the following?

    (A) A repetition of the speech of others
    (B) A loss of the ability to speak
    (C) A loss of the ability to visually integrate information
    (D) A loss of the ability to comprehend speech
    (E) An inability to solve verbal problems

2. In the neuron, the main function of the dendrites is to

    (A) release neurotransmitters to signal subsequent neurons
    (B) preserve the speed and integrity of the neural signal as it propagates down the axon
    (C) perform the metabolic reactions necessary to nourish and maintain the nerve cell
    (D) receive input from other neurons
    (E) connect the cell body to the axon

3. Veronica is having trouble balancing as she walks, and her muscles seem to have lost strength and tone. A neuroanatomist looking into her condition would most likely suspect a problem with Veronica's

    (A) medulla oblongata
    (B) right cerebral hemisphere
    (C) cerebellum
    (D) occipital lobes
    (E) thalamus

4. Which of the following neurotransmitters is generally associated with the inhibition of continued neural signaling?

    (A) Dopamine
    (B) Adrenaline
    (C) GABA
    (D) Serotonin
    (E) Acetylcholine

5. John is constantly overeating and can't seem to control his appetite, no matter how hard he tries. It is possible that John may have damage in which of the following brain structures?

    (A) Thalamus
    (B) Pons
    (C) Hypothalamus
    (D) Amygdala
    (E) Association areas

6. A demyelinating disorder, such as multiple sclerosis, would cause all of the following symptoms EXCEPT

    (A) a reduction of white matter in the central nervous system
    (B) an increased rate of neuronal conduction
    (C) a slower propagation of signals along the axon
    (D) a deficiency of sensation
    (E) a decreased neuronal insulation

7. Which area of the brain is responsible for coordinating complex motor functions?

    (A) Frontal lobe
    (B) Occipital lobe
    (C) Reticular activating system
    (D) Cerebellum
    (E) Temporal lobe

8. The brain wave patterns known as "sleep spindles" are most characteristic of which stage of sleep?

    (A) stage NREM 1 sleep
    (B) stage NREM 2 sleep
    (C) stage NREM 3 sleep
    (D) paradoxical sleep
    (E) REM sleep

9. If all external time cues are removed or blocked, the human circadian "free-running" rhythm tends to cycle every

    (A) 20 hours
    (B) 24 hours
    (C) 25 hours
    (D) 27 hours
    (E) 36 hours

10. All of the following are differences between nightmares and night terrors EXCEPT

   (A) nightmares typically occur during REM sleep, while night terrors typically occur during other sleep stages
   (B) nightmares are often recalled vividly and in detail upon waking, whereas night terrors are not
   (C) people are usually relatively still during nightmares, while they may move around quite a lot, even sleepwalk, during night terrors
   (D) while people may vocalize during nightmares, night terrors are more likely to involve screaming, crying, or shouting
   (E) nightmares are generally expressions of the dreamer's conscious issues, while night terrors reflect unconscious concerns

11. Which of the following is NOT a member of the class of psychoactive drugs collectively known as narcotics?

   (A) Codeine
   (B) Morphine
   (C) Heroin
   (D) Opium
   (E) Cocaine

12. Alcohol withdrawal syndrome occurs when an individual with a dependence on alcohol suddenly limits or stops their consumption of alcohol. Nervous symptoms of withdrawal include seizures and uncontrollable shaking of the extremities. What is the most plausible mechanism of action for these physical symptoms?

   (A) Chronic alcohol consumption causes down-regulation of GABA receptors, leading to a reduction in CNS inhibition, and excito-neurotoxicity.
   (B) Long-term alcohol abuse stimulates the autonomic nervous system, causing tremors.
   (C) Cessation of alcohol consumption leads to a reduction in dopamine production in the nucleus accumbens.
   (D) Alcohol is a hallucinogenic, and withdrawal causes the body to respond by relaxing, disinhibiting, and amplifying sensory information.
   (E) Alcohol is a depressant, decreasing inhibitory GABA-binding activity in the central nervous system.

13. A patient goes to the doctor's office citing symptoms of wakefulness in the night and tiredness during the day. Given these symptoms, which of the following might be a correct diagnosis?

   (A) Narcolepsy
   (B) Sleep apnea
   (C) Somnambulism
   (D) Paradoxical sleep
   (E) Night terrors

14. A 62-year-old female is on hypertension medication. Over the past three years, her dosage has increased twice. If she forgets to take her medication, her blood pressure increases dramatically. This increase in her blood pressure is an example of

   (A) addiction
   (B) psychological dependence
   (C) physical dependence
   (D) tolerance
   (E) stimulants

15. Paradoxical sleep occurs during

   (A) stage NREM 1 sleep
   (B) stage NREM 2 sleep
   (C) stage NREM 3 sleep
   (D) hypnotic states
   (E) REM sleep

16. Over the course of the night, which is true about the sleep cycles?

   (A) Stage NREM 3 eventually disappears while REM cycles lengthen to approximately one hour long.
   (B) Stages NREM 2 and NREM 3 eventually disappear while REM cycles lengthen to approximately 30 minutes long.
   (C) Stage NREM 3 eventually disappears while stages NREM 1 and NREM 2 lengthen to approximately 20 minutes each.
   (D) REM cycles eventually disappear while stage NREM 3 lengthens to approximately one hour long.
   (E) Stages NREM 1 and NREM 2 eventually disappear while stage NREM 3 lengthens to approximately 20 minutes.

17. If a person is supposed to press a button when he sees a red triangle but instead presses the button when he sees a green triangle, what is this called?

    (A) Opponent process
    (B) Hit
    (C) False alarm
    (D) Miss
    (E) Correct rejection

18. The five basic gustatory sensations that most animals possess are

    (A) bitter, salty, sweet, tangy, sour
    (B) salty, sweet, bitter, sour, umami
    (C) smooth, grainy, cold, hot, prickly
    (D) grain, fruit, meat, vegetable, dairy
    (E) salty, sharp, umami, sour, bitter

19. Cats tend to notice slight movements under low lighting conditions with greater ease than do humans; they do not, however, find it easy to distinguish colors. This is primarily due to their retinas containing, in comparison to humans,

    (A) relatively fewer amacrine cells and relatively more bipolar cells
    (B) relatively fewer ganglion cells and relatively more osmoreceptors
    (C) relatively fewer cilia and relatively more optic nerve cells
    (D) relatively fewer cones and relatively more rods
    (E) relatively fewer mechanoreceptors and relatively more ossicles

20. Which of the following would be the best illustration of Weber's law?

    (A) Most people can recognize the difference between a 40- and 42-decibel sound, but not an 80- and 82-decibel sound.
    (B) A person can recognize an imperceptible amount of perfume in a ten-foot-by-ten-foot room.
    (C) People cannot attend to more than one stimulus at a time.
    (D) A person has the ability to tell the difference between a 20-watt bulb and a 100-watt bulb 50 percent of the time.
    (E) All auditory stimuli above a certain frequency "sound" as if their frequencies are the same.

21. What structure in the middle ear generates vibrations that match the sound waves striking it?

    (A) Basilar membrane
    (B) Tympanic membrane
    (C) Cochlea
    (D) Malleus
    (E) Stapes

22. In the human visual pathway, what cell type comprises the bundle of fibers called the optic nerve?

    (A) Rods
    (B) Bipolar cells
    (C) Ganglion cells
    (D) Fovea cells
    (E) Cones

23. Laretta walks into a classroom and notices a strange odor. She sits down for class and, over time, forgets about the smell. When she returns to class the next day, she notices the odor again. This phenomenon is known as

    (A) habituation
    (B) dishabituation
    (C) adaptation
    (D) sensitization
    (E) desensitization

24. Subliminal perception is a form of preconscious processing that occurs when stimuli are presented too rapidly for us to be consciously aware of them. The fact that these stimuli were perceived and processed on some level can be demonstrated by

    (A) immediate recognition of these stimuli
    (B) subtle influence to do or say something that has been presented subliminally
    (C) inability of the stimuli to be subject to the tip-of-the-tongue phenomenon
    (D) greater tendency of these stimuli to be subject to proactive interference
    (E) slower recall of these stimuli in a matched-pairs trial

REFLECT

Respond to the following questions:

- Which topics in this chapter do you hope to see on the multiple-choice section or essay?

- Which topics in this chapter do you hope not to see on the multiple-choice section or essay?

- Regarding any psychologists mentioned, can you pair the psychologists with their contributions to the field? Did they contribute significant experiments, theories, or both?

- Regarding any figures given, if you were given a labeled figure from within this chapter, would you be able to give the significance of each part of the figure?

- Can you define the key terms at the end of the chapter?

- Which parts of the chapter will you review?

- Will you seek further help, outside of this book (such as from a teacher, Princeton Review tutor, or AP Students), on any of the content in this chapter—and, if so, on what content?

Chapter 8
Unit 2: Cognition

INTRODUCTION TO PERCEPTION

Perception refers to the way in which we recognize, interpret, and organize our sensations.

PERCEPTUAL PROCESSES

When we were describing sensory mechanisms, we talked about how environmental stimuli affect the receptor systems. This section deals with **perceptual processes**—how our mind interprets these stimuli. There are two main theories of perception: bottom-up and top-down.

Bottom-up processing achieves recognition of an object by breaking it down into its component parts. It relies heavily on the sensory receptors. Bottom-up processing is the brain's analysis and acknowledgment of the raw data. **Top-down processing**, by contrast, occurs when the brain labels a particular stimulus or experience. For example, let's think about the first time a person tastes the sourness of a lemon. In this example, the neurons firing to alert the brain of the presence of some taste in the mouth is a bottom-up process, whereas labeling it "sour" is the top-down process. However, the next time the person sees a lemon, they might salivate or wince before ever tasting the lemon. This is top-down processing because the expectation based on experience influences the perception of the lemon. Top-down processing can be a factor in optical illusions when people see what they expect to see rather than what is actually in front of them.

A **schema** is an organized unit of knowledge for a subject or event based on past experience. Schemas guide our perception of the world around us. A **perceptual set** refers to a mental predisposition or readiness to perceive stimuli in a particular way based on previous experiences, expectations, beliefs, and context. Both schemas and perceptual sets influence how we interpret and make sense of the barrage of sensory data we encounter. External factors are also involved in perception, including context and expectations based on experience or culture.

The visual system needs to perceive and recognize form: that is, size and shape. The **Gestalt approach** to form perception is based on a top-down theory. This view holds that most perceptions involve figure-ground relationships. Figures are those things that stand out, whereas the ground is the field against which the figures stand out. The famous vase-face example shows us that figure and ground are often reversible.

Some basic Gestalt principles of figure detection include the following:

- **Proximity**—the tendency to see objects near each other as forming groups

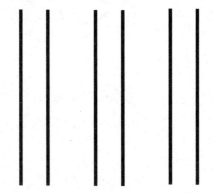

The Gestalt Principle of Proximity: We tend to see these as three pairs of lines, rather than as six individual lines.

- **Similarity**—the tendency to prefer grouping like objects together

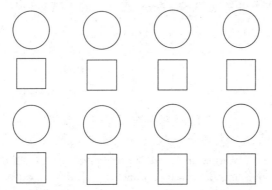

The Gestalt Principle of Similarity: We tend to see these as rows of circles and rows of squares, rather than as columns of circles and squares.

- **Symmetry**—the tendency to perceive forms that make up mirror images

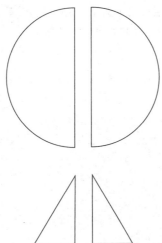

The Gestalt Principle of Symmetry: We tend to see the top figures as a single circle, and the lower figures as forming a single triangle.

- **Continuity**—the tendency to perceive fluid or continuous forms, rather than jagged or irregular ones

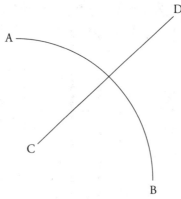

The Gestalt Principle of Continuity: We tend to see this as
a curve from point A to point B and a line from C to D,
rather than seeing angular paths from A to D and C to B.

- **Closure**—the tendency to see closed objects rather than those that are incomplete

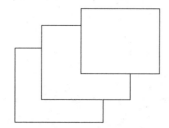

The Gestalt Principle of Closure: We tend to see this as three rectangles,
even though there is actually only one rectangle that is completely visible.

These Gestalt principles represent the **Law of Prägnanz**, which suggests that we tend to see objects in their simplest forms.

A different theory of form recognition is based on a **feature detector approach**. This approach differs from the Law of Prägnanz, which reduces an image to its simplest form, by positing that organisms respond to specific aspects of a particular stimulus. For example, when driving a car, we use feature detection to anticipate the movement of other cars and pedestrians that demand our immediate attention, helping us to be more aware of the environment.

ATTENTION

The term **attention** refers to the processing through cognition of a select portion of the massive amount of information incoming from the senses and contained in memory. In common terms, attention is what allows us to focus on one small aspect of our perceptual world, such as a conversation, while constantly being assailed by massive input to all of our sensory systems. Attention serves as a bottleneck, or funnel, that channels out some information in order to focus on other information. This process is essential because the brain is not equipped to process and pay attention to all of the information it is presented with at a particular moment. The fact that the brain must take shortcuts and focus on particular information is a key issue in perception, which explains why the brain can be tricked through illusions.

Selective attention, or focusing on one thing (like a movie) while ignoring another (like a loud talker), is a good example of this type of focus. Research has examined multiple theories as to why humans attend to certain stimuli and not to others. **Attentional resource theories** posit that we have only a fixed amount of attention, and this resource can be divided up as is required in a given situation. So, if you are deeply engrossed in this book, you are giving it nearly all of your attentional resources. Only strong stimulation could capture your attention. This theory is inadequate, however, because all attention is not equal.

For example, a conversation occurring near you is more likely to interfere with your reading than is some other nonverbal noise.

Filter theories propose that stimuli must pass through some form of screen or filter to enter into attention. Donald Broadbent proposed a filter at the receptor level. However, the notion of a filter at this level has generally been discarded, based on findings showing that meaningful stimuli, such as our own names, can catch our attention. Therefore, the filter must be at a higher processing level than that of the receptors because meaning has already been processed. Anne Treisman revised Broadbent's model to suggest that information not attended to is not actually filtered out. Rather, it is attenuated (Treisman's Attenuation Model of Attention), meaning that the volume is turned down on some stimuli and turned up on others.

> **Differentiating Messages**
> It is easiest for people to tell the difference between messages when they are physically different, such as when one message is spoken in a deep voice and one in a high-pitched one.

This model helped account for the **cocktail party phenomenon**, wherein a person can carry on and follow a single conversation in a room full of them but also still have their attention quickly drawn to another conversation by a key stimulus, such as someone saying their name. The ability to switch from an active conversation to one that you had not previously been focused on shows that a part of your brain was still attending to that information, just not as consciously.

This phenomenon has been studied in the laboratory with headphones, by playing a different message in each of a participant's ears, a task known as dichotic listening. The participant is instructed to repeat only one of the conversations. This repetition is referred to as **shadowing**. The message played into the nonshadowed ear is largely ignored; however, changes in that message or key words, like names, can draw attention to that message.

A classic video asks the viewer to pay attention to the number of times a basketball is passed. Most people who watch for this tend not to notice that someone in a gorilla costume walks right through the game.

Divided attention, trying to focus on more than one task at a time, is most difficult when attending to two or more stimuli that activate the same sense, as in watching TV and reading. The ability to successfully divide attention declines with age. A person's ability to multitask depends on task similarity, task difficulty, and task practice. **Inattentional blindness,** also known as change blindness, demonstrates a potential weakness of selective attention. Sometimes, when people focus too intently on specific stimuli, they can miss the bigger picture going on around them. There are many entertaining videos available online that display this phenomenon.

Binocular depth cues rely on both eyes viewing an image. They result from the fact that each eye sees a given image from a slightly different angle: this difference is called **retinal disparity.** When the brain fuses the images produced on the two separate retinas, it creates a three-dimensional or **stereoptic** image. **Retinal convergence** is a depth cue that results from the fact that your eyes must turn inward slightly to focus on near objects. The closer the object, the more the eyes must turn inward. The complement to stereopsis is **binocular disparity,** which results from the fact that the closer an object is, the less similar the information arriving at each eye will be. This process can be demonstrated by covering one eye, then the other, while looking at something directly in front of you. This procedure reveals two very different views of the object. Repeat this procedure with an object across the room, however, and the two views appear more similar.

Visual perception is quite complex. We need to perceive depth, size, shape, and motion. Depth perception is facilitated by various perceptual cues. Because of the limited ability of the brain to process information, it must take certain shortcuts and educated guesses based on how the world is normally structured. As such, the brain uses these cues but can also fall victim to illusions.

Visual perception cues can be divided into monocular and binocular cues. **Monocular depth cues** refer to the qualities of a visual scene that let you know how close or how far things are from you, using just one eye. **Relative size** refers to the fact that images that are farther from us project a smaller image on the retina than do those that are closer to us. Therefore, we expect an object that appears much larger than another to be closer to us. Related to this idea is the idea of **texture gradient.** Textures, or the patterns of distribution of objects, appear to grow more dense as distance increases. If we are looking at pebbles in the distance, they appear smooth and uniform, but close up may appear jagged and rough. Another monocular depth cue is **interposition,** also known as occlusion, which occurs when a near object partially blocks the view of an object behind it. **Linear perspective** is a monocular cue based on the perception that parallel lines seem to draw closer together as the lines recede into the distance. Picture yourself standing on a train track, looking at the two rails. As the rails move away from you, they appear to draw closer together. The place where the rails seem to join is called the **vanishing point.** This is the point at which the two lines become indistinguishable from a single line and then disappear. Objects present near the vanishing point are assumed to be farther away than

Nature, Nurture, and the Visual Cliff

Together, the binocular cues for vision enable us to have depth perception. To test whether depth perception was innate (nature) or learned (nurture), researchers Eleanor Gibson and Richard Walk developed the **visual cliff** to test depth perception. The visual cliff was a glass tabletop that appeared to be clear on one side and had a checkerboard design visible on the other side. Infants were placed on the checkerboard side of the "cliff," and researchers tracked whether they would crawl onto the clear side, thus going "over the cliff." Most infants refused to do so, which implies that depth perception is at least partially innate. Because the infants had to be a few months old, it was unclear how much learning had influenced depth perception. With other animals tested (chicks, pigs, kittens, turtles), it was concluded that the animal's visual skills depended on the importance of vision to the organism's survival.

those along the tracks at a point where they diverge greatly. **Relative clarity** is a perceptual clue that explains why less distinct, fuzzy images appear to be more distant.

Constancy is another important perceptual process. Constancy means that we know that a stimulus remains the same size, shape, brightness, weight, and/or volume even though it does not appear to. People who have never seen airplanes on the ground will have trouble perceiving the actual size of a plane because of their experience with the size of the object when airborne. The *ability* to achieve constancy, which is innate, and the *experience*, which is learned, both contribute to our development of the various types of constancy.

One of the most complex abilities we have is **motion detection**. We perceive motion through two processes. One records the changing position of an object as it moves across the retina. The other tracks how we move our heads to follow the stimulus. In both cases, the brain interprets the information with special motion detectors. A related issue is the perception of **apparent motion**. Examples of apparent movement include blinking lights on a roadside arrow, which give the appearance of movement (**phi phenomenon**); a motion picture, wherein still pictures move at a fast enough pace to imply movement (**stroboscopic effect**); and still light that appears to twinkle in darkness (**autokinetic effect**).

CONCEPTS

We are constantly being inundated with information about our surroundings. In order to organize all of this information, we devise concepts. A **concept** is a way of grouping or classifying the world around us. For example, chairs come in a large variety of sizes and shapes, yet we can identify them as chairs. The concept of chairs allows us to identify them without learning every possible trait of all chairs. **Typicality** is the degree to which an object fits the average. What are the average characteristics of a chair? When we picture "chair," an image emerges in our brain. This typical picture that we envision is referred to as a **prototype**. But we can imagine other images of a chair that are distant from the prototype to varying degrees. While a prototype can be thought of as an average of all our experiences of "chair," for example, an **exemplar** is a specific example of a specific chair that comes to mind when you think of "chair."

Concepts can be small or large, more or less inclusive. A **superordinate concept** is very broad and encompasses a large group of items, such as the concept of "food." A **basic concept** is smaller and more specific—for example, "bread." A **subordinate concept** is even smaller and more specific, such as "rye bread." Concepts are essential for thinking and reasoning. Without such categorization, we would be so overwhelmed by our surroundings that we would be incapable of any deeper thought.

A very basic problem-solving strategy we use is trial-and-error, which means we try random possible solutions and see what works. But trial-and-error is very time-consuming and does not always lead us to the answer. When solving well-structured problems, we often rely on **heuristics**, or intuitive rules that may or may not be useful in a given situation. There are a number of types of heuristics and all may lead to incorrect conclusions. The **availability heuristic** means that the conclusion is drawn from what events come readily to mind. For example, many people mistakenly believe that air travel is more dangerous than car travel because

> **Schemas: Assimilation and Accommodation**
> Part of the process of thinking is forming and modifying schemas through assimilation (taking in information) and accommodation (broadening of the schema). See more on page 174.

airplane crashes are so vividly and repeatedly reported. The **representativeness heuristic** also can lead to incorrect conclusions. In this case, we judge objects and events in terms of how closely they match the prototype of that object or event. For example, many people view high school athletes as less intelligent. However, most high school athletes must meet certain academic standards in order to participate in sports. A person's particular view of the athlete will determine whether the representativeness heuristic is leading to a correct or incorrect conclusion. Unfortunately, such erroneous conclusions are how racism, sexism, and ageism persist. Heuristics contrast with **algorithms**, which are systematic, mechanical approaches that guarantee an eventual answer to a problem.

Other obstacles to problem-solving include confirmation bias, hindsight bias, belief perseverance, and framing. **Confirmation bias**, the search for information that supports a particular view, hinders problem-solving by distorting objectivity. The **hindsight bias**, or the tendency after the fact to think you knew what the outcome would be, also distorts our ability to view situations objectively. Similarly, **belief perseverance** affects problem-solving. In this mental error, a person sees only the evidence that supports a particular position, despite evidence presented to the contrary. **Framing**, or the way a question is phrased, can alter the objective outcome of problem-solving or decision-making.

Subliminal perception is a form of preconscious processing that occurs when we are presented with stimuli so rapidly that we are not consciously aware of them. When later presented with the same stimuli for a longer period of time, we recognize them more quickly than stimuli we were not subliminally exposed to. Clearly, there was some processing occurring, even if we were not aware of it. This preconscious processing is known as **priming**.

Sink or Swim!

A perfect example of the sunk cost fallacy applies to those who keep working on a tough AP Psychology question in the hopes of solving it, all while spending more and more time that could've been better spent on other questions.

Gambler's fallacy refers to thinking that a certain event is more or less likely based on a series of events. However, this often leads to errors because each event should be considered independent and does not influence other events. The **sunk cost fallacy** is the tendency for people to continue doing something even when abandoning it would be more beneficial. Because we have invested our time, energy, or other resources, people feel they must stick with it. **Executive functions** are the cognitive processes in the brain that allow people to generate, organize, plan, and carry out goal-directed behaviors. The prefrontal cortex is primarily involved in these executive functions, which also enable people to think critically.

PROBLEM-SOLVING AND CREATIVITY

Problem-solving involves the removal of one or more impediments to the finding of a solution in a situation. The problems to be solved can be either well-structured, with paths to solution (for example, "What is the square footage of my room?"), or ill-structured, with no single, clear path to solution (for example, "How can I succeed in school?"). In order to solve problems, we must decide whether the problem has one or more solutions. If many correct answers are possible, we use a process known as **divergent thinking**. Brainstorming is an example of divergent thinking. If the problem can be solved only by one answer, **convergent thinking** must be used. Convergent thinking, then, requires narrowing of the many choices available.

Creativity can be defined as the process of producing something novel yet worthwhile. The elusive nature of creativity makes it a difficult topic to study. For example, what is truly novel, and who is the judge of what is or is not worthwhile? Briefly, creative people tend to be motivated to create primarily for the sheer joy of creation, rather than for financial or material gain. Creative people also seem to exhibit care and consideration when choosing a specific area of interest to pursue. Once they have chosen that area, they tend to immerse themselves in it and to develop extensive knowledge of all aspects of the topic. Creativity seems to correlate with nonconformity to the rules governing the area of creativity. For example, Copernicus had to disregard the common belief that the Earth was the center of the solar system to make his discoveries about planetary motion.

MEMORY

Memory describes all the processes involved with processing, storing, and retrieving information from what we experience. Information in the long-term can be stored in different ways, depending on the type of information it is. **Declarative** (or **explicit**) **memory** is a memory a person can consciously consider and retrieve, such as episodic and semantic memory. **Episodic memory** is our memory for events that we ourselves have experienced. **Semantic**, or declarative, **memory**, comprises facts, figures, and general world knowledge. In contrast, **nondeclarative** (or **implicit**) **memory** is beyond conscious consideration and would include procedural memory, priming, and classical conditioning. **Procedural memory** consists of skills and habits. Because these memories are stored in the striatum, these memories are less likely to be lost to injury or damage.

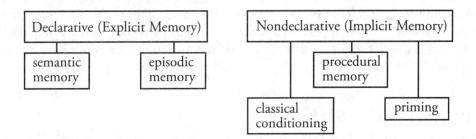

Prospective memory refers to remembering that one has to do something in the future. Retrospective memory refers to remembering the past.

At a given synapse, **long-term potentiation** involves both presynaptic and postsynaptic neurons. For example, dopamine is one of the neurotransmitters involved in pleasurable or rewarding actions. In operant conditioning, reinforcement activates the limbic circuits that involve memory, learning, and emotions. Because reinforcement of a good behavior is generally intrinsically pleasurable (like food or praise), the circuits are strengthened as dopamine floods the system, making it more likely the behavior will be repeated.

After long-term potentiation has occurred, passing an electrical current through the brain doesn't disrupt the memory associations between the neurons involved, although other memories will be wiped out. For example, when people receive a blow to the head resulting in a concussion, they lose their memory for events shortly preceding the concussion. This is due to the fact that long-term potentiation has not had a chance to occur (and leave traces of memory connections), while old memories, which were already potentiated, remain.

Many psychologists believe that the modal model of storage is too passive a model and does not account for all the activities involved in processing memory. Baddeley's Model of Working Memory posits short-term memory as **working memory**—a workbench of sorts—where our brains are actively manipulating sensory data for immediate use or encoding into long-term storage. Baddeley's model starts with a central executive, which controls the flow of information into three subservient systems: the phonological loop (for auditory and verbal data), the visuospatial sketchpad (for purely visual and spatial data), and the episodic buffer (which integrates information from multiple sources). These three systems then integrate with long-term memory stores.

Multi-Store Model of Memory

The multi-store model of memory is another way of conceptualizing memory by dividing the memory system into three distinct storage units: sensory memory, short-term memory, and long-term memory.

Sensory Memory

Sensory memory is the gateway between perception and memory. This store is quite limited. Information in sensory memory is referred to as **iconic** if it is visual and **echoic** if it is auditory. The iconic store lasts for only a few tenths of a second while the echoic store lasts for three or four seconds. The items in sensory memory are constantly being replaced by new input, with only certain items entering into short-term memory.

The nature of sensory memory is clarified by certain types of events. If you have ever watched someone jump rope quickly, you may have noticed the perception of the rope being at many points in its rotation at once. A quickly moving fan also may generate such a perception. This phenomenon is called **visual persistence**. Sensory information in sensory memory remains in attention briefly; the speed of the rope or fan causes the sensory information to run together.

Short-Term Memory (STM)

Short-term memory holds information from a few seconds up to about 30 seconds. Psychologist George Miller found that the information stored in this portion of memory is primarily acoustically encoded, regardless of the nature of the original source. Short-term memory can hold about seven items, plus or minus two (convenient for telephone numbers, which can still be useful to memorize in the event of an emergency). Items in the short-term store are maintained there by rehearsal.

Long-Term Memory (LTM)

Long-term memory is the repository for all of our lasting memories and knowledge, and it is organized as a gigantic network of interrelated information. It is capable of permanent retention for the duration of our lives. Evidence suggests that information in this store is primarily **semantically encoded**—that is, encoded in the form of word meanings. However, certain types of information in this store can be either **visually encoded** or **acoustically encoded**.

Elaborative rehearsal is more effective than maintenance rehearsal for ensuring short-term memory information is sent to long-term memory; therefore, it is a preferred way to study. Both types of rehearsal are forms of **effortful processing,** also known as controlled processing, when we make a conscious effort to retain information. This is distinguished from the **automatic processing** that can occur unconsciously when we are engaged with well-practiced skills, like riding a bicycle.

> **Everyday Example**
> Remembering song lyrics is an example of acoustic encoding.

The **levels of processing model** suggests that the way people encode information influences the ability to recall it. The deeper the level of processing, the easier it is for a person to recall that information. **Recognition memory** is a more superficial level of remembering. Think about things we recognize: faces, names, voices, patterns. Recognition memory is the strategy behind multiple choice tests. **Recall memory** is deeper level processing and is the strategy underlying short answer or essay tests. For example, it is easier to remember the general plot of a book than the exact words, meaning that semantic information (meaning) is more easily remembered than grammatical information (form) when the goal is to learn a concept. A **mnemonic device** can also help in this regard by compressing information into a format that's easier to recall, whether that's a rhyme or a bunch of short words or phrases that represent longer strings of information. For example, ROYGBIV is an acronym that is helpful in memorizing the colors of the rainbow (red, orange, yellow, green, blue, indigo, violet). A mnemonic device is any technique that makes it easier to learn and remember something.

The **dual-coding hypothesis** indicates that it is easier to remember words with associated images than either words or images alone. By encoding both a visual mental representation and an associated word, there are more connections made to the memory and there is more of an opportunity to process the information at a deeper level. For this reason, imagery is a useful mnemonic device. One aid for memory is to use the **method of loci**. This involves imagining moving through a familiar place, such as your home, and in each place, leaving a visual representation of a topic to be remembered. For recall, then, the images of the places could be called upon to bring into awareness the associated topics.

It is also easier to remember things that are personally relevant, known as the **self-reference effect**. We have excellent recall for information that we can personally relate to because it interacts with our own views or can be linked to existing memories. Another useful tool for memory, then, is to relate new information to existing knowledge by making it personally relevant.

An interesting feature of short-term memory is that its limit of about seven items is not as limiting as it would seem. The reason is that what constitutes an item need not be something as simple as a single digit. In fact, it can be a fairly large block of information. George Miller defined grouping items of information into units as **chunking**. For example, when learning a friend's phone number (typically seven digits), you probably chunk the information into a 3-digit and a 4-digit number in order to better retain the information. Encoding can also be improved by grouping information into categories or hierarchies.

The **spacing effect** describes how the time between study sessions can increase retention. **Distributed practice,** where information is studied over time with intervals in between, leads to better recall than **massed practice,** where material is encoded all at once. The **testing effect** refers to the finding that testing ourselves (or being tested) on material leads to better recall than simply restudying alone. **Metacognition** is being aware of one's own thinking processes. A person can use metacognition to determine the best ways an individual studies and learns and remembers.

An additional feature of short-term memory is that it seems to store items from a list sequentially. This sequential storage leads to our tendency to remember the first few and last few items in a list better than the ones in the middle. These effects are called the **primacy** (remembering the first items) and **recency** (remembering the last items) **effects**. The recency effect tends to fade in about a day; the primacy effect tends to persist longer. The overall effect is called the **serial position effect**.

The Serial Position Effect

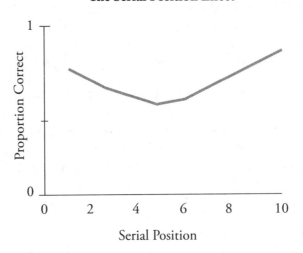

Rehearsal can be divided into two types: **maintenance rehearsal** and **elaborative rehearsal**. Maintenance rehearsal is simple repetition to keep an item in short-term memory until it can be used (as when you say a phone number to yourself over and over again until you can add it to your contacts). Elaborative rehearsal involves organization and understanding of the information that has been encoded in order to transfer the information to long-term memory (as when you try to remember the name of someone you have just met at a party).

Recalling items in long-term memory is subject to **context-dependent memory**. This principle states that information is more likely to be recalled if the attempt to retrieve it occurs in a situation similar to the situation in which it was encoded. For example, if you memorize information about psychology while in a classroom, you should remember it better in that same classroom than if the information was memorized at home. **State-dependent memory** also applies to states of mind, meaning that information memorized when under the influence of a drug is easier to access when in a similar state than when not on that drug. **Mood-congruent memory** refers to the ease in recalling memories when a person is in the same emotional mood as when the information was encoded.

Autobiographical memory is one's memory for events and experiences that happened to them. Much research points to autobiographical memory starting around the age of four. Autobiographical memory also lends support to the self-reference discussed above.

Hermann Ebbinghaus (1850–1909) studied the phenomenon of forgetting. His "forgetting curve" showed that most forgetting occurs immediately after learning, and he then showed that this could best be addressed by spaced review of materials. This has important implications for effective studying.

Items in short-term memory may be forgotten or they may be **encoded** (stored and able to be recalled later) into long-term memory. Items that are forgotten exit short-term memory either by **decay**—that is, the passage of time—or by **interference**—that is, they are displaced by new information. One type of interference is **retroactive interference**, in which new information pushes old information out of short-term memory. The opposite of retroactive interference is **proactive interference**, in which old information makes it more difficult to learn new information.

Long-term memory, like short-term memory, is subject to interference. To review what we discussed briefly in the short-term memory section: Retroactive interference occurs when newly memorized information interferes with the ability to remember previously memorized information. To give an example, when you learn a new language (such as Spanish), it can interfere with your memory of a language that you learned previously (for example, Italian). Proactive interference occurs when previously memorized information interferes with the ability to learn and memorize new information.

Another example of preconscious information processing can be seen in the **tip-of-the-tongue phenomenon**, in which we try to recall something, but find that it is not easily available for conscious awareness. Think of the last time you said something like this: "Hey, can you hand me the . . . um, . . . the . . . um, um, um . . . the remote?" This phenomenon demonstrates that certain preconscious information may be available to the conscious mind but quite difficult to access.

Most researchers believe that memory is a reconstructive process, not an objective photographic one. Sometimes what we remember happened only in part or even not at all. **Memory reconstruction** occurs when we fit together pieces of an event that seem likely. **Source confusion** (also called source amnesia) is one likely cause of memory reconstruction. In this case, we attribute the event to a different source than it actually came from. For example, if children read and reread a story, they may come to think the events of the story happened to them rather than to the character. Similarly, childhood memories of both trivial and serious events can be reconstructed (falsified) by repeated suggestion. Elizabeth Loftus and other psychologists are studying the existence of false or implanted memories. They have demonstrated that repeated suggestions and misleading questions can create false memories. This is called **framing**. Similarly, eyewitness accounts, thought to be very strong evidence in courts of law, are accurate only about half the time. This is particularly true when dealing with children as eyewitnesses. The degree of confidence in the testimony of the witness does not necessarily correlate to accuracy of the account. The **misinformation effect** refers to how memories of an event may be distorted when consistent but false information is introduced after an event.

In **anterograde amnesia**, a person cannot form new memories but may retain memories of the past. Most people with this condition cannot live on their own. In **retrograde amnesia**, a person cannot remember all or parts of their past before the illness or injury that led to the amnesia. **Alzheimer's disease** is a form of dementia that presents early on as problems with memory but then progresses into other neurocognitive impairments.

> Psychodynamic theories believe that information, notably trauma, can be repressed, or pushed out of conscious memory, in order to protect the ego from distress. See repression in personality theories.

INTELLIGENCE

Intelligence can be defined as goal-directed adaptive thinking. Such thinking is difficult to measure on a standardized test. In fact, the nature of intelligence itself is an issue of contention among psychologists. Before the advent of IQ tests, the anthropologist Francis Galton had attempted to measure intelligence by means of reaction time tests. This reflects the notion that **speed of processing** is an essential component of intelligence. Few psychologists would claim that the popular "intelligence" tests measure all aspects of intelligence. Alfred Binet was a French psychologist who first began to measure children's intelligence for the French government. Binet's test measured the "mental ages" of school-age children so that children needing extra help could be placed in special classrooms. An American psychologist and Stanford University professor named Lewis Terman modified Binet's test to create a test commonly referred to as the **Stanford-Binet Test**. The Stanford-Binet became the first widely administered intelligence test during World War I, when the United States Army used it to rank recruits. Most modern psychologists measure an aspect of intelligence, called the **IQ** or **intelligence quotient**. This quotient originally was conceived of as a ratio of mental age over chronological (physical) age, multiplied by 100. Mental age is a measure of performance based on comparing the participant's performance to that of an "average" person of a given age. Therefore, if you take a test and your score is comparable to that of an average 10-year-old, then your mental age is 10. IQ scores are normally distributed, with a mean, median, and mode of about 100, and a standard deviation of 15 or 16 points.

The most common intelligence tests given to children today are the Stanford-Binet Intelligence Scale and the Wechsler Intelligence Scale for Children (WISC-IV). There is also a version of the Wechsler specifically geared toward adults, the Wechsler Adult Intelligence Scale (WAIS). The WISC-IV and WAIS generally have six types of questions: information (how many wings does a bird have?), comprehension (what is the advantage of keeping money in a bank?), arithmetic (if 3 pencils cost $1, what will be the cost of 15 pencils?), similarities (in what ways are seals and sea lions alike?), vocabulary (what does retain mean?), and digit span questions in which subjects are asked to hold information in short-term memory. This reflects the idea that IQ tests tend to have a combination of abstract and verbal measures.

There has been an ongoing debate as to whether intelligence is one specific set of abilities or many different sets of abilities. In the early part of the 20th century, Charles Spearman proposed that there was a general intelligence (or **g factor**) that was the basis of all other intelligence. The *g* factor is the intelligence applied across mental activities, which is close to the standard definition for "intelligence." The *s* factor is the breakdown of this intelligence into a specific component, such as one's ability to process math equations or linguistic puns. Spearman used factor analysis, a statistical measure for analyzing test data. Robert Sternberg proposed that intelligence could be more broadly defined as having three major components: analytical, practical, and creative intelligence. Louis Thurstone, a researcher in the field of intelligence, posited that we need to think of intelligence more broadly because intelligence can come in many different forms. The most famous proponent of the idea of **multiple intelligences** is Howard Gardner of Harvard University. Gardner has identified the following types of intelligence: verbal and mathematical (these are the two traditionally measured by IQ tests) as well as musical, spatial, kinesthetic, environmental, interpersonal (people perceptive), and intrapersonal (insightful, self-awareness). Daniel Goleman, a psychologist at Rutgers, has done recent work on the importance of **emotional intelligence** (being able to recognize people's intents and motivations) and has created programs for enhancing one's emotional intelligence.

Those who are involved in **psychometrics**, or psychological testing, must be sure that they follow certain guidelines. Confidentiality must be protected. The purposes of the test must be clear to those administering and those taking the test. A group of individuals at each research institution sits on the Institutional Review Board, which combs through the proposed methodology of a study to determine whether there may be any unethical behavior in or adverse consequences of a scientist's research before granting them permission to perform any experiments. Questions should be asked and answered concerning who will see the results of the test and how the scores will be used. Furthermore, the impact of the scores should be ascertained before the test is given.

When we use tests designed to measure psychological characteristics, we need to know what the scores mean. For example, if a test measures your IQ, and you score a 125 on this IQ test, how do you know what your IQ is relative to the rest of the world? To determine such relative standing, tests are standardized. Standardization is accomplished by administering the test to a **standardization sample,** a group of people who represent the entire population. The data collected from the standardization sample is compared against **norms**, which are standards of performance against which anyone who takes a given test can be compared. Tests need to be restandardized when a new, different population takes the test. The **Flynn effect** supports the need to restandardize because the data indicates that the population has become smarter over the past 50 years. Thus, an IQ of 100 may mean different things in different years, depending on the standardization sample.

Some of the factors that may lead to the Flynn effect include better prenatal nutrition, as well as fewer siblings (parents can pay more attention to each child), better educational systems, and the complexity of the modern world.

IQ scores often vary more within a group than between groups. Poverty, discrimination, and educational inequalities have been shown to negatively influence intelligence scores around the world. IQ tests have been accused of displaying bias, which can affect the interpretation of scores. Intelligence scores have historically been used to limit access to jobs and the military as well as immigration.

Validity refers to the extent to which a test measures what it intends to measure. (This instance is known as construct validity.) Validity is calculated by comparing how well the results from a test correlate with other measures that assess what the test is supposed to predict. So, for example, if you just developed a new IQ test, and you wanted to know whether it was valid, you might compare your results to those that the same participants had achieved on other IQ measures. Even better, you might correlate the IQ test scores with school grades, on the notion that IQ test scores should predict school grades. It is possible to have a test that is reliable but not valid. Such a test consistently measures something, but not what it is intended to measure. However, it is impossible to have a test that is valid but not reliable. If individuals' scores fluctuate wildly, then they cannot consistently correlate with others' scores, whatever these other scores may be. **Internal validity** is the degree to which the subject's results are due to the questions being asked and not another variable. **External validity** is true validity—that is, the degree to which results from the test can be generalized to the real world. An IQ test would be externally valid if the findings applied in other settings. If it does, in fact, measure intelligence, rather than another construct like level of education, the IQ test is also high in construct validity.

Measuring IQs Today

Today, IQs are rarely computed as quotients, but rather are computed on the basis of the extent to which a person's score is above or below the average.

More Reliability Methods

Other methods of testing reliability include **split-half**, in which two halves of the same test are given to the same subjects, and the results are correlated, and **equivalent form**, in which different but similar tests covering the same concepts are given to the same group of subjects and the results are correlated.

Other Test Types

There are many other types of tests. **Achievement tests** assess knowledge gained; the Advanced Placement exams are of this type. In contrast to these are **aptitude tests**, which evaluate a person's abilities. A road test before getting a driver's license is an example of an aptitude test.

Tests used to measure any psychological trait or ability must be both reliable and valid. **Reliability** is a measure of how consistent a test is in the measurements it provides. In other words, reliability refers to the likelihood that the same individual would get a similar score if tested with the same test on separate occasions (disallowing for practice effects or effects due to familiarity with the test items from the first testing). In fact, reliability is often assessed by giving participants a test and later—preferably after they have forgotten the specific items—administering the same test again. The two sets of scores are compared and a correlation coefficient is computed between them. This is called the **test-retest method**. Tests that are perfectly reliable have a reliability coefficient of one. Reliabilities apply only to groups, however, so that even though a given test is highly reliable, a given individual may show substantial fluctuations in scores.

One distinction often made is between **fluid intelligence** and **crystallized intelligence**. Crystallized intelligence is accumulated knowledge. Fluid intelligence is the ability to process information quickly and to solve new problems. Fluid intelligence is likely to have earlier and more pronounced decay with aging than crystallized intelligence. Someone who has a **fixed mindset** about intelligence believes intelligence is fixed and therefore not subject to change or learning. Someone who has a **growth mindset** believes intelligence can be affected by learning and development. This can play a big role in academic achievement.

An issue that has received a great deal of attention in recent years is **stereotype threat.** This occurs when a message is sent, intentionally or unintentionally, to a group of people that their group tends to perform below average on a given measure. This often becomes a self-fulfilling prophecy, resulting in poorer performance than expected for members of that group. (There can also be **stereotype boost** if a group is told that its members tend to perform above average on a certain measure.)

KEY TERMS

Introduction to Perception
perception

Perceptual Processes
bottom-up processing
top-down processing
schema
perceptual set
Gestalt approach
  proximity
  similarity
  symmetry
  continuity
  closure
Law of Prägnanz
feature detector approach

Attention
selective attention
attentional resource theories
filter theories
cocktail party phenomenon
shadowing
divided attention
inattentional blindness
binocular depth cues
  retinal disparity
  stereoptic
  retinal convergence
  binocular disparity
visual perception
visual cliff
monocular depth cues
  relative size
  texture gradient
  interposition
  linear perspective
  vanishing point
  relative clarity
constancy
motion detection
apparent motion
  phi phenomenon
stroboscopic effect
  autokinetic effect

Concepts
typicality
prototype
exemplar
superordinate concept
basic concept
subordinate concept
heuristics
  availability heuristic
  representative heuristic
algorithms
confirmation bias
hindsight bias
belief perseverance
framing
subliminal perception
priming
gambler's fallacy
sunk cost fallacy
executive functions

Problem-Solving and Creativity
divergent thinking
convergent thinking

Memory
declarative (explicit) memory
episodic memory
semantic memory
nondeclarative (implicit) memory
procedural memory
prospective memory
long-term potentiation
working memory
sensory memory
  iconic
  echoic
  visual persistence
long-term memory
semantically encoded
visually encoded
acoustically encoded
effortful processing
automatic processing
levels of processing model
recognition memory
recall memory
mnemonic device

dual-coding hypothesis
method of loci
self-reference effect
chunking
spacing effect
distributed practice
mased practice
testing effect
metacognition
primacy effect
recency effect
serial position effect
maintenance rehearsal
elaborative rehearsal
context-dependent memory
state-dependent memory
mood-congruent memory
encoded
decay
interference
retroactive interference
proactive interference
tip-of-the-tongue phenomenon
memory reconstruction
source confusion
framing
misinformation effect
anterograde amnesia
retrograde amnesia
Alzheimer's disease

Intelligence
speed of processing
Stanford-Binet Test
intelligence quotient (IQ)
g factor
multiple intelligences
emotional intelligence
psychometrics
standardization sample
norms
Flynn effect
validity
internal validity
external validity
reliability
achievement tests
aptitude tests
test-retest method
fluid intelligence
crystallized intelligence
fixed mindset
growth mindset
stereotype threat
stereotype boost

Unit 2 Drill

See Chapter 12 for answers and explanations.

1. The Gestalt concept of perceptual continuity refers to

   (A) our tendency to see objects near to each other as belonging to the same group
   (B) our tendency to see objects that are closer to us as larger than objects that are farther away
   (C) our tendency to see fluid or complete forms rather than irregular or incomplete ones
   (D) our tendency to see similar-looking objects as part of the same group
   (E) our tendency to see two slightly different images from each of our eyes

2. In a given drawing, instead of perceiving a series of lines, humans perceive two shapes: a circle and a rectangle. What best accounts for this phenomenon?

   (A) The principles of Gestalt psychology
   (B) Bottom-up processing
   (C) Parallel processing
   (D) Weber's law
   (E) Summation

3. Claire views the figure above and reports seeing a triangle in the center supported by some concentric discs. Which Gestalt principle does Claire rely on most heavily to render this description?

   (A) Proximity
   (B) Symmetry
   (C) Similarity
   (D) Closure
   (E) Continuity

4. The main difference between auditory and visual sensory memory is that

   (A) visual memory dominates auditory memory
   (B) visual sensory memory lasts for a shorter period of time than auditory sensory memory
   (C) visual sensory memory has a higher storage capacity than auditory sensory memory
   (D) a phone number read to an individual will be lost before a phone number that was glanced at for 15 seconds
   (E) if both visual and auditory stimuli are presented at the same time, the visual stimulus is more likely to be transferred to the long-term memory than is the auditory stimulus

5. The greater likelihood of recalling information from memory while in the same or similar environment in which the memory was originally encoded is an example of

   (A) retroactive interference
   (B) chunking
   (C) elaborative rehearsal
   (D) context-dependent memory
   (E) procedural memory

6. Students are given a reasoning task in which they are asked, in 60 seconds, to come up with as many ways as possible to use a spoon that do not involve eating or preparing food. The number and diversity of responses could most accurately reflect the students'

   (A) divergent thinking abilities
   (B) convergent thinking abilities
   (C) intelligence quotients
   (D) working memories
   (E) subordinate concepts

7. Recalling the fact that Abraham Lincoln was the president of the United States during the Civil War is an example of

   (A) procedural memory
   (B) implicit memory
   (C) semantic memory
   (D) episodic memory
   (E) nondeclarative memory

8. Ben continues to get stuck on a physics problem, approaching it the same way every time. This is an example of

   (A) functional fixedness
   (B) a mental set
   (C) a representativeness heuristic
   (D) insight learning
   (E) framing

9. Which of the following is an example of a representativeness heuristic?

   (A) Kelly creates a perfect mental image of a rose in her mind and uses it to judge the roses she encounters.
   (B) Malik thinks that cancer is more deadly than heart disease because he sees advertisements for cancer research frequently.
   (C) Priscilla uses a box as a stepstool to reach the highest shelf.
   (D) In an effort to prove her theory true, Jennifer interprets the otherwise objective facts as supporting evidence for her claims.
   (E) Looking back, Justino feels he should have been able to predict the ending of the horror movie all along.

10. Sheldon memorizes organic chemistry functional groups by relating them to his passion and understanding of landscaping. This memorization technique is known as

    (A) functional fixedness
    (B) chunking
    (C) maintenance rehearsal
    (D) state-dependent memory
    (E) self-referential effect

11. In the context of psychometric testing, content validity is defined as

    (A) the extent to which the test actually measures what it is purported to measure
    (B) the degree to which there is a correlation between results on the test and future performance on another measure
    (C) the degree to which the test will yield similar results across administrations
    (D) the extent to which scores on two versions of the test are highly correlated
    (E) the degree to which scores on two sections of the same test are consistent with each other

12. Which of the following is an example of a projective test?

    (A) The Stanford-Binet Intelligence Scale
    (B) The Thematic Apperception Test (TAT)
    (C) The Minnesota Multiphasic Personality Inventory (MMPI)
    (D) The Strong Vocational Interest Blank
    (E) The F-scale

13. On a normal score distribution, an IQ score of 85 would be located

    (A) approximately one standard deviation above the mean
    (B) approximately one standard deviation below the mean
    (C) approximately two standard deviations above the mean
    (D) approximately two standard deviations below the mean
    (E) in a variable position—it would depend on the age of the respondent

14. Test standardization is accomplished by

    (A) administering the test to a sample chosen to reflect the characteristics of the population in question
    (B) administering different parts of the test to different samples meant to reflect different populations
    (C) correlating the results on the test with results on other tests that claim to measure the same dimension
    (D) correlating the consistency of scores given by different sets of graders
    (E) equilibrating the number of times each answer choice appears

15. Which of the following is NOT a dimension of intelligence in Howard Gardner's theory of multiple intelligences?

    (A) Environmental
    (B) Mathematical
    (C) Spatial
    (D) Musical
    (E) Emotional

16. Reliability measures

    (A) how consistently the test holds up over time
    (B) how well the test measures what it means to test
    (C) a way in which you can be sure that an experiment tests only one variable at a time
    (D) how consistently an individual will score on the same test on subsequent occasions
    (E) to what extent the findings of a study can be generalized to the whole population

17. A multiple-choice or a true/false question test is an example of a(n)

    (A) projective test
    (B) inventory-type test
    (C) intelligence test
    (D) hereditary test
    (E) environment test

18. Which of the following is necessary for a test to be ethical?

    (A) Confidentiality
    (B) Full disclosure of deception
    (C) Double-blind design
    (D) Internal validity
    (E) Generalization

19. Trivial Pursuit, a board game that asks for answers to questions about random facts, relies most heavily on which form of knowledge?

    (A) Assimilation
    (B) Crystallized intelligence
    (C) Internalization
    (D) Wisdom
    (E) Fluid intelligence

20. In a modern art museum, Mira comes across an abstract furniture exhibit. She sees one particular piece that looks like a desk, but is later told it is actually a bookshelf. After looking at the furniture piece a little longer, she then sees it can be a bookshelf. This concept of learning is called

    (A) functional fixedness
    (B) object permanence
    (C) a mental set
    (D) accommodation
    (E) assimilation

REFLECT

Respond to the following questions:

- Which topics in this chapter do you hope to see on the multiple-choice section or essay?

- Which topics in this chapter do you hope not to see on the multiple-choice section or essay?

- Regarding any psychologists mentioned, can you pair the psychologists with their contributions to the field? Did they contribute significant experiments, theories, or both?

- Regarding any theories mentioned, can you distinguish between differing theories well enough to recognize them on the multiple-choice section? Can you distinguish them well enough to write a fluent essay on them?

- Can you define the key terms at the end of the chapter?

- Which parts of the chapter will you review?

- Will you seek further help, outside of this book (such as from a teacher, Princeton Review tutor, or AP Students), on any of the content in this chapter—and, if so, on what content?

Chapter 9
Unit 3:
Development
and Learning

LIFE-SPAN APPROACH

The life-span approach to **developmental psychology** takes the view that development is not a process with a clear ending. For decades, development was thought to end with the onset of adolescence. Rather, it is now viewed as a process that continues from birth to death. From this perspective, developmental psychology can be defined as the study of the changes that occur in people's abilities and behaviors as they age. It is important to differentiate between **life-span psychologists** and **child psychologists**. Although both study development, the child psychologist has decided to focus on a particular earlier portion of the typical life span. Erik Erikson was the first to successfully champion the view that development occurs across an entire lifetime.

DEVELOPMENTAL ISSUES

Developmental psychology, like most aspects of psychology, must deal with the so-called **nature-nurture debate**. **Maturationists** emphasize the role of genetically programmed growth and development on the body, particularly on the nervous system. **Maturation** can best be defined as biological readiness. From their point of view, greater preprogrammed physiological development of the brain allows for more complex conceptualization and reasoning.

The opposing position is the learning perspective, and adherents to this position are sometimes referred to as **environmentalists**. The extreme form can be found in Locke's idea, which states that almost all development is the direct result of learning—infants are born as blank slates onto which experience etches its lessons. The organism develops more complex behaviors and cognition because it acquires more associations through learning.

The Feral Child

One famous example in favor of the critical period is Genie, the "feral child" who was isolated from other humans from infancy until age 13, preventing her from learning spoken language.

There are other issues to be considered when studying development. One is whether development is **continuous** or **discontinuous**—gradual or stage-oriented. Evidence of growth spurts and leaps of cognition support the discontinuous approach, but other studies show gradual development, particularly in social skill building. A **critical period** refers to a time during which a skill or ability must develop; if the ability does not develop during that time, it probably will never develop or may not develop as well. An example of a skill with a critical period is language. Scientists believe that, if a person is not exposed to language by roughly age 12, the ability to learn language significantly diminishes or disappears.

Culture also impacts development in important ways. A **collectivist culture** is one in which the needs of society are placed before the needs of the individual. Conversely, **individualist cultures** promote personal needs above the needs of society. It is important to realize that a developing child's relationship with her environment and culture is bidirectional, meaning that just as a child's social environment plays a role in how she develops, she also contributes to the society in which she is born.

Research Methods

Research methods in developmental psychology vary according to the questions being asked by the researcher. Some developmental psychologists are interested in studying **normative development**, which is the typical sequence of developmental changes for a group of people. For example, some developmental psychologists talk about development occurring in a series of stages, universal to human development. Other developmental psychologists are more interested in individual development, or the individual pattern of development, including differences among individuals during development. Often, the techniques and research methods useful for studying one type of development are not useful for studying other types of development.

Normative development is often studied using the **cross-sectional method**. The cross-sectional method seeks to compare groups of people of various ages on similar tasks. So, for example, a cross-sectional study might involve administering cognitive tests to a group of two-year-olds, a group of four-year-olds, and a group of six-year-olds, and then comparing the means of the groups. This approach can reveal the average ages at which certain skills or abilities appear. However, the data collected in cross-sectional studies tells us little about the actual development of any single individual.

To research the developmental process, many developmental psychologists use the **longitudinal method**. The longitudinal method involves following a small group of people over a long portion of their lives, assessing change at set intervals. As you might imagine, longitudinal research is more difficult and more expensive to conduct and, therefore, is conducted less frequently than cross-sectional research. However, the longitudinal method does have some benefits because the study of individuals over time rules out the differences between subjects that other studies include. It also allows for the study of the temporal order of events.

Physical Development

Physical development starts at conception. The zygote, or fertilized egg, goes through three distinct phases of gestation prior to birth. The first stage is the germinal stage, in which the zygote undergoes cell division, expanding to 64 cells and implanting itself in the uterine wall. This stage lasts about two weeks. The embryonic stage consists of organ formation and lasts until the beginning of the third month. In the fetal stage, sexual differentiation occurs and movement begins to develop. Growth is rapid in this stage. Various harmful environmental agents, known as **teratogens**, may affect fetal development. One such agent is alcohol. Some fetuses exposed to alcohol develop **fetal alcohol spectrum disorder (FASD)**, resulting in physical abnormalities and cognitive deficiencies. Other teratogens include cigarettes, over-the-counter and prescription medication, psychoactive drugs, infections and viruses, and environmental toxins and pollution. Teratogens can cause a variety of birth defects including cleft palate, brain and spinal cord abnormalities, and problems in physical and intellectual development.

> According to the new AP Psychology test, you won't need to know the specific stages, though you will need to know "the major physical and psychological milestones." We've included it all.

Children are born with a variety of **reflexes**, thought to be part of our evolutionary heritage. The rooting reflex is when you stroke the corner of the baby's mouth and the baby turns in that direction, which helps the baby find food. The sucking reflex occurs when the roof of the baby's mouth is stroked. The Moro reflex is also known as the startle reflex, where the baby's arms and legs fly out, the baby pulls back its head, and then brings the limbs and head back again. Often this will happen in response to a loud noise. The grasp reflex occurs when you stroke a baby's palm. The baby will then tightly grasp in response. **Rudimentary movements** are the first voluntary movements performed by a child. They occur in very predictable stages from birth to age 2, and they include rolling, sitting, crawling, standing, and walking. These form the foundation on which the fundamental movements are built and are primarily dictated by genetics (that is, these movements are more or less "pre-programmed").

Milestones in physical development involve changes and refinements in both gross and fine motor movements. **Gross motor movements** include running, jumping, and hopping. **Fine motor movements** include drawing, writing, and eating with utensils.

The **fundamental movement** stage occurs from age 2 to age 7; during this time, the child is learning to manipulate their body through actions such as running, jumping, throwing, and catching. This stage is highly influenced by environment, much more so than the rudimentary movement stage that precedes it. Children are typically in school at this stage, and physical activity and games are necessary for proper motor development. Movements initially start out uncoordinated and poorly controlled, but as the child advances in age, movements become more refined, coordinated, and efficient.

During the stage of **specialized movement**, children learn to combine the fundamental movements and apply them to specific tasks. This stage can be subdivided into two shorter stages: a **transitional substage** and an **application substage**. During the transitional substage, a combination of movements occurs; for example, grasping, jumping, and throwing are combined to take a shot in basketball. The application substage is defined more by conscious decisions to apply these skills to specific types of activity; for example, one child might choose to play basketball, whereas another might use the same set of skills and abilities to play baseball. Additionally, the application of strategy to movement is now possible; for example, a child choosing to delay shooting the basketball until she has a clear shot at the basket.

Ultimately, children progress to a lifelong application stage, typically beginning in adolescence and progressing through adulthood. During this time, movements are continually refined and applied to normal daily activities as well as recreational and competitive activities.

Both of these processes are dependent on neural development. There is evidence that the brain is still organizing itself in the months after birth. At birth, the brain is about 25 percent of its adult weight. By age 2, it is at 75 percent of its adult weight. By age 6, it is at 95 percent, and by age 7, it is at 100 percent. As the infant brain develops, the neurons increasingly undergo a process known as myelination, where **myelin**, a coating of fatty tissues, begins to envelop the axon of each neuron, facilitating faster and more efficient transmission of information. As the brain develops, **synaptic pruning** occurs, where the brain rids itself of connections it no longer needs (that is, old learning) to make room for new information. In fact, nervous system development continues into early adulthood. It is important to note that although perceptual and motor development depend on the development of the nervous system, the development of the nervous system depends on **environmental interaction** on the part of the child. It has been demonstrated that children raised in situations in which their ability to crawl or walk is restricted have impaired motor skills. This occurs, for example, in some institutions in countries without regulation of childcare facilities. Additionally, perceptual development can be delayed by lack of stimulation. An important theme in developmental psychology is that of the critical period—that for some parts of the brain, the phrase "use it or lose it" holds true.

Experiments with animals (see Hubel and Wiesel on page 162) have shown that depriving an eye of stimuli by covering it at the very beginning of life will lead to the underdevelopment of the part of the occipital lobe responsible for vision in that eye. As a result, that section of the brain will be allocated to another function. This **plasticity**, or changeability, of the brain is illustrated in an experiment in which a third eye was added to a frog. The occipital lobe flexibly responded by dividing the processing power of the occipital lobe among three eyes rather than two. This experiment worked only if the eye was introduced very close to birth, demonstrating the limited critical period during which some experience must occur for the brain to develop in a particular way.

> ### Nature, Nurture, and the Critical Period
> This phenomenon is informative with regard to the nature-nurture issue. The child is not born as a blank slate: it has some innate reflexes. However, the physiological development of the child depends on its interactions with the environment. Nature and nurture play complementary roles in development.

Puberty is another landmark of physical development. It is characterized by growth spurts, the development of secondary sex characteristics, and other physical developments. There are also social and cognitive changes that are discussed later in this section.

Most people peak physically in early adulthood. One just needs to look at professional athletes to recognize this fact. Adulthood is marked by gradual decrease of physical abilities, although a healthy lifestyle will slow this process. At approximately 50 years old, women experience menopause, a change in estrogen production causing menstruation to cease.

In the elderly population, the gradual diminution of adulthood reaches noticeable proportions. The senses lose much of their efficacy. For example, half of those over age 80 have lost their sense of smell. Diseases such as Alzheimer's can affect memory, cognition, and personality.

Sex Roles, Sex Differences

There are differences between the sexes at birth, and, although most observable sexual development occurs during adolescence, development starts at a much younger age.

Children develop **gender identity**, the awareness that they are boys or girls, by age two or three. The acquisition of sex-related roles, called **gender typing**, also occurs very early, from the ages of two to seven. This age range is also when children come to understand that there is **gender constancy**—that is, that gender is a fixed, unchangeable characteristic. At this age, children begin to understand that gender is a characteristic of the individual and that items such as clothes or even behavior do not define the sex of the individual. **Androgyny** may develop as children begin to blur the lines between stereotypical male and female roles in society. These individuals may adopt behaviors from both types of roles.

> Though the language around this topic is changing on a social level, this book intends to prepare you for the uses most commonly seen from the AP Psychology exam. We will update your free student tools accordingly should any new context for this subject be introduced to the test.

Socialization plays a large role in the social constructs of sex and gender roles. Another theory of how sex roles develop has been proposed by Albert Bandura. Bandura felt that, like violent behavior, sexual roles could be acquired through social or vicarious learning. Young boys see older boys being rewarded for being masculine and punished for being feminine. This pattern creates a self-perpetuating cycle, according to Bandura, with each successive generation providing the model for the following generation. This view has been supported by research showing that parents reward independence and competition in boys, while they reward nurturing and caring behaviors in girls.

It is important to consider that biological, social, and cognitive factors all play a role in sexual development. Additionally, we must consider that, when discussing sexual development, there is much disagreement on what is "normal." Theories of sexual development are often products of the culture and time in which they were developed and do not always reflect what is considered normal in modern society.

In the 1950s, Alfred Kinsey did extensive, and very widely read, work on the attitudes and behaviors of American adults pertaining to sexuality. He did this by conducting numerous subjective interviews. Among his important contributions was the **Kinsey Scale,** which posited that sexuality is not binary, either exclusively heterosexual or homosexual; rather, it exists along a continuum of attractions and practices. Kinsey's books played a role in liberalizing Americans' attitudes toward sexuality in the following decades.

Piaget's Stages of Development

Jean Piaget proposed an influential theory of the cognitive development of children. Piaget's developmental theory is based on the concept of **equilibration**. Equilibration is a child's attempt to reach a balance between what the child encounters in the environment and what cognitive structures the child brings to the situation. Children try to reach equilibration through **assimilation**, incorporating new ideas into existing schemas. For example, a child may develop a **schema**, or mental representational model, for animals after encountering dogs and cats. When he goes to the zoo and sees more exotic four-legged animals like elephants or giraffes, he must assimilate this new information into his existing category of animals. However, when facing information that does not easily fit into an existing schema, the child must modify the schema to include the new information. This process is called **accommodation**. For example, this child's schema of animal might go through a process of accommodation if he encounters a kangaroo that hops on two legs.

According to Piaget, children go through a series of developmental stages. Piaget believed that these stages occur in a fixed order, and a child can be in only one stage at any given time. The following are the four stages Piaget proposed, first presented as a chart and then in more detail.

Criticism of Piaget

Piaget's theory is not universally accepted. Other researchers have found flaws in his research methods and his underestimation of children's abilities, especially at ages four to five. Critics attest that some children that age can take another's perspective and are not so egocentric. Other criticisms include the failure of Piaget to recognize the environmental factors pushing child development.

Each stage can be categorized by the presence/absence of schemas, the types of mental operations the child can perform, and the presence or absence of theoretical thought.

Stage	Explanation	Schemas	Mental Operations	Theoretical Thinking
Sensorimotor	Act on objects that are present and begin to develop schemas but incapable of operations			
Preoperational	Able to use schemas not present (symbolic thought) but lacks ability to perform mental operations	X		
Concrete Operational	Able to access schemas and perform mental operations but still limited to experiences	X	X	
Formal Operational	Able to use schemas, understand operations, and apply both to theoretical questions not based on experiences	X	X	X

- **Sensorimotor Stage.** This stage usually occurs during the first two years of life and is typified by reflexive reactions and then circular reactions, which are repeated behaviors by which the infant manipulates the environment. For example, if an infant kicks its legs and hits the mobile on its crib with its foot, stimulating movement, the infant is likely to repeat the action in the future. **Object permanence**, which develops during this stage, is the knowledge that objects continue to exist when they are outside the field of view. For example, if a ball rolls under a chair, the child will continue to look for it. At this age, the child lacks the ability to access mental schemas or solve problems through performing a mental operation, which is the ability to represent and manipulate information in a person's mind. Schemas are acquired in the preoperational stage, while mental operations become accessible during the concrete operational stage. Another hallmark of the sensorimotor stage is the development of goal-oriented behavior. For example, a very young child who is able to roll over at will, but not yet able to crawl, may consciously roll over multiple times to reach a favorite toy.

- **Preoperational Stage.** The preoperational stage typically occurs from ages two to seven. Children generally begin this stage with the development of language. Language represents a shift to **symbolic thinking**, or the ability to use words to substitute for objects. Other characteristics of the stage are **egocentrism**, seeing the world only from one's own point of view, **artificialism**, believing that all things are human-made, and **animism**, believing that all things are living.

- **Concrete Operational Stage.** Typically occurring from ages seven to eleven, this is the stage when children develop the ability to perform a mental operation and then reverse their thinking back to a starting point, a concept called **reversibility**. Another important concept is **conservation**—the idea that the amount of a substance does not change just because it is arranged differently. For example, conservation of mass might be demonstrated by taking a large ball of clay and using it to create several smaller balls of clay. A child in the concrete operational stage will understand that the total amount of clay has not changed, while a child in the preoperational stage might think that there is more clay because there are more balls.

- **Formal Operational Stage.** This stage begins at about age 12. At this level, children are fully capable of understanding abstractions and symbolic relationships. They are also capable of **metacognition**, or the ability to recognize one's cognitive processes and adapt those processes if they aren't successful. The formal operational stage is also the point at which a child acquires hypothetical reasoning, which is the ability to figure out answers to problems with which a person does not have direct experience. For example, a child in the concrete operational stage would have great difficulty imagining how the world might change as a result of an alien invasion, while a 12-year-old could posit numerous theories on the issue.

Vygotsky's Social Factors of Development

Another influential theory of cognitive development was proposed by Lev Vygotsky. Piaget believed that biological maturation is the driving force in development. Vygotsky, on the other hand, stressed social factors as critical to the developmental process. Vygotsky believed that much of development occurs by **internalization**, the absorption of knowledge into the self from environmental and social contexts. Vygotsky also proposed the concept of a **zone of proximal development**, which is the range between the developed level of ability that a child displays and the potential level of ability of which the child is actually capable. These two levels are often referred to as the **actual development level** and the **potential development level**, respectively. Actual development rarely lives up to its potential because ability depends on input from the environment, and environmental input is rarely truly optimal. According to Vygotsky, the way in which a child realizes his potential is through the process of scaffolding. Scaffolding is the support system that allows a person to move across the zone of proximal development incrementally, with environmental supports, such as teachers and parents. If a person fails to advance, it might mean that the scaffolding steps are too high above the person's current abilities.

Older but Wiser

A related feature of adult cognitive development is **wisdom**. It is assumed in many cultures that older members of a society have a perspective or level of accumulated knowledge that gives them wisdom. Wisdom is a form of insight into life situations and conditions that results in good judgments about difficult life problems.

Life-span psychologists have realized that cognitive development continues into adulthood. Childhood and early adulthood are times marked by relatively rapid neural growth. However, we lose a small percentage of brain weight between our early 20s and our 80s. In the later years, many adults show a decrease in **fluid intelligence**—that is, the ability to think in terms of abstract concepts and symbolic relationships. This decrease, however, is accompanied by increased **crystallized intelligence**, or specific knowledge of facts and information.

Older adults see some cognitive changes with aging, even if they are relatively healthy. Some older adults may see a diminution of processing speed, less attention, and problems with memory.

LANGUAGE

Language is the arrangement of sounds, written symbols, or gestures to communicate ideas. Language has several key features.

- First, language is arbitrary—that is, words rarely sound like the ideas that they convey.

- Second, language has a structure that is additive in a certain sense. For example, words are added together to form sentences, sentences to form paragraphs, and so on.

- Third, language has multiplicity of structure, meaning that it can be analyzed and understood in a number of different ways.

- Fourth, language is productive, meaning that there are nearly endless meaningful combinations of words.

- Finally, language is dynamic, meaning that it is constantly changing and evolving.

Language can be broken down into subcomponents. **Phonemes** are the smallest units of speech sounds in a given language that are still distinct in sound from each other. Phonemes combine to form **morphemes**, the smallest semantically meaningful parts of language. **Grammar**, the set of rules by which language is constructed, is governed by syntax and semantics. **Syntax** is the set of rules used in the arrangement of morphemes into meaningful sentences; this can also be thought of as word order. **Semantics** refers to word meaning or word choice. **Prosody** is the rhythm, stress, and intonation of speech.

Children acquire language in stages. Infants make cooing noises, which consist of the utterance of phonemes that do not correspond to actual words, until roughly 4 months of age. The next stage after cooing is babbling, which is the production of phonemes only within the infants' own to-be-learned language. Sounds not relevant to this language drop out at this stage, which usually lasts until the first year of life. Soon the infant uses single words to convey demands and desires. These single words filled with meaning are called **holophrases**. Holophrases are single terms that are applied by the infant to broad categories of things: for example, an infant calling any passing woman "mama." This type of error is known as an **overextension**, and it results from the infant not knowing enough words to express something fully. **Underextension** is when a child thinks that their "mama" is the only "mama." Infants develop vocabulary as time goes on and tend to have up to 100 words in their vocabulary by 18 months.

At about two years of age, infants start combining words. Two- or three-word groups are termed **telegraphic speech**. This speech lacks many parts of speech. For example, a two-year-old would say, "mommy food," which means "mommy, give me food." This is called "telegraphic speech" because people used to remove words they deemed unnecessary when sending telegrams in order to save money.

Vocabulary is increasing rapidly at this point. By age 3, children know more than 1,000 words, but they frequently make **overgeneralization** errors. These are errors in which the rules of language are overextended, such as in saying, "I goed to the store." *Go* is an irregular verb, but the child applies the standard rules of grammar to it. By age 5, most grammatical mistakes in the child's speech have disappeared, and the child's vocabulary has expanded dramatically. At 10 years old, a child's language is essentially the same as an adult's.

SOCIAL-EMOTIONAL DEVELOPMENT

Social development involves the ability to interact with others and with the social structures in which we live.

Urie Bronfenbrenner developed the **ecological systems theory** positing that there are a series of nesting systems interacting in children's development. First there is the **microsystem**, people and groups who have direct contact with the person. The **mesosystem** involves relationships between the members of the microsystem. The **exosystem** are indirect factors influencing the child, such as government and the media. Finally, the **macrosystem** involves the cultural events that influence the child and important people in their lives, while the **chronosystem** is the individual's current stage of life.

Diana Baumrind has identified the following three types of parenting styles.

- **Authoritarian**—Parents have high expectations for their child to comply with rules without debate or explanation. This style is the most likely to use corporal punishment (like spanking) for disobedience. Children of these parents are socially withdrawn, lack decision-making capabilities, and lack curiosity. Authoritarian parents will exert a high level of control and low level of warmth.

- **Authoritative**—Parents also expect compliance to rules but explain rules and encourage independence. Parents set limits, give out punishments, and forgive. Children of these parents have high self-esteem, are independent, and are articulate. Authoritative parents will exert a high level of control and high level of warmth.

- **Permissive**—Parents have few expectations and are warm and non-demanding. Children are rarely punished, and parents consider themselves friends of the child. Children of these parents are not good at accepting responsibility, controlling their impulses, or being generous in social relationships. Permissive parents will exert a low level of control and high level of warmth.

Cultural differences play a role in how these parenting styles play out in practice and how they specifically influence children's development.

Erik Erikson tried to capture the complexities of social development in his psychosocial theory, which builds on Freud's theory, broadening and deepening it to include stages throughout the lifespan and account for sociocultural context. This theory is important not only for its description of the developmental process as a series of stages marked by the resolution of specific developmental "tasks," but also because it was the first theory to assert that development is a life-span process. Erikson's stages of **psychosocial development** include the following.

Trust versus Mistrust

This stage occurs during the first year of life. Infants decide whether the world is friendly or hostile, depending on whether or not they can trust that their basic needs will be met. Trust and hopefulness are the outcomes of positive resolutions of this stage.

Autonomy versus Shame and Doubt

Between the ages of one and three, the child must develop a sense of control over bodily functions as well as over the environment. Successful resolution of this stage involves learning how to use the toilet, to walk, and to perform other skills related to control of the self.

Initiative versus Guilt

This is the stage that occurs at about three to six years of age and often corresponds with a child's entry into a broader social world outside the home. Children at this stage must take initiative and learn to assert themselves socially, without overstepping their bounds. The successful resolution of this stage results in the development of a sense of purpose.

Industry versus Inferiority

Children from ages six to twelve are in this stage. They are now in school and are becoming accustomed to receiving feedback for their work. Thus, they must gain a sense of accomplishment and pride in their work. They begin to understand what they are capable of doing. The successful resolution of this stage produces a sense of competence.

Identity versus Role Confusion

This stage involves the adolescent search for identity. Adolescents question what type of people they are and begin to develop their own values at this stage. The resolution of this stage is **fidelity**, or truthfulness to one's self.

Intimacy versus Isolation

This is the stage of early adulthood when we attempt to form loving, lasting relationships. The successful resolution of this stage results in one's learning how to love in a mature, giving way. If this stage is not successfully resolved, feelings of isolation or a lack of intimacy may result.

Generativity versus Stagnation

This stage occurs during middle adulthood and brings with it the struggle to be productive in both career and home, and to contribute to the next generation with ideas and possibly with children. Being productive in these ways is called **generativity**. This is the stage where we try to leave our "mark" on the world. Failure to resolve this stage can result in feelings of **stagnation** or isolation.

Integrity versus Despair

This stage occurs during old age and brings with it the struggle to come to terms with one's life, which involves accepting both successes and failures. The positive outcome of this stage is wisdom, whereas the failure to resolve this stage can lead to bitterness and despair.

Study Tip

Freud's theory of psychosexual development is no longer covered on the revised AP Psychology exam, only the theory of psychosocial development. If studying the former helps you to better understand and articulate the latter, you might compare the two; otherwise, stick to what's on the test!

Erikson's is not the only social development theory. Some theories have been based on a child's **temperament,** the notion that some childhood behavior is biologically based rather than learned. Temperament is the early-appearing set of individual differences in reaction and regulation that form the nucleus of personality. For a trait to be considered part of temperament, it must be early appearing, stable, and constitutionally based, meaning that it is rooted in the physiology of the child. According to developmental psychologist Mary Rothbart, temperament is generally assessed on three scales: **surgency** (amount of positive affect and activity level), **negative affect** (amount of frustration and sadness), and **effortful control** (ability of a child to self-regulate moods and behavior). Jerome Kagan's work on the physiology of young children showed that children classified as low in effortful control were more likely to have higher baseline heart rates, more muscle tension, and greater pupil dilation. The stability of temperament is also quite remarkable, with surgency at 21 months correlating with the person's behavior at 18 years old. Beginning in the 1930s, Konrad Lorenz posited that much child attachment behavior is innate. Lorenz was an ethologist: he studied animal behavior and he based his ideas about attachment on his observations of imprinting in animals. In the 1950s, Harry and Margaret Harlow demonstrated that rhesus monkey infants need comfort and security as much as food. Through the use of artificial, inanimate surrogate mothers, Harlow ascertained that these infants become more attached to soft "mothers" without food than to wire ones with food. **Attachment** is defined as the tendency to prefer specific familiar individuals to others. John Bowlby is considered the father of attachment theory. He devoted extensive research to the concept of attachment and pioneered the psychoanalytic view that early experiences in childhood have an important influence on development and behavior later in life. Bowlby believed that a close and loving relationship between a child and a caregiver is critical to the infant's healthy development and provides a model that the growing child will use to build mutually beneficial relationships in their life. In contrast, a lack of responsiveness and physical support on the part of the parent will hurt the child in the short-term and the child's relationships in the long-term. In the 1970s, Mary Ainsworth studied human infant attachment. Using the **strange situation** in which a parent or primary guardian leaves a child with a stranger and then returns, Ainsworth recognized four attachment patterns.

> - **Secure**—The child is generally happy in the presence of the primary caretaker, is distressed when the caretaker leaves, and can be consoled again quickly after the caregiver returns.
>
> - **Avoidant**—The child may be inhibited in the presence of the primary caretaker, and may pretend to not be distressed when the caretaker leaves. (Blood pressure and cortisol analyses show that the child is, in fact, quite stressed out.)
>
> - **Ambivalent**—The child may have a "stormy" relationship with the primary caretaker, is distressed when the caretaker leaves, and has difficulty being consoled after the caretaker's return.
>
> - **Disorganized**—The child has an erratic relationship with the primary caretaker and with other adults. This attachment style is more common in cases of severe neglect and/or abuse. **Separation anxiety** is the normal apprehension experienced by a young child (usually six to 10 months old) when away (or facing the prospect of being away) from a person to whom they are attached.

Peer relationships develop over time. Early relationships often develop through play. **Parallel play** refers to when young toddlers and children play next to each other but don't actually interact or create joint narratives or games. As children get a little older, they engage in **pretend play**, where they make mental representations of the world through their games, which may involve more joint play with others. **Peer relationships** are invaluable to adolescents as they begin to develop their sense of identity. The **imaginary audience** is when an adolescent believes that others are consistently paying attention to them, scrutinizing every detail of their behavior and appearance, when it is actually not true. This is a manifestation of **adolescent egocentrism**, which involves tremendous self-consciousness.

Identity development includes all the different ways adolescents start figuring out who they are in terms of racial/ethnic identity, gender identity, sexual orientation, religious identity, occupational identity, and familial identity. James Marcia identified four processes in **adolescent identity development**: **achievement** (development of a true sense of self), **diffusion** (people who have been as yet unable to develop a true identity), **foreclosure** (people who have gained identity through guidance from an adult), and **moratorium** (where adolescents pause their search for true identity).

Adverse childhood experiences (ACEs) can impact the relationships people form throughout the lifespan. Adverse childhood experiences are negative experiences, usually traumatic, that happen in the first 17 years of life. ACEs can lead to issues such as mental health conditions, chronic physical health conditions and/or substance use disorder if not treated. Sociocultural differences influence what is considered an ACE and how ACEs affect a person's life.

Adult social interaction is another key area of human social-emotional development. The **social clock** refers to when major life events occur. Many of these life events, including marriage, children, and getting jobs, are culturally dependent. Adults form new families or family-like structures for social and emotional support. Studies of **adult attachment** indicate that the attachment patterns from childhood may still pay a role in adulthood in terms of how adults relate, securely or insecurely, to significant others in their lives.

LEARNING: AN OVERVIEW

Learning is a relatively permanent or stable change in behavior as a result of experience. Such changes may be associated with certain changes in the connections within the nervous system. Learning occurs by various methods, including classical conditioning, operant conditioning, and social learning. Cognitive factors are also implicated in learning, particularly in humans.

NONASSOCIATIVE LEARNING

Habituation is the process by which we become accustomed to a stimulus, and notice it less and less over time. **Dishabituation** occurs when a change in the stimulus, even a small change, causes us to notice it again. Dishabituation also occurs when a stimulus is removed and then represented. A good example of this pair of processes is in the noise from an air conditioner. We may notice a noisy air conditioner when we first enter a room, but after a few minutes, we stop noticing it; we have habituated to the noise. However, when the air conditioner's compressor turns on, slightly altering the sound being generated, we once again notice the noise. This noticing is dishabituation. Although habituation is not typically a conscious process, we can control it under certain circumstances. If, in the examples above, we are unaware of the air-conditioner noise, but then someone asks us whether the noise of the air conditioner sounds like something else, we can force ourselves to dishabituate, and again notice the noise. This control over our information processing is the key to distinguishing habituation from sensory adaptation: you cannot control sensory adaptation; for example, you cannot force your eyes to adapt to darkness by mere force of will. You can, however, force yourself to pay attention to things to which you have habituated.

Nonassociative learning occurs when an organism is repeatedly exposed to one type of stimulus. Two important types of nonassociative learning are habituation and **sensitization**.

Sensitization is, in many ways, the opposite of habituation. During sensitization, there is an increase in responsiveness due to either a repeated application of a stimulus or a particularly aversive or noxious stimulus. Instead of being able to "tune out" or ignore the stimulus so as to avoid reacting at all (as in habituation), the stimulus actually produces a more exaggerated response. Imagine that you attend a rock concert and sit near the stage. The feedback noise from the amplifier may at first be merely irritating, but as the aversive noise continues, instead of getting used to it, it actually becomes much more painful, to the point at which you have to cover your ears and perhaps even move. Sensitization may also cause you to respond more vigorously to similar stimuli. For example, as you leave the rock concert, an ambulance passes. The siren, which usually doesn't bother you, seems particularly loud and abrasive, as you've been sensitized to the noise of the rock concert. Thankfully, sensitization is usually temporary and unlikely to result in any long-term behavior change. **Desensitization** refers to a decreased responsiveness to an aversive stimulus after repeated exposure. This phenomenon may occur on its own or in the context of **desensitization therapy**. For example, if you have a phobia of snakes, you might engage in **systematic desensitization**: you look at a picture of a snake until your reaction is normal; then you come into a room with a snake until your reaction is normal. In various therapy sessions, you get closer and closer to the snake, eventually even handling it. By being exposed to the stimulus but having no bad outcomes, you can become desensitized to the stimulus and thus overcome your phobia.

BEHAVIORAL LEARNING: CLASSICAL CONDITIONING

Classical conditioning was first described by Ivan Pavlov and is sometimes called **Pavlovian conditioning**. Classical conditioning occurs when a neutral stimulus, paired with a previously meaningful stimulus, eventually takes on some meaning itself. For example, if you shine a light in your fish tank, the fish will ignore it. If you put food in the tank, they will all typically swim to the top to get the food. If, however, each time you feed the fish, you shine the light in the tank before putting in the food, the fish will begin to learn about the light. Eventually, the light alone will cause the fish to swim to the top, as if food had been placed in the tank. The previously neutral light has now taken on some meaning.

Psychologists use specific terms for the various stimuli in classical conditioning. The **conditioned stimulus (CS)** is the initially neutral stimulus—in our example, the light. The **unconditioned stimulus (US)** is the initially meaningful stimulus. In our example, the US is food. The response to the US does not have to be learned; this naturally occurring response is the **unconditioned response (UR)**. In our example, the UR is swimming to the top of the tank. The **conditioned response (CR)** is the response to the CS after conditioning. Again, in our example, the CR is swimming to the top. If you are having a difficult time understanding the different parts of classical conditioning, note that *conditioning* is another word for *learning*. For instance, *unconditioned response* is just another way of saying *unlearned response*.

John Watson and his assistant Rosalie Rayner demonstrated classical conditioning of emotions with a child known now as Little Albert. Albert was first tested and found to have no fear of small animals, though he did show fear whenever a steel bar was banged loudly with a hammer. Watson then presented Albert repeatedly with a small, harmless white rat and, at the same time, banged the steel bar, making the child cry. (Today, this procedure would not be considered ethical.) Afterward, Albert cringed and cried any time he was presented with the rat—even if the noise wasn't made. Furthermore, Albert showed that he was afraid of other white fluffy objects; the closer they resembled the white rat, the more he cried and cringed. This is known as **generalization**. If Albert could distinguish among similar but distinct stimuli, he would be exhibiting **discrimination**. We can use this example to demonstrate other terms related to classical conditioning. **Acquisition** takes place when the pairing of the natural and neutral stimuli (the loud noise and the rat) have occurred with enough frequency that the neutral stimulus alone will elicit the conditional response (cringing and crying). **Extinction**, or the elimination of the conditioned response, can be achieved by presenting the CS without the US

> **Teaching an Old Dog New Tricks**
>
> Pavlov famously demonstrated this conditioning by taking the reflexive response of dogs salivating when presented with food, and then pairing the food with light or sound. Over time, the dogs began to salivate when presented with only light or sound—the food didn't need to be there.

repeatedly (in other words, the white rat without the loud noise). Eventually, the white rat will not produce the unpleasant response. However, **spontaneous recovery**, in which the original response disappears on its own, but then is elicited again by the previous CS at a later time, is also possible under certain circumstances. Returning to the fish: if, after having taught them to associate a light with feeding, you shine a light and give no food a number of times, the fish will initially swim to the top looking for food, but will eventually ignore the light. However, after a period of time of not shining the light, if you shine the light again, the fish will again swim to the top. Notice that they do so spontaneously, without having been taught again. Of course, if there is no food, then the fish will even more quickly stop responding to the light. Spontaneous recovery demonstrates that even though the learning is not evident during the extinction period, the association between the CS and CR is still stored in the brain.

In **second-order conditioning**, a previous CS is used as the US. In our example, the fish would now be trained with a new CS, such as a tone, which would be paired with the light, which would now serve as the US. If the conditioning were successful, the fish would learn to swim to the top in response to the tone. Second-order conditioning is a special case of higher-order conditioning, which, in theory, can go up to any order as new CSs are linked to old ones. In practice, higher-order conditioning is rarely effective beyond the second order.

There are two distinct theories as to why classical conditioning works. Pavlov and Watson believed that the pairing of the neutral (eventual CS) and the natural (US) stimuli occurred because they were paired in time. This is the **contiguity approach**. Robert Rescorla believes that the CS and US get paired because the CS comes to predict the US. The fish from the initial example come to expect food upon seeing the light. This is known as the **contingency approach**.

An example of classical conditioning worthy of special mention is **conditioned taste aversion (CTA)**, also known as the **Garcia effect**, after the psychologist who discovered it. John Garcia demonstrated that animals that eat a food and then experience nausea induced by a drug or radiation will not eat that food if they ever encounter it again. This effect is profound and can be demonstrated with forward or backward conditioning. It is also highly resistant to extinction. A notable feature of this phenomenon is that it works best with food. It is hard to condition an aversion to a light paired with illness, for example. Psychologists have used this finding as evidence that animals are biologically predisposed to associate illness with food, as opposed to, say, light. This predisposition is a useful feature for a creature that samples many types of food, such as a rat. Humans also experience CTA. If you have ever eaten a food and vomited afterward, you may never want to eat that food again, even if you know that the food itself did not cause you to be ill.

BEHAVIORAL LEARNING: OPERANT CONDITIONING

Operant conditioning (also called **instrumental conditioning**) involves an organism's learning to engage in an action in order to obtain a reward or avoid punishment. B.F. Skinner pioneered the study of operant conditioning, although the phenomenon first was discovered by Edward L. Thorndike, who proposed the **law of effect**, which states that a behavior is more likely to recur if reinforced. Skinner ran many operant conditioning experiments. He often used a specially designed testing apparatus known as an operant conditioning chamber, or a Skinner box.

This box typically was empty except for a lever and a hole through which food pellets could be delivered. Skinner trained rats to press the lever (not a typical behavior for rats) in order to get food. To get the rats to learn to press a lever, the experimenter would use a procedure called **shaping**, in which a rat first receives a food reward for being near the lever, then for touching the lever, and finally for pressing the lever. In the end, the rat is rewarded only for pressing the lever. This process is also referred to as **differential reinforcement of successive approximations**.

In a typical operant conditioning experiment, pressing the level is the operant behavior, and food is the reinforcer. Food is a form of **natural reinforcement**; you don't have to learn to like it. These types of natural reinforcers, such as food, water, and sex, provide **primary reinforcement**. **Secondary reinforcement** is provided by learned reinforcers. Money is a good example of a secondary reinforcer. In nature, money is just paper or metal; it has no intrinsic value. We have learned, however, that money can be exchanged for primary reinforcers.

Reinforcement can be divided into positive and negative reinforcement. **Positive reinforcement** is a reward or event that increases the likelihood that a particular type of behavior will be repeated. For example, in the experiment in which a rat is given a food pellet every time it presses a lever, the food provides positive reinforcement, increasing the likelihood that the rat will press the lever again. **Negative reinforcement** is the removal of an aversive event in order to encourage the behavior. An example of negative reinforcement occurs in an experiment in which a rat is sitting on a mildly electrified cage floor. Pressing a bar in the cage turns off the electrical current. The removal of the negative experience (shock) is rewarding. **Omission training**, in contrast, seeks to decrease the frequency of behavior by withholding the reward until the desired behavior is demonstrated.

Like reinforcement, **punishment** is also an important element of operant conditioning, but the effect is the opposite: reinforcement increases behavior, while punishment decreases it. Punishment is an event that decreases the likelihood that the behavior will be repeated. Like reinforcement, punishment can be both positive AND negative. Positive punishment involves the application, or pairing, of an unpleasant stimulus with the behavior. For example, if cadets speak out of turn in military boot camp, the drill sergeant makes them do 20 push-ups. In contrast, negative punishment involves the removal of a reinforcing (desirable) stimulus after the behavior has occurred. For example, a child who breaks a window loses TV privileges for a week. Positive punishment adds something unpleasant and negative punishment subtracts something pleasant. Commonly, both reinforcement and punishment are used in conjunction when shaping behaviors; however, it is uncommon for punishment to have as much of a lasting effect as reinforcement. Once the punishment has been removed, it is no longer effective. Furthermore, punishment instructs only what not to do, whereas reinforcement instructs what to do. Reinforcement is therefore a better choice to encourage behavioral changes and learning.

	reinforcement (think reward)	punishment
positive (think addition!)	giving food, giving praise, giving money, giving a good grade, giving gold stars	giving pain, giving a chore, giving extra homework, giving a bad grade
negative (think subtraction!)	taking away a chore, ending a punishment, removing pain, canceling homework	taking away food, taking away money (a fine), taking away freedom (being grounded, getting a time-out)

Additionally, the processes described for classical conditioning (acquisition, extinction, spontaneous recovery, generalization, and discrimination) occur in operant conditioning, as well.

Instinctive drift refers to the phenomenon where animals that have been classical conditioned to perform behaviors similar to behaviors they might do naturally gradually revert back to those instinctive behaviors.

Superstitious behavior occurs when a being performs a behavior it thinks will lead to the reinforcement when in actually the reinforcement is not contingent on that behavior. For instance, Skinner found that pigeons that received food pellets on a fixed interval reinforcement schedule (so that the reinforcement was based on time rather than response) would repeat a behavior (turning around, pecking at the side of the cage, flapping wings) that the pigeon did immediately before the pellet dropped, even though these behaviors had no influence. **Learned helplessness** occurs when efforts consistently fail to bring rewards. If this situation persists, the subject will stop trying. Psychologist Martin Seligman's original experiment placed dogs in a room with an electrified floor. At first, the dogs would try to escape the room or avoid the floor, but they ultimately learned that there was nothing they could do to prevent being shocked. Eventually, when the dogs' leashes were removed, they still stayed on the electrified floor, even though they could have escaped. This fact shows that they had learned to be helpless. Seligman sees this condition as possibly precipitating depression in humans. If people try repeatedly to succeed at work, school, and/or relationships, and find their efforts are in vain no matter how hard they try, depression may result.

Let's further examine two specific types of operant learning: **escape** and **avoidance**. In escape, an individual learns how to get away from an unpredicted aversive stimulus by engaging in a particular behavior. This helps reinforce the behavior so they will be willing to engage in it again. For example, a child does not want to eat her vegetables (aversive stimulus), so she throws a temper tantrum. If the parents respond by not making the child eat the vegetables, then she will learn that behaving in that specific way will help her escape that particular aversive stimulus. On the other hand, avoidance occurs when a person performs a behavior to ensure a predicted aversive stimulus is not presented. For example, a child notices Mom cooking vegetables for dinner and fakes an illness so Mom will send him to bed with ginger ale and crackers. The child has effectively avoided confronting the aversive stimulus (the offensive vegetables) altogether. As long as either of these techniques work (meaning the parents do not force the child to eat the vegetables), the child is reinforced to perform the escape and/or avoidance behaviors.

Reinforcement can also lead to the development of superstitions. People can make specious connections between their behaviors and positive outcomes, leading to perpetuation of the "lucky" behaviors.

Behaviorists use various schedules of reinforcement in their experiments. A **schedule of reinforcement** refers to the frequency with which an organism receives reinforcement for a given type of response. In a **continuous reinforcement schedule**, every correct response that is emitted results in a reward. This produces rapid learning, but it also results in rapid extinction, where extinction is a decrease and eventual disappearance of a response once the behavior is no longer reinforced.

Schedules of reinforcement in which not all behaviors are reinforced are called **partial (or intermittent) reinforcement schedules**. A **fixed-ratio schedule** is one in which the reward always occurs after a fixed number of behaviors. For example, a rat might have to press a lever 10 times in order to receive a food pellet. This schedule is called a 10:1 ratio schedule. Fixed-ratio schedules produce strong learning, but the learning extinguishes relatively quickly, as the rat quickly detects that the reinforcement schedule no longer is operative. A **variable-ratio schedule** is one in which the ratio of operant behaviors to reinforcement is variable and unpredictable. A good example of this is slot machines. The operant behavior, putting in money and pulling the lever, is reinforced with a payoff in a seemingly random manner. Reinforcement can come at any time. This type of schedule takes longer to condition a behavior; however, the learning that occurs is resistant to extinction, which helps explain why people can become addicted to gambling. A **fixed-interval schedule** is one in which reinforcement is presented as a function of fixed periods of time, as long as there is at least one operant behavior. This schedule is similar to being a salaried employee. Every two weeks, the paycheck arrives regardless of your work performance (as long as you show up at all). Finally, in the **variable-interval schedule**, reinforcement is presented at differing time intervals, as long as there is at least one operant behavior. Variable-interval, like variable-ratio, is more difficult to extinguish than fixed schedules.

> **Variable-Interval in the Classroom**
> This schedule of reinforcement is illustrated by a teacher who gives pop quizzes. The time at which the quiz will be given is always changing.

> ## Study Tip
> Make sure that you can explain why the different partial reinforcement schedules produce different behaviors in people being reinforced. See whether you can apply it to your own life and how you are reinforced for various behaviors. For variable-ratio reinforcement, focus on the gambling example presented and try to imagine why this schedule can prove so addictive.

A combination of reinforcers and punishers designed to alter behavior is referred to as **behavior modification**. Operant conditioning techniques are used quite frequently in places that have controlled populations, such as prisons and mental institutions. Such an institution might set up a **token economy**—an artificial economy based on tokens (such as points or gold stars). These tokens act as secondary reinforcers, in that the tokens can be used for purchasing other primary or secondary reinforcers, such as food. The participants in a token economy are reinforced for desired behaviors (responses) with tokens; this reinforcement is designed to increase the number of positive behaviors that occur.

SOCIAL, COGNITIVE, AND NEUROLOGICAL FACTORS IN LEARNING

Social Learning

Classical and operant conditioning obviously do not account for all forms of learning. A third kind of learning is **social learning** (also called **observational learning**), which is learning based on observing the behavior of others as well as the consequences of that behavior. Because this learning takes place through observing others, it is also referred to as **vicarious learning**.

Albert Bandura conducted some of the most important research on social learning. In a classic study, Bandura had children in a waiting room with an adult **confederate** (someone who was "in" on the experiment). For one group of children, the adult would simply wait. For another group of children, the adult would punch and kick an inflatable doll (thus the experiment is now nicknamed the **Bobo Doll Experiment**). In both groups, the children were then brought into another room to play with interesting toys, but after a short time, the experimenters told the children they had to stop playing with the interesting toys, and were brought back to the initial waiting room. The idea was to frustrate the children, and then see how they managed their frustration. Many of the children who had witnessed an adult abusing the doll proceeded to abuse the doll themselves. But most of the children who had witnessed an adult quietly waiting proceeded to quietly wait themselves. This experiment illustrated the power of **modeling** in affecting changes in behavior. This finding calls into question the behaviorist assertion that learning must occur through direct experience.

> Bandura concluded that four conditions must be met for observational learning to occur. First, the learner must pay attention to the behavior in question. Second, there must be retention of the observed behavior, meaning that it must be remembered. Third, there must be a motivation for the learner to produce the behavior at a later time. Finally, the potential for reproduction must exist: that is, the learner must be able to reproduce the learned behavior.

Observational learning is a phenomenon frequently discussed in the debate over violence in the media. This issue is a particularly relevant one for television programs designed for children, as studies have shown that young children are particularly likely to engage in observational learning. However, even toddlers have shown unsolicited helping behaviors in experimental settings, suggesting that observational learning occurs in both desirable and undesirable directions.

Bandura's social cognitive theory is also known as reciprocal determinism—an interaction between a) thoughts, b) the environment, and c) behavior. Bandura discussed the importance of **self-efficacy** beliefs—the beliefs about how good or bad you think you are at performing a specific task. Another social cognitive theorist, Walter Mischel, experimented with **delay of gratification** in his famous **Marshmallow Test**. He gave children one marshmallow now but told them that if they waited they could have two. Children who were able to wait and delay gratification were believed to have on average more powerful executive control—they could keep a goal in mind, inhibit distractions, and focus.

Building on recent views that there are multiple types of intelligence, including emotional intelligence, a number of schools have developed programs in **social and emotional learning**. These programs are designed to help develop empathy and conflict resolution in students.

Another form of learning is **insight learning**. This occurs when we puzzle over a solution to a problem, unsuccessfully, and then suddenly the complete solution appears to us.

Other evidence for a cognitive component to learning derives from the work of Edward Tolman. Rats permitted to explore a maze without being reinforced would find the exit after following an indirect path; the time it took them to exit the maze without reinforcement decreased quite slowly. However, when reinforcers were applied after several trials without reinforcement, the rats' time to exit the maze decreased dramatically, indicating that the rats knew how to navigate to a specific location within the maze and so had formed a **cognitive map**, or mental representation of the maze. This demonstrates **latent learning**, or learning that is not outwardly expressed until the situation calls for it.

Biological Factors

The biological basis of learning is of great interest to psychologists. Neuroscientists have tried to identify the neural correlates of learning. In other words, what physiological changes are brought about when we learn?

In the 1960s, psychologists noticed that neurons themselves could be affected by environmental stimulation. Experiments were conducted in which some rats were raised in an enriched environment, while others were raised in a deprived environment. The enriched environment included things to explore and lots of room in which to move, whereas the deprived environment was just a small, empty cage. At the end of the experiment, the rats were sacrificed, and their brains were examined. The experimenters found that the rats from the enriched environment had thicker cortices, higher brain weight, and greater neural connectivity in their brains. This pattern of results suggests that neurons can change in response to environmental stimuli.

Donald Hebb proposed that human learning takes place through neurons forming new connections with one another or through the strengthening of connections that already exist. To study how learning affects specific neurons, scientists study the sea slug *Aplysia*. This is a good animal to study because it has only about 20,000 neurons, whereas humans have millions. *Aplysia* can be classically conditioned to withdraw its gill, a protective response. Eric Kandel, a neuroscientist, examined classical conditioning in *Aplysia*. Kandel paired a light touch (CS) with a shock (US). This pairing causes the *Aplysia* to withdraw its gill (UR). After training, the light touch alone can elicit the gill withdrawal (now a CR). Kandel found that when a strong stimulus, such as a shock, happens repeatedly, special neurons called modulatory neurons release neuromodulators. **Neuromodulators** strengthen the synapses between the sensory neurons (the ones that sense the touch) and the motor neurons (the ones that withdraw the gill) involved. Additionally, new synapses were created. In other words, the neurons sensing shock and those that withdrew the gill became more connected than they were before. This experiment illustrated a neural basis for learning: namely, a physiological change that correlates with a relatively stable change in behavior as a result of experience. This increased synaptic connection is known as **long-term potentiation** (LTP). The same basic process has been shown to be the neural basis of learning in mammals. An easy way to remember this information is that "neurons that fire together, wire together."

Long-term memory storage involves more permanent changes to the brain, including structural and functional connections between neurons. For example, long-term memory storage includes new synaptic connections between neurons, permanent changes in pre- and postsynaptic membranes, and a permanent increase or decrease in neurotransmitter synthesis. Furthermore, visual imaging studies suggest that there is greater branching of dendrites in regions of the brain thought to be involved with memory storage. Other studies suggest that protein synthesis somehow influences memory formation; drugs that prevent protein synthesis appear to block long-term memory formation.

The neural processes described above occur when animals or people learn new behaviors or change their behaviors based on experience (that is, environmental feedback). However, not all behaviors are learned: some are innate. These are the things we know how to do instinctively (or our body just does without us consciously thinking about it), not because someone taught us to do them (for example, breathing or pulling away from a hot stove). Further, innate behaviors are always the same between members of the species, even for those performing them for the first time.

Cognitive Processes in Learning

The behaviorist view, championed by Skinner, is that behavior is a series of behavior-reward pairings, and cognition is not as important to the learning process. In more recent years, many psychologists have abandoned this view. One more recent view of learning posits that organisms start the learning process by observing a stimulus; then they continue the process by evaluating that stimulus; then they move on to a consideration of possible responses; and finally, they make a response. Various lines of evidence indicate that cognitive factors play a role in both animal and human learning. For example, if humans could be conditioned to salivate to the word *style*, they also would be likely to salivate to the word *fashion*. These words are not acoustically similar, but rather semantically similar, meaning they have a related meaning instead of sounding alike, so this pattern of behavior results from cognitive evaluation.

Perhaps a more profound demonstration of a similar phenomenon comes from work with pigeons. Pigeons were shown pictures containing either trees or no trees. They were trained to peck a key for food, but only when a picture of a tree was shown. As you might expect, they would peck the key only when tree pictures were shown, even after reinforcement stopped. They even pecked at pictures of trees that they had never seen before. Therefore, the birds must have formed a concept of trees (a concept being defined as a cognitive rule for categorizing stimuli into groups). Any new stimuli were categorized according to the concept.

KEY TERMS

Life-Span Approach
developmental psychology
life-span psychologists
child psychologists

Developmental Issues
nature-nurture debate
maturationists
maturation
environmentalists
continuous development
discontinuous development
critical period
collectivist culture
individual culture
normative development
cross-sectional method
longitudinal method
physical development
teratogens
fetal alcohol spectrum disorder (FASD)
reflexes
rudimentary movements
gross motor movements
fine motor movements
fundamental movement
specialized movement
transitional substage
application substage
myelin
synaptic pruning
environmental interaction
plasticity
gender identity
gender typing
gender constancy
androgyny
Kinsey Scale
equilibration
assimilation
schema
accommodation
sensorimotor stage
  object permanence

preoperational stage
  symbolic thinking
  egocentrism
  artificialism
  animism
concrete operational stage
  reversibility
  conservation
formal operational stage
  metacognition
internalization
zone of proximal development
actual development level
potential development level
wisdom
fluid intelligence
crystalized intelligence

Language
phonemes
morphemes
grammar
syntax
semantics
prosody
holophrases
overextension
underextension
telegraphic speech
overgeneralization

Social-Emotional Development
ecological systems theory
  microsystem
  mesosystem
  exosystem
  macrosystem
  chronosystem
authoritarian parenting
authoritative parenting
permissive parenting
psychosocial development
fidelity
generativity
stagnation

temperament
  surgency
  negative affect
  effortful control
attachment
  strange situation
  secure
  avoidant
  ambivalent
  disorganized
  separation anxiety
parallel play
pretend play
peer relationships
imaginary audience
adolescent egocentrism
adolescent identity development
  achievement
  diffusion
  foreclosure
  moratorium
adverse childhood experiences (ACEs)
social clock
adult attachment

Learning

Nonassociative Learning
habituation
dishabituation
sensitization
desensitization
desensitization therapy
systematic desensitization

Classical (Pavlovian) Conditioning
conditioned stimulus (CS)
unconditioned stimulus (US)
unconditioned response (UR)
conditioned response (CR)
generalization
discrimination
acquisition
extinction
spontaneous recovery
second-order conditioning
contiguity approach
contingency approach
conditioned taste aversion (CTA)
Garcia effect

Operant (Instrumental) Conditioning
law of effect
shaping (differential reinforcement of successive
  approximations)
natural reinforcement
primary reinforcement
secondary reinforcement
positive reinforcement
negative reinforcement
omission training
punishment
instinctive drift
learned helplessness
escape
avoidance
schedule of reinforcement
  continuous reinforcement schedule
  partial (intermittent) reinforcement schedule
  fixed-ratio schedule
  variable-ratio schedule
  fixed-interval schedule
  variable-interval schedule
behavior modification
token economy

Social (Observational/Vicarious) Learning
confederate
Bobo Doll Experiment
modeling
self-efficacy
delay of gratification
Marshmallow Test
social and emotional learning
insight learning
cognitive map
latent learning

Biological Factors
neuromodulators
long-term potentiation (LTP)

Unit 3 Drill

See Chapter 12 for answers and explanations.

1. After having been struck by a car, a dog now exhibits fear responses every time a car approaches. The dog also exhibits a fear response to the approach of a bus, a truck, a bicycle, and even a child's wagon. The dog has undergone a process of

   (A) stimulus discrimination
   (B) stimulus generalization
   (C) spontaneous recovery
   (D) backward conditioning
   (E) differential reinforcement

2. Which of the following would be an example of second-order conditioning?

   (A) A cat tastes a sour plant that makes it feel nauseated and will not approach that plant again.
   (B) A horse that is fed sugar cubes by a particular person salivates every time that person walks by.
   (C) A pigeon that has received food every time a red light is presented exhibits food-seeking behavior when a yellow light is presented.
   (D) A rabbit that has repeatedly seen a picture of a feared predator paired with a musical tone exhibits a fear response to the musical tone as well as to a flashed light alone that had been repeatedly paired with the tone.
   (E) Wild rats instinctively avoid canine predators, but domesticated rats show little fear of the domesticated dogs they encounter, and may even join them in exploration or play.

3. The reinforcement schedule that generally provides the most resistance to response extinction is

   (A) fixed-ratio
   (B) fixed-interval
   (C) variable-ratio
   (D) variable-interval
   (E) continuous

4. The importance of enrichment and stimulation of the brain during critical periods in development can be seen in all of the following EXCEPT

   (A) an increase in the number of neurons
   (B) an increase in the number of connections between neurons
   (C) strengthening of already existing connections between neurons
   (D) an increase in the size of neurons
   (E) higher levels of neurotransmitters

5. According to Albert Bandura, observational learning can occur even in the absence of

   (A) observed consequences of behavior
   (B) direct attention to the behavior
   (C) retention of the observed behavior over time
   (D) ability to reproduce the behavior
   (E) motivation to reproduce the behavior at a later time

6. Jay joins a social media website to lose weight. He receives points based on the intensity of his daily exercise and praise from fellow users for each workout he logs on the website. This increases his exercise frequency and intensity. Eventually he stops logging onto the website, but continues to exercise with increased frequency. This is an example of

   (A) vicarious reinforcement
   (B) operant conditioning
   (C) innate behavior
   (D) classical conditioning
   (E) observational learning

7. Which of the following scenarios is an example of negative reinforcement?

   (A) After staying out past her curfew, Stephanie is grounded the next weekend.
   (B) When Toni finishes her homework, she does not have to take out the trash.
   (C) When Ben received an A for his research project, his family treated him to dinner at his favorite restaurant.
   (D) When Lola the dog jumps on her owner, the owner takes a step away from her.
   (E) When the rat in a Skinner box presses the lever, the box delivers an electric shock.

8. Chemotherapy is well known to cause nausea and vomiting. A chemotherapy patient's care team cautions the patient to eat only "novel" or new foods before treatment as opposed to food staples, like chicken, rice, or pasta. This is most likely due to

    (A) operant conditioning
    (B) taste aversion
    (C) Yerkes-Dodson Law
    (D) observational learning
    (E) stimulus generalization

9. Leigha, who is expecting college acceptance letters, knows the mail carrier comes every day around 1:30 P.M. Hoping that the mail arrives early, she checks the mailbox at 12:45, 1:15, and 1:40. She does not check again until the next day around the same time. This is an example of which reinforcement schedule?

    (A) Fixed-interval
    (B) Variable-interval
    (C) Fixed-ratio
    (D) Variable-ratio
    (E) Continuous

10. Kevin tries to teach his dog Muka to roll over. First, he teaches her to lie down. Then, he teaches her to lie on her side. Eventually, Kevin gets Muka to roll onto her back and, finally, all the way around. He gives her a treat with every step. This process is known as

    (A) habituation
    (B) discrimination
    (C) generalization
    (D) shaping
    (E) sensitization

11. The term given to that part of language composed of tones and inflections that add or change meaning without alterations in word usage is

    (A) syntax
    (B) grammar
    (C) phonemics
    (D) semantics
    (E) prosody

12. Which of the following would NOT be an example of a two-year-old's usage of telegraphic speech?

    (A) "Where ball?"
    (B) "Boy hurt."
    (C) "Milk."
    (D) "Mommy give hug."
    (E) "Go play group."

13. Stefano tries his hardest to learn German, but he continues to replace words with Spanish words by accident. This is most likely a result of

    (A) proactive interference
    (B) retroactive interference
    (C) telegraphic speech
    (D) surface structure of language
    (E) semantic encoding

14. In neonates, the response to a feeling of lost bodily support (like falling) that involves a splaying out of the limbs is called the

    (A) palmar reflex
    (B) Babinski reflex
    (C) orienting reflex
    (D) Moro reflex
    (E) rooting reflex

15. The belief that there is often a discrepancy between children's outward cognitive abilities and their true cognitive abilities is most closely associated with which of the following theorists?

    (A) Jean Piaget
    (B) Lev Vygotsky
    (C) Leon Festinger
    (D) Sigmund Freud
    (E) Julian Rotter

16. According to Erik Erikson, the major developmental task of school-age children before puberty is to develop

    (A) a sense of competence in their efforts
    (B) the ability to form stable intimate relationships
    (C) a feeling of trust that their basic needs will be met
    (D) control over basic bodily functions
    (E) a consistent self-view of identity and roles

17. Shyera, approaching the age of five, believes that all things, from people to animals to plants to objects, are alive, but she has trouble understanding circum-stances from these other "living" things' points of view. Piaget's theory would place Shyera

    (A) at the sensorimotor stage
    (B) at the preoperational stage
    (C) at the concrete operational stage
    (D) at the formal operational stage
    (E) at the latency stage

18. An infant cries when his mother leaves the room but is quickly consoled when she returns. The infant feels comfortable to explore and wander around when the mother is in the room. Mary Ainsworth would describe this infant as having

    (A) insecure attachment
    (B) avoidant attachment
    (C) secure attachment
    (D) disorganized attachment
    (E) generalized attachment

19. A school-age student is able to recognize that the water she poured from a short wide cup is still the same amount of water in a tall, skinny vase. This concept is known as

    (A) conservation
    (B) object permanence
    (C) conditioning
    (D) crystallized intelligence
    (E) egocentrism

20. Bandura believed which of the following statements about gender development?

    (A) Gender is a learned behavior that has a critical period right before puberty.
    (B) Gender is genetically based and does not have to do with socialization.
    (C) Gender is a result of hormonal fluctuations that happen during puberty.
    (D) Gender roles are a result of cognitive development only.
    (E) Gender roles are at least in part observed and rewarded through socialization.

21. Albert Bandura's famous Bobo Doll experiment shows the power of

    (A) observation
    (B) conformity
    (C) hostile aggression
    (D) dehumanization
    (E) instrumental aggression

REFLECT

Respond to the following questions:

- Which topics in this chapter do you hope to see on the multiple-choice section or essay?

- Which topics in this chapter do you hope not to see on the multiple-choice section or essay?

- Regarding any psychologists mentioned, can you pair the psychologists with their contributions to the field? Did they contribute significant experiments, theories, or both?

- Regarding any theories mentioned, can you distinguish between differing theories well enough to recognize them on the multiple-choice section? Can you distinguish them well enough to write a fluent essay on them?

- Can you define the key terms at the end of the chapter?

- Which parts of the chapter will you review?

- Will you seek further help, outside of this book (such as from a teacher, Princeton Review tutor, or AP Students), on any of the content in this chapter—and, if so, on what content?

Chapter 10
Unit 4: Social Psychology and Personality

ATTRIBUTION

Attribution refers to the way in which people assign responsibility for certain outcomes. Typically, attribution falls into two categories—dispositional (or individual) and situational. **Dispositional attribution** assumes that the cause of a behavior or outcome is internal. **Situational attribution** assigns the cause to the environment or external conditions. When students fail a test, they might attribute that failure to their own poor work habits or lack of intellectual abilities (a dispositional attribute), or they could attribute their failure to some external factor such as bad instruction (a situational attribute). **Explanatory style** refers to how people explain good and bad events that happen to themselves and to others. Explanatory style can be optimistic, where a person puts a positive spin on circumstances (e.g., I can cope, the problem is not a big deal, the problem will be over soon), or pessimistic, where the event is perceived as highly stressful and potentially threatening.

A **self-serving bias** sees the cause of actions as internal (or dispositional) when the outcomes are positive and external (or situational) when the results are negative. When a teacher's class fails a test, that teacher blames the students for their lack of initiative and motivation. However, when the class does very well, the teacher attributes the students' success to their own superior teaching and motivational ability. When your class gets back a paper, think about how often you've heard fellow students say things like, "I got an A" but "He gave me a C." A related concept is the **fundamental attribution error**. In this process of judging the behavior of others, people are more likely to overestimate the role of dispositional attributes and to underestimate the role of the situation. For example, if you are waiting for your friend to meet you at the movies and she is so late that the movie has already started, you would be more likely to blame your friend's lateness on her laziness or procrastination than on a traffic jam or car accident. Your judgment exemplifies a fundamental attribution error. The **actor-observer bias** is related to the fundamental attribution error. In the actor-observer bias, when a person behaves badly themselves, they attribute their bad behavior to the situation while when someone else behaves badly, they attribute the other person's bad behavior to their character or disposition.

Julian Rotter talked about **locus of control**—if you have an internal locus of control, you believe you have control over events. But if you have an external locus of control, you don't believe you have control. For example, you cannot control the weather (external locus of control) but you can control how you dress for the weather (internal).

PERSON PERCEPTION

Psychologists have studied **interpersonal attraction**, the tendency to positively evaluate a person and then to gravitate toward that person. Interpersonal attraction is obviously based on the characteristics of the person to whom we are attracted, but it may be subject to environmental and social influences, as well. Factors leading to interpersonal attraction include positive evaluation, shared opinions, good physical appearance, familiarity, and proximity of the individuals to each other. **Positive evaluation** refers to the fact that we all like to be positively evaluated and, therefore, we tend to prefer the company of people who think highly of us. **Shared opinions** as a basis for interpersonal attraction are typically thought of as a form of social reinforcement. If we are praised and rewarded by a person for our opinions, then we tend to prefer

Q: What factors may lend themselves to interpersonal attraction?

See answer on page 225.

their company. It is important to note that similarity across other factors, such as age and race, also tends to be a good predictor of interpersonal attraction. The variable of proximity is an interesting factor. It has been shown that people are more likely to be attracted to those in close physical proximity to them. Studies have shown that apartment building residents are much more likely to have friends who live on their floor than they are to have friends who live on other floors. This is an example of the **mere exposure effect**, which states that people tend to prefer people and experiences that are familiar.

Some attributions actually affect the outcome of the behavior, as in the case of the **self-fulfilling prophecy**. In a self-fulfilling prophecy, a person initially has a false belief about a situation, which evokes a new behavior, which makes the false belief come true. Because Person A expects Person B to achieve or fail, Person B is likely to do just that. This is especially true in education and is known as the **Rosenthal Effect**. When teachers are told that certain children are expected to achieve in the following year, those children tend to do better than others, even when there is actually no difference in ability levels.

Self-esteem is related to whom we compare ourselves to, which is posited by Leon Festinger in his **social comparison theory.** People can also inflate their self-esteem by basking in reflective glory, which is when someone takes pride in the accomplishments of an individual or group that the person strongly affiliates with in their life.

> **A:** Interpersonal attraction may occur as a result of positive evaluation, shared opinions, good physical appearance, familiarity, or proximity.

> **11 Domains of Competency**
> By the time we reach adulthood, self-esteem can be broken into 11 domains of competency within which we evaluate ourselves. These domains are morality, sociability, intimacy, athleticism, intelligence, sense of humor, nurturance, job competence, adequacy as a provider, physical appearance, and household management.

IDENTITIES AND GROUPS

Societies, organizations of individuals, each have a shared **culture**, a common set of beliefs, behaviors, values, and material symbols. Therefore, identities begin to form as collective **social identities** that are placed upon individuals by others, and individuals form their own **personal identities** about themselves. Personal identities are generally words that describe personality, such as *kind, generous, thoughtful, insightful,* etc., while social identities are how individuals are seen in the context of their society. Social identities can be related to religion, work, appearance, disability, gender, sexual orientation, immigration status, or any other label that societies have come to understand through their shared culture. For instance, someone's social identities might be lawyer, young adult, Muslim, and female. These traits do not have anything to do with personality traits, yet they are factors that influence how individuals are seen by others in society, which may color social interactions. These identities can give some individuals an inherent advantage in some societies, while other identities can be a disadvantage. For instance, those who have citizenship in a certain country have more power and rights than those who are considered immigrants, noncitizens, or undocumented. Similarly, in the United States, adults tend to hold more power in society than children or the very elderly. Individuals hold multiple social identities, and the effects and nature of these overlapping identities is referred to as **intersectionality**. Someone who identifies as female, Latina, and bisexual can provide a window into each of these social identities and how they intersect and create complexity when combined.

The closest group that individuals create with one another is called the **primary group**, which usually consists of family and close friends. These relationships are generally long-lasting and emotionally deep. Individuals spend time with others in their primary groups for the sake of spending quality time with them, not for any other gain. Most others fall into a **secondary group**, a group of friends and acquaintances who perhaps have shared interests or values. For instance, a person may take classes at school with classmates who have a shared interest in the material or take part in a running group with others who share a passion for running. Within societies, these identities underpin ideas of sameness and difference, which generate **in-groups** and **out-groups**. In-groups refer to groups of individuals with a shared identity. For example, teachers share an in-group with other teachers, while, to them, accountants would be considered an out-group. An additional type of group is a **reference group**.

Stereotypes refer to assumptions about a characteristic of an entire group. Stereotypes are usually negative and often lead to prejudice. **Prejudice** is a pre-conceived belief about a person or group based on group membership. **Discrimination** refers to engaging in unjust treatment of a person or group based on the prejudicial belief. Remember that prejudice is a belief while discrimination is a behavior based on the belief. **Implicit bias**, also known as implicit attitude, is a negative attitude against a specific social group. It is implicit because the person is not consciously aware of their negative beliefs but that bias manifests in their speech and actions. Group membership often has a lot to do with positive or negative feelings towards a group. **Outgroup homogeneity bias** is when a person perceives of all members of an outgroup as more similar than they actual are while members of one's in group are diverse. **Ingroup bias** is favoring members of one's ingroup over others. Related to these kinds of implicit attitudes is the concept of the **just-world phenomenon**, where one believes that people get what they deserve (e.g., if you pull out your wallet on the street to count your money and you get robbed, you deserve to be robbed because you didn't show street smarts). **Belief perseverance** affects problem-solving. In this mental error, a person sees only the evidence that supports a particular position, despite evidence presented to the contrary. Belief perseverance can affect any type of belief about how the world works but can be especially problematic with prejudicial beliefs.

Another cognitive theory of motivation concerns the need to avoid **cognitive dissonance**. People are motivated to reduce tension produced by conflicting thoughts or choices. Generally, they will change their attitudes to fit their behavioral patterns as long as they believe they are in control of their choices and actions. **Cognitive dissonance** occurs when attitudes and behaviors contradict each other. Generally, such tension is not pleasant, and people tend to change in order to achieve cognitive consistency. Leon Festinger studied this phenomenon and came to the conclusion that people are likely to alter their attitudes to fit their behavior. For example, law-abiding citizens speed frequently. A cognitive conflict exists. Which is going to change—their attitude toward the law or their over-the-limit driving? Generally, people adjust their attitudes and continue their behavior. Cognitive dissonance tends to occur only when the person feels that he has a choice in the matter. If someone feels that he is being forced to speed, his attitude will remain intact.

In a society, members have certain expectations for the behavior of its fellow members. These are the **social norms** of that society, and can change from society to society, as well as over time. For instance, in one society, the norm for greeting may be to say hello and shake hands while in another society the norm may be to silently bow to one another. **Social influence theory** proposes that society place pressure on its members to conform to certain standards of behavior or thought. Social influence may be **normative** (where people refer to others who they believe follow the norms) or **informational** (where people refer to others who they believe have more information).

PSYCHOLOGY OF SOCIAL SITUATIONS

Persuasion is the process by which a person or group can influence the attitudes of others. The efficacy of persuasion derives in part from the characteristics of the persuader. People who have positions of authority or who appear to be experts on a given topic are more likely to be viewed as persuasive. The motive of the persuader is also critical. If an author tries to convince you that authors are poor, and that you should donate five dollars to the poor authors' fund, you probably would not believe the author. Your disbelief would stem from your confidence that the author's motive is selfish. However, if an author asks for five dollars for disaster relief, you might be more likely to be persuaded because the motive seems more altruistic.

> **Marketing and Persuasion**
>
> Market researchers refer to the use of facts as the central route to persuasion.

An additional factor affecting persuasive ability is interpersonal attractiveness. More attractive, likable, trustworthy, and knowledgeable people are viewed as more persuasive. Most people are also swayed by the presentation of facts. Another factor influencing the persuasion process is the nature of the message. Repetition is an effective technique for achieving persuasion, which is why the same advertisements run so frequently. Fear is another motivator of attitudinal change. A prime example of the use of fear in persuasive attempts is the practice of putting cars wrecked in DWI (driving while intoxicated) accidents on display. The idea is that seeing the result of such an accident will induce an attitudinal change about drunk driving.

The **elaboration likelihood model** explains when people will be persuaded by the content of a message (or the logic of its arguments), and when people will be influenced by other, more superficial characteristics like the length of the message or the appearance of the person delivering it. Because persuasion can be such a powerful means for influencing what people think and do, much research has gone into studying the various elements of a message that might have an impact on its persuasiveness.

The three key elements are message characteristics, source characteristics, and target characteristics.

1. The message characteristics are the features of the message itself, such as its logic and the number of key points in the argument. This category also includes more superficial things, such as the length and grammatical complexity.

2. The source characteristics of the person or group delivering the message, such as expertise, knowledge, and trustworthiness, are also of importance. People are much more likely to be persuaded by a major study described in the *New England Journal of Medicine* than by something in the pages of the local supermarket tabloid.

3. Finally, the target characteristics of the person receiving the message (such as self-esteem, intelligence, and mood) have an important influence on whether a message will be perceived as persuasive. For instance, some studies have suggested that those with higher intelligence are less easily persuaded by one-sided messages.

The two cognitive routes that persuasion follows under this model are the **central route** and the **peripheral route**. Under the central route, people are persuaded by the content of the argument. They ruminate over the key features of the argument and allow those features to influence their decision to change their point of view. The peripheral route functions when people focus on superficial or secondary characteristics of the speech or the orator. Under these circumstances, people are persuaded by the attractiveness of the orator, the length of the speech, whether the orator is considered an expert in his field, and other features. The elaboration likelihood model argues that people will choose the central route only when they are both motivated to listen to the logic of the argument (they are interested in the topic) and not distracted, thus focusing their attention on the argument. If those conditions are not met, individuals will choose the peripheral route, and they will be persuaded by more superficial factors. Messages processed via the central route are more likely to have longer-lasting persuasive outcomes than messages processed via the peripheral route.

Finally, some people can be influenced to change their attitudes more easily than others. In general, people with high self-esteem are less easily persuaded than are those with low self-esteem. Thus, many hate groups recruit people who are considered outsiders or who have few friends. These people with low self-esteem are susceptible to being persuaded to change their attitudes on issues such as race to match those of the hate group.

Conformity is the modification of behavior to make it agree with that of a group. Solomon Asch performed studies on the nature of conformity. In these studies, participants thought that they were being evaluated on their perceptual judgments. Small groups of people sitting together were shown stimuli, such as lines of differing lengths. Each member of the group was to report which of several comparison lines matched a standard line in length. Each individual in the group was asked to respond orally in turn. The participants did not know that the other members of a given group were not naïve participants, but rather were confederates of the experimenter. The correct answers in the experiment were obvious. However, the confederates, pretending to be naïve participants, would purposely respond incorrectly. Asch found that, in general, the naïve participants agreed with the other members of the group, even though the answer they gave was obviously incorrect. Furthermore, Asch demonstrated that the participants knew that the answers they gave were wrong, but said them anyway.

Conformity Factors

Factors influencing conformity include group size, the cohesiveness of the group opinion, gender, social status, culture, and the appearance of unanimity.

Generally speaking, three or more members of a group are sufficient for conformity effects to occur. The desire to conform seems higher if the participants see themselves as members of a cohesive group. In general, women are more likely to conform than are men. People who view themselves as being of medium or low social status are more likely to conform than are those who perceive themselves as being of high social status. The cultural influence on conformity is also marked: people in more collective societies tend to conform more than do those in individualistic societies. Finally, unanimity is important. A participant is much less likely to conform if even one other person in the group did not conform.

Obedience was studied by Stanley Milgram in a series of famous experiments. The basic paradigm was as follows: participants were led to believe that their job was to administer shocks of increasing intensity to another participant if that participant performed poorly on a given learning task. The other participant was actually a confederate, intentionally performing badly, so that the real participant would be obliged to administer the shock. The confederate also acted as if the shocks were painful, pleading with the participant to stop. (In fact, no shocks were given.) The participant was instructed by the experimenter to continue the shocks, despite the obvious pain the "other participant" was enduring. You might think that you would not administer painful shocks in this paradigm, but a very high percentage of people did just that. Through additional studies, Milgram found that several factors were critical to whether or not the person would obey. The first was the perceived authority of the test administrator. For example, when the person overseeing the experiment introduced himself as a graduate student instead of as a scientist, the subject was much less likely to comply. Another factor was physical distance. If the subject was forced to sit in the room with the person receiving the shocks, his level of obedience dropped; the subject was also less likely to obey if the experimenter communicated the commands by phone instead of in person. Obedience also tended to go down if the subject was told that he was responsible for the outcome, if the subject witnessed someone else disobeying the experimenter, and if the experimenter instructed the subject to immediately apply a high level of voltage to the "learner." The major conclusion from this study was that people tended to be obedient to a figure of authority, but only if certain criteria were met. It also demonstrated that people are much less likely to obey when they feel that they have an ally in standing up to the pressure.

Culture also impacts social interaction in important ways. A **collectivist culture** is one in which the needs of society are placed before the needs of the individual. Conversely, **individualist cultures** promote personal needs above the needs of society. It is important to realize that a developing child's relationship with her environment and culture is bidirectional, meaning that just as a child's social environment plays a role in how she develops, she also contributes to the society in which she is born.

The Power of Groupthink

Another interesting phenomenon that may occur when people are in groups is what Irving Janis has referred to as "groupthink." **Groupthink** occurs when members of a group are so driven to reach unanimous decisions that they no longer truly evaluate the repercussions or implications of their decisions. Groupthink may be observed when the groups making decisions are isolated and homogeneous, when there is a lack of impartial leadership inside or outside the group, and when there is a high level of pressure for a decision to be made. Often, groups experiencing groupthink start to acquire feelings of invulnerability and omnipotence. They do not believe they can make a mistake and, as a result, often do. A **mindguard** in the group may take on the responsibility of criticizing or even ostracizing members of the group who do not agree with the rest. The groupthink hypothesis has been applied to understand political situations, such as how political leaders can make decisions that seem, in retrospect, so obviously bad to people outside of the group.

GROUP DYNAMICS

Group dynamics is a general term for some of the phenomena we observe when people interact. For example, **social facilitation** is an increase in performance on a task that occurs when that task is performed in the presence of others. You may have experienced this effect if you play sports. The opposite effect is called **social inhibition**, which occurs when the presence of others makes performance worse. Many people experience social inhibition when they give speeches. People experience social facilitation when they find a task to be easy or well-practiced, and they suffer from social inhibition when a task is overly difficult or novel.

Q: What is the bystander effect?

See answer on page 236

Another effect that occurs when people interact in groups is **social loafing**, or the reduced effort group members put into a shared task as a result of the size of the group. For example, when you are assigned a group project, you may put in less effort than you would if it were an individual project, hoping that the other group members will pick up some of your slack. People are prone to social loafing when they believe their performance is not being assessed or monitored.

Another interesting effect of being in groups is the exaggeration of our initial attitudes. This effect is known as **group polarization**. Group polarization occurs when a judgment or decision of a group is more extreme than what individual members of the group would have reached on their own. For example, if people with negative racial attitudes are placed into a group and told to discuss racial issues, those who started off the experiment with high prejudice often end up with an even higher prejudice after the discussion. **Peer pressure** occurs when an individual feels unduly influenced by their peers to engage in behaviors they otherwise would not. One example of peer pressure is someone encouraging a friend to try smoking. But peer pressure has a flip side: a friend can also inspire another to participate in positive activities. Motivating a friend to lose weight by becoming workout partners is an example. While more common in adolescence, peer pressure is also common in adulthood.

The Mob Mentality

The phenomenon of **deindividuation** is a common occurrence at riots and protests that have gotten angry. Even at a protest that started peaceably enough, when the crowd's emotions are running high in arousal, individuals tend to engage in behaviors they ordinarily would not when alone. These behaviors are often aggressive, and members of the crowd feel a low sense of personal responsibility. They also feel little risk of getting into trouble. ("They can't possibly arrest all of us. Give me a brick, I want to throw it!")

Some psychologists are interested in **altruism** and **helping behavior**. Research into these topics emerged in part as a result of the case of Kitty Genovese, a woman who was murdered outside of her apartment complex. According to media reports, between 15 and 41 neighbors saw or heard part of the attack, but many did not intervene or contact the police. Psychologists refer to this failure to act as the **bystander effect**. It occurs as a result of **diffusion of responsibility**. Simply put, each person assumes that someone else will (or should) help or call the police.

Altruism can help reduce the tendency toward the bystander effect. Altruism is selfless sacrifice, and it occurs more frequently than it might appear to. Altruism has been explained in terms of an empathic response to the plight of others. People place themselves in the positions of others in distress, and they act toward others as they would like others to act toward them.

The **false consensus** effect is when people believe their ideas and positions are more common than they actually are. **Social traps** are when people engage in behaviors that lead to negative outcomes but once the ball is rolling, it's hard to stop. Often the behaviors are motivated by short-term gain and self-interest.

Research has been conducted on the resolution of conflicts within groups. The most effective method to resolve a conflict between two groups is to have them cooperate toward a **superordinate goal**. For example, in the Robbers Cave experiment, campers who had been feuding for weeks were able to overcome their differences when they cooperated to solve problems, such as a water leak that threatened the whole camp. Another effective technique is **GRIT (Graduated and Reciprocated Initiatives in Tension-Reduction)**. This approach encourages groups to announce intent to reduce tensions and show small, conciliatory behaviors, as long as these reduced tensions and behaviors are reciprocated.

Industrial Organizational Psychology deals primarily with the workplace. I/O Psychologists evaluate companies to figure out best practices for employers and employees to manage coworker relationships, workloads, and company culture, and to try to help avoid **burnout**. The **equity theory** proposes a view whereby workers evaluate their efforts versus their rewards. Job satisfaction is often based on this concept. **Human factors research** deals with the interaction of person and machine. Many job-related accidents are caused by design flaws in equipment related to the expectancy of the worker. The **Hawthorne effect** indicates that workers being monitored for any reason work more efficiently and productively. This was demonstrated in an experiment that took place in a Western Electric plant. The study was intended to test whether levels of light increased or decreased worker productivity. The outcome, however, showed that worker productivity increased at all levels of light simply because of the presence of the monitors.

THEORIES OF PERSONALITY

Psychodynamic Theories

Sigmund Freud and those who followed his basic beliefs and practices typify **psychoanalytic** theories of personality. The term **psychodynamic** means a psychological approach based on a marriage of Freudian concepts, such as the unconscious, with more modern ideas. Freud, the first and most influential personality psychologist, believed that the mind can be divided broadly into the conscious and the unconscious. The unconscious, according to Freud, plays a major role in behavior; however, the contents of the unconscious mind are not readily accessible. People's motivations and the sources of their problems lie within the unconscious. A popular metaphor of the mind is to imagine it as an iceberg with the "conscious" brain sitting above the water and the dark recesses of the "unconscious" lying below. Although the unconscious is typically not open to scrutiny, certain events, according to Freud, allow for glimpses into the unconscious mind. When people make slips of the tongue or reveal the latent content of dreams, they provide brief looks into their unconscious minds. Freud also discovered that free association is a way to get a glimpse of the unconscious mind. In **free association**, a therapist actively listens, while the patient relaxes and reports anything that comes into his mind, no matter how absurd it might seem. The therapist then analyzes this seemingly random jumble of thoughts, looking for themes that may demonstrate some of what lies in the unconscious.

> **Stay Awake!**
> The AP Psychology exam will no longer feature any questions on the psychoanalytic theory of dreams.

Q: According to Freud, what are the three components of the mind?

Answer on page 233.

Freud was also a pioneer in the analysis of dreams, which he viewed as windows into the unconscious mind. Freud believed that the remembered parts of a dream, or the manifest content, amounted to a coded version of the real conflict, or the latent content. For example, knives and stabbing might symbolize male genitalia and intercourse, while boxes, ships, or other containers might symbolize the female uterus. Freud further described the mind as consisting of three distinct components: the id, the superego, and the ego. (Freud actually used regular German words to describe these mental structures; his English translators came up with these Latin terms. Since AP will test you on the Latin terms, we'll retain them.)

The **id** is the source of mental energy and drive. It encompasses all of the basic human needs and desires, including those for food and sex. The id operates on the **pleasure principle**, which is the desire to maximize pleasure while minimizing pain.

The **superego** is the internal representation of all of society's rules, morals, and obligations. The superego represents the polar opposite of the id.

The **ego**, according to Freud, is the part of the mind that allows a person to function in the environment and to be logical. It operates on the **reality principle**, which is that set of desires that can be satisfied only if the means to satisfy them exists and is available. The ego works as an intermediary between the id and the superego.

The ego is most involved in conscious thought and attempts to balance the interaction with the environment along with the opposing forces of the id and superego.

Freud hypothesized that the ego deals with the anxiety produced by the id-superego conflict using various defense mechanisms. Defense mechanisms often serve a useful purpose in helping the individual reduce tension and maintain a healthy outlook, even if they mean using self-deception. Repression is one of these defense mechanisms. **Repression** is the process by which memories or desires that provoke too much anxiety to deal with are pushed into the unconscious. For example, some people involved in terrible accidents have no memory of the accidents at all. The memory, according to Freudian theory, has been repressed.

Displacement is a defense mechanism that directs anger away from the source of the anger to a less threatening person or object. A boy who is angry with his father may not want to show hostility directly to his father; instead, he may yell at a friend or stuffed animal, thereby displaying his rage, but in a way that does not make his situation worse.

Reaction formation is another defense mechanism by which the ego reverses the direction of a disturbing desire to make that desire safer or more socially acceptable. For example, a person who unconsciously hates the poor might consciously experience this feeling as a strong desire to help the homeless. Or a lawmaker who is gay but closeted may speak and vote against gay rights. Other defense mechanisms include the following:

- **Compensation**—making up for failures in one area through success in others

- **Rationalization**—creating logical excuses for emotional or irrational behavior

- **Regression**—reverting to childish behaviors

- **Denial**—the refusal to acknowledge or accept unwanted beliefs or actions

- **Sublimation**—the channeling or redirecting of sexual or aggressive feelings into a more socially acceptable outlet

- **Projection**—when a person attributes feelings or beliefs to another person when they are actually the person's own feelings or beliefs

Freud's theory paved the way for a variety of psychodynamic theories, many of which were developed in direct response to Freud's own. Karen Horney, for example, pointed out the inherent male bias in Freud's work. She developed a theory of personality based on the need for security. According to Horney's theory, **basic anxiety**, or the feeling of being alone in an unfamiliar or hostile world, is a central theme in childhood. The interactions between the child and the parent, as the child deals with this anxiety, form the basis for adult personality. Children who find security in their relationships with their parents will find security in other adult relationships. Children who lack security in their relationships with their parents and their surroundings will grow up insecure and distrusting, and they are likely to end up with various unhealthy personality styles.

Carl Jung formulated another theory of personality that was, in part, a response to Freud's theory. Jung believed that the mind comprises pairs of opposing forces. For example, each person has a **persona,** the mask the person presents to the outside world, and a **shadow**, the deep, passionate, inner person (including the person's "dark side"). Jung also proposed that we each have an **anima** and an **animus**, a female and a male side to our personality. Jung believed that all of the opposing forces and desires of the mind were balanced by a force called the **Self**. Jung also divided the unconscious differently than Freud. Jung proposed that each of us has a **personal unconscious** comprised of repressed memories and clusters of thought and a **collective unconscious** of behavior and memory common to all humans and passed down from our ancient and common ancestors. **Archetypes** are the behaviors and memories in the collective unconscious. Reverence for motherhood is an example of an archetype.

> **A:** The id, the ego, and the superego

Alfred Adler, like other psychoanalytic psychologists, believed that childhood is the crucial formative period. He also thought, however, that all children develop feelings of inferiority because of their size and level of competence. He speculated that people spend the rest of their lives trying to overcome this inferiority and develop lifestyles suited to this purpose. Adler thought the best way to overcome inferiority is to develop a lifestyle of social interest; that is, one of contribution to society. Failure to make these accommodations may result in the development of an **inferiority complex**. Adler also saw personality as a product of birth order.

Tests used in psychology can be **projective tests**, in which ambiguous stimuli, open to interpretation, are presented, or **inventory-type tests**, in which participants answer a standard series of questions.

Two popular projective tests are the **Rorschach Inkblot Test** and the **Thematic Apperception Test (TAT)**. The Rorschach is a sequence of 10 inkblots, each of which the participant is asked to observe and then characterize. For example, a participant might see one inkblot as a bat or another as two people staring at each other. Sometimes, people see multiple images in a single inkblot. Different aspects of the participant's descriptions, such as form and movement of objects, are scored to yield an evaluation of the individual's personality.

Humanistic Theories

Humanistic theories of personality emphasize the uniqueness and richness of being human. These theories arose partially in response to behaviorism (see Chapter 5). As a result, they focus on subjective reality and subjective mental events. In contrast to behaviorism's attempts to reduce behavior to its smallest components, humanistic theories take a holistic view. They view people as unitary, not separable into learned reactions, and certainly not divisible into compartments such as the ego and superego. The final and most important concept in humanistic theories is the concept of self-actualization. **Self-actualization** is becoming, in a creative way, the person you are capable of being. According to humanistic theories, self-actualization is the ultimate purpose for existence.

Carl Rogers believed that the self constitutes the most important aspect of personality. Our **self-concept** is our mental representation of who we feel we truly are. Internal conflicts arise when we experience **incongruence**, or discrepancies between our self-concept and our actual thoughts and behavior, as well as feedback from our surroundings. Rogers believed that **conditions of worth**, or other people's evaluations of our worth, distort our self-concept. Parents and teachers play a critical role in child development, Rogers hypothesized, and should not impose conditions of worth on children. Instead, people should be treated with **unconditional positive regard**. This means that people, particularly children, should be loved despite failures. Saying, for example, "I love you only when you're good," creates poor self-concept.

Social-Cognitive Theories

Social-cognitive theories of personality are based on the assumption that cognitive constructs are the basis for personality. We bring constructs, such as expectations, to every social situation. These constructs are developed and modified through learning in social environments.

A representative example of a social-cognitive theory of personality was developed by Albert Bandura. Bandura focuses on the concept of self-efficacy as central to personality. **Self-efficacy** refers to a person's beliefs about their own abilities in a given situation. Basically, the belief that you can do a particular task greatly increases the chances that you actually can do it.

Trait Theories

Trait theories of personality provide quantitative systems for describing and comparing traits, or stable predispositions to behave in a certain way. A particular trait theory stipulates that certain traits are part of the person and are not typically environmentally dependent. Additionally, we each have traits in some degree or another. Trait theorists generally believe that traits are largely inherited, rather than acquired through experience. Trait theorists are divided over how to categorize traits. A relatively recent and influential theory focuses on the **Big Five** personality traits, which are the OCEAN:

- **O**penness to experience (are you open to change?)

- **C**onscientiousness (are you organized and do you pay attention to detail?)

- **E**xtraversion (are you energized by other people?)

- **A**greeableness (are you interested in and do you care about others?)

- **N**euroticism (are you anxious, stressed, or emotionally unstable?)

Two ways of researching traits are by **nomothetic** and **idiographic analysis**. Nomothetic traits such as the Big Five are thought to be universal. Idiographic traits are those that are unique to the individual, such as openness or curiosity. Gordon Allport, a trait theorist, identified three types of traits: **cardinal** (traits that override a person's whole being), **central** (the primary characteristics of the person), and **secondary** (traits that constitute interests). Raymond Cattell saw traits differently, because he believed that 16 **source traits** were the basis of personality. Source traits are the person's underlying characteristics. They give rise to clusters of **surface traits**, those readily seen in the individual. Walter Mischel recognized that traits are not necessarily consistent across various situations but often vary depending upon the circumstances.

Self-Efficacy and Success

Bandura has proposed that this theory has implications for education. Emphasizing accomplishments rather than failures should, according to self-efficacy theory, increase the likelihood of future successes.

Not So Neurotic

Though it doesn't make for as good of a mnemonic, you may see the term "emotional stability" used in place of "neuroticism" when discussing the Big Five traits.

Evaluation of the Various Personality Theories

Each of the personality theories provides some insight into the formation of personality, but each also has its flaws. The main problem with the psychoanalytic theory is that it was not developed through empirical testing, although recent psychologists have subjected Freud's theories to the scientific method. Testing supports some of his theories but not others. The humanistic theories also suffer from lack of empirical evidence in addition to what some believe is an overly optimistic outlook on life. Nevertheless, they are frequently the basis of counseling today. Cognitive theories, also popular in today's world, describe personality as a function of environmental perception and rational thought. However, critics suggest that this approach does not take into account the breadth of humanness. Trait theories face criticism that they are unable to explain the origin of personality.

A: The bystander effect asserts that the more people there are witnessing a crime, the less likely any one of them is to help the victim.

Other Theories

There are other theories of which you should be aware. Behaviorist theory, which you already know from the Foundations and Learning chapters, explains personality in much the way you would expect: personality characteristics that have proved successful are repeated, while those that have not been successful wither away. This is sometimes referenced within the Social-Cognitive Theories described above. Biological theories, noted in Chapters 5 and 7, suggest that personality is based on brain structure and chemistry (we are who we are due to balances or imbalances of neurotransmitters and/or hormones). Another explanation comes from Evolutionary Theory: our personalities are shaped by our genes and contain characteristics that enhanced our ancestors' chances of survival.

MOTIVATION

Motivation is defined as a need or desire that serves to energize or direct behavior.

Learning is motivated by biological and physiological factors. Without motivation, action and learning do not occur. **Evolutionary theory** states that animals are motivated to act by basic needs critical to the survival of the organism. For a given organism to survive, it needs food, water, and sleep. For the genes of the organism to replicate, reproductive behavior is needed to produce offspring and to foster their survival. Hunger, thirst, sleep, and reproduction needs are **primary drives**. The desire to obtain learned reinforcers, such as money or social acceptance, is a **secondary drive**.

The interaction between the brain and motivation was noticed when Olds and Milner discovered that rats would press a bar in order to send a small electrical pulse into certain areas of their brains. This phenomenon is known as intracranial self-stimulation. Further research demonstrated that if the electrode was implanted into certain parts of the limbic system, the rat would self-stimulate nearly constantly. The rats were motivated to stimulate themselves. This finding also suggests that the limbic system, particularly the nucleus accumbens, must play a pivotal role in motivated behavior, and that dopamine, which is the prominent neurotransmitter in this region, must be associated with reward-seeking behavior.

> Four primary theories attempt to explain the link between neurophysiology and motivated behavior: instinct theory, arousal theory, opponent process theory, and drive-reduction theory.

Arousal theory states that the main reason people are motivated to perform any action is to maintain an ideal level of physiological arousal. Arousal is a direct correlate of nervous system activity. A moderate arousal level seems optimal for most tasks, but keep in mind that what is optimal varies by person as well as task. The **Yerkes-Dodson law** states that tasks of moderate difficulty, neither too easy nor too hard, elicit the highest level of performance. The Yerkes-Dodson law also posits that high levels of arousal for difficult tasks and low levels of arousal for easy tasks are detrimental, while high levels of arousal for easy tasks and low levels of arousal for difficult tasks are preferred.

The **opponent process theory** is a theory of motivation that is clearly relevant to the concept of addiction. It posits that we start off at a motivational baseline, at which we are not motivated to act. Then we encounter a stimulus that feels good, such as a drug or even a positive social interaction. The pleasurable feelings we experience are the result of neuronal activity in the pleasure centers of the brain (the nucleus accumbens). We now have acquired a motivation to seek out the stimulus that made us feel good. Our brains, however, tend to revert back to a state of emotional neutrality over time. This reversion is a result of an opponent process, which works in opposition to the initial motivation toward seeking the stimulus. In other words, we are motivated to seek stimuli that make us feel emotion, after which an opposing motivational force brings us back in the direction of a baseline. After repeated exposure to a stimulus, its emotional effects begin to wear off; that is, we begin to habituate to the stimulus. The opponent process, however, does not habituate as quickly, so what used to cause a very positive response now barely produces one at all. Additionally, the opponent process overcompensates, producing withdrawal. As with drugs, we now need larger amounts of the formerly positive stimuli just to maintain a baseline state. In other words, we are addicted.

The **drive-reduction theory** of motivation posits that psychological needs put stress on the body and that we are motivated to reduce this negative experience. Another way to view motivation is using the homeostatic regulation theory. **Homeostasis** is a state of regulatory equilibrium. When the balance of that equilibrium shifts, we are motivated to try to right the balance. A key concept in the operation of homeostasis is the negative feedback loop. When we are running out of something, like fuel, a metabolic signal is generated that tells us to eat food. When our nutrient supply is replenished, a signal is issued to stop eating. The common analogy for this process is a home thermostat in a heating-cooling system. It has a target temperature, called the **set point**. The job of the thermostat is to maintain the set point.

An important intrinsic motivator is the need for **self-determination**, or the need to feel competent and in control. This need frequently conflicts with the pressures brought to bear by extrinsic motivators. The goal is to seek a balance between the fulfillment of the two categories of need.

Early theories on motivation relied on purely biological explanations of motivated behavior. Animals, especially less complex animals, are thought to be motivated by **instinct**, genetically programmed patterns of behavior. These early theories, along with arousal theory and drive-reduction theory, have given us an understanding of nature's role in motivating behavior.

Instinct theory, supported by evolutionary psychology, posits that the learning of species-specific behavior motivates organisms to do what is necessary to ensure their survival. For example, cats and other predatory animals have an instinctive motivation to react to movement in their environment to protect themselves and their offspring.

Cognitive Theories

Cognitive psychologists divide the factors that motivate behavior into **intrinsic** and **extrinsic factors**: that is, factors originating from within ourselves and factors coming from the outside world, respectively. A single type of behavior can be motivated by either intrinsic or extrinsic factors. Extrinsic motivators are often associated with the pressures of society, such as getting an education, having a job, and being sociable. Intrinsic motivators, in contrast, are associated with creativity

> **Intrinsic or Extrinsic?**
> We may read because we enjoy it. In this case, reading is a behavior motivated by an intrinsic need. However, we may read because we need to know some information that will be on a test. Here, reading is driven by extrinsic motivation.

and enjoyment. Over time, our intrinsic motivation may decrease if we receive extrinsic rewards for the same behavior. This phenomenon is called the **overjustification effect**. For example, a person may love to play the violin for fun but when he is a paid concert performer, he will play less for fun and view playing the violin as part of his job.

Related to the concept of self-determination is **self-efficacy**, or the belief that we can or cannot attain a particular goal. In general, the higher the level of self-efficacy, the more we believe that we can attain a particular goal and the more likely we are to achieve it, as well. Also closely related to this is **achievement motivation,** the need to reach realistic goals that we set for ourselves.

Although physiological needs form the basis for motivation, humans are not automatons, simply responding to biological pressures. Various theories have attempted to describe the interactions among motivation, personality, and cognition. Henry Murray believed that, although motivation is rooted in biology, individual differences and varying environments can cause motivations and needs to be expressed in many different ways. Murray proposed that human needs can be broken down into 20 specific types. For example, people have a **need for affiliation**. People with a high level of this need like to avoid conflicts, like to be members of groups, and dislike being evaluated. Closely linked to the need for affiliation are the damaging effects of social isolation and **ostracism**. Social isolation has been linked to poor health outcomes. Deliberately being excluded or shunned can have serious consequences in terms of reduced self-esteem and perhaps aggressive behavior on the part of the person being ostracized.

Social Theory

Another cognitive theory of motivation concerns the need to avoid **cognitive dissonance**. People are motivated to reduce tension produced by conflicting thoughts or choices. Generally, they will change their attitudes to fit their behavioral patterns, as long as they believe they are in control of their choices and actions.

Sometimes, motives are in conflict. **Kurt Lewin** classified **motivational conflicts** into four types. In an **approach-approach** conflict, one has to decide between two desirable options, such as having to choose between two colleges of similar characteristics. **Avoidance-avoidance** is a similar dilemma. Here, one has to choose between two unpleasant alternatives. In **approach-avoidance** conflicts, only one choice is presented, but it carries both pluses and minuses. For example, imagine that only one college has the major the student wants but that college is also prohibitively expensive. The last set of conflicts is **multiple approach-avoidance**. In this scenario, many options are available, but each has positives and negatives. Choosing one college out of many that are suitable, but not ideal, represents a multiple approach-avoidance conflict. **Sensation seeking theory** describes people who are consistently and impulsively looking for thrills and excitement. These people are often looking for adventures and/or to avoid feelings of boredom.

Hunger, Thirst, and Sex

The homeostatic regulation model provides a biological explanation for the efficacy of primary reinforcers such as hunger and sex. The brain provides a large amount of the control over feeding behavior. Specifically, the **hypothalamus** has been identified as an area controlling feeding. If body weight rises above the set point, the action of the **ventromedial hypothalamus** will send messages to the brain to eat less and to exercise more. Conversely, when body weight falls below the set point, the brain sends messages to eat more and exercise less through the **lateral hypothalamus**. This control can be demonstrated by lesion studies in animals. If the ventromedial hypothalamus (VMH) is lesioned, the animal eats constantly. The negative feedback loop that should turn off eating has been disrupted. If we damage a neighboring portion of the hypothalamus, the lateral hypothalamus (LH), then the animal stops eating, often starving to death. In more normal circumstances, **leptin** plays a role in the feedback loop between signals from the hypothalamus and those from the stomach. Leptin is released in response to a buildup of fat cells when enough energy has been consumed. This signal is then interpreted by the satiety center in the hypothalamus, working as a safety valve to decrease the feeling of hunger.

The feedback loop that controls eating can be broken by damaging the hypothalamus, but the operation of this mechanism raises the question of what is actually monitored and regulated in normal feeding behavior. Two prime candidates exist. The first candidate hypothesis is **blood glucose**. This idea forms the basis for the **glucostatic hypothesis**. Glucose is the primary fuel of the brain and most other organs. When **insulin** (a hormone produced by the pancreas to regulate glucose) rises, glucose decreases. To restore glucostatic balance, a person needs to eat something. If cellular fuel gets low, then it needs to be replenished. The glucostatic theory of energy regulation gains support from the finding that the hypothalamus has cells that detect glucose.

The glucostatic theory is not without flaws, however. Blood glucose levels are very transient, rising and falling quite dramatically for a variety of reasons. How could it be, then, that such a variable measure could control body weight, which remains relatively stable from early adulthood onward? Another phenomenon inconsistent with a glucostatic hypothesis is diabetes, a disorder of insulin production. Diabetics have greatly elevated blood glucose, but they are no less hungry than everyone else.

A second candidate hypothesis is called the **lipostatic hypothesis**. As you might have guessed, this theory states that fat is the measured and controlled substance in the body that regulates hunger. Fat provides the long-term energy store for our bodies. The fat stores in our bodies are fairly fixed, and any significant decrease in fat is a result of starvation. The lipostatic hypothesis gained support from the discovery of leptin, which is a hormone secreted by fat cells. Leptin may be the substance used by the brain to monitor the amount of fat in the body.

There are several disorders related to eating habits, body weight, and body image that have their roots in psychological causes. **Anorexia nervosa**, which is more prevalent in females, is an eating disorder characterized by an intense fear of gaining weight or becoming fat despite

The Great Motivator: Thirst

Another great motivator of action in humans and animals is thirst. A human can live for weeks without food, but only for a few days without water. Water leaves the body constantly through sweat, urine, and exhalation. This water needs to be replaced, and the body regulates our patterns of intake so that water is consumed before we are severely water depleted. The lateral hypothalamus is implicated in drinking. Lesions of this area greatly reduce drinking behavior. Another part of the hypothalamus, the preoptic area, is also involved. Lesions of the preoptic area result in excessive drinking.

The Long and the Short of It

In reality, both glucose and body fat are probably monitored, with glucostatic homeostasis responsible for the starting and stopping of individual meals and lipostatic homeostasis responsible for larger long-term patterns of eating behavior.

having a significantly low body weight for one's age, sex, developmental trajectory, and physical health. **Body dysmorphia**, or a distorted body image, is key to understanding this disorder. Another related eating disorder is **bulimia nervosa,** which is characterized by alternating periods of binging and purging. If there is no purging or over-exercising, it is likely to be a **binge-eating disorder**.

As mentioned earlier, biological drives are those that ensure the survival not only of the individual, but also the survival of the individual's genes. Like the motivations to eat and drink, the motivation to reproduce relies on the hypothalamus, which stimulates the **pituitary gland** and ultimately the production of androgens and estrogens. **Androgens** and **estrogens** are the primary sexual hormones in males and females, respectively. Without these hormones, sexual desire is eliminated in animals and is greatly reduced in humans.

THEORIES OF EMOTION

Emotions are experiential and subjective responses to certain internal and external stimuli. These experiential responses have both physical and behavioral components. Various theories have arisen to explain emotion.

Emotion consists of three components: a physiological (body) component, a behavioral (action) component, and a cognitive (mind) component. The physical aspect of emotion is one of physiological arousal, or an excitation of the body's internal state. For example, when being startled at a surprise party, you may feel your heart pounding, your breathing becoming shallow and rapid, and your palms becoming sweaty. These are the sensations that accompany emotion (in this instance, surprise). The behavioral aspect of emotion includes some kind of expressive behavior: for example, spontaneously screaming and bringing your hands over your mouth. The cognitive aspect of emotion involves an appraisal or interpretation of the situation. Upon first being startled, the thought "dangerous situation" or "fear" may arise, only to be reassessed as "surprise" and "excitement" after recognizing the circumstances as a surprise party. This describes how the situation is interpreted or labeled. Interestingly, many emotions share the same or very similar physiological and behavioral responses; it is the mind that interprets one situation that evokes a quickened heart rate and tears as "joyful" and another with the same responses as "fearful."

One class of theories relies on physiological explanations of emotion. The **James-Lange theory** posits that environmental stimuli cause physiological changes and responses. The experience of emotion, according to this theory, is a result of a physiological change. In other words, if an argument makes you angry, it is the physiological response (increased heart rate, increased respiratory rate) that prompts the experience of emotion.

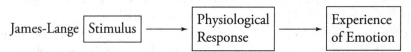

There are many reasons why we now know that this theory is incorrect. We know that a given state of physiological arousal is common to many emotions. For example, people might feel tenseness in their bodies as a result of being nervous, scared, or even excited. How, then, is it possible that the identical physiological state could lead to the rich variety of emotions that we experience? Another common experience that conflicts with the logic of the James-Lange theory is cutting onions. The physiological response to cutting onions is watering eyes; however, this physiological response does not make us sad.

The **Cannon-Bard theory** arose as a response to the James-Lange theory. The Cannon-Bard theory asserts that the physiological response to an emotion and the experience of emotion occur simultaneously in response to an emotion-provoking stimulus. For example, the sight of a tarantula, which acts as an emotion-provoking stimulus, would stimulate the thalamus. The thalamus would send simultaneous messages to both the autonomic nervous system and the cerebral cortex. Messages to the cortex produce the experience of emotion (fear), and messages to the autonomic nervous system produce physiological arousal (running, heart palpitations).

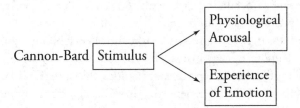

The **two-factor theory,** proposed by Schachter and Singer, adds a cognitive twist to the Cannon-Bard theory. The first factor is physiological arousal; the second factor is the way in which we cognitively label the experience of arousal. Central to this theory is the understanding that many emotional responses involve very similar physiological properties. The emotion that we experience, according to this theory, is the result of the label that we apply. For example, if we cry at a wedding, we interpret our emotion as happiness, but if we cry at a funeral, we interpret our emotion as sadness.

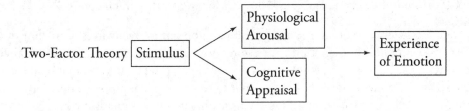

Study Tip

The three theories of emotion are often tested, so make sure that you understand them. When can your physiological arousal directly drive an emotional state? (James-Lange) When do the arousal and the emotion occur simultaneously? (Cannon-Bard) When do you experience arousal, but need to think about what brought it on in order to identify an emotion? (two-factor; Schachter and Singer)

According to more recent studies by Zajonc, Le Doux, and Armony, some emotions are felt before being cognitively appraised. A scary sight travels through the eye to the thalamus, where it is then relayed to the amygdala before being labeled and evaluated by the cortex. According to these studies, the amygdala's position relative to the thalamus may account for the quick emotional response. There are several parts of the brain implicated in emotional processing. The main area of the brain responsible for emotions is the limbic system, which includes the amygdala. The amygdala is most active when processing negative emotions, particularly fear.

Processing Emotions

Different sides of the brain also seem to be responsible for different emotional states. That is, the right brain is dominant in processing negative emotions, while the left brain seems to be more involved in processing positive emotions.

Although theorists have disagreed over time about how emotions are processed, there has been a great deal of agreement about the universality of certain emotions. Darwin assumed that emotions had a strong biological basis. If this is true, then emotions should be experienced and expressed in similar ways across cultures, and in fact, this has been found to be the case. A scientist and pioneer in the study of emotions, Paul Ekman, observed facial expressions from a variety of cultures and pointed out that, regardless of where two people were from, their expressions of certain emotions were almost identical. In particular, Ekman identified six **universal emotions** that appeared across cultures: anger, fear, disgust, surprise, happiness, and sadness. These findings suggest that emotions and how they are expressed are innate parts of the human experience. While research has identified these emotions as occurring cross-culturally, the **display rules** for emotions, or how a person expresses emotion, vary from culture to culture. For example, in some cultures, sadness may be expressed by uncontrolled sobbing, while in others, crying may be strictly frowned upon, opting instead for a more stoic display of sadness. Darwin's ideas also led to the **facial feedback hypothesis,** the idea that a person's facial expression can influence the actual emotion being experienced. These observations about facial expressions can also apply to other examples of body language.

The evolutionary basis for emotion is thought to be related to its adaptive roles. It enhances survival by serving as a useful guide for quick decisions. A feeling of fear one experiences when walking alone down a dark alley while a shadowy figure approaches can be a valuable tool to indicate that the situation may be dangerous. A feeling of anger may enhance survival by encouraging one to fight back against an intruder. Other emotions may have a role in influencing individual behaviors within a social context. For example, embarrassment may encourage social conformity. Additionally, in social contexts, emotions provide a means for nonverbal communication and empathy, allowing for cooperative interactions.

On a more subtle level, emotions are a large influence on our everyday lives. Our choices often require consideration of our emotions. A person with a brain injury to their prefrontal cortex (which plays a role in processing emotion) has trouble imagining their own emotional responses to the possible outcomes of decisions. This can lead to making inappropriate decisions that can cost someone a job, a marriage, or a life's savings. Imagine how difficult it could be to refrain from risky behaviors, such as gambling or spending huge sums of money, without the ability to imagine your emotional response to the possible outcomes.

The **broaden-and-build theory** of emotions comes from positive psychology and suggests that the more positive experiences a person has broadens their experiences of positive emotions and encourages more. Negative emotions do the opposite.

THE ROLE OF THE LIMBIC SYSTEM IN EMOTION

As mentioned in Chapter 7, the limbic system is a collection of brain structures that lie on both sides of the thalamus; together, these structures appear to be primarily responsible for emotional experiences. The main structure involved in emotion in the limbic system is the amygdala, an almond-shaped structure deep within the brain. The amygdala serves as the conductor of the orchestra of our emotional experiences. It can communicate with the hypothalamus, the brain structure that controls the physiological aspects of emotion (largely through its modulating of the endocrine system), such as sweating and a racing heart. It also communicates with the prefrontal cortex, located at the front of the brain, which controls approach and avoidance behaviors—the behavioral aspects of emotion. The amygdala plays an especially key role in the identification and expression of fear and aggression.

Emotion, Memory, Decision-Making, and the Autonomic Nervous System

Emotional experiences can be stored as memories that can be recalled by similar circumstances. The limbic system also includes the hippocampus, a brain structure that plays a key role in forming memories.

When memories are formed, the emotions associated with these memories are often also encoded. Take a second to close your eyes and imagine someone whom you love very much. Notice the emotional state that arises with your memory of that person. Recalling an event can bring about the emotions associated with it. Note that this isn't always a pleasant experience. It has an important role in the suffering of patients who have experienced traumatic events. Similar circumstances to a traumatic event can lead to recall of the memory of the experience, referred to as a **flashback.** Sometimes this recall isn't even conscious; for example, for someone involved in a traumatic car accident, driving past the intersection where the incident occurred might cause an increase in muscle tension, heart rate, and respiratory rate.

The **prefrontal cortex** is critical for emotional experience, and it is also important in temperament and decision-making. It is associated with a reduction in emotional feelings, especially fear and anxiety, and is often activated by methods of emotion regulation and stress relief. The prefrontal cortex is like a soft voice, calming down the amygdala when it is overly aroused. The prefrontal cortex also plays a role in executive functions—higher-order thinking processes such as planning, organizing, inhibiting behavior, and decision-making. Damage to this area may lead to inappropriateness, impulsivity, and trouble with initiation. This area is not fully developed in humans until they reach their mid-twenties, explaining the sometimes erratic and emotionally charged behavior of teenagers. The most famous case of damage to the prefrontal cortex occurred to a man in the 1800s named Phineas Gage. Gage was a railroad worker who, at age 25, suffered an accident in which a railroad tie blasted through his head, entering under his cheekbone and exiting through the top of his skull. After the accident, Gage was described as "no longer himself," prone to impulsivity, unable to stick to plans, and unable to demonstrate empathy. The accident severely damaged his prefrontal cortex, and while the reports about the change to his personality and behavior have been debated, this case led to the discovery of the role of the prefrontal cortex in personality.

The **autonomic nervous system** is responsible for controlling the activities of most of the organs and glands, and it controls arousal. As mentioned earlier, it answers primarily to the hypothalamus. The **sympathetic nervous system** provides the body with brief, intense, vigorous responses. It is often referred to as the **fight-or-flight response** because it prepares an individual for action. It increases heart rate, blood pressure, and blood sugar levels in preparation for action. It also directs the adrenal glands to release the stress hormones epinephrine and norepinephrine. The **parasympathetic nervous system** provides signals to the internal organs during a calm resting state when no crisis is present. When activated, it leads to changes that allow for recovery and the conservation of energy, including an increase in digestion and the repair of body tissues.

Many physiological states associated with emotion have been discussed. These include heart rate, blood pressure, respiratory rate, sweating, and the release of stress hormones. In order to measure autonomic function, clinicians can measure heart rate, finger temperature, skin conductance (sweating), and muscle activity. Keep in mind that different patterns tend to exist during different emotional states, but states such as fear and sexual arousal may display very similar patterns.

KEY TERMS

Attribution
dispositional attribution
situational attribution
explanatory style
self-serving bias
fundamental attribution error
actor-observer bias
locus of control

Person Perception
interpersonal attraction
positive evaluation
shared opinions
mere exposure effect
self-fulfilling prophecy
Rosenthal Effect
social comparison theory

Identities and Groups
societies
culture
social identities
personal identities
primary group
secondary group
in-group
out-group
reference group
stereotypes
prejudice
discrimination
implicit bias
outgroup homogeneity bias
ingroup bias
just-world phenomenon
belief perseverance
cognitive dissonance
social norms
social influence theory
  normative
  informational

Psychology of Social Situations
persuasion
elaboration likelihood model
central route
peripheral route
conformity
obedience

collectivist culture
individualist culture
groupthink
mindguard

Group Dynamics
social facilitation
social inhabition
social loafing
group polarization
peer pressure
deindividuation
peer pressure
altruism
helping behavior
bystander effect
diffusion of responsibility
false consensus
social traps
superordinate goal
Graduated and Reciprocated Initiatives in
  Tension-Reduction (GRIT)
burnout
equity theory
human factors research
Hawthorne effect

Psychodynamic Theories
psychoanalytic
psychodynamic
free association
id
pleasure principle
superego
ego
reality principle
repression
displacement
reaction formation
compensation
rationalization
regression
denial
sublimation
projection
basic anxiety
persona
shadow

anima
animus
Self
personal unconscious
collective unconscious
archetypes
inferiority complex
projective tests
inventory-type tests
Rorschach Inkblot Test
Thematic Apperception Test (TAT)

Humanistic Theories
self-actualization
self-concept
incongruence
conditions of worth
unconditional positive regard

Social-Cognitive Theories
self-efficacy

Trait Theories
Big Five
  openness
  conscientiousness
  extraversion
  agreeableness
  neuroticism (emotional stability)
nomothetic analysis
idiographic analysis
  cardinal traits
  central traits
  secondary traits
source traits
surface traits

Motivation
evolutionary theory
primary drives
secondary drive
arousal theory
Yerkes-Dodson law
opponent process theory
drive-reduction theory
homeostasis
set point
self-determination
instinct
instinct theory
intrinsic factors

extrinsic factors
overjustification effect
self-efficacy
achievement motivation
need for affiliation
ostracism

Social Theory
cognitive dissonance
motivational conflicts
  approach-approach
  avoidance-avoidance
  approach-avoidance
  multiple approach-avoidance
sensation seeking theory

Hunger, Thirst, and Sex
hypothalamus
ventromedial hypothalamus
lateral hypothalamus
blood glucose
glucostatic hypothesis
insulin
lipostatic hypothesis
anorexia nervosa
body dysmorphia
bulimia nervosa
binge-eating disorder
pituitary gland
androgens
estrogens

Theories of Emotion
James-Lange theory
Cannon-Bard theory
two-factory theory
universal emotions
display rules
facial feedback hypothesis
broaden-and-build

The Role of the Limbic System in Emotion
flashback
prefrontal cortex
autonomic nervous system
sympathetic nervous system
fight-or-flight response
parasympathetic nervous system

Unit 4 Drill

See Chapter 12 for answers and explanations.

1. An example of a secondary drive is

   (A) the satisfying of a basic need critical to one's survival
   (B) an attempt to get food to maintain homeostatic equilibrium related to hunger
   (C) an attempt to act only on instinct
   (D) an effort to obtain something that has been shown to have reinforcing properties
   (E) an effort to continue an optimal state of arousal

2. An example of the Yerkes-Dodson law is

   (A) the need to remain calm and relaxed while taking the SAT while letting adrenaline give a little boost
   (B) performing at the highest level of arousal in order to obtain a primary reinforcer
   (C) a task designed to restore the body to homeostasis
   (D) the need to remain calm and peaceful while addressing envelopes for a charity event
   (E) working at maximum arousal on a challenging project

3. Rhoni is a driven woman who feels the need to constantly excel in her career in order to help maintain the lifestyle her family has become accustomed to and in order to be seen as successful in her parents' eyes. The factors that motivate Rhoni's career behavior can be described as primarily

   (A) intrinsic
   (B) extrinsic
   (C) hierarchical
   (D) self-determined
   (E) instinctual

4. Sanju is hungry and buys a donut at the nearby donut shop. According to drive-reduction theory, she

   (A) has returned her body to homeostasis
   (B) will need to eat something else, since a donut is rich in nutrients
   (C) will continue to feel hungry
   (D) will have created another imbalance and feel thirsty
   (E) has raised her glucose levels to an unhealthy level

5. The hypothalamus does which of the following?

   (A) Serves as a relay center
   (B) Regulates homeostasis
   (C) Aids in encoding memory
   (D) Regulates most hormones to be secreted
   (E) Regulates fear and aggression

6. According to Freudian theory, which part of the mind operates according to the reality principle?

   (A) The superego
   (B) The ego
   (C) The id
   (D) The archetype
   (E) The shadow

7. The defense mechanism reaction formation is defined as

   (A) directing angry feelings away from the source of the anger to a less threatening object
   (B) reverting to behaviors more characteristic of childhood
   (C) attempting to make up for failures in certain areas by overcompensating efforts in other areas
   (D) creating excuses for irrational feelings or behaviors that sound logical
   (E) reversing the direction of a disturbing feeling or desire to make it safer or more socially acceptable

8. All of the following personality theorists can be considered psychodynamic in approach EXCEPT

   (A) Karen Horney
   (B) Carl Jung
   (C) Alfred Adler
   (D) Albert Bandura
   (E) Erik Erikson

9. According to Maslow and Rogers, the process by which human beings attain their full creativity and potential is termed

   (A) self-esteem
   (B) self-amplification
   (C) self-efficacy
   (D) self-actualization
   (E) self-reflection

10. Anne is terrible at riding a bike, but she knows that she has the ability to get better if she practices more often. This is an example of

    (A) high self-efficacy and an external locus of control
    (B) low self-efficacy and an internal locus of control
    (C) high self-efficacy and an internal locus of control
    (D) low self-efficacy and an external locus of control
    (E) low self-efficacy and learned helplessness

11. Lukas is a handsome guy who gets great grades and is the star of the football team. Ian assumes he is trustworthy, as well. This is most likely an example of

    (A) gender bias
    (B) an archetype
    (C) an inferiority complex
    (D) self-actualization
    (E) the halo effect

12. Tanya is a competitive figure skater trying to land her quadruple salchow. She gets frustrated with her coach and herself for not landing it and kicks the ice. This is an example of

    (A) displacement
    (B) sublimation
    (C) denial
    (D) regression
    (E) compensation

13. Carl Jung's theory of the anima and animus posits that

    (A) the self is a collection of archetypes from the collective unconscious
    (B) a person must first learn to trust their caregiver as an infant to thrive
    (C) there is both a male and female side to each personality
    (D) a positive self-worth comes from a balanced Self
    (E) individuals should not overcompensate for their weaknesses, but rather embrace them

14. Cara feels good about herself because she is going to become a doctor. This is an example of

    (A) self-efficacy
    (B) self-esteem
    (C) self-concept
    (D) rationalization
    (E) reaction formation

15. The "fundamental attribution error" phenomenon can best be seen in which of the following examples?

   (A) John blames his failure to get a job on his lack of appropriate skills and ill-preparedness.
   (B) Phyllis doesn't get the lead in the school play and blames her drama teacher for this failure.
   (C) Jane blames herself for forgetting that she has a term paper due in two days.
   (D) Bill doesn't hire John because he believes that John's lateness is a result of John's laziness and lack of respect for the job. In reality, John was late because he got a flat tire on the way to the interview.
   (E) Karen understands that her friend is late because she was caught in rush-hour traffic.

16. In the Asch conformity experiments, which of these was NOT a consistent factor influencing the degree to which conformity to the group answer would be shown by the experimental subject?

   (A) Unanimity of group opinion
   (B) Size of the group
   (C) The subjects' perceptions of their social status compared with that of group members
   (D) Age of the subject
   (E) Gender of the subject

17. Students are randomly designated by experimenters as likely to experience significant jumps in academic test scores in the coming semester, and this designation is communicated to their teachers. When actual test scores are examined at the end of the semester, it is found that these randomly designated students did indeed tend to experience jumps in performance. This phenomenon is known as

   (A) the Hawthorne effect
   (B) the Kandel effect
   (C) cognitive dissonance
   (D) self-fulfilling prophecy
   (E) the Ainsworth effect

18. An old woman carrying a number of packages trips and falls on a busy urban sidewalk and is having trouble getting back up. The fact that few people are likely to stop and offer her help is referred to by social psychologists as an example of

   (A) illusory correlation
   (B) diffusion of responsibility
   (C) cognitive dissonance
   (D) altruistic orientation
   (E) just-world hypothesis

19. Which of the following would illustrate the "foot-in-the-door" technique of facilitating compliance with a request?

   (A) A professional fundraiser, needing to get $10,000 from a foundation, first requests four times that amount, expecting to be turned down so that she can then ask for the lesser amount.
   (B) A teenager, wanting to extend his curfew from 10:00 P.M. to midnight, first asks whether it can be extended to 11:00 P.M. for a specific "special" occasion; he plans to ask for the further extension at a later date after pointing out to his parents that he was able to handle the 11:00 P.M. curfew.
   (C) A mother wishing to get her twins to do their homework each day upon coming home from school and before other activities tells each of them separately that the other twin has agreed to do just that.
   (D) An interviewee desperately needing to get a new job researches the mode of dress in each company he lands an interview with and always shows up at the meeting in that exact mode of dress.
   (E) A teacher wishing all her students to get their assignments in on time promises her class extra grading points for turning them in early.

20. According to Attribution Theory, which of the following is an example of the self-serving bias?

    (A) A man does not have health insurance, but is not worried because he is young and healthy.
    (B) A woman knows a man who does not have insurance. That man gets into a car accident, and medical expenses cause him to lose his home. She wonders why he didn't have insurance.
    (C) A toddler builds a tall tower with blocks and says "Me good!" when she completes the tower. However, she bumps it and it falls down. She frowns and says, "Bad blocks!"
    (D) Yuan's teacher believes he is well prepared for his history exam and offers encouragement to him as he approaches the final. Yuan continues to study hard for the exam and gets an A on the final.
    (E) A hurricane devastates an area of Mississippi and many residents seek grief counseling.

21. A group of five students and a group of three students, all roughly the same size and strength, engage in a game of tug of war. The game is equal for a long while, neither side immediately gaining an advantage. This is most likely an example of

    (A) social loafing
    (B) dehumanization
    (C) conformity
    (D) group polarization
    (E) social facilitation

22. A child tries to get a raise on his weekly allowance. When he first approaches his parents, he asks for $100 per week. His parents scoff and tell him this is out of the question. Then, he asks for $50 per week, and receives the same reply. Finally, he asks for $10 per week and his parents agree. This is an example of

    (A) foot-in-the-door phenomenon
    (B) central route of persuasion
    (C) peripheral route of persuasion
    (D) door-in-the-face phenomenon
    (E) elaboration likelihood model

23. Stanley Milgram's study involving the "teacher," "learner," and "experimenter" tested which of the following principles?

    (A) Conformity
    (B) Dehumanization
    (C) Groupthink
    (D) Role-playing
    (E) Obedience

REFLECT

Respond to the following questions:

- Which topics in this chapter do you hope to see on the multiple-choice section or essay?

- Which topics in this chapter do you hope not to see on the multiple-choice section or essay?

- Regarding any psychologists mentioned, can you pair the psychologists with their contributions to the field? Did they contribute significant experiments, theories, or both?

- Regarding any theories mentioned, can you distinguish between differing theories well enough to recognize them on the multiple-choice section? Can you distinguish them well enough to write a fluent essay on them?

- Regarding any figures given, if you were given a labeled figure from within this chapter, would you be able to give the significance of each part of the figure?

- Can you define the key terms at the end of the chapter?

- Which parts of the chapter will you review?

- Will you seek further help, outside of this book (such as from a teacher, Princeton Review tutor, or AP Students), on any of the content in this chapter—and, if so, on what content?

Chapter 11
Unit 5:
Mental and
Physical Health

Health psychology is the branch of psychology that looks at how physical health can impact behaviors, thoughts, and feelings.

STRESS

A concept related to emotion is the feeling of stress. **Stress** causes a person to feel challenged or endangered. Although this definition may make you think of experiences such as being attacked, in reality, most **stressors** (events that cause stress) are everyday events or situations that challenge us in more subtle ways. Stressors can be significant life-changing events, such as the death of a loved one, a divorce, a wedding, or the birth of a child. There are also many smaller, more manageable stressors, such as holidays, traffic jams, and other nuisances. Although these situations are varied, they share a common factor: they are all challenging for the person experiencing them.

As you may have inferred, the same situation may have different value as a stressor for different people. The perception of a stimulus as stressful may be more consequential than the actual nature of the stimulus itself. For example, some people find putting together children's toys or electronic items quite stressful, yet other people find relaxation in similar tasks, such as building models.

What is most important for determining the stressful nature of an event is its appraisal, or how the individual interprets it. When stressors are appraised as being challenges, as one may perceive the AP Psychology Exam, they can actually be motivating. On the other hand, when they are perceived as threatening aspects of our identity, well-being, or safety, they may cause severe stress. Additionally, events that are considered negative and uncontrollable produce a greater stress response than those that are perceived as negative but controllable.

Some stressors are **transient**, meaning that they are temporary challenges. Others, such as those that lead to job-related stress, are **chronic** and can have a negative impact on one's health. The physiological response to stress is related to the fight-or-flight response, a concept developed by Walter Cannon and enhanced by Hans Selye into the **general adaptation syndrome**. The three stages of this response to prolonged stress are alarm, resistance, and exhaustion. **Alarm** refers to the arousal of the sympathetic nervous system, resulting in the release of various stimulatory hormones, including **corticosterone,** which is used as a physiological index of stress. In the alarm phase, the body is energized for immediate action, which is adaptive for transient, but not chronic, stressors. **Resistance** is the result of parasympathetic rebound. The body cannot be aroused forever, and the parasympathetic system starts to reduce the arousal state. If the stressor does not relent, however, the body does not reduce its arousal state to baseline. If the stressor persists for long periods of time, the stress response continues into the **exhaustion** phase. In this phase, the body's resources are exhausted, and tissue cannot be repaired. The immune system becomes impaired in its functioning, which is why we are more susceptible to illness during prolonged stress.

Richard Lazarus developed a cognitive theory of how we respond to stress. In this approach, the individual evaluates whether the event appears to be stressful. This is called primary appraisal. If the event is seen to be a threat, a secondary appraisal takes place, assessing whether the individual can handle the stress. Stress is minimized or maximized by the individual's ability to respond to the stressor.

Research into stress has revealed that people generally show one of two different types of behavior patterns based on their responses to stress. The **Type-A pattern** of behavior is typified by competitiveness, a sense of time urgency, and elevated feelings of anger and hostility. The **Type-B pattern** of behavior is characterized by a low level of competitiveness, low preoccupation with time issues, and a generally easygoing attitude. People with Type-A patterns of behavior respond to stress quickly and aggressively. Type-A people also act in ways that tend to increase the likelihood that they will have stressful experiences. They seek jobs or tasks that put great demands on them. People with a Type-B pattern of behavior get stressed more slowly, and their stress levels do not seem to reach those heights seen in people with the Type-A pattern of behavior. There is some evidence that people with Type-A behavior patterns are more susceptible to stress-related diseases, including heart attacks, but may survive them more frequently than Type-Bs.

The **tend and befriend theory** of stress posits that when faced with a threat, humans and other beings will both tend to their children and rely on others for support. This contradicted the belief that the first response would be aggression. Researchers have found that this tend and befriend response is more prevalent in females than males. Other ways to deal with stress include problem-focused coping and emotion-focused coping. **Problem-focused coping**, as the name suggests, emphasizes working with the problem itself to find a solution and thus reduce stress. **Emotion-focused coping** emphasizes working with the feelings around the problem rather than the problem itself. Emotion-focused coping strategies may include medication to address stressful responses in the body, deep breathing, and meditation.

Meditation refers to a variety of techniques, many of which have been practiced for thousands of years, and which usually involve learning to train one's attention. Meditators may focus intensely on a single thing, such as their breathing, or they may broaden their attention and be aware of multiple stimuli, such as anything in their auditory field. Meditation has been utilized successfully to manage pain, stress, and anxiety disorders. Mindfulness-based stress reduction (MBSR) is a protocol commonly used in the medical setting to help alleviate stress; it incorporates meditation along with several other techniques. Meditators have increased alpha and theta waves while they are meditating (and to some extent sustain these increases above their baseline after stopping), with more experienced meditators showing greater improvements.

POSITIVE PSYCHOLOGY

Positive psychology is a more recent branch of psychology that focuses on the strengths a person or community possesses that enable them to thrive. The field was established by Martin Seligman, who is also known for his work on learned helplessness, and builds on some of the themes of humanistic psychology about helping people to reach their optimal potential. The field focuses on cultivating positive emotions and resilience. Research has shown, for example, that **gratitude** practices can increase a person's subjective well-being. Ryan Niemec has researched people's **signature strengths**, which are classified into six categories: wisdom, courage, humanity, justice, temperance, and transcendence. The idea is that cultivating one's signature strengths can also increase subjective well-being. The field of **post-traumatic growth** studies how people who have experienced trauma actually find ways to grow and develop through the suffering.

The *DSM-5-TR* is a text revision to the *DSM-5* that was published in 2022 with several new diagnoses and language that is more culturally sensitive. A full list of the disorders that were updated, including information on the newly added Prolonged Grief Disorder, can be found on the American Psychiatric Association's site (www.psychiatry.org/psychiatrists/practice/dsm/educational-resources/dsm-5-tr-fact-sheets). Note that the AP test-makers have not yet officially adapted the *DSM-5-TR* into the course so, for now, just knowing the *DSM-5* diagnoses is okay.

PSYCHOLOGICAL DISORDERS

When is behavior disordered? The definition of **disordered behavior** has four components. First, disordered behavior is unusual—it deviates statistically from typical behavior. Second, disordered behavior is maladaptive: that is, it interferes with a person's ability to function in a particular situation. Third, disordered behavior is labeled as abnormal by the society in which it occurs. Finally, disordered behavior is characterized by perceptual or cognitive dysfunction. In order for behavior to be disordered, it should meet all of these criteria. Behavior must be compared with the behavior of the society in which it occurs. So, for example, self-mutilation in this country is behavior that stands apart from what society considers normal. In other parts of the world, however, scarring is an important part of certain rituals.

Diagnosis of Psychopathology

The *Diagnostic and Statistical Manual of Mental Disorders (DSM-5)* is the American Psychiatric Association's handbook for the identification and classification of behavioral disorders. The *DSM-5* calls for the separate notation of important social factors and physical disabilities, in addition to the diagnosis of mental disorders. There are overarching categories in which specific disorders are classified. The **International Classification of Mental Disorders** (ICD) was developed by the World Health Organization to classify mental disorders and used throughout the world.

Theories of Psychopathology

Different schools of psychology have attempted to understand the causes of disordered behavior in different ways. Most psychologists integrate a variety of these perspectives into their practice based on what the individual patient or client needs. Sigmund Freud engaged in careful observation and analysis of people with varying degrees of behavioral abnormalities. Freud and the **psychoanalytic school** hypothesized that the interactions among conscious and especially unconscious parts of the mind were responsible for a great deal of disordered behavior. The power of unconscious motives drives behavior. To protect the ego, painful or threatening impulses are repressed into the unconscious. This repression stems from issues that arose during childhood. Generally speaking, if intrapsychic conflicts are not resolved, they may lead us to act abnormally. Much of Freud's writing described his analyses of maladaptive behavior.

The **humanistic school** of psychology suggests that disordered behavior is, in part, a result of people lacking social support or not being able to reach their highest potential. This tendency is related to people being unable to accept their own nature and having low self-esteem. This lack of acceptance may result, according to the humanistic view, from a lack of unconditional positive regard received as a child.

The **cognitive perspective** views disordered behavior as the result of faulty or illogical thoughts. Distortions in the cognitive process, according to this point of view, lead to misperceptions and misinterpretations of the world, which in turn lead to disordered behavior. The cognitive approach to treatment involves changing the contents of thought or changing the ways in which those contents are processed.

The **behavioral approach** to disordered behavior is based on the notion that all behavior, including disordered behavior, is learned. Disordered behavior has, at some point, been rewarded or reinforced, and has now been established as a pattern of behavior. Treatment involves the unlearning of the maladaptive behavior, or the modification of the learned responses to certain stimuli.

The **biological view** of disordered behavior, which is a popular one in the United States at the present time, views disordered behavior as a manifestation of abnormal brain function, due to either structural or chemical abnormalities in the brain. This point of view supports medication as providing appropriate treatment for various types of disordered behavior. The biological perspective also examines the role of genetics in psychological disorders.

The **sociocultural approach** holds that society and culture help define what is acceptable behavior.

The **biopsychosocial perspective** examines the interplay between biological, psychological, and sociocultural factors that impact psychological disorders. The **diathesis-stress model** examines psychological disorders from the perspective of the interplay between a diathesis, or underlying vulnerability, such as a genetic predisposition, with an external stressor that triggers that vulnerability to manifest.

There are commonalities among theories on psychopathology, though. Psychologists of all perspectives realize that disorders have multiple causes. One part of explaining a disorder is to look at the predisposing causes, which are the environmental or genetic influences that exist before the disorder begins and make people vulnerable to the disorder. The next factors to consider are the precipitating causes, which are the triggering events that bring about the disorder. Lastly, psychologists consider the maintaining causes, which are the factors that make the disorder more likely to continue.

Causes of Disorder	
Psychoanalytic	Negative early childhood experiences or a conflict between the superego and id
Humanistic	Low self-esteem or negative self-regard
Cognitive	Maladaptive thought processes
Behavioral	Reinforcement of depressive behavior
Biological	Neurons or neurotransmitters
Sociocultural	Cultural and environmental influences

CATEGORIES OF PSYCHOLOGICAL DISORDERS

Neurodevelopmental Disorders

The term *neurodevelopmental* refers to the developing brain. Related disorders manifest early in development, and may be due to genetic issues, trauma in the womb, or brain damage acquired at birth or in the first years of life. These disorders can range from very specific learning deficits to very global impairments to social skills or intelligence.

Autism spectrum disorder is a neurodevelopmental disorder that often manifests early on in childhood development. This may manifest itself in social communication deficits, both verbal and nonverbal, in which the individual has difficulty noticing social cues and has difficulty engaging others. ASD can also manifest itself in the form of restrictive or repetitive behaviors, difficulty coping with change, or difficulty with accepting change in activity. The spectrum varies widely from person to person, ranging from mild to severe. The term *Asperger's disorder* is no longer used.

Attention-deficit hyperactivity disorder (ADHD) is described as patterned inattention and/or hyperactivity-impulsivity. While everyone experiences spurts of inattention or impulsivity, ADHD interferes with an individual's ability to function at home, at work, at school, during activities, etc. It may sometimes interfere with friendships and relationships, and at least some symptoms must have been present before the age of 12 for diagnosis.

Other neurodevelopmental disorders include **communication disorders** such as language disorder, speech sound disorder, and fluency disorder (stuttering); **motor disorders** such as developmental coordination disorder, stereotypic movement disorder, and tics; and **specific learning disorders**.

Brain Changes

While less likely to be tested, cognitive symptoms represent the degenerative nature of this disease. There are structural and functional changes in the brain of a patient with schizophrenia that affect cognition, memory, attention, and inhibition. Symptoms may include disorganized thinking, inattention, and trouble with decision making. These are known as cognitive symptoms of schizophrenia. The structural changes include an enlargement of the ventricles in the brain and the functional changes are detected on PET or fMRI as low frontal-lobe activity.

Schizophrenia Spectrum And Other Psychotic Disorders

Although the term **schizophrenia** literally means "split brain," these disorders have nothing to do with what used to be called Multiple Personality Disorder. Rather, these disorders are marked by disturbances in thought, perception, and speech, as well as motor behavior and emotional experience.

It is important to distinguish between delusions and hallucinations. **Delusions** are beliefs that are not based in reality, such as believing that one can fly, that one is the president of a country, or that one is being pursued by the CIA (assuming that these things are not true). **Hallucinations** are perceptions that are not based in reality, such as seeing things or hearing voices that are not there, or feeling spiders on one's skin (assuming they are not really there).

Disorganized thinking and **disorganized speech** are typical. A person with such a disorder may switch from one topic to another in illogical fashion, may respond to questions with irrelevant answers, and may produce streams of speech that have little or no coherence ("word salad").

It is important to distinguish between **positive symptoms** and **negative symptoms**. Just as with Skinner's learning theory, the terms *positive* and *negative* here have nothing to do with good or bad, but rather refer to adding and subtracting. A positive symptom of schizophrenic disorders refers to something that a person has that typical people do not. Thus, delusions and hallucinations are positive symptoms. A negative symptom refers to something that typical people do have, but that one does not have. In schizophrenic disorders, a limited range of emotion and the lack of desire to initiate activities are both particularly noticeable. **Catatonia**, or disorganized motor behavior, can be a positive or negative symptom depending on whether it manifests as lack of movement or excessive movement. A number of antipsychotic medications can alleviate the positive symptoms of schizophrenia spectrum disorders.

The specific causes of schizophrenia are unknown but there seems to be a combination of a genetic or biological predisposition interacting with environmental stressors, such as viruses or childhood trauma, in many cases of schizophrenia. There are also changes in the brain visible in many cases of schizophrenia.

Depressive Disorders

Unlike the everyday-language use of the term ("I'm so depressed about that test"), **depressive disorders** involve the presence of a sad, empty, or irritable mood, combined with changes in thinking and bodily functioning that significantly impair one's ability to function. These disorders go far beyond normal sadness or grief and last longer than usual periods of sadness. Separate or combined treatments such as psychotherapy (in particular cognitive-behavioral therapy) and antidepressant medications may assist in recovery. One diagnosis in this category is Major Depressive Disorder (MDD), which includes nine different criteria: a depressed mood, loss of interest or pleasure in activities (known as anhedonia), weight gain or loss, insomnia or hypersomnia, suicidal ideation, fatigue, feelings of worthlessness, psychomotor changes, and decreased concentration. A person who experiences a majority of these symptoms for most days over a period of two weeks straight would likely be diagnosed with MDD. **Persistent depressive disorder**, formerly known as dysthymia, is chronic, long-term depressive symptoms. The criteria for PDD are similar to MDD but the differences are the duration of episode and the severity of the symptoms.

As with the schizophrenia disorders, the causes of depressive disorders are linked to a combinations of biological, genetic, sociocultural, behavioral, or cognitive factors.

Bipolar And Related Disorders

Bipolar disorders, as the name suggests, involves movement between two poles: depressive states on the one hand and manic states on the other hand. Mania is a very elevated state of being where a person may speak very quickly, go for days without sleep, and experience a very elevated mood. Because manic states often have psychotic features such as delusions of grandeur or feeling invincible, the *DSM-5* now regards bipolar disorders as a bridge between the psychoses and the major depressive disorders. Bipolar Disorder I includes cycling between full mania and major depression. In Bipolar Disorder II, the manic phases are milder. These disorders are often treated with mood-stabilizing medication as well as psychotherapy. Again, the causes of bipolar disorders are linked to a combination of biological, genetic, sociocultural, behavioral, or cognitive issues.

Anxiety Disorders

Fear is an emotional response to something present; anxiety is a related emotional response, but to a future threat or a possibility of danger. In a state of anxiety, the nervous system wants to get into fight-or-flight mode, but there is nothing there to fight and nothing to flee from. Physical effects of anxiety may include but are not limited to muscle tension, hyperalertness for danger signs, and avoidance behaviors. Sleep disturbances, irritability, and inability to concentrate are common related symptoms.

Treatments vary from behavioral modification in the case of specific phobias to cognitive-behavioral therapy to psychotherapy to medical treatment through **anxiolytics**, anti-anxiety medications.

Panic disorder is an anxiety disorder characterized by recurring **panic attacks**, as well as the constant worry of another panic attack occurring. While panic attacks last only a few minutes, they are debilitating. They are accompanied by sweating, increased heart rate, and a general feeling of being paralyzed with fright. **Ataque de nervios** is a form of panic disorder that is culturally linked and experienced mainly by people of Caribbean or Iberian descent.

Generalized anxiety disorder (GAD) is an anxiety disorder characterized by an almost constant state of autonomic nervous system arousal and feelings of dread and worry.

Specific phobias, or persistent, irrational fears of common events or objects, are also anxiety disorders. Phobias include fear of objects, such as snakes, and fear of situations. **Agoraphobia**, for example, is the fear of being in open spaces, public places, or other places from which escape is perceived to be difficult.

Social anxiety is diagnosed when a person has a specific fear of social situations and may engage in avoidance behaviors to prevent the anxious feelings. **Taijin kyofusho** is a culture-bound anxiety disorder experienced mainly by Japanese people. In this disorder, people are afraid that others are judging their bodies as displeasing.

Anxiety disorders are linked to behavioral causes, such as learned associations, cognitive causes, especially maladaptive thinking, as well as biological factors.

Obsessive-Compulsive And Related Disorders

As the name suggests, these disorders involve **obsessions** and/or **compulsions**. Be clear on the difference between these terms: obsessions are thoughts; compulsions are actions. Specifically, obsessions are intrusive (unwanted) thoughts, urges, or images that plague the individual. Compulsions are repetitive behaviors (or mental acts) that one feels compelled to perform, often in relation to an obsession. For example, intrusive thoughts about germs could lead to repeated hand-washing. This is the textbook example for **obsessive-compulsive disorder (OCD)**. OCD is characterized by involuntary, persistent thoughts or obsessions, as well as compulsions, or repetitive behaviors that are time consuming and maladaptive, that an individual believes will prevent a particular (usually unrelated) outcome. Related disorders include **body dysmorphic disorder** and **hoarding disorder**, which involve obsessive thoughts about bodily defects or the need to save possessions. Some other specific related disorders involve hair-pulling and skin-picking. The causes of OCD are similar to those of anxiety disorders: maladaptive thinking, learned associations, and other biological and/or genetic factors.

Dissociative Disorders

What gets dissociated in dissociative disorders is primarily consciousness or identity. In many cases, these disorders appear following a trauma and may be seen as the mind's attempt to protect itself by splitting itself into parts. Thus, one might experience **derealization**, the sense that "this is not really happening," or **depersonalization**, the sense that "this is not happening to me." Significant gaps in memory may be related to **dissociative amnesia** with or without **fugue** (where a person with dissociative amnesia winds up in an unexpected place), an inability to recall life events that goes far beyond normal forgetting. Perhaps the most extreme of these disorders is **dissociative identity disorder** (formerly known as multiple personality disorder), in which one may not only "lose time," but also manifest a separate personality during that lost time. This disorder is most often associated with significant trauma or abuse in childhood.

Trauma- And Stressor-Related Disorders

By definition, these disorders follow a particularly disturbing event or set of events (the trauma or the stressor), like war or violence. Although it is completely normal for people to respond to a stressful event with stress symptoms, some people recover naturally, whereas others develop symptoms. The best-known such disorder is **post-traumatic stress disorder (PTSD),** which can involve intrusive thoughts or dreams related to the trauma, irritability, avoidance of situations that might recall the traumatic event, sleep disturbances, diminished interest in formerly pleasurable activities, and social withdrawal. These PTSD symptoms, in turn, lead to a decreased ability to function as well as to a general detachment from reality.

Feeding And Eating Disorders

Anorexia nervosa (commonly called anorexia) involves not only restriction of food intake, but also intense fear of gaining weight and disturbances in self-perception, such as thinking one looks fat, when one does not. The self-starvation behavior associated with this disorder can lead to life-threatening medical conditions. **Bulimia nervosa** (commonly called bulimia) involves eating large amounts of food in short amounts of time, followed by inappropriate behaviors to prevent weight gain, such as self-induced vomiting (**purging**), using laxatives, or intense exercising. There is usually a heightened sense of shame in connection with both binging and purging. Self-image is also unduly affected by body shape and weight. **Binge-eating disorder** might be thought of as bulimia without purging. But this occurs in both normal-weight and overweight/obese people. There is a loss of control associated with the binge-eating in this disorder. While it is not clear why this occurs, it is most likely a result of biochemical, physiological, and cultural factors.

Personality Disorders

Consider data that suggests that 15% of U.S. adults have at least one personality disorder. This is roughly one in seven people. While we do not encourage you to start diagnosing people without training, you might think about the people you have met as you study personality disorders.

A personality disorder refers to a stable (and inflexible) way of experiencing and acting in the world, one that is at variance with the person's culture, that starts in adolescence or adulthood, and leads to either personal distress or impairment of social functioning. (It is important to note that, by definition, children cannot have personality disorders. Think of it this way: children are still developing their personalities.) Ten personality disorders are organized into three clusters. You might think of them as the three Ws: the weird, the wild, and the worried.

Cluster A includes paranoid, schizoid, and schizotypal personality disorders. These individuals appear to be markedly odd or eccentric. With **paranoid personality disorder**, there may be a pattern of general distrust of others that is not justified by real circumstances. **Schizoid personality disorder** is marked by disturbances in feeling (detachment from social relationships, flat affect, does not enjoy close relationships with people), whereas **schizotypal personality disorder** is marked by disturbances in thought (odd beliefs that do not quite qualify as delusions, such as superstitions, belief in a "sixth sense," etc.; odd speech; eccentric behavior or appearance).

Cluster B includes antisocial, borderline, histrionic, and narcissistic personality disorders. These individuals appear to be dramatic, emotional, or erratic. Terms like *psychopath* and *sociopath* have been used to describe people with **antisocial personality disorder**, which is characterized by a persistent pattern of disregard for, and violation of, the rights of others. Lying, cheating, stealing, and having no remorse are common. **Borderline personality disorder** involves a very stormy relationship with the world, with others, and with one's own feelings. People with this disorder have a regular pattern of instability in relationships, often involving frantic efforts to avoid abandonment (imagined or real), alternating between extremes of idealization and devaluation ("You're the best ever!" → "I hate you!") with the same person, identity disturbance, impulsivity, chronic feelings of emptiness, and anger control issues. **Histrionic personality disorder** involves a pattern of excessive emotionality and attention-seeking, beyond what might be considered normal (even in a "culture of selfies"). **Narcissistic personality disorder** involves an overinflated sense of self-importance, fantasies of success, beliefs that one is special, a sense of entitlement, a lack of empathy for others, and a display of arrogant behaviors or attitudes.

Cluster C includes avoidant, dependent, and obsessive-compulsive personality disorders. These individuals appear to be anxious or fearful. **Avoidant personality disorder** involves an enduring pattern of social inhibition, feelings of inadequacy, and hypersensitivity to real or perceived criticism, which lead to avoidance behavior in relation to social, personal, and intimate relationships. **Dependent personality disorder** is marked by an excessive need to be cared for, leading to clingy and submissive behavior and fears of separation. People with this disorder may feel unable to make everyday decisions without constantly consulting others and getting their advice and approval. Finally, **obsessive-compulsive personality disorder (OCPD)** is marked by a rigid concern with order, perfectionism, control, and work, at the expense of flexibility, spontaneity, openness, and play. In distinction to OCD, which involves unwanted or intrusive thoughts along with unwanted or intrusive compulsions, OCPD can involve similar thoughts and compulsions, but they are not seen by the person as intrusive. Rather, the person with OCPD may think that the problem lies with other people who do not see the need for things to be ordered in a certain way.

In many cases, people do not seek treatment for their personality disorders. But if their disorder leads them to become depressed or anxious due to social or occupational impairments, they may seek help for depression or anxiety and may become diagnosed in that way.

> **Study Tip**
>
> It can seem quite daunting to know all of the disorders listed in the *DSM-5*. Focus on the ones highlighted in this chapter. More and more in modern times, famous people have been open about their diagnoses and their struggles with some of these conditions. If you are aware of such individuals, it may be helpful to link these disorders with real-world people as a way to remember the associated symptoms.

In Addition

We have only given an overview and selection of the disorders listed in the *DSM-5*. Other disorders include the following: elimination disorders; sleep-wake disorders; sexual dysfunctions; gender dysphoria; disruptive, impulse-control, and conduct disorders; substance-related and addictive disorders; neurocognitive disorders; paraphilic disorders; and others.

TREATMENT APPROACHES

Treatments for various disordered behaviors described in the previous chapter can be viewed from varying perspectives. Meta-analyses of different therapeutic approaches show the efficacy of psychotherapy. Therapists, regardless of their theoretical orientation, should be trained to be culturally sensitive and should work to establish a therapeutic alliance (i.e., a good working relationship) with their patients or clients.

Psychological treatments have evolved tremendously, especially over the last 100 years or so. Prior to the 20th century, institutionalization without treatment was essentially the norm. Social movements of the 19th century advocated for more humane treatments. Psychoanalysis, developed at the end of the 19th and beginning of the 20th century, revolutionized treatment with its idea of talk therapy. By the mid-20th century, **psychosurgery** was quite popular. Perhaps the most well-known form of psychosurgery is the **prefrontal lobotomy**, in which parts of the frontal lobes are cut off from the rest of the brain. It frequently left patients in a zombie-like or catatonic state. Its use marked a controversial chapter in the history of psychotherapy. But with the development of new pharmacological treatments, many more people can receive treatment for psychological disorders on an outpatient basis with medication and psychotherapy.

Professional organizations for psychologists, social workers, counselors, and other mental health providers oblige their members to follow ethical codes of conduct to protect the well-being of, show respect for, and uphold the dignity of patients and clients.

Insight Therapies: Psychoanalytic and Humanistic Approaches

The psychoanalytic approach to the treatment of disordered behavior is rooted in the concept of **insight**. Insight into the cause of the problem, according to this theory, is the primary key to eliminating the problem.

Psychoanalysis

Psychoanalysis, or psychoanalytic therapy, as it is sometimes called, was first developed by Freud and focuses on probing past defense mechanisms of repression and rationalization to understand the unconscious cause of a problem. Primary tools for revealing the contents of the unconscious include dream analysis and also **free association**, in which the patient reports any and all conscious thoughts and ideas. Within the pattern of free associations are hints to the nature of the unconscious conflict. The insight process does not occur quickly, however, as patients exhibit resistance to the uncovering of repressed thoughts and feelings.

In psychoanalytic therapy, the therapist strives to remain detached from the patient, resisting emotional or personal involvement. This detachment is intended to encourage **transference**, which occurs when the patient shifts thoughts and feelings about certain people or events onto the therapist. This process is thought to help reveal the nature of the patient's conflicts. **Counter-transference** may occur if the therapist transfers their own feelings onto the patient. In order to avoid countertransference, psychotherapists have typically undergone analysis themselves and many continue to do so while practicing therapy.

Humanistic Therapy

The humanistic school of psychology takes a related, yet different, approach to the treatment of disordered behavior. Rather than treating the person seeking help as a patient, the humanistic approach treats the individual as a client. **Client-centered therapy** was invented by Carl Rogers and involves the assumption that clients can be understood only in terms of their own realities. This approach differs from the Freudian approach in its focus on the client's present perception of reality, rather than the past and its analysis of conscious, instead of unconscious, motives. The goal of the therapy is to help the client realize full potential through self-actualization. In order to accomplish this, the client-centered therapist takes a somewhat different approach from that of the Freudian. Rather than remaining detached, the therapist is open, honest, and expressive of feelings with the client (an active listener). Rogers referred to this way of relating to the client as **genuineness**.

The next key for successful client-centered therapy, according to Rogers, is **unconditional positive regard**. Rogers believed that unconditional positive regard for the child by the parent was critical for healthy development. The therapist provides this unconditional positive regard to help the client reach a state of unconditional self-worth.

The final key to successful therapy is **accurate empathic understanding**. Rogers used this term to describe the therapist's ability to view the world from the eyes of the client. This empathy is critical to successful communication between the therapist and client.

A different type of approach toward treatment is **Gestalt therapy**, which combines both physical and mental therapies. Fritz Perls developed this approach to blend an awareness of unconscious tensions with the belief that one must become aware of and deal with those tensions by taking personal responsibility. Clients may be asked to physically "act out" psychological conflicts in order to make them aware of the interaction between mind and body.

Cognitive Therapy

Cognitive approaches to the treatment of disordered behavior rely on changing cognitions, or the ways people think about situations, in order to change behavior. One such approach is **cognitive therapy,** formulated by Aaron Beck, in which the focus is on maladaptive schemas. These schemas cause clients to experience cognitive distortions, which in turn lead them to feel worthless or incompetent. Beck asserted that there is a **negative triad** of depression that involves a negative view of self, of the world, and of the future. This view is learned through experiences and then becomes a cycle of response that needs to be addressed through cognitive therapy. Maladaptive schemas include **arbitrary inference**, in which a person draws conclusions without evidence, and **dichotomous thinking**, which involves all-or-nothing conceptions of situations. An example might be that of a person, faced with the stress of a job interview, who thinks, "If I don't get this job, I'll be a complete failure." The goal of cognitive therapy is to eliminate or modify the individual's maladaptive schemas.

Dialectical behavioral therapy combines standard cognitive behavioral therapy techniques with distress tolerance and emotional regulation. DBT evolved out of a need for an effective treatment approach to help suicidal patients, who were not responding to traditional CBT methods.

Another cognitive approach is **rational-emotive behavior therapy (REBT)** (sometimes called simply **RET**, for **rational-emotive therapy**), formulated by Albert Ellis. REBT is based on the idea that when confronted with situations, people recite statements to themselves that express maladaptive thoughts. The maladaptive thoughts result in maladaptive emotional responses. The goal of REBT is to change the maladaptive thoughts and emotional responses by confronting the irrational thoughts directly. Incorrect thoughts are changed in a simple way: the patient is told that they are incorrect and why. Some examples of maladaptive thoughts are, "I always have to be perfect in everything I do" and "Other people's opinions are crucial to my happiness."

Behavioral Therapy

Behavioral therapy stands in dramatic contrast to the insight therapies. First, behavioral therapy is a short-term process, whereas the insight approaches are extended over long periods of time, often spanning years. Secondly, behavior therapy treats symptoms because, in this school of thought, there is no deep underlying cause of the problem. The disordered behavior itself is both the problem and symptom. To change behavior, behavioral therapists use specific techniques with clearly defined methods of application and clear ways to evaluate their efficacy.

Counterconditioning is a technique in which a response to a given stimulus is replaced by a different response. For example, if a patient seeks behavioral therapy to stop drinking alcohol, the therapist must take the learned responses, the positive feelings generated by drinking alcohol, and replace them with a new reaction, namely, negative feelings concerning alcohol.

Counterconditioning can be accomplished in a few ways. One is to use **aversion therapy**, in which an aversive stimulus is repeatedly paired with the behavior that the client wishes to stop. So, to use our alcohol example, the therapist might administer a punishment to the patient each time the patient drinks alcohol.

Another method used for counterconditioning is **systematic desensitization**. This technique involves replacing one response, such as anxiety, with another response, such as relaxation. In order to achieve this goal, a therapist constructs, with the help of the client, a hierarchical set of mental images related to the stressful stimulus. These mental images are laid out in an order such that each one is slightly more anxiety-inducing than the previous one. The patient then learns a deep-relaxation technique. Next, the therapist asks the patient to bring to mind the least stressful of the mental images. As the client imagines the scene, they may become anxious. The client is instructed to practice the relaxation technique the moment the feelings of anxiety begin and to continue using the relaxation technique until they feel fully relaxed while imagining the scene. The therapist, over time, systematically helps the client work up the hierarchy until they are able to imagine the most stressful scene in the hierarchy without experiencing anxiety. This technique relies on learning mechanisms to associate the formerly anxiety-provoking stimuli with relaxation.

Other forms of behavioral therapy involve **extinction procedures**, which are designed to weaken maladaptive responses. One way of trying to extinguish a behavior is called **flooding**. Flooding involves exposing a client to the stimulus that causes the undesirable response. If, for example, a client has come to a therapist to try to overcome a fear of spiders, the therapist will actually expose the client to spiders. Of course, the client will have a high anxiety level, but after a few minutes of being near the spider without any negative consequences, the client will presumably realize that the situation is not dangerous. **Implosion** is a similar technique, in which the client imagines the disruptive stimuli rather than actually confronting them.

Operant conditioning is a behavior-control technique that we discussed in the chapter on learning. A related approach is **behavioral contracting**, in which the therapist and the client draw up a contract by which they both agree to abide. The client must, according to the contract, act in certain ways, such as not exhibiting undesirable behaviors; meanwhile, the therapist must provide stated rewards if the client holds up their end of the bargain.

Modeling is a therapeutic approach based on Bandura's social learning theory. This technique is based on the principle of vicarious learning. Clients watch someone act in a certain way and then receive a reward. Presumably, the client will then be disposed to imitate that behavior.

Applied behavioral analysis combines many of the behavioral interventions discussed above and has been shown to be very effective in the treatment of many disorders, notably autism spectrum disorder. In **biofeedback**, people learn a variety of techniques, including deep breathing and guided visualization, to learn to have more control over autonomic nervous system functions, and thus have more control over anxious or depressive responses. Research supports the use of **hypnosis** for pain control and anxiety reduction.

MODES OF THERAPY

Not all forms of therapy involve an individual client seeing a therapist. **Group therapy**, in which clients meet together with a therapist as an interactive group, has some advantages over individual therapy. It is less expensive, and the group dynamic may be therapeutic in and of itself. Of course, the psychological effect of the therapist also may be diluted across the members of the group because attention is focused on the group rather than on a specific individual. One area in which group therapy has gained popularity is in the treatment of substance abuse. **Twelve-step programs** are one form of group therapy, although they are usually not moderated by professional psychotherapists. These programs, modeled after Alcoholics Anonymous, are a combination of spirituality and group therapy. The twelve-step programs focus on a strong social support system of people who are experiencing or who have experienced addictions or other types of maladaptive adjustments to life. Twelve-step groups are a type of peer support group. Peer support groups usually do not have a professional psychologist or social worker facilitating them. Rather, people who have experience with particular conditions simply share their experience and strength with each other.

Another form of therapy in which there is more than a single client is **couples** or **family therapy**. This type of treatment arose out of the simple observation that some dysfunctional behavior affects the afflicted person's loved ones. Couples therapy approaches the couple dyad as a system that involves complex interactions. Family therapy has distinct advantages in that it allows family members to express their feelings to one another and to the therapist simultaneously. This behavior, in turn, encourages family members to listen to one another in a way that might not occur in other settings.

Alternative Therapies

Did you know that biofeedback is often used to treat disorders like anxiety, chronic pain, and ADHD? It is a non-invasive technique that may reduce or eliminate the need for medications, and it enables patients to feel in control of their health. Other alternative therapies include therapeutic touch, eye movement desensitization and reprocessing (EMDR), and light therapy.

Biological Therapies

Biological therapies are medical approaches to behavioral problems. Biological therapies are typically used in conjunction with one of the previously mentioned forms of treatment.

Psychopharmacology is the treatment of psychological and behavioral maladaptations with drugs. There are four broad classes of **psychotropic**, or psychologically active **drugs:** antipsychotics, antidepressants, anxiolytics, and lithium salts.

Antipsychotics, including first-generation medications such as Thorazine and Haldol, reduce the symptoms of schizophrenia by blocking the neural receptors for dopamine. You may recall that dopamine is implicated in schizophrenia and in movement disorders. Unfortunately, jerky movements, tremors, and muscle stiffness are among the side effects of these drugs. The clinician must decide which is worse—the psychological disorder being treated or the side effects of the drugs. Second-generation antipsychotics, known as atypical antipsychotics—such as Risperidone, Clozapine, Abilify, and Seroquel—have fewer side effects than the older drugs.

Antidepressants can be grouped into three types: monoamine oxidase (MAO) inhibitors, tricyclics, and selective reuptake inhibitors. **MAO inhibitors,** such as Eutron, work by increasing the amount of serotonin and norepinephrine in the synaptic cleft. They produce this increase by blocking monoamine oxidase, which is responsible for the breakdown of many neurotransmitters. These drugs are effective but toxic and require special dietary modifications. **Tricyclics,** like Norpramin, Amitriptyline, and Imipramine increase the amount of serotonin and norepinephrine.

The third class of antidepressants, **selective reuptake inhibitors** (often called the selective serotonin reuptake inhibitors, or **SSRIs**, for the neurotransmitter most affected by them) also work by increasing the amount of neurotransmitter at the synaptic cleft, in this case by blocking the reuptake mechanism of the cell that released the neurotransmitters. Prozac (Fluoxetine) is one example of such a drug. The indirect mechanism of action of these drugs means that they have fewer side effects. They are the most frequently prescribed class of antidepressant drugs in the United States. SNRIs (serotonin norepinephrine reuptake inhibitors), such as Effexor and Cymbalta, and atypical antidepressants, such as Wellbutrin, are also frequently prescribed for depression.

Anxiolytics depress the central nervous system and reduce anxiety while increasing feelings of well-being and reducing insomnia. A commonly prescribed anti-anxiety medication is Xanax. Anxiolytics also include barbiturates, which are rarely used because of their potential for addiction and their danger when mixed with other drugs. **Benzodiazepines**, which also include Valium (Diazepam) and Librium (Chlordiazepoxide), cause muscle relaxation and a feeling of tranquility.

Lithium carbonate, a salt, is effective in the treatment of bipolar disorder. The mechanism of action is not known, however.

The use of psychoactive medication requires doctors and patients to do a cost-benefit analysis to see if the side effects are worse than the treatment. For instance, some psychoactive medications are linked to a disorder called **tardive dyskinesia**, which is a movement disorder related to the regulation of dopamine. Weight gain and extreme sleepiness are other common side effects.

Surgical or invasive procedures are still performed in more treatment resistant cases. While psychosurgery is no longer in favor, one treatment used is **electroconvulsive therapy (ECT)** is a form of treatment in which fairly high voltages of electricity are passed across a patient's head. This treatment causes temporary amnesia and can result in seizures. It has been successful in the treatment of major depression, but today it is used only when all other means of treating depression have failed because of the risks involved with memory loss. **Transcranial magnetic stimulation** involves using a magnet to stimulate nerve cells and has been demonstrated effective in many cases of treatment-resistant depression.

KEY TERMS

health psychology

Stress

stressors

transient

chronic

general adaptation syndrome

alarm

corticosterone

resistance

exhaustion

Type-A pattern

Type B-pattern

tend and befriend theory

problem-focused coping

emotion-focused coping

Positive Psychology

gratitude

signature strengths

post-traumatic growth

Psychological Disorders

disordered behavior

Diagnostic and Statistical Manual of Mental Disorders (DSM-5)

International Classification of Mental Disorders (ICD)

Theories of Psychopathology

psychoanalytical school

humanistic school

cognitive perspective

behavioral approach

biological view

sociocultural approach

biopsychosocial perspective

diathesis-stress model

Categories of Psychological Disorders

autism spectrum disorder

attention-deficit hyperactivity disorder (ADHD)

communication disorders

motor disorders

specific learning disorders

Schizophrenia Spectrum and Other Psychotic Disorders

schizophrenia

delusions

hallucinations

disorganized thinking

disorganized speech

positive symptoms

negative symptoms

catatonia

Depressive Disorders

persistent depressive disorder

Bipolar and Related Disorders

Anxiety Disorders

anxiolytics

panic disorder

panic attacks

ataque de nervios

generalized anxiety disorder (GAD)

specific phobias

agoraphobia

social anxiety

tajin kyofusho

Obsessive-Compulsive and Related Disorders

obsessions

compulsions

obsessive-compulsive disorder (OCD)

body dysmorphic disorder

hoarding disorder

Dissociative Disorders

derealization

depersonalization

dissociative amnesia

fugue

dissociative identity disorder

Trauma- and Stressor-Related Disorders

post-traumatic stress disorder (PTSD)

Feeding and Eating Disorders

anorexia nervosa

bulimia nervosa

purging

binge-eating disorder

Personality Disorders
Cluster A
  paranoid personality disorder
  schizoid personality disorder
  schizotypal personality disorder
Cluster B
  antisocial personality disorder
  borderline personality disorder
  histrionic personality disorder
  narcissistic personality disorder
Cluster C
  avoidant personality disorder
  dependent personality disorder
  obsessive-compulsive personality disorder
  (OCPD)

Treatment Approaches
psychosurgery
prefrontal lobotomy
insight
psychoanalysis
  free association
  transference
  counter-transference
client-centered therapy
  genuineness
  unconditional positive regard
  accurate empathetic understanding
Gestalt therapy
cognitive therapy
  negative triad
  arbitrary inference
  dichotomous thinking
rational-emotive behavior therapy (REBT/RET)
behavioral therapy
  counterconditioning
  aversion therapy
  systematic desensitization
  extinction procedures
  flooding
  implosion
  operant conditioning
  behavioral conditioning
  modeling
  applied behavioral analysis
  biofeedback
  hypnosis

Modes of Therapy
group therapy
twelve-step programs
couples therapy
family therapy
biological therapies
  psychopharmacology
  psychotropic
  drugs
    antipsychotics
    antidepressants
    MAO inhibitors
    tricyclics
    selective reuptake inhibitors (SSRIs)
    anxiolytics
    benzodiazepines
    lithium carbonate
    tardive dyskinesia
electroconvulsive therapy (ECT)
transcranial magnetic stimulation

Unit 5 Drill

See Chapter 12 for answers and explanations.

1. All of the following are symptoms of chronic stress EXCEPT

    (A) hypertension
    (B) immunosuppression
    (C) chronic fatigue
    (D) tissue damage
    (E) suppressed appetite

2. A man claims to hear voices telling him to run for president. He is most likely experiencing

    (A) delusions
    (B) obsessions
    (C) hallucinations
    (D) compulsions
    (E) inceptions

3. Which of the following are most characteristic of a dissociative disorder?

    (A) A persistent, irrational fear of objects or situations
    (B) Difficulties in forming lasting personal relationships
    (C) Involuntary and persistent thoughts that interfere with daily activity
    (D) Auditory and tactile hallucinations
    (E) Memory dysfunction and/or altered perceptions of identity

4. Depression has been associated with low levels of the neurotransmitter

    (A) acetylcholine
    (B) GABA
    (C) serotonin
    (D) chlorpromazine
    (E) dopamine

5. Which of the following is NOT characterized by the *DSM-5* as an anxiety disorder?

    (A) Phobia
    (B) Social phobia
    (C) Anxious personality disorder
    (D) Panic disorder
    (E) Generalized anxiety disorder

6. A high-school girl goes missing, and when she is found in a town 100 miles away a week later, she has assumed a new personality and has no apparent recollection of her life at home. Which category of disorder is she most likely suffering from?

    (A) Somatic symptom disorder
    (B) Delusional disorder
    (C) Personality disorder
    (D) Dissociative disorder
    (E) Schizophrenia

7. All of the following are Cluster B personality disorders EXCEPT

    (A) borderline personality disorder
    (B) schizoid personality disorder
    (C) histrionic behavior disorder
    (D) narcissistic personality disorder
    (E) antisocial personality disorder

8. A child shows difficulty engaging with other children and needs to follow a very strict routine every day to function properly. If the routine is broken, he cries and has a very difficult time adjusting. These symptoms may satisfy which of the following diagnoses?

    (A) Attention-deficit hyperactivity disorder
    (B) Reactive attachment disorder
    (C) Obsessive-compulsive disorder
    (D) Adjustment disorder
    (E) Autism spectrum disorder

9. The concept of *accurate empathic understanding* is most closely associated with which of the following therapeutic approaches?

    (A) Psychoanalytic therapy
    (B) Inductive therapy
    (C) Client-centered therapy
    (D) Implosion therapy
    (E) Reductionist therapy

10. Behavioral therapeutic approaches, such as systematic desensitization, have been most often used with those experiencing or diagnosed with

    (A) fugue
    (B) dementia
    (C) dissociative disorder
    (D) schizophrenia
    (E) phobia

11. A psychoanalytically oriented therapist would most likely be in accord with which of the following criticisms regarding behaviorally oriented therapies?

   (A) Behaviorally oriented therapies often take years to complete and create an onerous financial burden for the patient.
   (B) Behaviorally oriented therapies are concerned solely with the modification of troubling behavioral symptoms and do not address the underlying problems which may have produced those symptoms.
   (C) Behaviorally oriented therapies can be performed only by therapists who have had the longest and most rigorous training and, as a result, can never impact as many people as can other treatment approaches.
   (D) Behaviorally oriented therapies are relatively uninterested in the development of an egalitarian client-therapist relationship and miss opportunities to promote emotional growth and empowerment.
   (E) Behaviorally oriented therapies avoid the technique of role-playing and may not be suitable for group or family therapy situations.

12. The cognitively oriented therapeutic approach known as rational-emotive behavior therapy is most closely associated with

   (A) Julian Rotter
   (B) Albert Ellis
   (C) Abraham Maslow
   (D) Raymond Cattell
   (E) Rollo May

13. Which of the following is NOT a major class of drugs used for psychotherapeutic effect?

   (A) Anticoagulants
   (B) Anxiolytics
   (C) Monoamine oxidase inhibitors
   (D) Lithium salts
   (E) Selective reuptake inhibitors

14. Judy has acrophobia, a fear of heights. A behavioral therapist creates a treatment plan to take her to the top of the Empire State Building on the first session, where she will remain until her reaction to the stimulus subsides. This technique is known as

   (A) systematic desensitization
   (B) aversion therapy
   (C) flooding
   (D) implosion
   (E) behavior contracting

15. A behavioral therapist uses which of the following techniques?

   (A) Free association
   (B) Dream analysis
   (C) Hypnosis
   (D) Extinction procedures
   (E) Unconditional positive regard

16. Selective serotonin reuptake inhibitors, more commonly known as SSRIs, are generally effective in treating which of the following?

   (A) Depressive disorders
   (B) Anxiety disorders
   (C) Bipolar disorder
   (D) Feeding and eating disorders
   (E) Schizophrenic disorders

17. Carl Rogers is most closely identified with which of the following therapy perspectives?

   (A) Humanistic therapy
   (B) Psychoanalytic therapy
   (C) Behavioral therapy
   (D) Cognitive behavioral therapy
   (E) Biological therapy

REFLECT

Respond to the following questions:

- Which topics in this chapter do you hope to see on the multiple-choice section or essay?

- Which topics in this chapter do you hope not to see on the multiple-choice section or essay?

- Regarding any psychologists mentioned, can you pair the psychologists with their contributions to the field? Did they contribute significant experiments, theories, or both?

- Regarding any theories mentioned, can you distinguish between differing theories well enough to recognize them on the multiple-choice section? Can you distinguish them well enough to write a fluent essay on them?

- Can you define the key terms at the end of the chapter?

- Which parts of the chapter will you review?

- Will you seek further help, outside of this book (such as from a teacher, Princeton Review tutor, or AP Students), on any of the content in this chapter—and, if so, on what content?

Chapter 12
Chapter Drills:
Answers and
Explanations

CHAPTER 1

Understand the Question/Key Words Drill

3. What's a scientist who's into the (physical basis) of (psychological phenomena) called?

10. One of the (primary tools) of the school of (structuralism) was

18. Binocular cues help you see (depth) because

35. What type of effect is this: person (only remembers) words from the (beginning and end) of a list?

47. The (recognition-by-components) theory asserts that we categorize objects by breaking them down into their component parts and then

   We break stuff down and then do what?

56. The fact that V. can (ignore) the crowd is called what?

70. Which of the following was (true) of Stanley (Milgram's studies of obedience?)

88. In their discussions of the (process of development,) the advocates of (the importance of nurture) in the (nature-nurture controversy) emphasize which of the following?

   Nurture emphasizes what?

Easy Questions Drill

1. Understand the Question/Key Words: Freud = which perspective?
   Predict the Answer: Psychoanalytic
   Answer: **(B)** Easy enough.

2. Understand the Question/Key Words: When you stop using a drug, you go through what?
   Predict the Answer: Withdrawal
   Answer: **(C)** Be careful not to rush through and accidentally pick another answer.

3. Understand the Question/Key Words: Conditioning: when the dog salivates at what?
   Predict the Answer: The light without the food
   Answer: **(B)** Watch for (A) and (C). Both are wrong, but close enough to trip up someone who is rushing. If you picked (D) or (E), better hit the books.

4. Understand the Question/Key Words: Circle *basic unit* and *nervous system.*

    Predict the Answer: Neuron

    Answer: **(D)** Watch out for the others—(A), (B), and (E) are all parts of the neuron, while (C) is too general—a neuron is a type of cell.

5. Understand the Question/Key Words: Circle *methods of research* and *central to the behaviorist.*

    Predict the Answer: Experimenting

    Answer: **(E)** Again, if you don't know, start reviewing. POE should easily get rid of (B), (C), and (D).

Medium Questions Drill

33. Understand the Question/Key Words: What regulates hunger and thirst?

    Predict the Answer: I'm not sure, but I know what it's not (use POE).

    Answer: **(C)** Using POE, you should have been able to get rid of at least (D) and (E), and most likely (A).

34. Understand the Question/Key Words: Which psychologists were into viewing things as part of a whole?

    Predict the Answer: Don't remember, but I know all the main perspectives well (use POE).

    Answer: **(D)** If you know your perspectives well, you could easily have gotten rid of at least (A), (B), and (C). Cognitive socialist doesn't make sense, so the answer must be (D).

35. Understand the Question/Key Words: What's wrong with the study: Survey comp sci class to find out who in the school has computers.

    Predict the Answer: The sample is biased.

    Answer: **(B)** It's the closest answer to yours. Use POE for the rest.

36. Understand the Question/Key Words: Looking out the window stimulates which two parts of the brain?

    Predict the Answer: Occipital and another (use POE)

    Answer: **(E)** Knowing occipital gets it down to two answer choices. If you don't know it from there, guess and move on (review Chapter 7).

37. Understand the Question/Key Words: Circle behaviorism and true of.

    Predict the Answer: Experimenting, everything is learned, consequences

    Answer: **(C)** It's the closest answer to yours. Choice (A) is psychodynamic, (B) is a sort of cognitive behaviorism, (D) is wrong, and (E) is silly.

CHAPTER 2

Put It All Together

Our Sample Evidenced Based Question Essay

Research has shown that having a pet or a companion animal is beneficial for increased mental and physical well-being like decreased heart rate or lowered cortisol levels. However, there have been some mixed findings in the literature about attachment to animals, likely due to different populations, measures, paradigms, and social situations studied. For instance, most studies recruit college students to look at these benefits (Sources B & C). Such studies might increase their generalizability if they sampled more variable populations and different age groups.

Further, studies have primarily looked at the benefits to individual participants, but few have investigated how having a pet might promote overall well-being in families, particularly families that report stress and conflict. One study (Source A) attempted to discover the relationship between family conflict and attachment to pets among primary care-givers. Despite using archival data, the study did find a positive correlation between high family conflict and deeper attachment to pets (Source A). This suggests that people with more family conflict will seek more time with a pet, which might decrease the negative effects of family stress, especially in teenagers (e.g., depression, impaired social interactions, increased risk of substance abuse).

While there was more attachment to pets among primary care givers with high family conflict, it was more evident for men than for women (Source A). A possible explanation for that finding is that women have more care-giver responsibilities than men do and men, therefore, have more time to bond with a pet. Nonetheless, creating a stronger bond to a pet through interaction (e.g., petting) or seeking comfort from the pet in high-conflict situations might reduce some of the effects of stress (e.g., lowered cortisol), which in turn might lower the risk for developing a physical illness.

Study A also found that primary care-givers with higher attachment to the pet tended to be non-white, despite making up only about 42% of the sample. This speaks to potential sociocultural differences people of color might face that creates more family strife. And the finding suggests that having an attachment to one's pet might lessen the psychological stress one feels when there is more family conflict. One reason this study might not be replicable is that it uses survey data from a previous study. Another is that very few questions were asked of the participants regarding family conflict and pet attachment (5 in total). The results of this study might generalize better if different age groups, like children and teenagers, in addition to primary care-givers, were surveyed using lengthier and more established questionnaires.

Other studies have shown that, in addition to a reduction in cortisol, petting a companion animal increases oxytocin, which has many health benefits. Among these is a reduction in inflammation, anxiety and stress responses to adverse situations; all of which will activate the parasympathetic nervous system, returning a person to a more homeostatic state. Study B showed that petting a live Labrador Retriever versus a stuffed teddy bear lowered state anxiety in two high-stress scenarios. This will reduce not only cortisol, but likely epinephrine, again returning participants to homeostasis.

The researchers in Study B manipulated stress levels by requiring participants to spend five minutes writing a five minute speech they had to give on camera in front of some judges. Then, the participants completed difficult math problems. During all of this, the participants were petting either the teddy bear or the dog. Because the stuffed animal was not a dog, but a teddy bear, it may have been a poor control against the live dog. It was also much smaller than the real dog (1/3 its size). Had it been a stuffed dog, and had the live dog been smaller (or the stuffed animal larger), the study might have better generalizability. Then too, looking at other types of animals (e.g., cats) might replicate the effect attachment and contact with a companion animal have on stress.

Study B also found that heart rate and blood pressure were affected by both the tasks and the pet condition, but only for those high in trait anxiety. In other words, those participants that are typically anxious (trait anxiety is relatively stable over the lifespan), and were petting the teddy bear, had significantly higher heart rate, blood pressure, and state anxiety scores during peak stress of the experiment. This study would better generalize if there was a control group that also had to perform the high-stress tasks, but weren't petting anything; then researchers could determine if it is the animal, the toy, or the act of petting (like a placebo effect) that reduces stress and brings health benefits.

CHAPTER 4

Drill 1: Understand the Question/Key Words

7. Psychoanalytic vs. behaviorist: How are they different?

22. What technology should you use to look at different regions of the brain?

39. The ⟨somatosensory cortex⟩ is the ⟨primary⟩ area of the

   The circled words mean what?

58. To know what a picture is, the info has to get to which part of the brain?

78. What's it called when someone doesn't give false positives—if there is no sound, there is no report?

89. The ⟨lower⟩ the ⟨p-value⟩ of a study, the
   Lower *p*-value means what?

Drill 2: Predict the Answer

5. How will Thomas learn to make a big meal using the stuff he knows?

   He can link together what he knows (called *chaining*, if you remember that).

22. What does the endocrine system do?

   It secretes hormones into the body.

35. What big thing did Wilhelm Wundt do for psychology?

   He created the first psychology lab in 1879, and he is considered the father of experimental psychology.

45. Why do taste buds need to be able to replace themselves?

   Otherwise, if you burned your mouth, you would lose your sense of taste forever.

72. What technology should you use to study brain waves?

   Electrosomething...(Electroencephalogram or EEG, if you remember)

Drill 3: Using All Three

15. Of the following (variables,) which typically requires a measurement that is more complex?

Understand the Question/Key Words:	*Which variable requires more complex measurement?*
Predict the Answer:	*The complex one—not categorical.*
Answer:	**(B) It's continuous.** Choice (A) is out, (C) doesn't make sense, and (D) and (E) aren't those kinds of variables.

35. Which of the following most accurately states the role of the (iris)?

Understand the Question/Key Words:	*What does the iris do?*
Predict the Answer:	*It opens and closes the pupil (controls amount of light, if you remember).*
Answer:	**(B) It says to open and close the pupil and regulate the entrance of light.** Choice (A) is way off. Choice (C) describes the lens, (D) is basically just the inside of the eyeball, and (E) is the optic nerve.

42. The nature-nurture controversy concerns

Understand the Question/Key Words:	*What is the nature-nurture debate about?*
Predict the Answer:	*It's about which is more important: genes or environment. Inborn and external processes determine behavior.*
Answer:	**(C) It's the closest to yours: "inborn processes" (genes) and "environmental factors" (environment).** Be careful of (A): it is a similar idea, but not the same. Choice (B) is way off base, (D) is a silly trap answer (using the words *natural* and *nurture* to lure you), and (E) doesn't answer the question at all.

66. Prior to the fall of the Berlin Wall, East Berlin schools de-emphasized the (individuality) of the student. As a result, many of the children from those schools tend to have a(n)

Understand the Question/Key Words:	*What happens if kids are taught to not be individuals?*
Predict the Answer:	*They depend on others for their self-identity and self-esteem.*
Answer:	**(D) They have an external locus of control—looking to others for their self-esteem and self-identity.** Choices (A) and (B) are not close to yours (no optimism, pessimism). Choice (C) is the opposite of what you want, and (E) is just filler.

85. A ⟨prototypic example⟩ of a ⟨category⟩ is called a(n)

Understand the Question/Key Words:	*A major example of something is called what?*
Predict the Answer:	*I don't know—a major example.*
Answer:	**(E) Exemplar—a major example.** Choice (A) does not mean a major example. Choice (B) is only a feature, not an example of the whole category. Choice (C) is weak. Don't pick (D)! *It's a verbal trap.*

Drill 4: POE

4. **B** Can obese people have *fewer* fat cells than average-weight people?

27. **B** Your key word from the question is "connectionist approaches." Would connectionists think things occurred in individual segments or in a bunch of networks simultaneously?

47. **A** Your key word is "chunking." Even if you don't remember this memory technique, (A) sounds more like chunking than (B).

85. **C** Your key word is "person-centered psychotherapy." Even without that clue, suppressing negative feelings of a client or using a didactic approach are not typically the chosen methods of most psychotherapists.

92. **B** Even without a clue, it's understood in the field of psychology that counselors do not do either (A) or (C) for clients.

CHAPTER 5 DRILL

1. **D**   A cognitive psychologist is primarily interested in thought processes and products, and (D), involving word association, is most directly connected to such processes and products. Choice (A) is more the province of biological psychologists, (B) that of humanistic psychotherapists, (C) that of clinical psychotherapists or behaviorists, and (E) that of developmental psychologists.

2. **C**   The idea of *tabula rasa* is most closely associated with the philosopher John Locke. Choice (A), David Hume, was a philosopher who speculated on the nature of knowledge and perception; (B), Charles Darwin, is more closely identified with the theory of natural selection and evolution of species; (D), Sigmund Freud, was the founder of psychoanalytic theory; and (E), Erich Fromm, was one of the theorists influenced by Freud.

3. **B**   The concept of dualism refers to the division of the world and all things in it into two parts: body and spirit. Choice (C) refers to two ways of conceptualizing the structure and function of the mind and (E) to two different types of experimental variables.

4. **D**   Humanistic psychologists are primarily concerned with the impact of free will on behavior. Choice (A), childhood experiences, are emphasized in the psychoanalytic approach. Choice (B), biological predispositions, refers to either the biological/medical model or the behavioral-genetics approach. The cognitive approach focuses on how maladaptive thoughts, (C), can influence behavior, and the social-cognitive approach centers on the interaction of cultural experiences, (E), and behavior.

5. **C**   Proponents of the psychoanalytic or psychodynamic approach believe that the source of all current trauma can be traced back to childhood through repressed memories. Choice (A), the cognitive approach, stresses the importance of thought processes and schemas in evaluating behaviors. Choice (B), behaviorists, believe in the power of learning and other environmental influences on behavior. Choice (D), the sociocultural perspective, focuses instead on individuals' cultures and how those shape them into who they are; (E), the medical/biological approach, seeks physiological answers in brain and body chemistry to explain behavior.

6. **B**   Circle the key words *behavior* and *learned*. These words indicate that the answer is associated with behaviorism. The person synonymous with behaviorism is B.F. Skinner, (B).

7. **E**   First, eliminate anything that is not a defense mechanism: self-actualization, (B), and consciousness, (D). Because denial is a state that dismisses an event as unimportant or trivial, but does not involve the individual not remembering what happened, you can eliminate (A). Projection is placing one's problems onto someone else's actions or emotions. This is not the case in this situation, so cross out (C). The answer choice left is repression, (E), the correct answer; repression is a defense mechanism in which the subconscious keeps painful memories from surfacing.

8. **C** Carl Rogers is one of the major players in the humanistic approach to psychology, so the correct answer is (C). He coined the term *unconditional positive regard*, (A), meaning a therapist's proper regard toward his patients, always viewing them in a positive light. However, this is not a psychological approach. Cognitive psychology is focused on cognition and thought processes. While maladaptive thoughts are part of treating the whole person, that is not the only component of what makes up a person, so eliminate (B). The sociocultural components of a person, (D), are also another aspect of an individual's experience, but Carl Rogers sought to treat the individual rather than systemic problems. Behaviorism, (E), is associated with B.F. Skinner.

9. **E** According to Maslow's hierarchy of needs, the physiological needs of a person, such as the needs for food and water, are at the base of the pyramid. Maslow suggested that if a person cannot have these basic needs satisfied, it is much more difficult to accomplish a sense of belonging, esteem, and potentially self-actualization.

10. **B** Behavioral genetics often involves the study of identical twins separated at birth. This allows researchers to examine the contributions of genetics versus those of environment in the development of various traits.

CHAPTER 6 DRILL

1. **D** By definition, a double-blind experimental design is one in which neither the researchers nor the experimental subjects know whether the subjects have been assigned to an experimental group or a control group; this is done to minimize the chance that either the researchers will influence the results through their own expectations or the subjects will influence the results by trying to act in accordance with what is thought to be desired. Choice (B) describes a single-blind experimental design; (E) is completely nonsensical.

2. **B** In a normal statistical curve, about 68 percent of all scores will fall within one standard deviation of the mean; this includes scores both above and below the mean. Choice (A) is the percentage that would occur between the mean and one standard deviation above or below it only; (C) is the percentage that would occur within two standard deviations of the mean.

3. **B** This is the definition of a Type II error—concluding there is no difference when in fact there is a difference. Choice (A) is the definition of a Type I error. Choice (E) is an erroneous conclusion drawn when, in fact, a Type I error has been made.

4. **C** All of the other answers are standard tenets for designing and carrying out ethically acceptable research. Choice (C) has nothing to do with ethics, though it would not be very good for the research design in another way—if both the subjects and the researchers knew which of the former would be part of the experimental group, there would be a great likelihood of expectancy effects confounding the study.

5. **B** A correlation of −0.84 implies that as one variable increases, the other is likely to decrease—positive correlations indicate that two variables vary directly, while negative correlations indicate that two variables vary inversely. Remember the famous research statement, "correlation does not imply causation," and you'll know that neither (D) nor (E) is correct.

6. **C** The behavior of the subjects is measured here as the outcome of the study. The control and independent variables in this study are the violent and nonviolent video games and the behavior supposedly "depends" on which games were played. Therefore, the behavior of the subjects is the dependent variable, (C). Of course, there are most likely some confounding variables and possibly some sampling bias in this study, but the behavior must be classified as the dependent variable.

7. **D** External validity measures the real-life applicability of an experimental study. The other forms of validity measure how well the experiment itself is designed, but do not measure what might be true outside of the experiment. Reliability measures whether one gets the same results across tests or among raters.

8. **D** Circle the key words here: *different regions* and *socioeconomic statuses*. Since the study seeks to look at different backgrounds and regions of the country, researchers are seeking to measure a large cross-sectional population. Longitudinal studies measure the same subjects over a long period of time, and there is no lapse in time here, so eliminate (A). There is not enough information about the design of this study to know whether it is experimental or not (though it's most likely correlational), so eliminate (B) and (C), as well. Choice (E), a case study, studies only one subject or a few subjects at a time. This is not true of this study, so the correct answer is (D).

9. **E** As you most likely noticed, there are many things wrong with this method of procuring subjects for a study. Eliminate (A) because there is a pre-screening bias with weight-loss studies. People who respond to this ad most likely already want to or are trying to lose weight. The answer cannot be (B) because the people inquiring about the ad have control over whether they participate in the study, so they are self-selecting. Selection bias is also present here because these ads are only in New York City buses and subways. Many people visit New York City, but this area is not representative of the entire country. Therefore, eliminate (C). The healthy user bias may or may not be as large of a factor here. However, potential subjects who already engage in a healthy lifestyle or are in the process of losing weight can make this supplement look more effective than unhealthy subjects can. Eliminate (D). Courtesy bias applies to people answering surveys who respond in ways that they think are more socially or politically correct than their true responses. Since this is a study and does not involve a survey, the correct answer is (E).

10. **A** A normal bell curve has most of the data around the middle of the graph, creating a symmetrical bell shape. Since this is not the case, eliminate (C). If the peak of a bell curve is not centered but rather in the lower end of the chart, it is called a positive skew. If the curve sits to the right of the graph's center, it is a negative skew. The curve described here is a positive skew, since many subjects scored low totals. The correct answer is (A).

CHAPTER 7 (UNIT 1) DRILL

1. **B**   Broca's area, which is on the left side of the frontal lobe of the cortex, controls the muscles of speech. Choice (A), repetition of the speech of others, is often referred to as echolalia. Choice (C), the loss of the ability to visually integrate information, or prosopagnosia, is often the result of damage to the occipital lobe. Choice (D), the loss of the ability to comprehend speech, refers to damage in the Wernicke's area of the temporal lobe, and (E), the inability to solve verbal problems, stems from some kind of damage to the left hemisphere.

2. **D**   The dendrites are attached to the cell body, and their purpose is to receive signals and information from other neurons, usually by receiving neurotransmitters; these signals will determine whether or not the neuron will "fire." Choice (A) is the function of the terminal buttons, (B) is that of the myelin sheaths, (C) is that of the cell body, and (E) is that of the axon hillock.

3. **C**   The cerebellum is the part of the brain most involved with maintaining balance and muscular strength and tone. Choice (A) is the part of the brain that controls heart rate, swallowing, breathing, and digestion; (B) is the part, in most people, that is specialized for spatial and intuitive processing; (D) is involved in processing visual input; and (E) is the brain's primary relay station for sensory information.

4. **C**   GABA is the neurotransmitter most associated with inhibitory neural processes; the others generally act to excite neurons further.

5. **C**   The hypothalamus, part of the limbic system, controls motivated behaviors such as hunger, thirst, and sex. Choice (A), the thalamus, routes sensory information to the sensory areas of the brain; (B), the pons, connects the lower brain regions with the higher functioning areas of the brain. Choice (D), the amygdala, controls fear and aggression via the limbic system, and (E), the association areas of the brain, match existing information with incoming information already stored in the brain.

6. **B**   Myelin is an insulating sheath wrapped around the axons of neurons. White matter in the central nervous system is composed of myelinated axons; thus, a reduction in myelination would result in a decrease in white matter and neuronal insulation—(A) and (E), as symptoms, can be eliminated. Gaps in the myelin sheath (called nodes of Ranvier) allow depolarization of the axon and conduction of neuronal signals along the length of the axon. Myelination speeds the movement of the action potential along the length of the axon in a process called saltatory conduction. Choice (C) would be a symptom and can be eliminated; a reduction in myelination would decrease (not increase) saltatory conduction (which makes (B) the correct answer choice). This would decrease sensation, as sensory information from the peripheral nervous system would be hindered from reaching the central nervous system. Choice (D) is a symptom and can be eliminated.

7. **D**   The cerebellum, located behind the pons and below the cerebrum, receives input from the primary motor cortex in the forebrain and coordinates complex motor function, making (D) correct. The frontal lobes contain the primary motor cortices, which are responsible for initiating movement, but do not coordinate complex motor functions, so (A) is wrong. The occipital lobes are responsible for vision, ruling out (B), and the reticular activating system is responsible for arousal and wakefulness, which eliminates (C). The temporal lobes are involved in processing sensory input related to visual memories, language comprehension, and emotion, so it's not (E).

8. **B** The specific pattern of brain waves known as sleep spindles is characteristic of stage NREM 2 sleep, and it is associated with a relaxation of the skeletal musculature. Stage NREM 1 sleep and REM sleep characteristically show the smaller, less regular theta waves, and stage NREM 3 is more likely to show the longer, slower delta waves. Paradoxical sleep is the paralysis of the voluntary muscles during REM sleep.

9. **C** Though the natural day/night cycle of humans and most other organisms matches the 24-hour cycle of the Earth and the Sun, if all cues (such as sunshine) are removed, humans and many other organisms tend to follow a free-running rhythm that cycles approximately every 25 hours, which can be demonstrated through varying body temperature and hormonal levels.

10. **E** There is no evidence that there is any distinction between what kinds of concerns give rise to nightmares versus night terrors. The hypothesis that one of the functions of dreams is to express conscious or unconscious concerns has its roots in Freudian or psychoanalytic theory, and it is only one of a number of competing theories of dream function, none of which has yet proven conclusive. Choices (A), (B), (C), and (D) all represent characteristic differences between nightmares and night terrors.

11. **E** Cocaine is a strong stimulant, not a narcotic. Narcotics, such as those mentioned in (A), (B), (C), and (D), are derived originally from the opium poppy and tend to have analgesic and relaxation effects that depress the central nervous system.

12. **A** Alcohol is a depressant that inhibits neural activity, so eliminate (D). GABA receptors in the central nervous system respond to GABA, an inhibitory neurotransmitter. Alcohol acts on GABA receptors, inhibiting neuronal signaling. Chronic alcohol consumption causes a down-regulation of GABA receptors; therefore, once the artificial depressant (alcohol) is removed from the system, the CNS no longer has an inhibitory influence and excito-neurotoxicity occurs, which can result in seizures and tremors, so (A) is the answer. Alcohol is a depressant and does not stimulate the autonomic nervous system, so (B) cannot be correct. While alcohol consumption does promote dopamine release in the nucleus accumbens (which stimulates the reward pathway in the brain and helps to explain why alcohol is addictive), and cessation of alcohol consumption would surely lead to a decrease in dopamine, this does not explain the physical symptoms of withdrawal described in the question stem, ruling out (C). While alcohol is a depressant, decreasing GABA activity would be excitatory, not inhibitory. Furthermore, this explanation would not account for the symptoms seen in alcohol withdrawal, and so (E) can be eliminated.

13. **B** The doctor needs to ask more questions before diagnosing the patient, but their first thought should be insomnia or sleep apnea. None of the other terms listed in the answer choices constitutes periods of wakefulness during the night. Narcolepsy is overwhelming periods of sleep needed during the day, so eliminate (A). Somnambulism and night terrors happen during sleep, so even though the person seems to be active, they would not report being awake, eliminating (C) and (E). Paradoxical sleep occurs during dreaming, so eliminate (D). The correct answer is (B), sleep apnea.

14. **C**   The question does not mention that the woman is in any state of psychological dependence or addiction, so eliminate (A) and (B). Her body has grown tolerant to the drug, as shown by her dosage being increased twice, but that is not the reason for this increase in her blood pressure. Blood pressure medications are different from stimulants. You can cross out (D) and (E). The clear reason for this increase is that she forgets to take her medication, and the physical symptom that results is an example of physical dependence, (C).

15. **E**   Paradoxical sleep occurs during dreaming. The mind is active, but the paradox is that the body remains almost still. REM sleep represents this sleep state.

16. **A**   Stage NREM 3 is the deepest stage of sleep and, over the course of the night, the cycles contain less and less of it until the cycles contain mostly REM. The REM period can last up to approximately an hour toward the morning hours. The correct answer is (A).

17. **C**   If the individual hits the button to indicate that he has seen a particular stimulus when it was not present, this is called a false alarm.

18. **B**   Choice (B) is the only one that contains the five basic taste sensations—bitter, salty, sweet, sour, and umami; relative combinations of these result in the full range of taste sensations. Choice (C) refers to types of touch sensations and (D) to the five basic food groups.

19. **D**   Know your retinal receptor cells; the rods are sensitive to low light conditions and to movement, while the cones are responsible for color vision and work best at higher illumination levels. Choice (A) contains two other types of cells found in the retina, but not the ones that make the distinction noted here. The same is true of the ganglion cells, (B), and osmoreceptors sense thirst, anyway. In (E), mechanoreceptors sense physical touch and ossicles are bones of the middle ear.

20. **A**   Weber's law relates to the issue of thresholds in sensation and perception. The law states that the greater the magnitude of the stimuli, the larger the differences must be if we are to distinguish among the stimuli. Recognition of an imperceptible amount of perfume, (B), relates to the issue of absolute threshold. People not attending to more than one stimulus at a time, (C), focuses on selective attention. The ability to tell the difference between 20- and 100-watt bulbs 50 percent of the time, (D), refers again to the absolute threshold. All auditory stimuli sounding the same above a certain frequency, (E), negates frequency theory in audition.

21. **B**   The tympanic membrane (also known as the eardrum), located in the middle ear, generates vibrations that match the sound waves striking it, so (B) is correct. Vibrations generated in the tympanic membrane pass through three small bones—the malleus (hammer), the incus (anvil), and the stapes (stirrup); these bones magnify the incoming vibrations by focusing them onto a structure known as the oval window, which means that (D) and (E) are wrong. Once the vibrations pass through the oval window, they enter the cochlea, a fluid-filled spiral structure in the inner ear, so (C) can be eliminated. The base of the cochlea is lined with a long, fluid-filled duct known as the basilar membrane, which rules out (A).

22. **C**   The axons of ganglion cells in the retina make up the optic nerve, which carries visual information to the brain, so (C) is correct. Photoreceptors such as rods and cones are specialized cells in the retina that transduce light energy into nerve cell activity and synapse with bipolar cells, but none of those are a part of the optic nerve, which rules out (A), (B), and (E). The fovea is the area of highest visual acuity and contains a high concentration of cones, which are a type of photoreceptor and do not comprise the optic nerve, thereby eliminating (D).

23. **B**   When Laretta sits down in class and eventually forgets about the odor, this is known as habituation. However, when the stimulus is removed and then re-presented (e.g., when she leaves the class and returns to notice the smell again), this is known as dishabituation. The correct answer is (B).

24. **B**   Subliminal information is presented just below the threshold. This information is often referred to as imperceptible, yet it is believed to influence behavior. Choice (A), immediate recognition of the stimuli, refers to the absolute threshold. Choice (C) mentions the tip-of-the-tongue phenomenon, which is another kind of preconscious processing, but the inability of a stimulus to be on the tip of the tongue would not be an indication of its presence. There is no evidence that there is proactive interference or that recall of these stimuli is slower in a matched-pairs trial, so eliminate (D) and (E).

CHAPTER 8 (UNIT 2) DRILL

1. **C**   Among the Gestalt principles of perception, continuity refers to our tendency to perceive fluid or continuous forms preferentially, rather than jagged or irregular ones—we would tend to see an image as two lines that cross at a point, rather than as two angles sharing a vertex. Choices (A) and (D) are two other Gestalt perceptual principles—proximity and similarity, respectively, and (E) refers to binocular disparity, a depth perception cue.

2. **A**   Gestalt psychology proposes that humans tend to see objects in their entirety, and our visual processing systems and brain will superimpose a larger organization or structure that makes holistic sense. The "shapes" are technically composed of a series of unconnected lines, but according to Gestalt psychologists, humans are more likely to use both top-down and bottom-up processing to perceive them as a complete circle or a complete rectangle, so (A) is the answer. Bottom-up processing begins with the sensory receptors and works up to the complex integration of information occurring in the brain; while bottom-up processing is a requirement of perceiving the lines in the figure, it does not explain why we see two shapes instead of perceiving many unconnected lines, which makes (B) incorrect. Parallel processing refers to the brain's capability to process multiple sensory inputs simultaneously, and Weber's law explains that the greater the magnitude of the stimuli, the larger the difference must be for their difference to be perceptible; neither accounts for the phenomenon described in the question stem, and so (C) and (D) are both wrong. Summation, also referred to as frequency summation, is related to neuronal signal conduction, when the combined polysynaptic potential of multiple excitatory and inhibitory neurotransmitters determines whether or not an action potential is generated, thereby eliminating (E).

3. **D**   Oddly enough, there is not a triangle drawn, but Claire reports seeing a triangle because people have a natural tendency to want to see closed figures as opposed to incomplete figures. This supports the law of closure. She could have said she sees three incomplete concentric discs, but her mind configured it in a way that organizes the information as closed, complete figures.

4. **B**   Visual sensory memory is referred to as *iconic*, and auditory sensory memory is called *echoic*. Iconic memory has a shorter duration than echoic memory, making (A) inaccurate. Visual and auditory memory have approximately the same capacity before encoding, so eliminate (C). The phone number read out loud (echoic) should have a longer duration than visually presented information, so eliminate (D). Choice (E) is wrong because if both auditory and visual information are presented at the same time, auditory information is more likely to be transferred to long-term memory.

5. **D**   The principle of context-dependent memory states that information is more likely to be recalled if the attempt to retrieve it occurs in a situation similar to the situation in which it was first encoded. Choice (A) refers to the process of new information pushing old information out of short-term memory; (B) to the grouping of items of information in order to better hold them in short-term memory; (C) to organizing short-term memory items in order to transfer them to long-term memory; and (E) to the memory for motor skills and habits.

6. **A**   Divergent thinking is the name we give to the problem-solving process used when there are many possible solutions. In contrast, (B) is the process used when the problem has only one solution, such as is the case with most math problems. The intelligence quotient, (C), was originally conceived of as a ratio of mental age over chronological age, multiplied by 100; this was determined by comparing performance to that of others over a range of problem-solving tasks, which might involve both divergent and convergent abilities.

7. **C**   This type of knowledge is a fact to be recalled, so it must be part of the explicit memory. Eliminate (A), (B), and (E). Episodic memory refers to memories the person has experienced, and semantic memory is the memory of facts and figures (remember, semantic is meaning-making). No one living today was around to experience Abraham Lincoln's presidency, so it cannot be episodic. The fact is, instead, semantic. The correct answer is (C).

8. **B**   Ben cannot get past this physics problem because he is approaching it the same way instead of thinking outside the box. This is known as a mental set, (B). Functional fixedness is a type of mental set; however, it is specifically concerning an object's intended use versus its other creative uses, so eliminate (A). A representativeness heuristic is using a prototypical representation of an image or concept to judge a particular case, so eliminate (C), and insight learning refers to having a sudden understanding of a problem or a potential strategy for solving a problem. The question does not state that Ben has solved the problem, so eliminate (D). Framing involves either false memories or leading questions, so eliminate (E), as well. The correct answer is (B).

9. **A**   A representativeness heuristic is using a prototypical representation to judge a particular case. The mental image of a rose is an example of this, so (A) is the correct answer. Choice (B) is an example of an availability heuristic, which pulls upon readily available images or memories, such as seeing advertisements recently. Choice (C) shows someone who is not limited by functional fixedness and thus is able to solve her dilemma. Choice (D) describes a confirmation bias, and (E) describes hindsight bias.

10. **E** Sheldon is relating new knowledge to something he already understands. Functional fixedness refers to only using an object for its intended use, so (A) cannot be the answer. Choice (B) is more related to grouping pieces of information, and there is no evidence of this in the question. Maintenance rehearsal is related to short-term memory only and state-dependent memory depends on the mental state a person is in when learning the information. Choices (C) and (D) can be eliminated. The self-referential effect works here because Sheldon is relating the new information to something he is familiar with. This is (E).

11. **A** Content validity is a measure of the degree to which material on the test is balanced and is measuring what it is said to measure. Choice (B) refers to another type of validity—predictive validity. Choices (C), (D), and (E) refer not to measures of test validity, but to measures of test reliability.

12. **B** A projective test is one in which ambiguous stimuli, which are open to various kinds of interpretation, are presented, in contrast to the more common inventory-type tests in which participants answer a standard series of questions. The Thematic Apperception Test (TAT) is a well-known projective test; it involves a series of pictures of people in ambiguous relationships with other people, and the respondent's task is to generate a story for each picture, including what led up to the scene in the picture, what is happening now, and what might occur next. All of the other choices are inventory-style tests in which participants are faced with standardized answer choices.

13. **B** IQ scores over a population are distributed along a normal curve, with the mean, median, and modal scores at 100 and a standard deviation of roughly 15 to 16 points; therefore, a score of 85 would be located approximately one standard deviation below the mean. Choice (E) is deceptive, as the original definition of IQ as mental age divided by physical age multiplied by 100 makes it attractive, but physical age would have no effect on where an IQ score is located relative to established means, medians, modes, or standard deviations.

14. **A** Test standardization is used to set the norms for a given population of subjects; these norms can then be used to compare the test results of groups or individuals with specific characteristics to the whole population. In order to set these norms, the test is administered to a (usually fairly large) standardization sample which, as much as is feasible, possesses characteristics reflective of the entire population. Choice (C) actually refers to the measurement of validity, (D) is more of a way of ensuring reliability on tests where scoring is not computerized, and (E) has more to do with the format of the test than the population.

15. **E** Howard Gardner's theory of multiple intelligences—not just verbal and mathematical, the dimensions measured by most intelligence tests—posits that there are measurable intelligences in all of the dimensions listed except for (E), which is a dimension added by two other theorists, Peter Salovey and John Mayer.

16. **D** Reliability measures how consistent the results will be if the same subject takes the test multiple times. Choice (A) calls into question current versus noncurrent practices, while (B) describes validity instead. Choice (C) should be true of any experiment. Choice (E) describes generalizability. The correct answer is (D).

17. **B** A true/false or other type of multiple-choice test is one that does not allow for much creativity, so you can eliminate (A). Since there is a very clear-cut answer to each question through multiple-choice responses, the correct answer is (B), inventory-type test. The test could be about intelligence, environment, or hereditary information, but none of these are the name for a multiple-choice test, eliminating (C), (D) and (E).

18. **A** There are several components to making sure the administration of a test is done ethically, but the key component is that the subjects must be protected under confidentiality no matter what, (A). Choice (B) refers to a concern of studies, not tests; usually tests don't involve deception unless it has to do with how they are used within a study. Double-blind design is a characteristic of experiments, not tests, and it has more to do with eliminating confounding variables than with ethics, so eliminate (C). Validity and generalization have nothing to do with ethics, but rather effectiveness in what a test intends to measure internally and in a general population. Methodology is not included in these two terms, so eliminate (D) and (E). The correct answer is (A).

19. **B** Knowledge of certain facts and figures is crystallized intelligence. Perhaps you reasoned your way to a good guess and chose fluid intelligence, but remember, fluid intelligence is mental agility, problem-solving ability, and other qualities that are not necessarily parroting back facts. Assimilation is a type of learning, incorporating information into mental schemas. Wisdom is knowledge that comes from life experiences.

20. **D** Since Mira learns to understand that the object is in fact a bookshelf instead of a desk, she is accommodating this information, making adjustments to her already preexisting schema. If it were, in fact, a desk, as she originally thought, this would have been assimilation. But it wasn't, so you can cross out (E). Functional fixedness is a type of mental set, but there is no problem-solving in this question, so eliminate (A) and (C). Choice (B) is a milestone from Jean Piaget's preoperational stage. The correct answer is (D).

CHAPTER 9 (UNIT 3) DRILL

1. **B** The fact that the dog is now exhibiting a fear response to any moving, wheeled vehicle represents a stimulus generalization. Choice (A) is the opposite process—if the dog was originally struck by a blue van of a certain make, for example, and did not show a fear response to any vehicle but that type of blue van. Choice (C) refers to the process whereby a conditioned response was made extinct by removing a conditioned stimulus, but might be elicited by a presentation of that stimulus at a later time. Choice (D), backward conditioning, occurs when an unconditioned stimulus is presented before a conditioned one and has nothing to do with this situation.

2. **D** Second-order conditioning occurs when a previously conditioned stimulus—originally neutral, but now response-eliciting—acts as an unconditioned stimulus and is paired with a new neutral stimulus to be conditioned; eventually, this second stimulus is successful at eliciting a conditioned response. In (D), the rabbit was conditioned to fear the musical tone; then the musical tone was paired with a flashed light; and eventually the flashed light elicited fear even in the absence of the tone. Choice (A) is an example of conditioned taste aversion; (B) is a simple classic conditioning paradigm; (C) is stimulus generalization; and (E), which may be a result of social learning, does not apply to this situation.

3. **C** A variable-ratio reinforcement schedule is one in which the ratio of responses to reward is variable and therefore unpredictable. Although the original conditioning may take longer, the response is quite resistant to extinction. In a fixed-ratio schedule (A), rewards always come after a certain number of correct responses; learning is quick but so is extinction, as it is easy to determine when the reinforcement schedule is no longer operative. This can also be said for (E), a continuous schedule. Choice (B), fixed-interval schedules, with rewards presented after a set time period, have a similar learning/extinction profile to fixed-ratio schedules. Choice (D), variable-interval schedules, with rewards presented at variable time periods, are more resistant to extinction than fixed-interval schedules but not as resistant as variable-ratio schedules.

4. **A** The number of neurons does not increase with learning; in fact, the number of neurons is at its highest for most animals at birth—neurons do not reproduce under normal circumstances. However, they do grow in size and number of connections, alter the strength of already existing connections, and produce higher levels of neurotransmitters in response to learning. Neurons that wire together, fire together.

5. **A** Though there are many social or observational learning situations that involve rewards or punishments, Bandura's experiments showed that such learning can occur even if there were no rewards or punishments—that is, consequences—to the observed behaviors. According to Bandura, attention to the behavior, retention of it, the ability to reproduce it, and the motivation to reproduce it at some point are what is necessary for observational learning.

6. **B** Operant conditioning, (B), is accomplished when someone receives a reward after performing a task; after the person has performed the task and received the reward enough times, they will perform the task without the reward, as occurs here. Choice (A), vicarious reinforcement, involves watching another person receive a reward for their behavior; there is no mention of Jay being motived by other people getting rewarded. Choice (C), an innate behavior, is one that does not need to be conditioned and therefore not what is being described in the question stem. Choice (D), classical conditioning, is accomplished by pairing two stimuli, one that is neutral with another that is unconditioned. Over time, the neutral stimulus becomes the conditioned stimulus. Because the question is not describing the pairing of two stimuli, nor is a stimulus presented before the behavior, classical conditioning does not explain the behavior described in the question stem. Choice (E), observational learning, involves the observation of a behavior or set of behaviors and a subsequent modification of behavior on the part of the observer in modeling what they've seen.

7. **B** Negative reinforcement occurs when an unpleasant stimulus is removed. Remember, negative is equivalent to taking something away from a situation and positive is equivalent to adding something in reinforcement terms. Choice (A) describes negative punishment, since Stephanie's weekend privileges are revoked for the next weekend. Choice (B) works because the negative stimulus, taking out the trash, is removed in order to reinforce a behavior. In (C), Ben receives positive reinforcement, because he is rewarded with a pleasant stimulus for having done good work on his project. Choice (D) is another example of negative punishment because the dog does an undesirable behavior and the owner removes himself from contact. Choice (E) introduces something unpleasant to the situation, an example of positive punishment. The correct answer is (B).

8. **B** The care team does not want the patient to develop a taste aversion to food staples or favorite foods. The unconditioned stimulus in this case would be the chemotherapy, but the patient would likely associate the foods (a neutral stimulus) with the nausea. While stimulus generalization is part of the concept of taste aversion, the care team is trying to keep the association from occurring in the first place, not to keep it from becoming generalized before the connection is in place.

9. **A** When dealing with periods of time, always think of "interval" to decipher reinforcement schedules. For number of instances, think "ratio." In this scenario, the mail comes consistently at the same time every day, so it must be an interval schedule, eliminating (C) and (D). Choice (E) is incorrect because continual reinforcement is a reward for every single instance, and she doesn't receive mail every time she goes to the mailbox. Since the time interval between mail deliveries is consistent, this is a fixed-interval schedule. The correct answer is (A).

10. **D** The process of teaching a skill through gradually molding specific behavior is called shaping, (D). Kevin rewards the dog for accomplishing intermediate steps along the way, which shapes Muka's behavior to learn a new trick.

11. **E** Prosody is the term given to the tones and inflections added to language that elaborate meaning with no word alterations. Choice (A), syntax, refers to the set of rules in a language for arranging words into sentences; (B), grammar, is the set of rules by which language is constructed, which includes syntax and semantics; (C) indicates the study of the smallest units of speech sounds in a language that are still distinct from one another; and (D) refers to the meanings of chosen words, not their expressed tone.

12. **C** Telegraphic speech is a common occurrence in toddlers who are combining words for the first time; it consists of two- or three-word utterances that are composed mostly of salient nouns, verbs, and adjectives with an absence of articles, conjunctions, and prepositions, and a limited use of pronouns. All of the answers except (C) involve two- or three-word utterances that fit that definition; (C) is an example of a holophrase—a single-word utterance of younger children that has a broad meaning.

13. **A** Stefano's knowledge of Spanish is interfering with his effort to speak German. In other words, his prior knowledge is hindering his ability to retain new knowledge, so this is an example of proactive interference.

14. **D** The Moro reflex in newborns is the startle response that involves the splaying of limbs in response to a falling sensation. Choice (A) is the neonatal reflex of grabbing anything placed in the hand; (B), the Babinski reflex, is produced when stroking the bottom of the neonate's foot results in a splaying out of the toes; and (E) is the reflex that causes a newborn to turn in the direction of a touch on the cheek. While the orienting reflex, (C), may be elicited by a loud noise, it occurs whenever there is any other sudden change in the environment, as well.

15. **B** The cognitive theory of Vygotsky stresses social and environmental, not just biological/maturational, factors as critical to development; he proposed the concept of a zone of proximal development, which is the range between the developed level of ability a child displays and the potential, or latent, level of ability a child is actually capable of. He further theorized that this latent level is hard to elicit due to a lack of optimal environmental circumstances. Choices (A), Jean Piaget, and (D), Sigmund

Freud, created alternate theories of development; (C), Leon Festinger, is most closely identified with the theory of cognitive dissonance and (E), Julian Rotter, with the concept of locus of control.

16. **A**   Erik Erikson's psychosocial theory of development describes a series of "conflicts" or "tasks" at each stage of life, from infancy to old age. In his theory, the successful resolution of each developmental task results in the development of a certain ability or belief, which serves as the foundation for the resolution of the next "task." The developmental task for school-age children is termed "industry vs. inferiority," and the resolution of this stage produces a sense of competence in one's own efforts and work. Choice (B) is the resolution of the task of early adulthood—"intimacy vs. isolation"; (C) is the resolution of the task of infancy—"trust vs. mistrust"; (D) is the resolution of the task of toddlerhood—"autonomy vs. shame/doubt"; and (E) is the resolution of the task of adolescence— "identity vs. role confusion."

17. **B**   According to the developmental theory of Jean Piaget, a child of about five would generally be at the preoperational stage, characterized by both animism—the belief that all things are alive—and egocentrism—the ability to see the world only from one's own point of view. Choices (A), (C), and (D) are other stages of Piaget's developmental model. Choice (E) is a developmental stage in Sigmund Freud's theory.

18. **C**   An infant who is securely attached will feel secure when he is around his mother, as evidenced by his comfort when his mother is in the room. When she leaves the room, the infant cries, but is easily consoled upon her return. If the child were insecurely attached, his reaction would differ. In the "strange situation" experiment, the insecurely attached children had varied reactions. Some children did not react as much when the mother left the room, and other children did a combination of both behaviors (disorganized behavior). The correct answer is (C).

19. **A**   Conservation is the concept that the amount of a material is still the same in different forms. In this case, it is the same amount of water in both the cup and the vase, though the water level may change.

20. **E**   Bandura's name is synonymous with observational learning. Through this perspective, Bandura posited that gender roles are at least partially observed by the individual. Choice (A) alludes to a behavioral perspective since it involves learning, so eliminate (A). Choice (B) is also incorrect because Bandura was not concerned with genetics. Choice (C) is also an incomplete explanation for the complex subject of gender, aside from it not relating to Bandura's theories. Choice (D) is too extreme because of the word *only,* and does not address the observational nature of Bandura's work. Only (E) is consistent with Bandura's research.

21. **A**   Though Bandura was measuring aggressive behavior in the children, the crucial part of the experiment was the children's observation of the adults. If the children observed the adults behaving aggressively toward the bobo doll, they were more apt to act aggressively themselves. If they observed the adults behaving nonaggressively, they were also less likely to act aggressively.

CHAPTER 10 (UNIT 4) DRILL

1. **D** Secondary drives, like secondary reinforcers, are learned by association with primary drives and primary reinforcers. Satisfying basic needs, as in (A), is a primary drive, as is the attempt to maintain homeostatic equilibrium, as in (B). Choice (C), instinct, refers to unlearned behaviors and (E), optimal arousal, refers to biological theory.

2. **A** The Yerkes-Dodson law relates levels of arousal and task difficulty. Here, a high-difficulty task (SAT) requires low levels of arousal (calm and relaxed). Arousal and obtaining a primary reinforcer, as in (B), is an inaccurate comparison for this theory. Tasks related to homeostasis, as in (C), involve drive-reduction theory. Choices (D) and (E) give scenarios opposite to what the law dictates: low arousal and low difficulty in (D) and high arousal and high difficulty in (E).

3. **B** An extrinsic factor is one that motivates behavior but does not originate within the individual performing the behavior; it instead originates from the outside world. In Rhoni's case, feeling the need to excel at her career in order to keep up her family's lifestyle and her parents' opinion of her qualifies as being primarily from outside of her (though she may enjoy the lifestyle herself). Choice (A) would be a factor that originated within the individual displaying the behavior; (D) and (E) would also describe such internal factors.

4. **A** According to drive-reduction theory, the drive is hunger in this case, so to reduce the need, Sanju needs to eat something. Since she does this, theoretically, she will return to homeostasis, as in (A). Yes, she may be thirsty as well, but that is not stated in the question, nor will a donut necessarily cause thirst. The donut may increase insulin levels in the body, but it is not certain that they will be raised to unhealthy levels, so (A) is the only provable response.

5. **B** The hypothalamus is mostly in charge of maintaining homeostasis in the body, (B). Choice (A) describes the thalamus, (C) the hippocampus, (D) the pituitary gland, and (E) the amygdala. The correct answer is (B).

6. **B** In Freudian theory, the ego is the part of the mind that mediates between the wants/demands of the part of the mind known as the id, (C); the internal representation of rules, morals, and social obligations known as the superego, (A); and the realities of the outside world. The ego involves conscious thought and choice, and attempts to find acceptable ways to satisfy desires. Choices (D) and (E) are not parts of the mind in Freudian theory; they are concepts from Jungian theory.

7. **E** Reaction formation is the psychodynamic defense mechanism that involves the ego reversing the direction of a disturbing or unacceptable desire to make that desire safer and more acceptable, as when a person who unconsciously hates children might feel the need to volunteer at a day-care center. The other answers are all definitions of other defense mechanisms: (A) is displacement, (B) is regression, (C) is compensation, and (D) is rationalization.

8. **D** Albert Bandura is identified with a social-cognitive, rather than psychodynamic, theory of personality; his theory does not concern itself very much with unconscious desires and mechanisms, as psychodynamic theories do, but rather focuses on an individual's concepts and beliefs. Horney, Jung, Adler, and Erikson are all psychodynamic theorists who expanded on or modified Freud's original conception of personality.

9. **D** In the personality and therapeutic theories of Carl Rogers, self-actualization refers to the process by which individuals learn and grow over time in ways that allow them to reach their full potential and ability. To humanistic theorists, such as Rogers, self-actualization is the ultimate purpose of human existence. Choice (A) refers to the value we place on ourselves—often a product of self-actualization, but not the actual process. Choice (C), self-efficacy, refers to a person's belief in their own competence in a given situation.

10. **B** Anne is not very competent at riding a bike, which shows she has a low self-efficacy, so eliminate (A) and (C). However, she knows she is in control of getting better at riding a bike if she practices. This means that she has an internal locus of control; she has control over her improvements. The correct answer is (B).

11. **E** The concept of the halo effect is that multiple positive attributes will surround a person who already possesses some. Since Lukas has good looks, grades, and athleticism, the halo effect suggests that he has other positive attributes as well, such as being trustworthy. The correct answer is (E).

12. **A** When Tanya kicks the ice instead of her coach or herself, she is showing displacement, since she directs her anger toward the ice. The correct answer is (A).

13. **C** In Jung's theory, the anima and animus are the male and female qualities that lie in each personality. This supports (C). Beware of the recycled Jungian language in (A) and (D). Neither addresses the subject of this question, but test-makers hope that those key words might be enticing. Choice (B) describes Erikson's trust versus mistrust, and (E) is more of a humanistic viewpoint.

14. **B** Cara feels good about herself, showing that she is exhibiting positive self-esteem, (B). The question does not show whether she is proficient at a task or not, so eliminate self-efficacy, (A). The self-concept is a larger umbrella including self-esteem, efficacy, schemata, etc., so eliminate (C) as well. Choices (D) and (E) are incorrect because those are defense mechanisms of psychoanalysis. The correct answer is (B).

15. **D** The fundamental attribution error is defined as the tendency of people to overestimate a person's disposition and to underestimate the situational circumstances when evaluating another person's behavior. Both (A) and (C) are examples of an internal locus of control. Choice (B), blaming a teacher for one's failures, is an example of an external attribution. In evaluating her friend's behavior, Karen is balancing personal and situational attributes, so eliminate (E) as well.

16. **D** In the Asch conformity experiments, many factors influenced the degree to which an experimental subject would show conformity to the obviously wrong group opinion, but the subject's age did not show a consistent effect in this regard. Choice (A) certainly did—unanimity was very important; only one dissenting opinion drastically reduced the tendency of the subject to go along with the rest of the group; (B), size of the group, had an influence in that it seemed to take a group of at least three members for such conformity to be shown consistently; (C), the subjects' perceptions of their own social status versus that of the group, was important—subjects who perceived themselves as of low/medium status were much more likely to conform than those who perceived themselves as of high status; and (E), gender of the subject, was an influencing factor, with females more likely to conform than males.

17. **D** The self-fulfilling prophecy refers to the scenario in the question—students randomly labeled as likely to experience significant jumps in academic test scores in the coming semester did indeed seem to perform to those expectations on those tests at the end of the semester. Choice (A), the Hawthorne effect, refers to the observation that students or workers who know they are being monitored tend to perform better, even if they do not know why they are being monitored. Choice (B), the Kandel effect, is associated with research into learning and neurophysiology in sea slugs; (C), cognitive dissonance, refers to the discomfort that comes from conflicting behavior and beliefs; and (E), the Ainsworth effect, comes from studies of attachment in human infants.

18. **B** Diffusion of responsibility, also sometimes referred to as the bystander effect, occurs when every person in a crowded social situation defers to another to make the effort to mount a response to the situation. It can also occur when members of a group perform negative behaviors that no specific individual or individuals will take responsibility for. Choice (D), an altruistic orientation, usually refers to the decision-making paradigm in which individuals wish to maximize the outcome for others, but it could also be applied to this situation as a countervailing force to the diffusion of responsibility. Choice (A), illusory correlation, refers to the false presumption that certain groups are associated with certain stereotypes or behaviors, and (E), the just-world hypothesis, is the belief that because the world is basically fair, people deserve whatever befalls them, positive or negative. Choice (C), cognitive dissonance, deals with conflicting beliefs and behaviors, not responsibility.

19. **B** The "foot-in-the-door" technique involves making requests in small increments that people are more likely to initially comply with, and then working from those up to bigger requests; the incremental approach seems to work better than "going for the whole ball of wax all at once." This is what the teenager is trying to do in getting his curfew extended in small increments until he gets the curfew he actually wants. Choice (A) is an example of the "door-in-the-face" technique, in which one asks for much more than what one actually wants, expecting to be turned down; one can then ask for the smaller, "more reasonable" request, which is more likely to be granted. People also tend to be more likely to comply with or be persuaded by those they feel they are similar to, as in (D), or by those they will receive a desired reward from (hardly a surprise), as in (E).

20. **C** The man who does not have health insurance in (A) thinks nothing bad will happen to him, which is known as an optimism bias. The woman observing the man who loses his house in (B) most likely feels for the man, but exhibits the just-world bias since she most likely thinks the man failed to act on obtaining health insurance. Choice (C) is the clearest example of the self-serving bias, since the toddler attributes building the block tower to herself, but blames the blocks instead of herself when they tumble to the ground. Remember, the self-serving bias is when a person takes credit for positive achievements and attributes something or someone else as the cause of negative ones. Choice (D) most clearly shows a self-fulfilling prophecy and the Rosenthal Effect, in which the teacher believes in Yuan, and he then goes and studies for his exam. Finally, (E) is an example of a situational attribution, in which the environment causes conditions that affect a large number of the residents described in the answer choice. The correct answer is (C).

21. **A** Since both groups remained equal for a while, the group that had five members shows evidence of social loafing. The more people assigned to that side of the rope, the less force they thought they needed to exert individually. The three students on the other side of the rope felt more individually responsible and had an increased need to contribute.

22. **D**   The child in this question uses the door-in-the-face technique to get what he wants from his parents. This technique is named for his parents metaphorically "slamming the door in his face" at his outrageous request of $100 per week. However, when he asks for less money, he is met with less resistance.

23. **E**   Stanley Milgram's study involved a significant amount of deception, tricking the subjects into thinking they were participating in a study on learning. They played roles within the experiment, though this was not the point of the experiment, so eliminate (D). There is not a group in the experiment, so conformity, dehumanization, and groupthink are not factors here either, eliminating (A), (B), and (C). The point of the experiment was to test obedience to the "experimenter" when he told the subject (the "teacher") to administer what the subject believed to be an electric shock to the "learner" (a confederate to the experimenter in another room). A large percentage of subjects obeyed the experimenter and administered the highest level of electric shock. The correct answer is (E).

CHAPTER 11 (UNIT 5) DRILL

1. **E**   Suppressed appetite is not a symptom of chronic stress, though it may be one of acute stress, which lasts for only a short amount of time. Remember that chronic stress is defined as lasting for weeks, months, or even years.

2. **C**   This person is most likely experiencing a psychotic episode. Choices (B) and (D), obsessions and compulsions, refer to a different disorder. Choice (A), delusions, are relevant to psychosis, but they are beliefs not based in reality, and the question stem explicitly says he hears voices, not that he believes anything in particular. Choice (E), inceptions, is not a psychological concept. Only (C), hallucinations, fits the question stem.

3. **E**   Dissociative disorders, such as amnesia, fugue, or dissociative identity disorder, are characterized by dysfunction of memory and disruption in the sense of identity. Choice (A) is more characteristic of phobias, (C) of obsessive disorders, and (D) of certain types of schizophrenia. Choice (B) might be descriptive of some individuals with dissociative disorders, but it is not a diagnostic criterion or a widely seen characteristic of the disorder (many with such disorders have quite extensive social networks).

4. **C**   Serotonin is a neurotransmitter that influences mood and seems to be present at lower-than-usual levels in many of those diagnosed with depression (at least, unipolar depression). Choice (A), acetylcholine, has, at least in some studies, been associated with the expression of bipolar behavior when present in greater-than-average amounts. Dopamine deficits have been implicated in Parkinson's disease, and may be implicated in certain instances of schizophrenia, but not depression, so eliminate (E).

5. **C**   By *DSM-5* definition, anxiety disorders are characterized by feelings of tension, nervousness, fear, and sometimes panic. All of the choices here qualify except for anxious personality disorder, which is made up.

6. **D**   The girl is most likely suffering from dissociative fugue (a type of dissociative disorder, (D)), which causes her to experience personal amnesia. Sufferers of dissociative fugue tend to wander or travel and often establish new identities based on who they believe they are. Choice (A), somatoform disorder, involves physical illness or injury. Choice (B), delusional disorder, is a psychotic illness that is characterized by non-bizarre delusions, with no accompanying hallucinations, mood disturbances, or flattening of affect; furthermore, amnesia is not a symptom of a delusional disorder. Choice (C), personality disorder, is characterized by a set of personality traits that deviates from cultural norms, impairs functioning, and causes distress; there are three major clusters of personality disorders, none of which accurately explain the girl described in the question stem. Although it is possible that the girl's symptoms are feigned in an attempt to seek attention, a possible symptom of histrionic personality disorder, the question stem would need to provide concrete information to draw this conclusion, which it does not. Also, there is no direct evidence of schizophrenia demonstrated in the question stem, so eliminate (E).

7. **B**   Schizoid personality disorder, (B), is classified under Cluster A personality disorders. This person will likely be markedly detached from friends and family members and have a flat affect, whereas Cluster B disorders are more emotional and dramatic.

8. **E**   Many diagnoses, such as obsessive-compulsive disorder, are diagnosed only in adulthood. This is a child, so this must be a neurodevelopmental disorder, narrowing options to (A) and (E). The child is not exhibiting impulsivity/hyperactivity or inattention, but rather restrictive behavior and difficulty in social situations, since he is having difficulty engaging with peers. This is descriptive of ASD. The correct answer is (E).

9. **C**   Client-centered therapy, as an outgrowth of the humanistic school of psychology, is very concerned with trying to understand the client's view of the world and how it affects them, in order to facilitate the client's own tendencies toward growth and fulfillment. Therapists utilizing this approach see accurate empathic understanding—the therapist's ability to view the world through the eyes of the client—as critical to successful communication between client and therapist. While (A), psychoanalytic therapy, also considers communication and understanding the client's view of the world important, it tends to discourage emotional or personal involvement with the patient through such empathy. Psychoanalytic therapists believe a stance of detachment is best for the encouragement of transference, which helps to reveal the nature of the patient's conflicts. Choice (D), implosion therapy, is a behavioral approach with little emphasis on the kind of client–therapist relationship considered essential to client-centered therapy.

10. **E**   Behavioral approaches to therapy are concerned with treating maladaptive or troubling symptoms, rather than underlying causes, and in this school of thought, there are no hidden, "deep" underlying causes—the disordered behavior itself is the problem. As such, behavioral therapies have been most often used with those who seek to change specific behaviors, such as those who suffer from phobias. While behavioral approaches might be tried for individuals with some of the other conditions listed, the more symptom-oriented behavioral techniques are usually not the treatment of choice with conditions that involve more than just a specific maladaptive behavior and/or altered mental states.

11. **B**   Psychoanalytic therapy focuses on probing past defense mechanisms to understand the unconscious roots of problems; indeed, its practitioners believe that troubling behaviors or symptoms cannot possibly cease until a patient gains insight into such unconscious roots. In this approach, treating just symptoms through behavioral methods without addressing the underlying hidden causes will not result in a lasting "cure" and may instead result in symptoms returning or new ones manifesting. Choices (A) and (C) are not generally criticisms leveled at behavioral therapy by psychoanalysts; indeed, for those it's the other way around—these are criticisms of psychoanalytic approaches often made by behaviorists. The criticism in (D) would more likely be made by humanistic or client-centered therapists.

12. **B**   Rational-emotive behavioral therapy, or simply rational-emotive therapy, is primarily associated with Albert Ellis, who formulated this cognitive approach, which concentrates on modifying incorrect thoughts or cognitions that lead to maladaptive emotional and behavioral responses. Choice (A), Julian Rotter, is associated with the concept of locus of control; (C), Abraham Maslow, with the concepts of hierarchy of needs and self-actualization; (D), Raymond Cattell, with a trait theory of personality and the 16 PF Questionnaire; and (E), Rollo May, with the existential approach to psychotherapy.

13. **A**   Anticoagulants are not drugs used for psychotherapeutic purposes; they are, instead, used to modulate the ability of the blood to clot and form vessel blockages. Both (C) and (E) are classes of drugs that belong to the larger family of antidepressants; (B), anxiolytics, as the name implies, are used primarily for the reduction of anxiety; and (D), lithium salts, are useful in the treatment of some cases of bipolar disorder.

14. **C**   There is nothing systematic or progressive about going to the top of the Empire State Building on a first therapy session for acrophobia. Instead, the therapist is choosing a situation in which Judy will most likely have a very strong reaction at first, but will hopefully have less of a reaction the longer she realizes she will not fall off the ledge. This is a technique called flooding, (C). Choice (B) is not the answer because the therapist is not trying to condition Judy not to like something. Choice (D), implosion, is similar to flooding, but it uses visualization techniques instead of physically going to a location or confronting a stimulus. There is not a contract in the question stem either, eliminating (E).

15. **D**   A behavioral therapist will seek to modify behavior by extinguishing maladaptive behaviors and conditioning more adaptive ones. Therefore, extinction procedures will be used to modify behaviors. Choices (A), (B), and (C) are specific to psychoanalysis, while (E) is most closely associated with humanistic therapy. The correct answer is (D).

16. **A**   SSRIs are most commonly used as antidepressants. Therefore, they would most likely be used for depressive disorders.

17. **A**   Carl Rogers is synonymous with humanistic therapy. If you were unsure, remember that he coined the phrase *unconditional positive regard*, so he was most concerned with treating other humans with the utmost respect and compassion. Hence, the term humanism came forth.

Part VII
Practice Test 2

- Practice Test 2
- Practice Test 2: Answers and Explanations

Practice Test 2

AP® Psychology Exam

SECTION I: Multiple-Choice Questions

DO NOT OPEN THIS EXAM UNTIL YOU ARE TOLD TO DO SO.

DISCLAIMER: The official AP Psychology exam will be administered digitally. Instructions for the digital exam may differ from this practice test.

At a Glance

Total Time
90 minutes
Number of Questions
75
Percent of Total Grade
66.6%

Instructions

Section I of this exam contains 75 multiple-choice questions. Fill in only the ovals for numbers 1 through 75 on your answer sheet.

Indicate all of your answers to the multiple-choice questions on the answer sheet. Give only one answer to each question. If you change an answer, be sure that the previous mark is erased completely. Here is a sample question and answer.

Sample Question   **Sample Answer**

Omaha is a

(A) state
(B) city
(C) country
(D) continent

Use your time effectively, working as quickly as you can without losing accuracy. Do not spend too much time on any one question. Go on to other questions and come back to the ones you have not answered if you have time. It is not expected that everyone will know the answers to all of the multiple-choice questions.

GO ON TO THE NEXT PAGE.

PSYCHOLOGY
Section I
Time—90 minutes
75 Questions

Directions: Each of the questions below is followed by four answer choices. Select the one that is best in each case.

---

1 ☐ Mark for Review

Mr. Weber discovered that he was about to lose his job, as his company decided to replace his entire team with AI. The first week after hearing this news, he had difficulty sleeping. In the three weeks following, though, he worked on his résumé and applied to 34 new jobs. By the end of the month, he was terminated but had not found a new job. Two months later, after depleting his savings account to afford rent and basic necessities, he started catching one cold after another. Which of the following best describes what Mr. Weber was experiencing?

(A) Eustress

(B) General Adaptation Syndrome

(C) Generativity vs. Stagnation

(D) Major depressive disorder

---

2 ☐ Mark for Review

Sean, preparing to study for an AP Psychology exam, is attempting to learn all ten personality disorders. His friend Teresa suggests that he draw a comic strip with ten characters who represent each of the personality disorders. Her suggestion involves which of the following?

(A) Iconic memory

(B) Elaborative rehearsal

(C) Mnemonic device

(D) Prospective memory

---

3 ☐ Mark for Review

Dr. Merken conducted a study to determine the noticeable difference in volume levels. She played songs by Taylor Swift, Shinee, Rammstein, and Nemo; participants pressed a button whenever they perceived an increase in volume, whether during or between songs. Dr. Merken found that volume increases of 10% or more were almost always noticed, whereas volume increases of 3% or less were almost never noticed. Volume increases of 5% were noticed about half of the time. What was the independent variable in this research study?

(A) The actual change in volume

(B) The perceived change in volume

(C) The type of music heard

(D) The number of correct button presses

GO ON TO THE NEXT PAGE.

Questions 4 through 6 refer to the following.

Dr. Rätsel conducted a study to investigate problem solving. Three participants were sent at different times to a locked room filled with various objects, including a sign stating that "volume is the key." If the participant had not solved the puzzle after 20 minutes, they were released from the room. Participant A tried one object after another to open the door. Participant B tried using the largest objects (those with the greatest volume) to open the door. Participant C tried various tactics, then suddenly thought to stand near the door and yell loudly (at a high volume). The data collected on the time each group spent in the room are displayed in the table.

Group	Time in minutes
A	20
B	20
C	5

4 ☐ Mark for Review

Which of the following terms would a psychologist use to identify the problem-solving strategy of participant A?

(A) Mental set

(B) Heuristic

(C) Algorithm

(D) Functional fixedness

5 ☐ Mark for Review

What was the median escape time?

(A) 10

(B) 12.5

(C) 15

(D) 20

6 ☐ Mark for Review

Which of the following concepts best explains the outcome for participant C?

(A) Insight learning

(B) Latent learning

(C) Convergent thinking

(D) Inductive reasoning

GO ON TO THE NEXT PAGE.

7 ⬚ Mark for Review

Hanna goes to Bread and Cheese, a sandwich shop, on the way home from school about twice a week. She likes it partly because she gets a card that is punched every time she purchases a sandwich. When she buys a dozen, she gets the 13th free. Bread and Cheese encourages Hanna's business using which of the following reinforcement schedules?

(A) Variable-ratio

(B) Fixed-interval

(C) Variable-interval

(D) Fixed-ratio

8 ⬚ Mark for Review

Which of the following psychological perspectives would best help researchers answer questions about an organism's ability to learn novel behaviors through observation, rather than through direct reward and punishment?

(A) Social-cognitive

(B) Behaviorist

(C) Psychoanalytic

(D) Humanistic

9 ⬚ Mark for Review

In the 1960s, a psychologist led participants in an experiment to believe that they would act as a "teacher" to another participant. Whenever the "student" delivered a wrong answer on a vocabulary test, the "teacher" was supposed to press a button that would give an increasingly intense electric shock to the "student." In reality, no shocks were delivered—the "student" was in on the experiment. If the "teacher" wanted to stop, the experimenter would state: "You must continue." About two-thirds of participants continued to deliver shocks to the highest levels ("severe danger" and "XXX"). Which of the following concepts best describes the behavior of the majority of "teachers"?

(A) Conformity

(B) Obedience

(C) Cognitive dissonance

(D) Social facilitation

10 ⬚ Mark for Review

As Goldie was hiking through the woods, she suddenly heard a rustling sound behind her. When she turned to locate the source of the sound, she saw something brown and furry moving. She ran home as quickly as she could and told her friends how scared she had been to nearly encounter a bear. Which of the following was most directly responsible for Goldie's flight reaction?

(A) Sympathetic nervous system

(B) Central nervous system

(C) Parasympathetic nervous system

(D) Efferent nervous system

GO ON TO THE NEXT PAGE.

11 ☐ Mark for Review

Siblings Alice, Beth, and Carla are stressed out by the upcoming SAT. Alice starts making more time to listen to her friends. Beth starts listening to more lo-fi beats and practicing deep breathing. Carla starts making charts to sketch out a study plan. Which of the following best describes Beth's behavior?

Ⓐ Tend and befriend

Ⓑ Problem-focused coping

Ⓒ Emotion-focused coping

Ⓓ Avoidant detachment

GO ON TO THE NEXT PAGE.

Questions 12 through 14 refer to the following.

Researchers investigated the extent to which 30 pairs of identical and fraternal male twins shared personality traits of agreeableness and emotional stability with their twin. Twins separately completed a 50-item version of the "Big Five" personality inventory. Researchers found that 12 out of 15 pairs of identical twins and 3 out of 15 pairs of fraternal twins had similar levels of agreeableness and emotional stability. These results were shared with the twins' parents and teachers.

12 Mark for Review

Which of the following appropriate ethical procedures appears to have been neglected?

(A) The researchers failed to seek approval from an institutional review board.

(B) The researchers failed to obtain an informed consent from the participants.

(C) The researchers failed to keep participant information confidential or anonymous.

(D) The researchers failed to protect participants from harm.

13 Mark for Review

Which of the following conclusions can be made based on the data collected in this study?

(A) Identical twins are less likely than fraternal twins to develop high degrees of agreeableness.

(B) One twin having a high degree of emotional stability will cause the other to also have a high degree of emotional stability.

(C) Environment appears to be more strongly correlated with personality traits.

(D) Heredity appears to be more strongly correlated with personality traits.

14 Mark for Review

Which of the following personality traits was also likely tested on the "Big Five" personality inventory?

(A) Conscientiousness

(B) Anxiousness

(C) Genuineness

(D) Optimism

GO ON TO THE NEXT PAGE.

15 ☐ Mark for Review

In which of the following categories is Autism Spectrum Disorder classified?

Ⓐ Neurodevelopmental disorders

Ⓑ Obsessive-compulsive disorders

Ⓒ Neurocognitive disorders

Ⓓ Somatic symptom disorders

16 ☐ Mark for Review

Dr. Erbe wanted to know the relative contribution of heredity and environment to personality traits. She located a set of identical twins who had been separated at birth and raised in different households; she then administered a validated personality test to both. Results suggested a partial genetic contribution toward the trait of emotional stability. Which of the following best describes Dr. Erbe's research design?

Ⓐ Experimental, because participants were tested with a valid tool

Ⓑ Non-experimental, because participants cannot be assigned to conditions

Ⓒ Meta-analysis, because statistical analysis of data was performed

Ⓓ Naturalistic observation, because data gathered in this way are not artificial

17 ☐ Mark for Review

Dr. Klug wanted to see whether the Beck Depression Inventory could be used to measure general intelligence. She recruited 100 participants in February, administered the exam, then had them return in May and take the exam again. She found that for each participant, the scores were very similar at the two times. As a measure of intelligence, which of the following does the Beck Depression Inventory have?

Ⓐ Reliability

Ⓑ Content validity

Ⓒ Standardization

Ⓓ Face validity

18 ☐ Mark for Review

Dr. Plauder drops his children off at their respective schools on the way to his laboratory. His teenage daughter says, "Bruh, why I gotta go to school anyway?" In response, his three-year old son proudly announces: "I go school!" The pre-schooler's utterance is an example of which of the following?

Ⓐ Phoneme

Ⓑ Morpheme

Ⓒ Babbling

Ⓓ Telegraphic speech

GO ON TO THE NEXT PAGE.

19   ▢ Mark for Review

Ms. Spalt, 46 years old, reports to a psychologist that she has recurrent gaps in her recall of everyday events. In addition, her friends report that she sometimes switches from seeming happy and energetic to seeming angry and resentful. Medical tests show that her memory symptoms are not related to the effects of a substance or a medical condition. Which of the following diagnoses would the psychologist be most justified in making?

(A) Personality disorder

(B) Trauma- and stressor-related disorder

(C) Schizophrenic spectrum disorder

(D) Dissociative disorder

GO ON TO THE NEXT PAGE.

Questions 20 through 22 refer to the following.

Dr. Rauch conducted a study examining the effects of smoking on heart rate and perceived hunger. Participants reported how many cigarettes they had smoked that day and also indicated their hunger levels (no hunger, low hunger, moderate hunger, extreme hunger). Participants' heart rates were measured at the same time. The data collected are displayed in the graphs below.

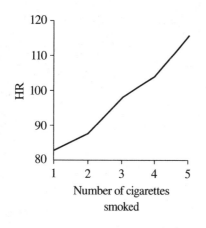
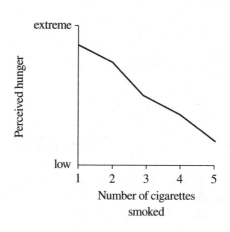

20 ☐ Mark for Review

Dr. Rauch found that smoking correlates to a faster heartbeat. This phenomenon is most likely due to which of the following?

(A) Dopamine

(B) GABA

(C) Acetylcholine

(D) Norepinephrine

21 ☐ Mark for Review

Based on the table, what is the relationship between number of cigarettes smoked and perceived hunger?

(A) Positive correlation

(B) Negative correlation

(C) No correlation

(D) Direct correlation

22 ☐ Mark for Review

When perceived hunger increases, people are likely to go look for something to eat. Which of the following brain areas is most involved in the motivation to eat?

(A) Hypothalamus

(B) Amygdala

(C) Medulla

(D) Hippocampus

GO ON TO THE NEXT PAGE.

23 ☐ Mark for Review

Peter is studying for a biology test. He remembers the information much better when he actually goes into the biology classroom, rather than staying in the library. This is most likely an example of which of the following?

(A) Mood-congruent memory

(B) State-dependent memory

(C) Procedural memory

(D) Context-dependent memory

24 ☐ Mark for Review

Harriet is on the soccer team. The coach requires daily workouts, which she praises each student for. Harriet likes the praise and shows up for each workout, doing more than asked. Eventually, Harriet does the workout every day even in the off-season, when the coach isn't around. This is an example of which of the following?

(A) Operant conditioning

(B) Vicarious conditioning

(C) Classical conditioning

(D) Negative reinforcement

25 ☐ Mark for Review

Paula is a gymnast who has been practicing hard for the state finals. When the judges give her an average score of 9, she attributes the high score to her hard work, thinking, "All my practice paid off!" But in one trial, her average falls to 5. She fumes, "They shortchanged me on the balance beam." Which of the following explains her reasoning?

(A) Actor-observer bias

(B) Fundamental attribution error

(C) Self-fulfilling prophecy

(D) Self-serving bias

26 ☐ Mark for Review

Drs. Gibson and Walk designed a plexiglass table that had a "shallow" and a "deep" side. They conducted a study with healthy infants with normal vision. They found that infants would readily crawl across the "shallow" side but that most would not crawl further across the "deep" side. Which of the following were they testing?

(A) Binocular cues

(B) The rooting reflex

(C) Monocular cues

(D) Depth perception

GO ON TO THE NEXT PAGE.

27 ☐ Mark for Review

Larry and Pat are both 52. Their children are in college. They are developing a plan to sell their home and go to work with the poor in other countries. Their plan corresponds to which following stages?

(A) Integrity vs. despair

(B) Post-conventional

(C) Generativity vs. stagnation

(D) Industry vs. inferiority

28 ☐ Mark for Review

Ivan's aunt had a stroke last week. Since then, the family noticed that she has difficulty speaking and writing, though she does understand other people's speaking and writing. Which area of the brain was likely damaged by the stroke?

(A) Broca's area

(B) Brodmann's area

(C) Wernicke's area

(D) Limbic system

29 ☐ Mark for Review

Jayden is learning to sail, but he experiences nausea every time he encounters open water. He is working with a therapist on ways to manage it. The therapist mentions that he should never eat favorite foods (chocolate, pizza) while sailing. This recommendation is made to help avoid which of the following?

(A) Biofeedback

(B) Taste aversion

(C) Desensitization

(D) Habituation

GO ON TO THE NEXT PAGE.

Questions 30 through 32 refer to the following.

Although antipsychotic drugs and improved therapeutic techniques represent great advances in the treatment of schizophrenia, they do not help everyone. Even when successful, they typically mitigate only psychotic effects, leaving many patients severely disabled from their negative and cognitive symptoms. Neuroscientists know that schizophrenia has a strong genetic component, because studies show that having a relative with schizophrenia dramatically increases the risk of developing the disease.

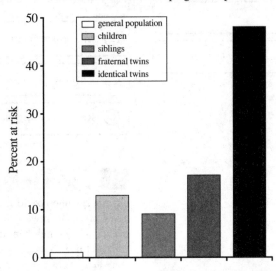

Lifetime Risk of Developing Schizophrenia

---

30 ☐ Mark for Review

The data in the graph above display the risk of someone developing schizophrenia in relation to whether they have a relative who has also developed schizophrenia. Based on the data in the graph, which of the following statements is true?

(A) There is a strong positive correlation between genetic similarity and risk of developing schizophrenia.

(B) Having children somewhat increases the risk of developing schizophrenia.

(C) If one has a fraternal twin with schizophrenia, one is at greater risk of developing this disorder than if one has a non-twin sibling with schizophrenia.

(D) Almost half of identical twins of someone with schizophrenia will also develop schizophrenia.

---

31 ☐ Mark for Review

Conventional antipsychotic drugs such as Thorazine have been found to help reduce positive symptoms of schizophrenia. Which of the following symptoms are most likely to be lessened through the use of Thorazine?

(A) Disintegration of memory and consciousness

(B) Flat affect and anhedonia

(C) Hallucinations and delusions

(D) Short attention span and impaired working memory

GO ON TO THE NEXT PAGE.

32 ☐ Mark for Review

Many antipsychotic drugs target dopamine receptors. Which of the following is a common side effect of dopamine antagonists?

(A) Gastrointestinal difficulties

(B) Weight changes

(C) Sleep issues

(D) Tardive dyskinesia

33 ☐ Mark for Review

Buster and Dave are driving on a highway to a shopping area. They see a hill in the distance and, as they approach, they see a neon light forming a small arc. They assume that the lights are broken and that the sign is actually a full circle, which is the logo of the shopping center. Which of the following best explains why they perceive a complete sign?

(A) Binocular disparity

(B) Linear perspective

(C) Closure

(D) Retinal convergence

34 ☐ Mark for Review

Dr. Aberglauben performed an experiment with pigeons. In a first phase, he rewarded pigeons with food whenever they pecked a lever and then immediately cooed. The pigeons learned this behavior rapidly and engaged in it whenever they were hungry. In a second phase, he rewarded the pigeons with food approximately every 3 minutes, no matter what they were doing. He noted that the pigeons began engaging in various unusual behaviors, from wing flapping to walking in circles. Which of the following concepts best describes the pigeons' behavior?

(A) Secondary reinforcement

(B) Superstition

(C) Successive approximation

(D) Instinctive drift

GO ON TO THE NEXT PAGE.

35 🔖 Mark for Review

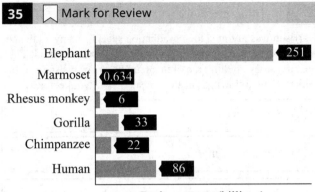

Brain neurons (billions)

The data in the graph display an estimated number of neurons in the brains of several species. Within these data, what is the median number of brain neurons?

Ⓐ 22 billion

Ⓑ 27.5 billion

Ⓒ 33 billion

Ⓓ 66.4 billion

36 🔖 Mark for Review

Dr. Seligman believes that psychology has been overly focused on problem behaviors; he proposes that the field should also focus on concepts such as well-being, resilience, and psychological health. One of his recent studies supports the claim that people who regularly express gratitude have better physical health. Which of the following best describes Dr. Seligman's area of research?

Ⓐ Positive reinforcement

Ⓑ Positive correlation

Ⓒ Positive psychology

Ⓓ Positive symptoms

37 🔖 Mark for Review

Sebastian is on his feet screaming, "Go! Go! Go!" as his favorite basketball team fights against the clock to win the game. He interprets his screaming and adrenaline as enthusiasm rather than anger or aggression. Which aspect of theories of emotion best explains this?

Ⓐ Cognitive label

Ⓑ The broaden-and-build theory

Ⓒ Universal emotions

Ⓓ Display rules

GO ON TO THE NEXT PAGE.

38 ☐ Mark for Review

Some research into schizophrenia suggests an interruption to the development of protective covering around the neuron, which can lead to problems in neural connectivity. According to this research, which of the following neural components is most clearly compromised?

Ⓐ Axons

Ⓑ Dendrites

Ⓒ Myelin sheath

Ⓓ Terminal buttons

39 ☐ Mark for Review

Harrison was giving a long graduation speech. Many audience members listened but didn't pay attention to what he said. The next day, they couldn't recall the main points of his speech. In which of the following did storage successfully take place?

Ⓐ Sensory memory

Ⓑ Semantic memory

Ⓒ Procedural memory

Ⓓ Working memory

GO ON TO THE NEXT PAGE.

Questions 40 through 42 refer to the following.

Researchers examined the influence of attachment security on student academic success over their first four years in college. Eighty-five first-semester students provided their attachment dimensions and psychological indices at the beginning of their college careers. Students' academic records were accessed throughout the four-year period. Retention (staying in college) rates were also tracked. The results indicate that attachment security had a significant effect on students' four-year cumulative GPA.

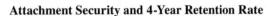

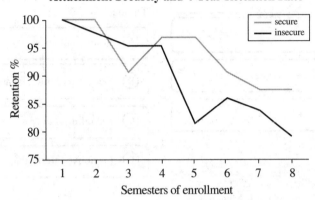

Attachment Security and 4-Year Retention Rate

40 ☐ Mark for Review

Based on the data in the figure above, which of the following statements is true?

(A) Secure attachment is positively associated with retention.

(B) Insecure attachment causes a lowering in retention.

(C) Both attachment styles lead to a lowering in retention.

(D) It is unclear whether there is a significant effect of attachment styles on retention.

41 ☐ Mark for Review

Which of the following best describes the research design?

(A) Cross-sectional

(B) Meta-analytic

(C) Longitudinal

(D) Ethnographic

42 ☐ Mark for Review

In which stage of psychosocial development would the participants likely be?

(A) Autonomy and shame and doubt

(B) Industry and inferiority

(C) Intimacy and isolation

(D) Trust and mistrust

GO ON TO THE NEXT PAGE.

43 ☐ Mark for Review

Ever since sophomore year, Brianna has felt it very comforting to come home and fix 10 pieces of cinnamon toast. She eats them in her bedroom and later vomits all of them up so she doesn't gain weight. Brianna likely has which of the following?

(A) Pica

(B) Anorexia nervosa

(C) Binge-eating disorder

(D) Bulimia nervosa

44 ☐ Mark for Review

Three students are taking an AP Chemistry test. Megan is very nervous about the test, as she wants to be a doctor, and a good chemistry score is essential. Zach has been talking to his parents about taking a gap year and hasn't really paid much attention to the test. Tamika wants to do well and is slightly anxious but knows she has done well in class and that her overall GPA and essay are more likely to affect her chances at college. Tamika gets the highest score. Which of the following best explains her performance?

(A) Type B behavior

(B) Classical conditioning

(C) Yerkes-Dodson Law

(D) Self-actualization

45 ☐ Mark for Review

Thomas is a 55-year-old journalist. When he was young, he learned that all periods at the ends of sentences should be followed by two spaces. His 27-year-old editor learned that one space is correct. She gets very frustrated with Thomas because she's told him many times to just use one. Thomas shrugs and says, "I can never remember that." What best explains Thomas's response?

(A) Source amnesia

(B) Retroactive interference

(C) Encoding failure

(D) Proactive interference

GO ON TO THE NEXT PAGE.

Questions 46 through 48 refer to the following.

Dr. Schlaf conducted a study to investigate the relationship between stress and sleep disturbances. Nine participants rated their stress levels and then underwent a sleep study. The data collected on reported stress levels and observed number of sleep disturbances are displayed in the table.

Participant	Reported stress level	Number of sleep disturbances
A	high	6
B	high	7
C	high	6
D	medium	3
E	medium	2
F	medium	3
G	low	0
H	low	1
I	low	0

46 ☐ Mark for Review

Which of the following is most involved in regulating sleep?

(A) Thalamus

(B) Cerebellum

(C) Reticular activating system

(D) Limbic system

47 ☐ Mark for Review

Do the data in the table support the conclusion that increased stress causes sleep disturbances?

(A) Yes, because there is a positive correlation between reported stress level and the number of sleep disturbances.

(B) Yes, because there is a negative correlation between reported stress level and the number of sleep disturbances.

(C) No, because sleep disturbances could also be the cause of increased stress.

(D) No, because stress and sleep disturbances have not been found to be correlated.

48 ☐ Mark for Review

Sleep studies often involve an electroencephalogram. Which of the following are researchers most likely to observe in the moments after participants first fall asleep?

(A) REM sleep

(B) NREM sleep

(C) Paradoxical sleep

(D) Dreaming

GO ON TO THE NEXT PAGE.

49 ☐ Mark for Review

Olivia's family moves to a new house very near an airport. For the first week, all the family members are distressed that the sound of planes taking off is so loud. When a friend comes to visit the third week and complains about the noise, Olivia realizes she doesn't even notice it anymore. This is likely due to which phenomenon?

(A) Habituation

(B) Dishabituation

(C) Discrimination

(D) Shaping

50 ☐ Mark for Review

Ayesha's new job requires employees to punch in a numeric code to enter certain rooms. She repeats the code over and over to herself to remember it. Ayesha is using which of the following?

(A) Elaborative rehearsal

(B) Maintenance rehearsal

(C) Method of loci

(D) Chunking

51 ☐ Mark for Review

Whenever her father leaves the house, Koshka runs to the door and cries. When her father returns, she rushes to be near him but also cries, sometimes simultaneously hugging him and hitting him. Which of the following appears to be her attachment style?

(A) Secure

(B) Avoidant

(C) Anxious

(D) Disorganized

52 ☐ Mark for Review

Dr. List wanted to study the effect of a new weight loss drug on hypothalamus activity. Twenty participants enrolled in the study; all of them signed documents that indicated that they might receive injections. He injected ten participants with the experimental drug and ten participants with a saline solution. Dr. List found mild changes in hypothalamus activity in the saline condition and moderate changes in hypothalamus activity in the drug condition. Participants were then sent home. Based on this description, did this research follow appropriate ethical procedures?

(A) Yes, because the participants all gave their informed consent to participate in the study.

(B) Yes, because the researcher ensured that no participants were harmed during the study.

(C) No, because participants' anonymity could be compromised after the study.

(D) No, because participants were not properly debriefed at the end of the study.

53 ☐ Mark for Review

Gordon keeps his grades very high because of his belief that this is inherently a good thing. His classmate Jordan keeps her grades very high to please her parents and keep her scholarship. Her motivation can be described as

(A) Instinctual

(B) Extrinsic

(C) Autonomous

(D) Intrinsic

GO ON TO THE NEXT PAGE.

Questions 54 through 56 refer to the following.

Data from the 2019–2021 National Health Interview Survey (NHIS) show that from 2019 to 2021, the total percentage of adults who had received any mental health treatment (defined as having either taken medication for mental health, received counseling or therapy, or both) increased by 2.4%. Among adults aged 18–44, the percentage who had received any mental health treatment increased by 4.7%. Among adults aged 45–64, the percentage who had received any mental health treatment increased by 1%. Among adults aged 65 and over, the percentage who had received any mental health treatment decreased by 0.5%.

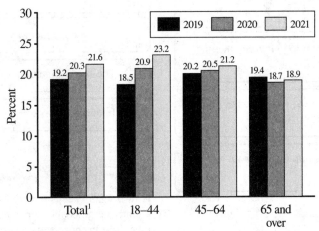

[1]Significant linear trend by year (p < 0.05)

---

54 ☐ Mark for Review

The data in the graph display the percentage of adults who had received any treatment for mental health, by age group and year, for the United States. Based on the data in the graph, which of the following statements is true?

(A) The total percentage increase was significant.

(B) The total percentage increase was not significant.

(C) The percentage increase for ages 45 and over was significant.

(D) The percentage increase for ages 18–44 was not significant.

---

55 ☐ Mark for Review

Which of the following perspectives would be most relevant to psychotherapeutic treatment that focuses on latent emotional conflicts in order to explain and treat mental disorders?

(A) Trait

(B) Applied behavior analysis

(C) Cognitive-behavioral

(D) Psychodynamic

GO ON TO THE NEXT PAGE.

56 ☐ Mark for Review

Alexander has developed an abnormal fear of thunder and lightning. Which of the following clinicians most likely believes that his phobia has a biological basis?

(A) Dr. Allgood, who encourages him to replace his thoughts of "I'm scared! The lightning is going to strike me" with "I'm perfectly safe; the lightning is actually not near."

(B) Dr. Bene, who encourages him to join group therapy with other phobic people

(C) Dr. Cando, who has him listen to recordings of thunder and prescribes a regular dose of Xanax

(D) Dr. Dormir, who encourages him to talk about his dreams

57 ☐ Mark for Review

When Ashleigh was 4, she watched a movie over and over again about a little girl whose grandmother lets her wear a tiara as a reward for good behavior. Now that she's 15, she thinks that her grandmother gave her a tiara for being a good girl when she was little. Which of the following best explains this?

(A) Retrograde amnesia

(B) Constructive memory

(C) The forgetting curve

(D) Infantile amnesia

58 ☐ Mark for Review

A K–6 school keeps boxes of juice for snacks. Each contains 4 ounces of juice, but some are in long, thin juice boxes and others are in short, squat juice boxes. Some kindergartners who get a long, thin box are upset, because they think they are getting less juice than their classmates. But all the 10-year-olds understand they have equal amounts of juice. Which milestone of cognitive development does this scenario highlight?

(A) Formal operations

(B) Object permanence

(C) Conservation

(D) Theory of mind

GO ON TO THE NEXT PAGE.

59 ⬜ Mark for Review

Ken is in training for the state wrestling finals. It's been challenging to remain in the range for his weight class. Two days before his weigh-in, he throws a party for his eighteenth birthday, which includes his favorite type of cake. Of course, he wants to eat the cake—it's his birthday!—but he's also worried about the effect on the weigh-in, 48 hours away. This is an example of which of the following?

(A) Approach-approach conflict

(B) Approach-avoidance conflict

(C) Avoidance-avoidance conflict

(D) Multiple approach-avoidance

60 ⬜ Mark for Review

Julio is an A student who received early admission to the college of his choice. He still thinks he needs to be perfect in everything he does in class this spring, even though his GPA has already secured him a place in higher education. He has such extreme anxiety that a therapist suggests he replace every thought of "I've got to nail this assignment" with "It needs to just be good enough to graduate." The therapist is using which of the following approaches?

(A) Client-centered

(B) Behaviorist

(C) Psychoanalytic

(D) Cognitive-behavioral

61 ⬜ Mark for Review

Sitting in a medical waiting room, Barbara noticed that another patient, Ken, was loudly arguing with the receptionist about how long he had been waiting to see the doctor. Barbara thinks to herself, "What a jerk he is!" What sort of attribution did Barbara make of Ken?

(A) Dispositional

(B) Optimistic

(C) Situational

(D) Pessimistic

62 ⬜ Mark for Review

Addison was in a car accident and sustained a brain injury. Since then, he can't feel much difference between hot and cold temperatures. His neuroanatomist suspects that the head injury caused damage to which of the following?

(A) Occipital lobe

(B) Temporal lobe

(C) Parietal lobe

(D) Frontal lobe

GO ON TO THE NEXT PAGE.

Questions 63 through 65 refer to the following.

Researchers have described children as gender detectives: children are skilled in using cues about gender to form expectations about other people and to develop personal standards for behavior. By the age of 5, children develop an impressive constellation of stereotypes about gender (often amusing and incorrect) that they apply to themselves and others. They use these stereotypes to form impressions of others, to help guide their own behavior, to direct their attention, and to organize their memories. In one study, after being shown equal numbers of pictures of people engaged in gender-stereotypic activities (e.g., a girl sewing) and gender-inconsistent activities (e.g., a boy cooking), children were three times more likely to misremember the inconsistent than the stereotypic pictures. For example, instead of remembering that they had been shown a picture of a girl sawing wood, children reported having seen a picture of a boy sawing wood.

Source for research study:

Martin, C. and Ruble, D. (2004). Children's Search for Gender Clues. Cognitive Perspectives on Gender Development. Current Directions in Psychological Science, 13.2, 67-70.

---

63 ☐ Mark for Review

Which of the following terms would cognitive psychologists most likely use to explain the memory failures described above?

(A) Gender roles

(B) Accommodation

(C) Gender discrimination

(D) Myelination

---

64 ☐ Mark for Review

Dr. Weiblich replicated the study, using children from the preschool next to his practice in New York City. He found similar results and concluded that children in New York develop inflexible gender schemas early in life. Which of the following might make one question the research design?

(A) The study was a controlled experiment and thus may not accurately represent real-life conditions.

(B) The participants are from a random sample and thus may not accurately represent the population.

(C) The study was not a controlled experiment and thus does not provide reliable data.

(D) The participants are from a convenience sample and thus may not accurately represent the population.

---

65 ☐ Mark for Review

The results of the study are most relevant to which of the following concepts?

(A) Group polarization

(B) Obedience

(C) Conformity

(D) Social facilitation

GO ON TO THE NEXT PAGE.

66 ☐ Mark for Review

Jeremiah doesn't study if he doesn't feel like it, but he also doesn't take responsibility for getting low scores on his high school tests. His parents don't care about his grades, viewing themselves as his friends. Which of the following likely describes their parenting style?

- (A) Authoritative
- (B) Authoritarian
- (C) Permissive
- (D) Disorganized

67 ☐ Mark for Review

Leticia has developed a fear of heights. But her environmental science class is going on a field trip, hiking in the Rocky Mountains, and she doesn't want to miss it. She starts therapy to get over her fear. First, the therapist tells Leticia to visualize standing on a mountain path. Second, she'll start hiking on gradual inclines. Finally, Leticia will go with a guide up a steep mountain for a short while, and then gradually lengthen the hikes. Which technique is her therapist using?

- (A) Systematic desensitization
- (B) Flooding
- (C) Psychopharmacology
- (D) Extinction

GO ON TO THE NEXT PAGE.

Questions 68 through 70 refer to the following.

Research has shown that global face characteristics influence social attributions. For example, adult faces with a baby-faced appearance are perceived as physically weak, submissive, honest, and warm. Similar findings have been obtained for other global attributes such as attractiveness, which people associate with competence and intelligence, and gender categorization, which people associate with dominance levels. In one study, participants from North America were asked to categorize computer-generated faces on dominance (1 "not at all dominant" to 9 "very dominant") and sex/gender (0 male to 1 female). A correlation of −0.78 was found.

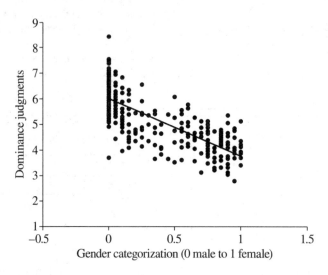

Source for research study:

Todorov, A., et al. (2015). Social Attributions from Faces: Determinants, Consequences, Accuracy, and Functional Significance. *Annual Review of Psychology*, 66, 519-545.

---

68 ☐ Mark for Review

Which of the following explanations best describes the data in the scatterplot?

(A) A more "female" appearance leads to a positive correlation with dominance judgments.

(B) A more "male" appearance has a negative correlation with dominance judgments.

(C) Gender appearance and dominance judgments have no correlation.

(D) Dominance judgments appear to be correlated to gender categorization.

---

69 ☐ Mark for Review

Dr. Geschlecht replicates the study in Denmark and finds a weaker correlation. Which of the following explanations is most likely correct?

(A) Denmark has more gender equality; cultural norms might thus explain a weaker correlation between the study's categories.

(B) The Danish language has more gendered nouns than does English; this language difference could lead to perceptual differences.

(C) The sample of Danish people does not necessarily represent the population of all people; this discrepancy might lead to skewed data.

(D) It is unclear whether the study used double-blind procedures; this could lead to social desirability bias.

GO ON TO THE NEXT PAGE.

70 ☐ Mark for Review

If a participant were unable to tell the difference between the computer-generated faces, what would this participant be likely experiencing?

(A) Prosopagnosia

(B) Dementia

(C) Catatonia

(D) *Ataque de nervios*

71 ☐ Mark for Review

Sophie always has difficulty coming up with ideas for her research papers at the end of the term. Her teacher suggests that she jot down five ideas quickly, without trying to critically assess whether they'll work or not, as a first step. Her teacher is suggesting what type of thinking?

(A) Critical

(B) Convergent

(C) Divergent

(D) Fixed

72 ☐ Mark for Review

Caleb is taking part in a psychology experiment. He is to stare at a green dot on a page for 30 seconds. Then he is shown a blank white page and asked what he sees. He tells the researcher he sees a red dot. Which of the following best explains Caleb's perception?

(A) Color blindness

(B) Trichromatic theory

(C) Serial processing

(D) Opponent process theory

GO ON TO THE NEXT PAGE.

Questions 73 through 75 refer to the following.

Researchers performed a field experiment to measure racial discrimination in the labor market. They responded with fictitious résumés to help-wanted ads in Boston and Chicago newspapers. To manipulate perception of race, each otherwise identical résumés was assigned either a very African American sounding name or a very white sounding name. Researchers found that white names received 50 percent more callbacks for interviews. They also found that race affects the benefits of a better résumé. For white names, a higher quality résumé elicited 30 percent more callbacks whereas for African Americans, it elicited a far smaller increase. Federal contractors and employers who listed "Equal Opportunity Employer" in their ad discriminated as much as other employers.

Source for research study:

Bertrand, M. and Mullainathan, S. (Sept. 2004). Are Emily and Greg More Employable than Lakisha and Jamal? A Field Experiment on Labor Market Discrimination. The American Economic Review, 94.4, 991-1013.

73 ☐ Mark for Review

The study suggests that the stereotypical white or African American names had an effect on the companies' résumé reviewers. Which of the following describes relying on internal, likely unconscious prototypes in decision making?

(A) Representativeness heuristic

(B) Availability heuristic

(C) Gambler's fallacy

(D) Mental set

74 ☐ Mark for Review

Which of the following conclusions can be made based on the data collected in this study?

(A) Compared to white job applicants, African American job applicants have only half the chance of receiving interview callbacks.

(B) White male job applicants have a greater chance than Black female job applicants to receive interview callbacks.

(C) Racial discrimination appears to be a prominent feature of the labor market in areas like Boston and Chicago.

(D) Racial discrimination appears to be a prominent feature of the labor market in most United States cities.

75 ☐ Mark for Review

Which of the following psychological perspectives would best help researchers answer questions about the development of stereotypes connected to "African American" or "white"?

(A) Cognitive

(B) Psychodynamic

(C) Humanistic

(D) Behavioralist

END OF SECTION I

Section II: Free-Response

Article Analysis Question (AAQ)

Your response to the question should be provided in six parts: A, B, C, D, E, and F.

Write the response to each part of the question in complete sentences. Use appropriate psychological terminology in your response.

Using the source provided, respond to all parts of the question.

(A) Identify the research method used in the study.

(B) State the operational definition of negative health-taste belief.

(C) Describe how researchers attempted to increase generalizability of Experiment 1 with the second experiment.

(D) Identify at least one ethical guideline applied by the researchers or one potential ethical concern in either experiment.

(E) Explain how internal and external factors (e.g., culture) apply to perception of tastiness in this research.

(F) Propose a potential confound found in this research that might provide an alternate explanation for the results.

GO ON TO THE NEXT PAGE.

Source

Introduction
Attitudes and expectations often lead to misconceptions toward food. This is particularly the case for perceived taste of unhealthy versus healthy foods across different, contrasting contexts (e.g., unhealthy, tasty foods are plentiful in one context, like a fast-food restaurant, but rare in another, as in a hospital cafeteria). Research has shown that people expect healthy foods just don't taste as good as unhealthy ones, depending on the context. This has held true even when healthy foods taste better than unhealthy ones in *both* contexts. One explanation of this has been linked to strongly-held Protestant beliefs (e.g., strict self-discipline ethic and the notion that fun/enjoyable things are less wholesome and less healthy). To add to that finding, two experiments were conducted to determine if misconceptions develop regarding how tasty unhealthy versus healthy food is within a single context.

Participants
Experiment 1:
One-hundred thirty-four people were recruited; 114 were undergraduate psychology students at the University of Vienna and 20 were volunteers. The students received course credit for participation and all participants were German speakers that were not currently dieting. More than 50% of the sample were women and the mean age for the total sample was 22.97 years old. The entirety of their participation was conducted in a laboratory setting.
Experiment 2:
The first study was partially replicated using 208 German-speaking consumers (49.04% women; M = 45.06 years old). None of the participants was actively dieting and they participated exclusively online.

Method
All participants completed informed consent forms and were debriefed on the nature of the experiment at the conclusion.
Researchers were testing the hypothesis that people will mistakenly rate unhealthy foods as tastier than healthy foods (i.e., negative health-taste belief) when more unhealthy food options are available—even when there are an equal number of healthy versus unhealthy tasty ratings among the food options. They expected to find this when investigated in a single context (e.g., at a restaurant or while using an online app).
Experiment 1:
Participants were shown 104 photographs of complex meals from a fictitious new restaurant. The stimuli included a health and taste rating for each meal. There were three groups being compared including a 'tasty healthy,' 'tasty unhealthy,' and an 'equally tasty, non-tasty, and healthy and unhealthy' food condition (the 3rd condition served as a control group). Each of the three groups was shown twice as many tasty foods as non-tasty—relative to how many foods they were shown in total. This controlled for any potential correlation between tasty ratings and health.
Researchers took two measures of health-taste belief: one indirect and one direct. The indirect measure required participants to recall percentage of foods they saw that were healthy/tasty, unhealthy/tasty, healthy/non-tasty, and unhealthy/non-tasty. The direct measure gave participants a slider scale to rate tastiness, for each meal (on a continuum from −.50 to +.50, with negative values representing tasty unhealthy foods & positive values tasty healthy ones).
Experiment 2:
Researchers partially replicated their study to increase the generalizability of the findings in Experiment 1. The procedure differed from Experiment 1 in several ways: the sample worked exclusively online, their Protestant ethic was assessed, and, instead of looking at photos of meals from a new restaurant, participants viewed pictures of 16 meals from a fictitious new food-delivery app. Each stimulus included a rating for tastiness and health.
As in Experiment 1, participants' belief of the relationship between health and tastiness of the 16 meals was (directly) measured.

GO ON TO THE NEXT PAGE.

Results and Discussion
Experiment 1: In line with their hypothesis, researchers found participants did perceive a stronger relationship between tastiness and unhealthy foods in the condition that presented participants with more unhealthy food options than healthy ones. Experiment 2: The results of the second experiment supported those of the first. Participants held stronger negative beliefs about the relationship between health and tastiness (i.e., unhealthy foods are tastier than healthy ones). Although, contrary to their prediction, those with stronger Protestant convictions considered healthier meals to be tastier. This effect was small, however, and was mitigated after researchers controlled for participants' Protestant beliefs. Results of both experiments indicate that, within a single context, false beliefs about food are easily formed based on the environment in which food is presented. In other words, if more unhealthy foods choices are available, people mistakenly believe they will taste better than healthier alternatives. This argument was somewhat contradicted with the finding that participants' with strong a Protestant ethic considered healthier foods to be tastier when using an online delivery app.

Adapted from *Appetite*:
Kunz, S., Pivecka, N., Dietachmair, C., & Florack, A. (2024). Seeing is misbelieving: Consumers wrongly believe that unhealthy food tastes better when there is more of it. *Appetite*, 197(1), 1-8. DOI: https://doi.org/10.1016/j.appet.2024.107295

GO ON TO THE NEXT PAGE.

Evidence-Based Question (EBQ)

This question has three parts: Part A, Part B, and Part C. Use the three sources provided to answer all parts of the question.

For Part B and Part C, you must cite the source that you used to answer the question. You can do this in two different ways:

- Parenthetical Citation:
  For example: "...(Source A)"
- Embedded Citation:
  For example: "According to Source A,..."

Write the response to each part of the question in complete sentences. Use appropriate psychological terminology.

Using the sources provided, develop an argument that shows the generalizability of findings in the famous Solomon Asch conformity experiments of the 1950s in the United States (US).

(A) Identify a specific and defensible claim based in psychological science that responds to the question.

(B) (i) Support your claim using at least one piece of specific and relevant evidence from one of the sources.

(ii) Explain how the evidence from Part B (i) supports or refutes your claim using a psychological perspective, theory, concept, or research finding learned in AP Psychology.

(C) (i) Support your claim using an additional piece of scientific and relevant evidence form a different source than the one that was used in Part B (i).

(ii) Explain how the evidence from Part C (i) supports or refutes your claim using a different psychological perspective, theory, concept, or research finding learned in AP Psychology than the one that was used in Part B (ii).

GO ON TO THE NEXT PAGE.

Source A

Introduction
Conformity studies have been conducted since the 1950s. Researchers have replicated Solomon Asch's work primarily in the US, but few studies have been conducted over the last 20 or so years. A team of researchers wondered if the original findings in the 1950s were exclusive to students in the US. They also investigated whether those findings could be generalized to modifications of the original studies (e.g., monetary incentives, political opinions, & personality characteristics).

Participants
Participants were recruited from the University of Bern in Switzerland (N=210, female = 61%, M = 22.6 years old). Verbal informed consent was obtained prior to participation, for which they all received 20 Swiss francs. All participants were debriefed via email at the conclusion of the study.

Method
The experiment was conducted in three parts. Part 1 of the study replicated the original line judgment task Asch conducted (1955). There were five confederates, and one naïve participant seated side-by-side in one room. The confederates were instructed ahead of time to get six out of ten line judgment decisions incorrect (the same 6). In Part 2, the six individuals were confronted with five moderate and general political, 'yes' or 'no' questions. Again, confederates were instructed to answer a specific way ("yes" to the 1st and "no" to the rest of the questions = Sequence 1, or vice versa = Sequence 2). Finally, in Part 3, all participants (5 confederates & the 1 naïve participant) were brought into separate rooms to answer a questionnaire on the Big Five personality traits (which also included items on self-esteem, intelligence, & need for social acceptance measures).
The sample of 210 participants was randomly split into two groups. Group 1 received no additional renumeration for participation, whereas Group 2 received one Swiss franc for each correct answer provided in the line judgment task. However, data from eight participants were excluded from analyses due to failure to follow directions or having recognized the true nature of the study (i.e., that some participants were confederates). The number of participants included in the final analyses totaled 202.

Results and Discussion
According to analyses, participants without monetary incentive (Group 1) conformed to near identical levels as Asch's participants in 1955 (33%) on the line judgment task. And while the participants that received extra remuneration (Group 2) showed a lower rate of conformity (25%) than Group 1 for that task, providing monetary incentive did not remove the effect of bowing to social pressure. So, the effect seems not to be exclusive to students in the US and the phenomenon is valid many decades after the seminal Asch studies. The phenomenon is robust even in the face of monetary reward. Further, the entire sample showed an average conformity level of 38% for the 2nd task on political opinions. This suggests pressure to follow majority opinion is not exclusive to perceptual tasks. (See the bar graph below.)
Finally, results for Part 3 of the study showed those participants high in openness were less likely to conform. None of the other Big Five personality traits, nor the measures on self-esteem, intelligence, and need for social approval were correlated with conformity.

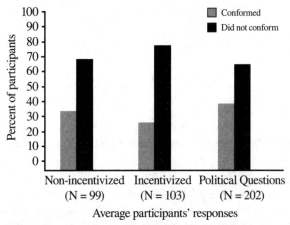

Adapted from *PLoS ONE.*
Franzen A., Mader S. (2023). The power of social influence: A replication and extension of the Asch experiment. *PLoS ONE 18*(11): e0294325.
DOI: https://doi.org/10.1371/journal.pone.0294325

GO ON TO THE NEXT PAGE.

Source B

Introduction
Historically, conformity studies have focused on in-person interactions, where participants performing a perceptual task would change a response or opinion based on erroneous majority response or opinion. Researchers in the current study wanted to investigate whether similar phenomena occur in an online environment when participants are tasked with making moral judgments instead of perceptual ones.

Participants
Study 1
The researchers used the online labor market Amazon Mechanical Turk (MTurk) to recruit 592 US participants that took a survey on the platform Qualtrics. No demographic information was collected for the current study, because research shows that typical MTurk users are more diverse than traditional US college students (e.g., 36% non-White, 55% female; mean age = 32.8 years).
Study 2
A larger sample of 1002 US participants were recruited from MTurk for this study, and they too completed a survey on Qualtrics.
All participants provided signed informed consent satisfying requirements of the IRB at Duke University. Participants from both samples were compensated 10 cents for their involvement.

Method
Both studies used the same two ethical vignettes and randomly assigned participants to one or the other scenario (purity or harm domains). Scenario A described a purity dilemma in which a family must decide whether to eat their recently deceased pet dog to survive. Scenario B provided a different ethical situation in which a group of stranded lifeboat passengers must decide whether to sacrifice one, overweight and seriously injured passenger to save the others.
Study 1
Participants in both Scenario A and B were further randomly divided into three conditions: a baseline condition or one of two prime conditions (condemnable or acceptable). For both scenarios, the baseline condition required participants to simply rate how morally condemnable the decision in the scenario was (on a scale from 0-10, 0 being *completely acceptable*).
The two prime conditions for Scenario A were as follows: Participants were told that "*58 people who previously took this survey rated it as morally condemnable [acceptable]*," and then rated the dilemma using the same scale those in the baseline condition used. Participants in Scenario B followed the same procedure, but they were told that *65* people previously took the survey and rated it as morally condemnable or acceptable before rating it themselves.
Study 2
Instead of providing participants in either scenario with merely statistical information about its condemnability, researchers provided two types of arguments for each scenario: one that was impassioned (emotional) or logical (rational). This resulted in a total of five conditions: baseline, acceptable/emotional, acceptable/rational, condemnable/emotional, or condemnable/rational. An example of an argument for the condemnable/emotional experimental condition in Scenario B was: '75 people who previously took this survey rated it as morally condemnable and said something similar to, "Those barbaric passengers committed a horrible murder!"'
Participants in all five conditions used the same 0-10 rating scale as those in Study 1. Researchers anticipated that emotional arguments would result in more conformity.

Results and Discussion
Study 1
Participants in both Scenarios A and B in the condemnable group ("58" or "65 people who previously took this survey rated it as morally condemnable," respectively) gave significantly higher ratings than either the acceptable or baseline groups. They found their respective scenario even MORE condemnable than social-media statistics showed (i.e., showing a higher rate of conformity).
Study 2
Overall, ratings of acceptability versus condemnability echoed that of Study 1 (i.e., more conformity was found with participants in the condemnable groups). Contrary to their hypothesis, emotional arguments resulted in less conformity than rational arguments did. Researchers interpreted this finding to indicate that reasoned judgments assisted participants in discounting emotional arguments with no justification when they made their own moral assessment of the ethical scenario.

Adapted from *Social Influence.*
Kelly, M., Ngo, L., Chituc, V., Huettel, S., & Sinnott-Armstrong, W. (2017). Moral conformity in online interactions: Rational justifications increase influence of peer opinions on moral judgments. *Social Influence, 12*(2–3), 57–68. DOI: https://doi.org/10.1080/15534510.2017.1323007

GO ON TO THE NEXT PAGE.

Source C

Introduction
The current study investigated whether participants would conform in their decisions to ethical dilemmas in an online environment using the Zoom meeting platform, partially replicating Asch's original work in the 1950s. This was testing what researchers call the *moral conformity effect* (i.e., does the power of suggestion change participants' moral judgments even in an on-line venue?).

Participants
Using local websites, including Facebook and Instagram, as well as local newspapers, 120 Polish participants were recruited for this study (59% female, M = 26.18 years). No monetary compensation was provided for participation and exclusionary criteria were used such that no undergraduate or graduate psychology students were permitted to participate to keep them naïve to the nature of the study. All participants completed a signed informed consent form online, prior to the start of the experiment.

Method
The entirety of the study was conducted in a Zoom meeting. Participants were randomly assigned to either the experimental or control condition.
The experimental condition contained one real participant and four confederates (2 men, 2 women). The confederates were told ahead of time how to respond to each of 12 ethical dilemmas. All 12 dilemmas were referred to as 'sacrificial' in nature (i.e., forfeiting or surrendering the well-being or life of one individual in favor of another individual or group of people). In eight of these (experimental dilemmas), confederates were instructed to answer contrary to popular opinion based on data taken from a previous study.
Half of these eight experimental scenarios were testing a utilitarian ethicality (i.e., actions could be justified if the outcome benefits the most people or society as a whole). The other half were testing deontological ethics, which states an action is judged as moral or not based on the action itself and not the consequences (e.g., it is never OK to kill someone). Utilitarian versus deontological is referred to as 'direction of conformity pressure."
To the other four ethical dilemmas (called 'filler' trials) confederates were instructed to answer with mixed or obvious responses (e.g., "yes, it is wrong to kill an innocent person to save a sculpture"). Using filler scenarios was meant to ensure the true participant did not catch onto the deception. In the control condition, participants met one-on-one with the researcher and responded to the same 12 ethical dilemmas.
The task required participants in both conditions to determine if the solution to each dilemma was acceptable or not, using oral 'yes' or 'no' responses with their camera turned on. In the experimental condition, the true participant always provided their response last.

Results and Discussion
There was no conformity among participants in the four filler scenarios, and none was expected in those instances in either the experimental or control conditions.
A significant main effect was found between types of ethicalities tested (i.e., direction of conformity pressure), showing that only one sacrificial dilemma was justified in the deontological category, where three out of four were justified in the utilitarian.
There was also an interaction effect found between the direction of conformity pressure and the experimental conditions. In four of the eight experimental dilemmas, participants that rendered their decisions in the presence of confederates showed more conformity than did participants that worked one-on-one with the researcher.
Researchers provided several caveats on interpretation of their results, not the least of which is their having used sacrificial ethical dilemmas only. The also made suggestions to expand generalizability of their findings (e.g., include other types of ethical scenarios, focus on social-media messages, & test the reasons behind participants' decisions).

Adapted from *Current Psychology*.

Paruzel-Czachura, M., Wojciechowska, D. & Bostyn, D. (2024). Online moral conformity: How powerful is a group of strangers when influencing an individual's moral judgments during a video meeting? *Current Psychology 43*, 6125–6135. DOI: https://doi.org/10.1007/s12144-023-04765-0

WHEN YOU ARE FINISHED WRITING, CHECK YOUR WORK ON SECTION II IF TIME PERMITS.

STOP
END OF EXAM

Practice Test 2:
Answers and
Explanations

PRACTICE TEST 2 ANSWER KEY

1.	B		39.	A
2.	C		40.	D
3.	A		41.	C
4.	C		42.	C
5.	D		43.	D
6.	A		44.	C
7.	D		45.	D
8.	A		46.	C
9.	B		47.	C
10.	A		48.	B
11.	C		49.	A
12.	C		50.	B
13.	D		51.	C
14.	A		52.	D
15.	A		53.	B
16.	B		54.	A
17.	A		55.	D
18.	D		56.	C
19.	D		57.	B
20.	C		58.	C
21.	B		59.	B
22.	A		60.	D
23.	D		61.	A
24.	A		62.	C
25.	D		63.	A
26.	D		64.	D
27.	C		65.	C
28.	A		66.	C
29.	B		67.	A
30.	C		68.	D
31.	C		69.	A
32.	D		70.	A
33.	C		71.	C
34.	B		72.	D
35.	B		73.	A
36.	C		74.	C
37.	A		75.	A
38.	C			

PRACTICE TEST 2: ANSWERS AND EXPLANATIONS

Section I: Multiple Choice

Note: The explanations in this section make use of the smart-tester strategies introduced in Part IV. Please refer to pages 71–84 first in order to make the most of this section.

1. **B** *Understand the Question/Key Words*: This question asks which term describes someone developing poor health due to chronic stress. *Predict the Answer*: This sounds like the General Adaptation Syndrome. *Use POE*: Eustress might be tempting, but it refers to a good kind of stress, like having people watch one perform at a sporting event—the stress enhances performance. Eliminate (A). Choices (C) and (D) are irrelevant to a question about stress, so eliminate (C) and (D). Choice (B) is correct.

2. **C** *Understand the Question/Key Words*: This question asks which mnemonic technique Teresa suggests using. *Predict the Answer*: Her suggestion that Sean "draw a comic strip with ten characters who represent each of the personality disorders" is a mnemonic device that involves dual coding as well as semantic coding. *Use POE*: Choices (A) and (D) are not mnemonic devices; they represent types of memory storage. Choice (B) entails linking new information to be learned with old long-term memories. Choice (C) is correct.

3. **A** *Understand the Question/Key Words*: This question asks for the independent variable. *Predict the Answer*: Since the researcher manipulated (controlled) volume levels, that would be your prediction. *Use POE*: The dependent variable would be the number of button presses, which reflect a perceived change in volume, so eliminate (B) and (D). Although the researcher did select the types of music heard, this was not changed or manipulated, so it is not an independent variable; eliminate (C). Choice (A) is correct.

4. **C** *Understand the Question/Key Words*: This question asks which term best describes the problem-solving strategy of participant A, who "tried one object after another to open the door." *Predict the Answer*: An algorithm involves trying every strategy until a solution is found. *Use POE*: A heuristic is a problem-solving strategy that involves rules of thumb, so eliminate (B). Mental set and functional fixedness are not problem-solving strategies at all, so eliminate (A) and (D). Choice (C) is correct.

5. **D** *Understand the Question/Key Words*: This question asks you to calculate the median from data in a graph. *Predict the Answer*: The median is the middle value of an odd group of numbers or the average of the two middle values of an even set of numbers. The middle value of this odd set of numbers is 20. *Use POE*: The mean of these numbers would be 15, so (C) is a logical trap answer. Choice (D) is correct.

6. **A**   *Understand the Question/Key Word*: This question asks which concept best explains the outcome for participant C, who "tried various tactics, then suddenly thought to stand near the door and yell loudly." Participant C got out of the room after only 5 minutes. *Predict the Answer*: You might think of a "eureka" moment, divergent thinking, or a flash of insight. These are all good predictions. *Use POE*: Convergent thinking is the opposite of your prediction, so eliminate (C). There is no evidence of latent learning, so eliminate (B). If you have never heard of inductive reasoning, then assume that (D) is incorrect. Choice (A) is correct.

7. **D**   *Understand the Question/Key Words*: This question asks which reinforcement schedule the sandwich shop is using. *Predict the Answer*: After Hanna buys 12 sandwiches, she gets a 13th sandwich free. Thus, she's being rewarded on a fixed-ratio schedule. *Use POE*: Choices (A), (B), and (C) describe other reinforcement schedules. Choice (D) is correct.

8. **A**   *Understand the Question/Key Words*: This question asks which psychological perspective relates to learning novel behaviors through observation, rather than through direct reward and punishment. *Predict the Answer*: This sounds like observational learning, which is part of the cognitive-behavioral perspective. *Use POE*: Behaviorism (not otherwise specified) fits direct reward and punishment, so eliminate (B). Psychoanalytic and humanist perspectives are not relevant here, so eliminate (C) and (D). Choice (A) is correct.

9. **B**   *Understand the Question/Key Words*: This question asks which concept is most relevant to a famous experiment on the extent to which participants would obey orders from an authority figure. *Predict the Answer*: Something involving obedience would make sense. *Use POE*: Choice (A) refers to a different famous experiment, and choices (C) and (D) are irrelevant. Choice (B) is correct.

10. **A**   *Understand the Question/Key Words*: This question asks what is most directly responsible for a flight reaction. *Predict the Answer*: The sympathetic nervous system is involved in fight-or-flight reactions. *Use POE*: The parasympathetic system is involved in rest-and-digest reactions, so eliminate (C). Both the sympathetic and parasympathetic systems are part of the peripheral nervous system, as opposed to the central nervous system, so eliminate (B). If you haven't learned about the efferent nervous system, then assume it's not the right answer and eliminate (D). Choice (A) is correct.

11. **C**   *Understand the Question/Key Words*: This question asks which best describes the behavior of someone who deals with stress by "listening to more lo-fi beats and practicing deep breathing." *Predict the Answer*: She is managing her feelings of stress, so look for an answer that matches that idea. *Use POE*: Choices (A) and (B) are different coping mechanisms. Choice (D) is a made-up term. Choice (C) is correct.

12. **C**   *Understand the Question/Key Words*: This question asks which ethical procedures appear to have been neglected in the study. *Predict the Answer*: The results of a personality test were shared with the participants' parents and teachers. Nothing else in the research design seems to raise concerns. *Use POE*: Choices (A) and (B) could be true, but the scenario doesn't give you a reason to be concerned about the institutional review board or about informed consent. That is, these ethical

concerns do not appear to have been neglected. Since there is no expectation of harm, eliminate (D). Because (C) seems like an adequate rewording of the scenario's final sentence, choice (C) is correct.

13. **D** *Understand the Question/Key Words*: This question asks which conclusion can be made based on the data collected in the study. *Predict the Answer*: Since 12 of 15 pairs of identical twins scored similarly on personality traits, compared to only 3 of 15 pairs of fraternal twins, it seems possible that genetic identity plays a role in determining personality traits. *Use POE*: Choices (A) and (C) are both the opposite of your prediction. Choice (B) claims too much—the data show a correlation, while (B) claims that there is causation. Choice (D) sounds like your prediction, and thus (D) is correct.

14. **A** *Understand the Question/Key Words*: This question asks which personality trait was also likely tested on the "Big Five" personality inventory. *Predict the Answer*: The "Big Five" are Openness to Experience, Conscientiousness, Extraversion, Agreeableness, and Emotional Stability (formerly Neuroticism). *Use POE*: Eliminate any answers that don't fit. Thus, eliminate (B), (C), and (D). Choice (A) is correct.

15. **A** *Understand the Question/Key Words*: This question asks in which category Autism Spectrum Disorder is classified. *Predict the Answer*: ASD is a neurodevelopmental disorder. *Use POE*: Choices (B), (C), and (D) refer to other categories. Choice (A) is correct.

16. **B** *Understand the Question/Key Words*: This question asks for the best description of a research design. *Predict the Answer*: Because this study involves testing identical twins separated at birth, it might be easier to look for wrong answers than to predict a right answer. *Use POE*: Because the researcher didn't separate them at birth, this is not an experiment, so eliminate (A). Because this is just one study, rather than an analysis of many studies, eliminate (C). Since they are not just observing the twins but instead testing them, eliminate (D). Choice (B) is correct.

17. **A** *Understand the Question/Key Words*: This question asks which characteristic a depression test has, given that the researcher was attempting to measure intelligence and that participant scores were similar at two different times. *Predict the Answer*: Reliability refers to the likelihood of getting similar scores at different times. *Use POE*: Using a depression test to measure intelligence is not remotely valid, so eliminate (B) and (D). Choice (C) is irrelevant to the question. Choice (A) is correct.

18. **D** *Understand the Question/Key Words*: This question asks which concept best describes the utterance "I go school!" of a three-year-old. *Predict the Answer*: Telegraphic speech describes the development of 2- or 3-word phrases. *Use POE*: Choices (A) and (B) describe other aspects of language, and (C) describes speaking during infancy. Choice (D) is correct.

19. **D** *Understand the Question/Key Words*: This question asks which diagnosis would be most justified for someone who "has recurrent gaps in her recall of everyday events" and "sometimes switches from seeming happy and energetic to seeming angry and resentful," but whose memory symptoms

are "not related to the effects of a substance or a medical condition." *Predict the Answer*: This sounds like Dissociative Identity Disorder. *Use POE*: Because Dissociative Identity Disorder used to be called Multiple Personality Disorder, (A) might be tempting, but a Personality Disorder is a different thing entirely. Choices (B) and (C) do not typically present with the symptoms mentioned in this scenario, so eliminate (A), (B), and (C). Choice (D) is correct.

20. **C**   *Understand the Question/Key Words*: This question asks what likely causes a faster heartbeat. *Predict the Answer*: If you know that acetylcholine relates to muscles, then this would be your prediction. *Use POE*: If you know that dopamine relates to feelings of pleasure, and/or that GABA relates to anxiety, you can eliminate (A) and (B). If you don't remember learning about norepinephrine, then assume that (D) is incorrect. Choice (C) is correct.

21. **B**   *Understand the Question/Key Words*: This question asks about the relationship between two variables in one of the graphs. *Predict the Answer*: The data suggest a downward trend, which implies a negative correlation, so this would be your prediction. *Use POE*: An upward trend would imply a positive correlation, also known as a direct correlation, so eliminate (A) and (D). And if there were no correlation, there would be no visible trend, so eliminate (C). Choice (B) is correct.

22. **A**   *Understand the Question/Key Words*: This question asks which brain area is most involved in the motivation to eat. *Predict the Answer*: If you remember that it is the hypothalamus, then that is your prediction. *Use POE*: If you remember that the medulla is involved with automatic muscle movements like breathing, that the amygdala is involved in emotions, and/or that the hippocampus is involved in memory, you can eliminate (B), (C), and (D). Choice (A) is correct.

23. **D**   *Understand the Question/Key Words*: This question asks why Peter remembers information for a biology test much better when he is in the biology classroom rather than the library. *Predict the Answer*: Context-dependent memory describes such a scenario. *POE*. Choices (A) and (B) describe other factors relevant to memory; (C) describes a type of memory storage. Choice (D) is correct.

24. **A**   *Understand the Question/Key Words*: This question asks why Harriet continues engaging in a behavior even in the absence of continuous reinforcement. *Predict the Answer*: Operant conditioning involves an increase in behavior after partial reinforcement. *Use POE*: Choices (B) and (C) describe other kinds of conditioning, and (D) mentions negative rather than positive reinforcement. Choice (A) is correct.

25. **D**   *Understand the Question/Key Words*: This question asks why Paula attributes her success to her own hard work but attributes her failure to other people. *Predict the Answer*: This is a classic instance of self-fulfilling prophecy. *Use POE*: The actor-observer bias and the fundamental attribution error describe other sorts of attribution, so eliminate (A) and (B). Self-fulfilling prophecy is not relevant to attribution, so eliminate (C). Choice (D) is correct.

26. **D** *Understand the Question/Key Words*: This question asks why infants would stop crawling across a plexiglass table when they reached the "deep" side. *Predict the Answer*: This is a classic experiment showing that depth perception might be, in part, innate. *Use POE*: Choices (A) and (C) relate to vision but not to this experiment. Choice (B) refers to an instinctual behavior observed in infants, but not this behavior. Choice (D) is correct.

27. **C** *Understand the Question/Key Words*: This question asks which stage fits 52-year-olds who are planning to reorganize their lives to do something meaningful. *Predict the Answer*: This sounds like the generativity vs. stagnation stage of psychosocial development. *Use POE*: Integrity vs. despair is a psychosocial stage describing the elderly, so eliminate (A). Post-conventional describes a stage of moral development, so eliminate (B). Industry vs. inferiority describes a psychosocial stage of school-aged children, so eliminate (D). Choice (C) is correct.

28. **A** *Understand the Question/Key Words*: This question asks what brain area was likely damaged in someone who has difficulty producing language but no difficulty understanding language. *Predict the Answer*: Damage to Broca's area would cause these symptoms. *Use POE*: Damage to Wernicke's area would cause problems with understanding language, so eliminate (C). Damage to the limbic system would cause other sorts of problems, likely with emotion or memory, so eliminate (D). If you have never heard of Brodmann's area, then assume it's not the right answer and eliminate (B). Choice (A) is correct.

29. **B** *Understand the Question/Key Words*: This question asks what the therapist is trying to help Jayden avoid by not eating his favorite foods while sailing. *Predict the Answer*: Taste aversion occurs when one associates a taste with an unpleasant experience. *Use POE*: Choices (A), (C), and (D) describe other terms. Choice (B) is correct.

30. **C** *Understand the Question/Key Words*: This question asks which statement is true based on data in the graph. *Predict the Answer*: Since the graph shows the highest risk of developing schizophrenia being for identical twins (vs. fraternal twins, children, siblings, and the general population), look for an answer that reflects that fact. *Use POE*: Choice (A) may look tempting, but neither "genetic similarity" nor a correlation coefficient is listed on the graph. Choice (B) has no support. Choice (C) may not grab your attention immediately, but it is supported, so keep it for now. Choice (D) makes a prophecy about what "will" happen, making it an extreme answer choice. Choice (C) is correct.

31. **C** *Understand the Question/Key Words*: This question asks which are positive symptoms of schizophrenia. *Predict the Answer*: Positive symptoms are abnormal phenomena that are present. *Use POE*: Choice (A) does not describe schizophrenia. Choice (B) describes negative symptoms of schizophrenia. Choice (D) describes cognitive symptoms of schizophrenia. Choice (C) is correct.

32. **D** *Understand the Question/Key Words*: This question asks what a common side effect of dopamine antagonists is. *Predict the Answer*: A dopamine antagonist works against dopamine, so side effects could include motor symptoms like those involved in Parkinson's disease. *Use POE*: Choices (A), (B), and (C) are not specific to low dopamine. Choice (D) is correct.

33. **C** *Understand the Question/Key Words*: This question asks why Buster and Dave perceive a complete sign, even though they are only seeing a small arc. *Predict the Answer*: According to Gestalt theory, the law of closure explains why one can perceive a whole shape when presented with only a partial shape. *Use POE*: Choices (A) and (D) name binocular cues for depth perception; (B) describes a monocular cue for depth perception. Choice (C) is correct.

34. **B** *Understand the Question/Key Words*: This question asks what best describes the behavior of pigeons who were rewarded every 3 minutes, no matter what they were doing, and who then begin engaging in unusual behaviors. *Predict the Answer*: Research in operant conditioning shows that animals can display behavior that looks like "superstitious" behavior in humans. *Use POE*: Choices (A), (C), and (D) describe other terms related to operant conditioning. Choice (B) is correct.

35. **B** *Understand the Question/Key Words*: This question asks you to calculate the median from data in a graph. *Predict the Answer*: The median is the middle value of an odd group of numbers or the average of the two middle values of an even set of numbers. The two middle values of this even set of numbers are 22 and 33; the average of 22 and 33 is 27.5. *Use POE*: Eliminate (A), (C), and (D). Choice (B) is correct.

36. **C** *Understand the Question/Key Words*: This question asks which area of psychological research focuses on "well-being, resilience, and psychological health" rather than being overly focused on problem behaviors. *Predict the Answer*: This sounds like positive psychology. *Use POE*: Positive reinforcement refers to presenting a reward for a desired behavior, so eliminate (A). Positive correlation refers to an increase in one variable predicting an increase in another variable, so eliminate (B). Positive symptoms of schizophrenia include hallucinations and delusions, so eliminate (D). Choice (C) is correct.

37. **A** *Understand the Question/Key Words*: This question asks which concept best explains someone interpreting their screaming and adrenaline as enthusiasm rather than anger or aggression. *Predict the Answer*: Something involving thinking (cognition, labeling, framing, assessment) would make sense. *Use POE*: Choices (B), (C), and (D) are not relevant to the prediction. Choice (A) is correct.

38. **C** *Understand the Question/Key Words*: This question asks which term refers to the protective coating around the neuron. *Predict the Answer*: If you remember that myelin is a protective coating around the neuron, then that's your prediction. *Use POE*: If you remember that axons are long slender projections, that dendrites are the branches where neurons receive input from other cells, and/or that terminal buttons are small knobs at the end of the axon, you can eliminate (A), (B), and (D). Choice (C) is correct.

39. **A** *Understand the Question/Key Words*: This question describes audience members hearing but not paying attention to a speech, then forgetting its main points after one day; the question asks what sort of storage *did* successfully occur. *Predict the Answer*: If they heard the speech then, by definition, sensory memory storage took place. *Use POE*: One has to pay attention for information to get into working memory, so eliminate (D). Both semantic and procedural memory are forms of long-term memory, so eliminate (B) and (C). Choice (A) is correct.

40. **D**   *Understand the Question/Key Words*: This question asks which statement is true based on data in a figure. *Predict the Answer*: Both secure and insecure attachment show a downward trend with 4-year retention rate; insecure attachment shows lower retention rates after four semesters. The correct answer should involve a negative correlation. *Use POE*: Choice (A) involves a positive correlation, and (B) and (C) claim that there is a causal relationship, which one cannot infer from a correlation. Choice (D) is correct.

41. **C**   *Understand the Question/Key Words*: This question asks what best describes the research design. *Predict the Answer*: Researchers tracked college students over four years, so predict longitudinal design. *Use POE*: Choices (A), (B), and (D) describe other sorts of research design. Choice (C) is correct.

42. **C**   *Understand the Question/Key Words*: This question asks in which stage of psychosocial development college students would be. *Predict the Answer*: Either Identity and Role Confusion or Intimacy and Isolation could fit the typical age of college students. *Use POE*: Choice (A), (B), and (D) refer respectively to toddlers, school-age children, and infants. Choice (C) is correct.

43. **D**   *Understand the Question/Key Words*: This question asks what disorder someone has who takes comfort in eating a lot and vomiting to not gain weight. *Predict the Answer*: From your study of AP Psychology, you should know that anorexia and bulimia nervosa are tested, and that bulimia nervosa would be a good answer here. *Use POE*: If you have never seen (A) and (C) before, don't worry about it. Choice (B) is not what you predicted, and (D) is, so eliminate (A), (B), and (C). Choice (D) is correct.

44. **C**   *Understand the Question/Key Words*: This question asks why someone moderately nervous performs better on a test than both someone extremely nervous and someone rather relaxed. *Predict the Answer*: The Yerkes-Dodson Law describes the optimum level of arousal as a "sweet spot" between extreme nervousness and extreme relaxation. *Use POE*: Choices (A), (B), and (D) do not fit this prediction. Choice (C) is correct.

45. **D**   *Understand the Question/Key Words*: This question asks why Thomas has trouble learning a spacing rule different from one he learned previously. *Predict the Answer*: The old information is interfering with the new information. *Use POE*: Choices (A) and (C) are not relevant to this scenario. Choice (B) refers to new information interfering with old information. Choice (D) is correct.

46. **C**   *Understand the Question/Key Words*: This question asks which brain area is most involved in regulating sleep. *Predict the Answer*: If you remember that the reticular activating system is involved in wakefulness and sleep, then that's your prediction. *Use POE*: If you remember that the thalamus is a sensory relay center, that the cerebellum is involved with balance, and that the limbic system is involved with emotions, you can eliminate (A), (B), and (D). Choice (C) is correct.

47. **C**   *Understand the Question/Key Words*: This question asks whether the data in the table support the conclusion that increased stress causes sleep disturbances. *Predict the Answer*: Because low stress level is associated with 0–1 sleep disturbances, medium stress level is associated with 2–3 sleep

disturbances, and high stress level is associated with 6–7 sleep disturbances, these data show a positive correlation between stress and sleep disturbances. But we do not know that stress causes sleep disturbances—it could be that having disturbed sleep causes stress. *Use POE*: Note that (A) confuses correlation with causation, (B) gets the correlation wrong, (C) expresses a valid reason why the data do not support the conclusion, and (D) does not correctly describe the data. So eliminate (A), (B), and (D). Choice (C) is correct.

48. **B** *Understand the Question/Key Words*: This question asks what is most likely to be observed in the moments after someone first falls asleep. *Predict the Answer*: If you remember that NREM sleep comes first, then that's your prediction. *Use POE*: If you remember that REM sleep and dreaming come later, you can eliminate (A) and (D). If you remember that paradoxical sleep is a term used to describe eye movement combined with muscle paralysis during REM sleep and dreaming, you can eliminate (C). Choice (B) is correct.

49. **A** *Understand the Question/Key Words*: This question asks why Olivia doesn't notice the sound of planes taking off after three weeks of exposure to that stimulus. *Predict the Answer*: Habituation is when one gets used to a stimulus and no longer notices it. *Use POE*: Choices (B), (C) and (D) describe other concepts relating to non-associative, classical, and operant conditioning. Choice (A) is correct.

50. **B** *Understand the Question/Key Words*: This question asks which mnemonic technique Ayesha is using. *Predict the Answer*: Because she "repeats the code over and over," she is utilizing maintenance rehearsal. *Use POE*: Choices (A), (C), and (D) represent other sorts of mnemonic technique. Choice (B) is correct.

51. **C** *Understand the Question/Key Words*: This question asks what the attachment style is of someone who rushes to be near an attachment figure who has been gone for some time, but reacts ambivalently ("sometimes simultaneously hugging him and hitting him"). *Predict the Answer*: This sounds like anxious or anxious-ambivalent attachment. (Both terms are used in the literature.) *Use POE*: Choices (A), (B), and (D) describe different attachment styles. Choice (C) is correct.

52. **D** *Understand the Question/Key Words*: This question asks whether the research followed appropriate ethical procedures. *Predict the Answer*: Ethical research ensures that participants give informed consent, that they are not harmed, that their anonymity is not compromised, and that they are debriefed at the end of the study. This scenario seems to show that they did give informed consent. There is no mention of anything that suggests the presence or absence of harm or of compromised anonymity. But participants were immediately sent home, apparently without knowing whether they had received a drug or a placebo. *Use POE*: Eliminate both (A) and (B), even though the second half of (A) is true. Choice (C) has no support in the text. Choice (D) is correct.

53. **B** *Understand the Question/Key Words*: This question asks which type of motivation describes Jordan, who keeps her grades high to please her parents and keep her scholarship, as opposed to Gordon, who keeps his grades high because he believes that this is a good thing per se. *Predict the Answer*: Something external would make sense. *Use POE*: Choice (A) is irrelevant, and both (C) and (D) relate to internal factors. Choice (B) is correct.

54. **A** *Understand the Question/Key Words*: This question asks which statement is true based on data in a graph. *Predict the Answer*: In this case, go straight to the next step. *Use POE*: The answer choices label certain trends as significant or not significant. Note that the footnote marks the total percentage and the 18–44 group as significant. Thus, (B), (C), and (D) are not supported. Choice (A) is correct.

55. **D** *Understand the Question/Key Words*: This question asks which perspective would be most relevant to psychotherapeutic treatment that focuses on latent emotional conflicts in order to explain and treat mental disorders. *Predict the Answer*: Psychoanalytic or psychodynamic therapies focus on bringing latent content into consciousness. *Use POE*: Choices (A), (B), and (C) describe other modes of therapy. Choice (D) is correct.

56. **C** *Understand the Question/Key Words*: This question asks which clinician most likely believes that a phobia of thunder and lightning has a biological basis. *Predict the Answer*: Whichever clinician talks about biological causes or treatments would be a good choice. *Use POE*: Dr. Allgood seems to be a cognitive-behavioral therapist, so eliminate (A). Dr. Bene does not seem to have a biological focus, so eliminate (B). Dr. Dormir seems to be a psychoanalytic therapist, so eliminate (D). Choice (C) is correct.

57. **B** *Understand the Question/Key Words*: This question asks why Ashleigh mistakes a movie scene for an autobiographical memory. *Predict the Answer*: When people remember, they often add or change details, which means that memory is constructive. *Use POE*: Choices (A), (C), and (D) refer to different types of memory loss, rather than memory alteration. Choice (B) is correct.

58. **C** *Understand the Question/Key Words*: This question asks which milestone of cognitive development involves children learning that liquids in different containers contain the same volume. *Predict the Answer*: This is called conservation. *Use POE*: Choices (A) and (B) involve a later and an earlier stage, respectively. Choice (D) involves a different concept altogether. Choice (C) is correct.

59. **B** *Understand the Question/Key Words*: This question asks for the best description of ambivalent feelings: both wanting to eat birthday cake and wanting to not gain weight. *Predict the Answer*: Something that describes mixed feelings would make sense. *Use POE*: Choices (A) and (C) describe similar things, so eliminate (A) and (C). Choice (D) seems like a made-up term, so eliminate (D). Choice (B) is correct.

60. **D** *Understand the Question/Key Words*: This question asks which therapeutic technique involves replacing perfectionistic thoughts with more realistic thoughts. *Predict the Answer*: Something cognitive would make sense. *Use POE*: Choices (A), (B), and (C) refer to other therapy models. Choice (D) is correct.

61. **A** *Understand the Question/Key Words*: This question asks what sort of attribution Barbara makes when she thinks that Ken is a jerk after he argues with a receptionist. *Predict the Answer*: This seems like a classic instance of the fundamental attribution error, which involves assuming someone else's behavior is due to internal, dispositional reasons, rather than external, situation reasons. *Use POE*: Choices (C) and (D) are the opposite of your prediction, and (B) is irrelevant. Choice (A) is correct.

62. **C**   *Understand the Question/Key Words*: This question asks which brain area is likely damaged when one can't feel temperature differences. *Predict the Answer*: Sensory information is processed in the parietal lobe. *Use POE*: The occipital lobe is for vision, the temporal lobe is for hearing and language, and the frontal lobe is for higher-level thinking, so eliminate (A), (B), and (D). Choice (C) is correct.

63. **A**   *Understand the Question/Key Words*: This question asks which term best explains children misremembering pictures of "gender inconsistent" activities. *Predict the Answer*: Part of socialization involves learning about gender roles, so "gender inconsistent" activities might be less likely to be remembered accurately. *Use POE*: Choice (C) mentions gender, but this scenario has nothing to do with discrimination. Choices (B) and (D have nothing to do with the scenario. Choice (A) is correct.

64. **D**   *Understand the Question/Key Words*: This question asks why one might question the research design of a study using participants who all come from a preschool next to the researcher's practice. *Predict the Answer*: The sample does not seem like it represents the population. *Use POE*: Choice (A) describes a research design flaw that doesn't fit this particular scenario. Choice (C) is extreme in assuming that only controlled experiments provide reliable data. Choices (B) and (D) both correctly describe the concern, but (B) incorrectly identifies the participants as being part of a "random" sample. A random sample would be desirable. Choice (D) is correct.

65. **C**   *Understand the Question/Key Words*: This question asks which concept is most relevant to the results of the study. *Predict the Answer*: Since the results involve memory failures for gender-inconsistent pictures, the correct answer should be relevant to that issue. *Use POE*: Choices (A), (B), and (D) are irrelevant to that issue. Choice (C) is correct.

66. **C**   *Understand the Question/Key Words*: This question asks which parenting style is likely for parents who don't care about their kid's grades and view themselves as his friends. *Predict the Answer*: This describes a permissive parenting style. *Use POE*: Choices (A) and (B) describe other parenting styles. Choice (D) describes an attachment style. Choice (C) is correct.

67. **A**   *Understand the Question/Key Words*: This question asks which therapeutic technique involves overcoming a hiking phobia in gradual steps (from visualizing to small hikes to longer ones). *Predict the Answer*: This sounds like behavioralism in general and systematic desensitization in particular. *Use POE*: Choices (B) and (C) describe other sorts of therapy. Choice (D) describes what might happen to her anxiety reactions, but it does not describe the therapy style itself. Choice (A) is correct.

68. **D**   *Understand the Question/Key Words*: This question asks which explanation best describes the data in the scatterplot. *Predict the Answer*: The data show a negative correlation between dominance judgments and femininity. *Use POE*: Choice (A) is too strong, claiming that one variable "leads to" another. This implies causation, which one cannot do based on correlation. Choice (B) is the opposite of your prediction. Choice (C) goes against your prediction. Choice (D) fits your prediction and says nothing wrong, so (D) is correct.

69. **A** *Understand the Question/Key Words*: This question asks which conclusion is most likely correct, given that Dr. Geschlecht replicates the study in Denmark and finds a weaker correlation. *Predict the Answer*: Since the original study was done in North America and the replication is done in Denmark, presumably something about the different locations is contributing to the difference in results. *Use POE*: Different cultural norms could fit your prediction, so keep (A) for now. Linguistic relativity doesn't seem relevant to your prediction, so eliminate (B). The fact that Danish people don't represent all people also doesn't seem relevant, so eliminate (C). The issue of double-blind procedures also seems irrelevant, so eliminate (D). Choice (A) is correct.

70. **A** *Understand the Question/Key Words*: This question asks what a participant who is unable tell the difference between the computer-generated faces would likely be experiencing. *Predict the Answer*: Face blindness (also known as prosopagnosia) would be an obvious prediction. *Use POE*: Choices (B), (C), and (D) do not sound like face blindness. Choice (A) is correct.

71. **C** *Understand the Question/Key Words*: This question asks what type of thinking characterizes quickly generating multiple ideas. *Predict the Answer*: You might think of this as "creative" brainstorming. *Use POE*: Choice (A) is contradicted by the question stem ("without trying to crucially assess"). Choices (C) and (D) both involve limiting one's options, rather than expanding them. Choice (C) is correct.

72. **D** *Understand the Question/Key Words*: This question asks why someone would stare at something green, then see something red when looking at a white surface. *Predict the Answer*: Opponent process theory explains that after seeing one color for a long time, the relevant receptors become fatigued and their opposing cells start firing, such that one sees an afterimage in "opposite" colors. *Use POE*: The trichromatic theory of color does not explain afterimages, so eliminate (B). Since Caleb sees colors, he is not colorblind; eliminate (A). Serial processing has nothing to do with this scenario, so eliminate (C). Choice (D) is correct.

73. **A** *Understand the Question/Key Words*: This question asks which term involves reliance on internal, likely unconscious prototypes in decision making. *Predict the Answer*: You might think of one of the heuristics, so that could be your initial prediction. If you know that the representativeness heuristic involves precisely this, then that's your answer. *Use POE*: Gambler's fallacy, an erroneous assumption about the probability of an event happening, is irrelevant here, so eliminate (C). Mental set, a tendency to only see solutions that have worked in the past, is irrelevant here, so eliminate (D). The availability heuristic, a tendency to incorrectly estimate probabilities due to relying on information recently presented, does not fit the question, so eliminate (B). Choice (A) is correct.

74. **C** *Understand the Question/Key Words*: This question asks which conclusion can be made based on the data collected in a study. *Predict the Answer*: The study found that "White names received 50 percent more callbacks for interviews." It also found that "[f]or White names, a higher quality résumé elicited 30 percent more callbacks whereas for African Americans, it elicited a far smaller increase." Finally, the study also found that "federal contractors and employers who listed 'Equal Opportunity Employer' in their ad discriminated as much as other employers." Keep this data in mind. *Use POE*: Choice A mischaracterizes the data: half the chance is not the same as 50% more.

Choice B introduces the variable of gender; the study did not discuss this. In addition, both (A) and (B) also use more definite language ("have") than the study does. By contrast, both (C) and (D) use more tentative, careful language ("appears to be"). But (D) claims without basis that this study applies to "most United States cities," when the study was done in Boston and Chicago. Choice (C) is correct.

75.   **A**   *Understand the Question/Key Words*: This question asks which perspective is most relevant to the development of racial stereotypes. *Predict the Answer*: Since stereotypes are fixed and oversimplified ideas, a perspective that focuses on ideas would make the most sense. *Use POE*: Since the cognitive perspective focuses primarily on ideas, and the others do not, eliminate (B), (C), and (D). Choice (A) is correct.

Section II: Free Response

1. Credit is awarded for responses that incorporate the following points:

    (A) Identify the research method used in the study.

        a. Accurately identifies between-groups design set of experiments.

    (B) State the operational definition of negative health-taste belief.

        a. The response states the operational definition of negative health-taste belief as the perception unhealthy foods taste better than healthy ones; this may include mention of the direct and indirect measures taken in Experiment 1 (e.g., sliding scale from −.50 – +.50 where negative values equal unhealthy foods). The response may also include this false belief occurs when more unhealthy food options are available than healthy ones.

    (C) Describe how researchers attempted to increase generalizability of Experiment 1 with the second experiment.

        a. Accurately describes the changes made from the first experiment to include method of data collection (i.e., online vs. lab setting), a measure of Protestant ethic was assessed, and/or a different stimulus set was used. Further, the response may mention a different population of interest was sampled (e.g., consumers vs. students).

    (D) Identify at least one ethical guideline applied by the researchers or one potential ethical concern in either experiment.

        a. Accurately identifies that the researchers used informed consent, or that they were debriefed at the conclusion of each experiment. An ethical concern might have occurred in Experiment 2 with the measure of Protestant ethic.

    (E) Explain how internal and external factors (e.g., culture) apply to perception of tastiness in this research.

        a. References any cognitive perceptual theories/constructs like relying on internal prior expectations or external sensory information. May also mention contexts and cultural experiences (i.e., Protestant ethic) that affect attitudes and beliefs about eating and food (e.g., whether food is seen as necessary purely for survival or for socialization).

    (F) Propose a potential confound in this research that might provide an alternate explanation for the results.

        a. Notes that different cultures might have different attitudes toward the relationship between food and enjoyment that could alter perceptions on how tasty healthy versus unhealthy foods might be. Additionally, researchers manipulated frequency of available healthy and unhealthy foods in both experiments, potentially leading participants to conclude the fictitious restaurant or delivery app represents venues that specialize in unhealthy foods and are therefore particularly good at making that unhealthy food. This would lead to an erroneous conclusion then, that those unhealthy meals taste better.

2. Credit is awarded for responses that incorporate the following points .

A. Identify a specific and defensible claim based in psychological science that responds to the question.

    (1) "Asch's experiments have been replicated for decades, although not in the last 20 or so years. It's possible the effects of social pressure on participant decisions may persist even today."

    (2) "The original studies did not compensate participants with money that might motivate giving non-conformist responses to questions."

    (3) "Using participants from other countries, volunteers that are not students, conducting the research online rather than in person, and requiring activities that are not simple perceptual tasks might show similar results to the original Asch findings."

B. (i) Support your claim using at least one piece of specific and relevant evidence from one of the sources.

    (1) Source A: "Group 1 received no additional renumeration for participation, whereas Group 2 received one Swiss franc for each correct answer provided in the line judgment task. While the participants that received extra remuneration (Group 2) showed a lower rate of conformity (25%) than Group 1 for that task, providing monetary incentive did not remove the effect of bowing to social pressure."

    (ii) Explain how the evidence from Part B (i) supports or refutes your claim using a psychological perspective, theory, concept, or research finding learned in AP Psychology.

        1. "This evidence refutes the claim that paying people to give a genuine response to a question is sufficient to eliminate conformity; it merely attenuates it."

C. (i) Support your claim using an additional piece of scientific and relevant evidence from a different source than the one that was used in Part B (i).

    (1) Source C: "The current study investigated whether participants would conform in their decisions to ethical dilemmas in an online environment using the Zoom meeting platform, partially replicating Asch's original work in the 1950s."

    (ii) Explain how the evidence from Part C (i) supports or refutes your claim using a different psychological perspective, theory, concept, or research finding learned in AP Psychology than the one that was used in Part B (ii).

        1. "Participant responses conformed in three out of four utilitarian ethical dilemmas. This is evidence that the power of suggestion is applicable in an online environment and for more than simple perceptual tasks, replicating the original Asch findings of the 1950s."

Appendix: Bonus Drill Questions

BONUS DRILL: QUESTIONS

1. A behavior that is elicited automatically by an environmental stimulus is called a(n)

   (A) conditioned response
   (B) condition
   (C) aversive stimulus
   (D) reflex
   (E) drive

2. Six-month-old Sasha loves to play "peek-a-boo" with her mother, an indication that she has developed a sense of

   (A) play versus learning
   (B) transitivity
   (C) metacognition
   (D) attachment anxiety
   (E) object permanence

3. Studying a few subjects in great depth to investigate a rare condition is known as

   (A) an experiment
   (B) a case study
   (C) naturalistic observation
   (D) correlational research
   (E) longitudinal research

4. A group of participants in a sleep study are to be deprived of sleep for four days. After their second sleepless night, participants may begin reporting which of the following?

   (A) Hunger
   (B) Thirst
   (C) Lack of coordination
   (D) Hallucinations
   (E) Increased respiration

5. Conflicting attitudes or behaviors that create tension within a person's mind are referred to in terms of

   (A) persuasion
   (B) general adaptation syndrome
   (C) serial position
   (D) cognitive dissonance
   (E) fluid intelligence

6. Nell decides not to throw her stuffed animal into the toilet after she witnesses her brother Matthew being punished for putting his stuffed animal into the toilet. Nell's decision exemplifies

   (A) prepared conditioning
   (B) tutelage
   (C) scheduled reinforcement
   (D) shaping
   (E) vicarious learning

7. Which of the following lobes of the brain is central to visual sensation and perception?

   (A) Occipital
   (B) Temporal
   (C) Parietal
   (D) Frontal
   (E) Cerebral

8. In order for the mean, mode, and median of a data set to be equal, the distribution must be

   (A) positively skewed
   (B) asymmetrical
   (C) negatively skewed
   (D) normal
   (E) abnormal

9. The adaptive response of a six-month-old child who shows distress when an attachment figure leaves is known as

   (A) attachment anxiety
   (B) reactive attachment disorder
   (C) object permanence
   (D) separation anxiety
   (E) detachment adaptation

10. Which of the following most accurately describes the firing of a neuron?

   (A) It occurs gradually as the neuron reaches hyperpolarization.
   (B) It has an all-or-none quality: it either happens, or it does not.
   (C) Its strength diminishes as it travels along the soma.
   (D) It occurs only in the post-synaptic neuron.
   (E) Stronger stimulations make a neuron fire harder.

11. At the outset of a study on eating habits, a researcher asks participants a variety of questions, including whether they typically eat breakfast. Whether or not a person eats breakfast is a(n)

    (A) categorical variable
    (B) continuous variable
    (C) dependent variable
    (D) independent variable
    (E) conditioned variable

12. Hypnosis has been used effectively to diminish

    (A) antisocial personality disorder
    (B) chronic pain
    (C) night terrors
    (D) kinesthetic abilities
    (E) Alzheimer's disease

13. Which of the following terms describes the behavioral component of negative attitudes toward particular groups?

    (A) Bias
    (B) Conditioning
    (C) Catharsis
    (D) Passive aggression
    (E) Discrimination

14. A doctor who smokes cigarettes knows that it is unhealthy, but thinks that he can keep smoking, since he eats healthily. Which concept best explains this thought process?

    (A) Reaction formation
    (B) Affective retraining
    (C) Cognitive dissonance
    (D) Obsessive compulsion
    (E) Psychotic delusion

15. After a big Thanksgiving dinner replete with turkey, stuffing, and all, Karmina becomes violently ill. In the weeks that follow this event, Karmina feels an unexplainable aversion to chicken, one of her favorite dishes. Karmina's feeling about chicken reflects

    (A) response generalization
    (B) latent learning
    (C) prepared learning
    (D) unconditioned stimulus response
    (E) stimulus generalization

16. Lynda is a confident, capable woman who takes responsibility for her own actions. Lynda has a(n)

    (A) manic coping strategy
    (B) discriminative expectancy
    (C) internal locus of control
    (D) external locus of control
    (E) generalized expectancy

17. A longitudinal study would be useful in assessing which of the following?

    (A) Age differences
    (B) Gender differences
    (C) Cultural environments
    (D) Changes in behavior over time
    (E) Sequential studies

18. Calvin's fear of dogs was so great that he could not even visit his friends who had dogs or who lived in a neighborhood that had a lot of dogs. Once he sought help, he worked to overcome this fear first by witnessing his counselor playing with a dog and then, after a while, by actually touching and petting a dog himself. The method used to help Calvin overcome his fears is known as

    (A) countertransference
    (B) peer-counselor alliance
    (C) rational-emotive therapy
    (D) flooding
    (E) systematic desensitization

19. Asia has just seen a brief video entitled "Twelve Steps to a Better You" that she found on YouTube. She is now talking to her friend Joyce and trying to relay the steps. She is doing well in recounting the first few and the last few, but she finds herself unsure about elements of steps 5 to 8. This is an example of

    (A) motivated forgetting
    (B) proactive interference
    (C) retroactive interference
    (D) serial position effect
    (E) source monitoring error

20. Myron has been depressed recently and he schedules an appointment with Dr. Smith, a psychiatrist. After meeting with Myron, Dr. Smith concludes that the major reason that Myron is depressed is that he categorizes events as "catastrophic" or "wonderful," more often "catastrophic," with no in-between. Dr. Smith is relying on which psychological perspective to make this determination?

    (A) Psychoanalytic
    (B) Behaviorist
    (C) Cognitive
    (D) Humanist
    (E) Evolutionary

21. When a person experiences a discrepancy between an attitude and a behavior, the person experiences

    (A) cognitive dissonance
    (B) dissociation
    (C) behavioral dysfunction
    (D) metacognition
    (E) countertransference

22. Which of the following most accurately explains why a pool with water temperature of 82 degrees may feel cool to a person who has been sunbathing, yet warm to a person who has been inside in the air conditioning?

    (A) Sensory restriction
    (B) Perceptual constancy
    (C) Relative clarity
    (D) Absolute threshold
    (E) Sensory adaptation

23. Psychoactive substances are drugs that alter consciousness by

    (A) inducing the secretion of excitatory hormones into the bloodstream
    (B) imitating the behaviors of various pheromones
    (C) facilitating or inhibiting neural transmission at the synapse
    (D) increasing an individual's hypnotic susceptibility
    (E) flooding post-synaptic receptors with subliminal commands

24. A child is frightened by the sudden barking of a neighbor's dog. Once her mother picks her up, the child begins to calm down as which of the following biological processes occurs?

    (A) The parasympathetic nervous system resumes control and reverses the sympathetic responses.
    (B) The sympathetic nervous system resumes control and reverses the parasympathetic responses.
    (C) The autonomic nervous system resumes control and reverses the peripheral responses.
    (D) The peripheral nervous system resumes control and reverses the autonomic responses.
    (E) The endocrine system resumes control and reverses the responses brought on by neurotransmitters.

25. Which of the following is an example of a result of operant conditioning?

    (A) Milo starts at the sound of a buzzer because it sounds very similar to the alarm clock that wakes him every morning.
    (B) Paula is promoted to vice president of her company and vows to not lose touch with her employees.
    (C) Rebecca cancels her credit card to avoid paying the annual fee but plans to reinstate it in the new year.
    (D) Ashmed speaks louder than usual when he talks to his mother on the phone because she is hard of hearing.
    (E) Pika avoids eating red meat after she hears several horror stories about mad cow disease.

26. Detection of a just noticeable difference (JND) depends on the

    (A) presence of a "no stimulus" control and the sensitivity of the signal-detection equipment
    (B) initial determination of the absolute threshold and the variation of the difference threshold
    (C) frequency of the existing stimulus and the presence of one or more sensory modalities
    (D) establishment of a 50 percent "hit" rate and a long enough series of trials
    (E) intensity of the new stimulus and that of the stimulus already present

27. Lizette and her family watch the sunset over the ocean. While walking home in the increasing darkness, Lizette notices that she can no longer distinguish the colors of objects. Which of the following best explains why Lizette cannot see color in dim light?

(A) Rods, which are specialized for color vision, require more light to be activated, whereas cones, which produce images in black, white, and gray, allow for vision in dim light.

(B) Cones, which are specialized for color vision, require more light to be activated, whereas rods, which produce images in black, white, and gray, allow for vision in dim light.

(C) Cones, which are specialized for black and white vision, require a small amount of light to be activated, whereas rods, which produce images in color, require greater amounts of light for vision.

(D) The receptive fields in the retina respond to the loss of light through light adaptation, the process of rapidly adjusting to a diminution of light.

(E) In order to perceive aspects of color such as hue, brightness, and saturation, rods require a great deal of light, while cones can perceive images in black, white, and gray with little light.

28. The "cocktail party effect" refers to

(A) the impact of alcohol on the dopamine reward system

(B) altered perceptual constancies

(C) multitasking by trying to listen to several conversations at once

(D) selective attention in trying to focus on one of several conversations

(E) a loosening of social inhibitions

29. Which of the following is an example of imprinting?

(A) A mother eagle will fly under her young while they are learning to fly in case they begin to fall.

(B) A newborn gosling will "attach" to the first moving object it sees, usually its mother.

(C) An infant who is left by its primary caregivers for significant periods of time develops an indifference to their presence.

(D) A mother cat teaches her kittens how to clean themselves.

(E) A premature infant grows rapidly in part as a result of constantly being held by a primary caregiver.

30. Max was typically out of control whenever he attended preschool. Teachers tried time-outs and other punishments to no avail. His parents and the school decided to work with Max by giving him a sticker each time he behaved for a full hour. Once he accumulated ten stickers, he could present them to his parents who would give him a reward. The method the school and parents chose to employ is referred to as

(A) negative reinforcement
(B) a token economy
(C) a point value system
(D) negative punishment
(E) classical conditioning

BONUS DRILL: ANSWERS AND EXPLANATIONS

1. **D** *Understand the Question/Key Words*: An automatic reaction to something is called a... *Predict the Answer*: Reflex. Rephrasing the question makes the answer much more obvious. Now use POE to quickly scan the answers. Watch out for (C), aversive stimulus, and (E), drive.

2. **E** *Understand the Question/Key Words*: She plays peek-a-boo, which means what, developmentally? *Predict the Answer*: She knows that the fact that she cannot see her mother does not mean her mother is gone. In other words, she has developed object permanence. If you don't remember the term, use POE. Would a sense of (A), playing versus learning, mean she knows her mother is not gone? No. Cross it off. Would a sense of (B), transitivity, mean she knows her mother is not gone? No, it is something to do with transience or changing. Would a sense of (C), metacognition, mean she knows her mother is not gone? She is too young for this level of complex thought. Would a sense of (D), attachment anxiety, mean she knows her mother is not gone? No, it would mean the opposite. Would a sense of (E), object permanence, mean she knows her mother is not gone? Bingo.

3. **B** *Understand the Question/Key Words*: Psychologists who study a few subjects in great depth are using... *Predict the Answer*: A case study. Choice (A), an experiment, shows cause and effect relationships. Choice (C), naturalistic observation, is often used by anthropologists to study people and animals in their natural environment. Choice (D), correlational research, is used to study the relationship between or among variables. Choice (E), longitudinal research, is used by developmental psychologists to assess change over time.

4. **D** *Understand the Question/Key Words*: If you don't sleep for two days, you may begin to experience... *Predict the Answer*: Hallucinations. If you are unsure, use POE. Sleepless doesn't mean without food or water, so get rid of (A), hunger, and (B), thirst. Choice (E) is also way off base.

5. **D** *Understand the Question/Key Words*: When you struggle between what you want to do and what you believe you ought to do, you are experiencing... *Predict the Answer*: cognitive dissonance. Watch out for (B), which is a trap answer. The general adaptation syndrome concerns chronic stress, and the word "tension" in the question may trick you into thinking about stress. None of the other answer choices come close to cognitive dissonance.

6. **E** *Understand the Question/Key Words*: Nell doesn't want to get in trouble like her brother did, so she won't throw her stuffed animal into the toilet. What is this called? *Predict the Answer*: Nell is learning by watching her brother's experience (vicariously through her brother). This is called vicarious conditioning. If you are unsure, use POE. Would (A), prepared conditioning, mean learning from watching her brother's experience? No, this is not a psychological concept. Cross it off. Would (B), tutelage, mean learning from watching her brother's experience? No. Would (C), scheduled reinforcement, mean learning from watching her brother's experience? No, that is not taking place here. Would (D), shaping, mean learning from watching her brother's experience? Again, shaping is more direct. Would (E), vicarious learning, mean learning from watching her brother's experience? Yup.

7. **A** *Understand the Question/Key Words*: Circle *visual*. Which lobe is involved in vision? *Predict the Answer*: Occipital lobe. If you don't know, use POE to get rid of (D), frontal (you probably know that the frontal lobe is used for a variety of more-complex tasks), and (E), cerebral, because this isn't a lobe of the brain.

8. **D** *Understand the Question/Key Words*: When are mean, median, and mode equal? *Predict the Answer*: In a normal distribution. If you don't remember, use POE. Choices (A) and (C) represent distributions where scores are overwhelmingly low or high, respectively. Choice (B), asymmetrical, is a generic term for a skewed distribution. Choice (E), abnormal, is not generally a term used to describe distributions.

9. **D** *Understand the Question/Key Words*: When a six-month-old gets upset when Mom leaves, it's called… *Predict the Answer*: Separation anxiety. Watch out for (A), attachment anxiety, and (B), reactive attachment disorder. Choices (C), object permanence, and (E), detachment adaptation, would require a different response from the child.

10. **B** *Understand the Question/Key Words*: Circle *firing of a neuron*. *Predict the Answer*: All or nothing. Use POE to get rid of answers that don't make sense. Get rid of (A) because firing does not occur gradually, (C) because this is also a false statement, and (E) because a neuron cannot fire "harder." Choice (D) is also a false statement.

11. **A** *Understand the Question/Key Words*: What kind of variable is eating breakfast in this study? *Predict the Answer*: Eating breakfast is an either/or thing, so it is a categorical variable. Even if you are not sure, POE can get rid of (C), dependent variable, because it is not being observed and measured, (D), independent variable, because it is not being manipulated, and (E), conditioned variable, because it is not conditioned.

12. **B** *Understand the Question/Key Words*: Circle *hypnosis* and *diminish*. *Predict the Answer*: Chronic pain. If you don't remember this, use common-sense POE to get rid of (A), antisocial personality disorder, (D), kinesthetic abilities, and (E), Alzheimer's disease.

13. **E** *Understand the Question/Key Words*: What is the term used to describe when prejudices are acted upon? *Predict the Answer*: Discrimination. Your clue is "behavioral component." Choices (A), bias, (B), conditioning, and (C), catharsis, are not directly related to the question. Choice (D), passive aggression, is way off base, so (E), discrimination, is the best answer.

14. **C** When one's behavior and one's thinking are not in alignment, there are two ways one can bring them into alignment. An obvious way, but also often a hard way, is to change one's behavior to fit one's thinking. The fact that many New Year's resolutions are quickly abandoned shows how difficult it can be to change one's behavior to fit one's ideas. The other way to minimize this conflict between behavior and thought is to change one's thought process to justify the bad behavior. The name of this feeling of conflict is "cognitive dissonance." The other concepts are either irrelevant or made-up.

15. **E** *Understand the Question/Key Words*: Turkey made her sick. Why would chicken also make her queasy? *Predict the Answer*: Turkey and chicken are similar—stimulus generalization. If you don't remember the term, use POE. Choices (B), latent learning, and (C), prepared learning, are obviously out. Does (A), response generalization, mean associating similar stimuli? Be careful—it says response generalization. Does (D), unconditioned stimulus response, mean associating similar stimuli? Again, this is talking about a response. The answer must be (E), stimulus generalization.

16. **C** *Understand the Question/Key Words*: She is confident and self-directed. Therefore she has…*Predict the Answer*: An internal locus of control. If you don't remember the term, use POE. Would a confident, self-directed person have a manic coping strategy, as in (A)? No, that strategy would be dysfunctional. Cross this answer off. Would a confident, self-directed person have a discriminative expectancy, as in (B)? This term doesn't make sense. Cross it off. Would a confident, self-directed person have an internal locus of control, as in (C)? Hopefully this answer jogs your memory. Even if you aren't sure, the term sounds possible, so keep it and check the others. Would a confident, self-directed person have an external locus of control, as in (D)? No, that would involve looking to others for your own direction or self-worth. This answer is the opposite of what you want. Would a confident, self-directed person have generalized expectancy, as in (E)? No. Choice (C) is correct.

17. **D** *Understand the Question/Key Words*: Which needs to be studied over a long period of time? *Predict the Answer*: Anything that is related to changes over time. Use POE to find an answer that is close to yours. Be careful on (A)—age differences could be measured by studying groups of people at different ages, not necessarily the same people at different ages. Look for an answer that is more clear. Choice (D), changes in behavior over time, is the closest to yours.

18. **E** *Understand the Question/Key Words*: He slowly got over his fear by gradual exposure and eventual participation. This is called…*Predict the Answer*: Systematic desensitization. If you don't remember the term, use POE. Could (A), countertransference, mean gradual exposure and participation? No. Could (B), peer-counselor alliance, mean gradual exposure and participation? No, so cross it off. Could (C), rational-emotive therapy, mean gradual exposure and participation? Sounds possible. Keep it, and check the rest. Could (D), flooding, mean gradual exposure and participation? It doesn't sound very gradual. Cross it off. Could (E), systematic desensitization, mean gradual exposure and participation? Yes. This refers to a process of gradual exposure to a fear stimulus.

19. **D** When a list being processed to short-term, or working, memory exceeds "Miller's Magic Number," seven plus or minus two, people have a tendency to remember items at the beginning or end of the list better than items in the middle. Choice (D) is the correct answer.

20. **C** The cognitive explanation for depression involves people engaging in selective perception, "all-or-nothing" thinking, and "catastrophizing." The psychoanalytic approach would emphasize childhood traumas and repressed memories. The behaviorist approach would emphasize how depressive tendencies could be reinforced by the person's environment. The humanist approach would emphasize obstacles preventing someone from achieving a coherent "self." The evolutionary approach would not apply.

21. **A** *Understand the Question/Key Words*: Circle *discrepancy between an attitude and a behavior*. If someone thinks one thing but does something else, they may experience...*Predict the Answer*: Cognitive dissonance—mental conflict. If you don't remember the term, use POE. Could (A), cognitive dissonance, mean mental conflict? Sure, that sounds right. Keep it, and check the others. Could (B), dissociation, mean mental conflict? No, cross it off. Could (C), behavioral dysfunction, mean mental conflict? No, it's about behavior. Cross it off. Could (D), metacognition, mean mental conflict? No, there is nothing about conflict here. Could (E), countertransference, mean mental conflict? No. It must be (A).

22. **E** *Understand the Question/Key Words*: Why does the water feel cool to the person who's been in the heat, but warm to the person who's been inside with the air conditioning? *Predict the Answer*: Sensory adaptation, (E). When a person has been sunbathing, the thermoreceptors that register heat "tire out," or experience adaptation. Thus the move into the relatively cooler pool leads one to feel that the water is cool. When a person has been in the air conditioning, the thermoreceptors that register cool experience adaptation. Thus the relatively warmer pool leads one to feel that the water is warm.

23. **C** *Understand the Question/Key Words*: How do psychoactive drugs work? *Predict the Answer*: Kind of like neurotransmitters. Choice (A) is out because of hormones, (B) is way out, and (D) and (E) are silly.

24. **A** *Understand the Question/Key Words*: She begins to calm down as what system takes back over? *Predict the Answer*: Her emergency response systems are turned off, and her parasympathetic system takes over. Don't confuse (B) with (A). Central and peripheral are not the right systems, so (C) and (D) are out. Get rid of (E)—the endocrine system does not control neurotransmitters.

25. **D** *Understand the Question/Key Words*: Circle *operant conditioning*. What does it mean? *Predict the Answer*: It has to do with "day-to-day operations" as opposed to classical conditioning. Use POE to eliminate (B) and (C) because they have nothing to do with conditioning. Choice (A) is an example of classical conditioning.

26. **E** *Understand the Question/Key Words*: Noticing a change in a stimulus depends on what? *Predict the Answer*: How intense the new stimulus is as compared with that of the existing stimulus. Choices (A) and (D) try to confuse you with technology—get rid of them. Choice (C) is silly—if you are present, so are your sensory modalities. Choice (B) is a "confuse the test-taker" answer.

27. **B** *Understand the Question/Key Words*: Why can't she see color in dim light? *Predict the Answer*: Color transduction (cones) requires more light than does the transduction of black and white images (rods). If you know that cones are color and rods are black and white, you can get rid of (A), (C), and (E). You can tell (D) is wrong because of "rapidly adjusting" to light changes.

28. **D** This is the phenomenon of trying to home in on a conversation of particular interest. It is the opposite of (C). It is not related to the effects of alcohol, as anticipated in (A), (B), and (E).

29. **B**   *Understand the Question/Key Words*: Circle *imprinting*. What does it mean? *Predict the Answer*: An animal will attach to the first moving object it sees, presumably its mother. If you don't know imprinting, you can still guess the meaning and use POE. Get rid of (A) and (C) because they don't sound like imprinting. Choice (E) is more of an example of a physiological response to positive attachment.

30. **B**   *Understand the Question/Key Words*: They used behavior modification that involved small rewards that can be traded in for bigger rewards. This is known as…*Predict the Answer*: Token economy. You should know that it is not (D) and (E) even if you are not sure what it is. It is also different from negative reinforcement, plus that is too easy an answer for question 99, so get rid of (A). Choice (C) might look good, but unfortunately, it's not a psychological concept. Token economy is the correct name.

Completely darken bubbles with a No. 2 pencil. If you make a mistake, be sure to erase mark completely. Erase all stray marks.

1. YOUR NAME: _____
(Print)   Last   First   M.I.

SIGNATURE: _____ **DATE:** ___/___/___

HOME ADDRESS: _____
(Print)   Number and Street

_____
City   State   Zip Code

PHONE NO. : _____
(Print)

IMPORTANT: Please fill in these boxes exactly as shown on the back cover of your test book.

2. TEST FORM
_____

6. DATE OF BIRTH

Month		Day		Year	
○ JAN					
○ FEB					
○ MAR	⓪	⓪	⓪	⓪
○ APR	①	①	①	①
○ MAY	②	②	②	②
○ JUN	③	③	③	③
○ JUL		④	④	④
○ AUG		⑤	⑤	⑤
○ SEP		⑥	⑥	⑥
○ OCT		⑦	⑦	⑦
○ NOV		⑧	⑧	⑧
○ DEC		⑨	⑨	⑨

3. TEST CODE   4. REGISTRATION NUMBER

⓪	Ⓐ	⓪	⓪	⓪	⓪	⓪	⓪	⓪	⓪	⓪
①	Ⓑ	①	①	①	①	①	①	①	①	①
②	Ⓒ	②	②	②	②	②	②	②	②	②
③	Ⓓ	③	③	③	③	③	③	③	③	③
④	Ⓔ	④	④	④	④	④	④	④	④	④
⑤	Ⓕ	⑤	⑤	⑤	⑤	⑤	⑤	⑤	⑤	⑤
⑥	Ⓖ	⑥	⑥	⑥	⑥	⑥	⑥	⑥	⑥	⑥
⑦		⑦	⑦	⑦	⑦	⑦	⑦	⑦	⑦	⑦
⑧		⑧	⑧	⑧	⑧	⑧	⑧	⑧	⑧	⑧
⑨		⑨	⑨	⑨	⑨	⑨	⑨	⑨	⑨	⑨

5. YOUR NAME

First 4 letters of last name				FIRST INIT	MID INIT
Ⓐ	Ⓐ	Ⓐ	Ⓐ	Ⓐ	Ⓐ
Ⓑ	Ⓑ	Ⓑ	Ⓑ	Ⓑ	Ⓑ
Ⓒ	Ⓒ	Ⓒ	Ⓒ	Ⓒ	Ⓒ
Ⓓ	Ⓓ	Ⓓ	Ⓓ	Ⓓ	Ⓓ
Ⓔ	Ⓔ	Ⓔ	Ⓔ	Ⓔ	Ⓔ
Ⓕ	Ⓕ	Ⓕ	Ⓕ	Ⓕ	Ⓕ
Ⓖ	Ⓖ	Ⓖ	Ⓖ	Ⓖ	Ⓖ
Ⓗ	Ⓗ	Ⓗ	Ⓗ	Ⓗ	Ⓗ
Ⓘ	Ⓘ	Ⓘ	Ⓘ	Ⓘ	Ⓘ
Ⓙ	Ⓙ	Ⓙ	Ⓙ	Ⓙ	Ⓙ
Ⓚ	Ⓚ	Ⓚ	Ⓚ	Ⓚ	Ⓚ
Ⓛ	Ⓛ	Ⓛ	Ⓛ	Ⓛ	Ⓛ
Ⓜ	Ⓜ	Ⓜ	Ⓜ	Ⓜ	Ⓜ
Ⓝ	Ⓝ	Ⓝ	Ⓝ	Ⓝ	Ⓝ
Ⓞ	Ⓞ	Ⓞ	Ⓞ	Ⓞ	Ⓞ
Ⓟ	Ⓟ	Ⓟ	Ⓟ	Ⓟ	Ⓟ
Ⓠ	Ⓠ	Ⓠ	Ⓠ	Ⓠ	Ⓠ
Ⓡ	Ⓡ	Ⓡ	Ⓡ	Ⓡ	Ⓡ
Ⓢ	Ⓢ	Ⓢ	Ⓢ	Ⓢ	Ⓢ
Ⓣ	Ⓣ	Ⓣ	Ⓣ	Ⓣ	Ⓣ
Ⓤ	Ⓤ	Ⓤ	Ⓤ	Ⓤ	Ⓤ
Ⓥ	Ⓥ	Ⓥ	Ⓥ	Ⓥ	Ⓥ
Ⓦ	Ⓦ	Ⓦ	Ⓦ	Ⓦ	Ⓦ
Ⓧ	Ⓧ	Ⓧ	Ⓧ	Ⓧ	Ⓧ
Ⓨ	Ⓨ	Ⓨ	Ⓨ	Ⓨ	Ⓨ
Ⓩ	Ⓩ	Ⓩ	Ⓩ	Ⓩ	Ⓩ

1. Ⓐ Ⓑ Ⓒ Ⓓ
2. Ⓐ Ⓑ Ⓒ Ⓓ
3. Ⓐ Ⓑ Ⓒ Ⓓ
4. Ⓐ Ⓑ Ⓒ Ⓓ
5. Ⓐ Ⓑ Ⓒ Ⓓ
6. Ⓐ Ⓑ Ⓒ Ⓓ
7. Ⓐ Ⓑ Ⓒ Ⓓ
8. Ⓐ Ⓑ Ⓒ Ⓓ
9. Ⓐ Ⓑ Ⓒ Ⓓ
10. Ⓐ Ⓑ Ⓒ Ⓓ
11. Ⓐ Ⓑ Ⓒ Ⓓ
12. Ⓐ Ⓑ Ⓒ Ⓓ
13. Ⓐ Ⓑ Ⓒ Ⓓ
14. Ⓐ Ⓑ Ⓒ Ⓓ
15. Ⓐ Ⓑ Ⓒ Ⓓ
16. Ⓐ Ⓑ Ⓒ Ⓓ
17. Ⓐ Ⓑ Ⓒ Ⓓ
18. Ⓐ Ⓑ Ⓒ Ⓓ
19. Ⓐ Ⓑ Ⓒ Ⓓ
20. Ⓐ Ⓑ Ⓒ Ⓓ
21. Ⓐ Ⓑ Ⓒ Ⓓ
22. Ⓐ Ⓑ Ⓒ Ⓓ
23. Ⓐ Ⓑ Ⓒ Ⓓ
24. Ⓐ Ⓑ Ⓒ Ⓓ
25. Ⓐ Ⓑ Ⓒ Ⓓ

26. Ⓐ Ⓑ Ⓒ Ⓓ
27. Ⓐ Ⓑ Ⓒ Ⓓ
28. Ⓐ Ⓑ Ⓒ Ⓓ
29. Ⓐ Ⓑ Ⓒ Ⓓ
30. Ⓐ Ⓑ Ⓒ Ⓓ
31. Ⓐ Ⓑ Ⓒ Ⓓ
32. Ⓐ Ⓑ Ⓒ Ⓓ
33. Ⓐ Ⓑ Ⓒ Ⓓ
34. Ⓐ Ⓑ Ⓒ Ⓓ
35. Ⓐ Ⓑ Ⓒ Ⓓ
36. Ⓐ Ⓑ Ⓒ Ⓓ
37. Ⓐ Ⓑ Ⓒ Ⓓ
38. Ⓐ Ⓑ Ⓒ Ⓓ
39. Ⓐ Ⓑ Ⓒ Ⓓ
40. Ⓐ Ⓑ Ⓒ Ⓓ
41. Ⓐ Ⓑ Ⓒ Ⓓ
42. Ⓐ Ⓑ Ⓒ Ⓓ
43. Ⓐ Ⓑ Ⓒ Ⓓ
44. Ⓐ Ⓑ Ⓒ Ⓓ
45. Ⓐ Ⓑ Ⓒ Ⓓ
46. Ⓐ Ⓑ Ⓒ Ⓓ
47. Ⓐ Ⓑ Ⓒ Ⓓ
48. Ⓐ Ⓑ Ⓒ Ⓓ
49. Ⓐ Ⓑ Ⓒ Ⓓ
50. Ⓐ Ⓑ Ⓒ Ⓓ

51. Ⓐ Ⓑ Ⓒ Ⓓ
52. Ⓐ Ⓑ Ⓒ Ⓓ
53. Ⓐ Ⓑ Ⓒ Ⓓ
54. Ⓐ Ⓑ Ⓒ Ⓓ
55. Ⓐ Ⓑ Ⓒ Ⓓ
56. Ⓐ Ⓑ Ⓒ Ⓓ
57. Ⓐ Ⓑ Ⓒ Ⓓ
58. Ⓐ Ⓑ Ⓒ Ⓓ
59. Ⓐ Ⓑ Ⓒ Ⓓ
60. Ⓐ Ⓑ Ⓒ Ⓓ
61. Ⓐ Ⓑ Ⓒ Ⓓ
62. Ⓐ Ⓑ Ⓒ Ⓓ
63. Ⓐ Ⓑ Ⓒ Ⓓ
64. Ⓐ Ⓑ Ⓒ Ⓓ
65. Ⓐ Ⓑ Ⓒ Ⓓ
66. Ⓐ Ⓑ Ⓒ Ⓓ
67. Ⓐ Ⓑ Ⓒ Ⓓ
68. Ⓐ Ⓑ Ⓒ Ⓓ
69. Ⓐ Ⓑ Ⓒ Ⓓ
70. Ⓐ Ⓑ Ⓒ Ⓓ
71. Ⓐ Ⓑ Ⓒ Ⓓ
72. Ⓐ Ⓑ Ⓒ Ⓓ
73. Ⓐ Ⓑ Ⓒ Ⓓ
74. Ⓐ Ⓑ Ⓒ Ⓓ
75. Ⓐ Ⓑ Ⓒ Ⓓ

The Princeton Review®

1. YOUR NAME:
(Print)   Last   First   M.I.

SIGNATURE: _____ DATE: ___/___/___

HOME ADDRESS: _____
(Print)   Number and Street

_____
        City   State   Zip Code

PHONE NO. : _____
(Print)

IMPORTANT: Please fill in these boxes exactly as shown on the back cover of your test book.

2. TEST FORM

_____

6. DATE OF BIRTH

Month	Day		Year	
○ JAN				
○ FEB				
○ MAR	⓪	⓪	⓪	⓪
○ APR	①	①	①	①
○ MAY	②	②	②	②
○ JUN	③	③	③	③
○ JUL		④	④	④
○ AUG		⑤	⑤	⑤
○ SEP		⑥	⑥	⑥
○ OCT		⑦	⑦	⑦
○ NOV		⑧	⑧	⑧
○ DEC		⑨	⑨	⑨

3. TEST CODE   4. REGISTRATION NUMBER

⓪	Ⓐ	⓪	⓪	⓪	⓪	⓪	⓪	⓪	⓪	⓪
①	Ⓑ	①	①	①	①	①	①	①	①	①
②	Ⓒ	②	②	②	②	②	②	②	②	②
③	Ⓓ	③	③	③	③	③	③	③	③	③
④	Ⓔ	④	④	④	④	④	④	④	④	④
⑤	Ⓕ	⑤	⑤	⑤	⑤	⑤	⑤	⑤	⑤	⑤
⑥	Ⓖ	⑥	⑥	⑥	⑥	⑥	⑥	⑥	⑥	⑥
⑦		⑦	⑦	⑦	⑦	⑦	⑦	⑦	⑦	⑦
⑧		⑧	⑧	⑧	⑧	⑧	⑧	⑧	⑧	⑧
⑨		⑨	⑨	⑨	⑨	⑨	⑨	⑨	⑨	⑨

5. YOUR NAME

First 4 letters of last name				FIRST INIT	MID INIT
Ⓐ	Ⓐ	Ⓐ	Ⓐ	Ⓐ	Ⓐ
Ⓑ	Ⓑ	Ⓑ	Ⓑ	Ⓑ	Ⓑ
Ⓒ	Ⓒ	Ⓒ	Ⓒ	Ⓒ	Ⓒ
Ⓓ	Ⓓ	Ⓓ	Ⓓ	Ⓓ	Ⓓ
Ⓔ	Ⓔ	Ⓔ	Ⓔ	Ⓔ	Ⓔ
Ⓕ	Ⓕ	Ⓕ	Ⓕ	Ⓕ	Ⓕ
Ⓖ	Ⓖ	Ⓖ	Ⓖ	Ⓖ	Ⓖ
Ⓗ	Ⓗ	Ⓗ	Ⓗ	Ⓗ	Ⓗ
Ⓘ	Ⓘ	Ⓘ	Ⓘ	Ⓘ	Ⓘ
Ⓙ	Ⓙ	Ⓙ	Ⓙ	Ⓙ	Ⓙ
Ⓚ	Ⓚ	Ⓚ	Ⓚ	Ⓚ	Ⓚ
Ⓛ	Ⓛ	Ⓛ	Ⓛ	Ⓛ	Ⓛ
Ⓜ	Ⓜ	Ⓜ	Ⓜ	Ⓜ	Ⓜ
Ⓝ	Ⓝ	Ⓝ	Ⓝ	Ⓝ	Ⓝ
Ⓞ	Ⓞ	Ⓞ	Ⓞ	Ⓞ	Ⓞ
Ⓟ	Ⓟ	Ⓟ	Ⓟ	Ⓟ	Ⓟ
Ⓠ	Ⓠ	Ⓠ	Ⓠ	Ⓠ	Ⓠ
Ⓡ	Ⓡ	Ⓡ	Ⓡ	Ⓡ	Ⓡ
Ⓢ	Ⓢ	Ⓢ	Ⓢ	Ⓢ	Ⓢ
Ⓣ	Ⓣ	Ⓣ	Ⓣ	Ⓣ	Ⓣ
Ⓤ	Ⓤ	Ⓤ	Ⓤ	Ⓤ	Ⓤ
Ⓥ	Ⓥ	Ⓥ	Ⓥ	Ⓥ	Ⓥ
Ⓦ	Ⓦ	Ⓦ	Ⓦ	Ⓦ	Ⓦ
Ⓧ	Ⓧ	Ⓧ	Ⓧ	Ⓧ	Ⓧ
Ⓨ	Ⓨ	Ⓨ	Ⓨ	Ⓨ	Ⓨ
Ⓩ	Ⓩ	Ⓩ	Ⓩ	Ⓩ	Ⓩ

---

1. Ⓐ Ⓑ Ⓒ Ⓓ
2. Ⓐ Ⓑ Ⓒ Ⓓ
3. Ⓐ Ⓑ Ⓒ Ⓓ
4. Ⓐ Ⓑ Ⓒ Ⓓ
5. Ⓐ Ⓑ Ⓒ Ⓓ
6. Ⓐ Ⓑ Ⓒ Ⓓ
7. Ⓐ Ⓑ Ⓒ Ⓓ
8. Ⓐ Ⓑ Ⓒ Ⓓ
9. Ⓐ Ⓑ Ⓒ Ⓓ
10. Ⓐ Ⓑ Ⓒ Ⓓ
11. Ⓐ Ⓑ Ⓒ Ⓓ
12. Ⓐ Ⓑ Ⓒ Ⓓ
13. Ⓐ Ⓑ Ⓒ Ⓓ
14. Ⓐ Ⓑ Ⓒ Ⓓ
15. Ⓐ Ⓑ Ⓒ Ⓓ
16. Ⓐ Ⓑ Ⓒ Ⓓ
17. Ⓐ Ⓑ Ⓒ Ⓓ
18. Ⓐ Ⓑ Ⓒ Ⓓ
19. Ⓐ Ⓑ Ⓒ Ⓓ
20. Ⓐ Ⓑ Ⓒ Ⓓ
21. Ⓐ Ⓑ Ⓒ Ⓓ
22. Ⓐ Ⓑ Ⓒ Ⓓ
23. Ⓐ Ⓑ Ⓒ Ⓓ
24. Ⓐ Ⓑ Ⓒ Ⓓ
25. Ⓐ Ⓑ Ⓒ Ⓓ

26. Ⓐ Ⓑ Ⓒ Ⓓ
27. Ⓐ Ⓑ Ⓒ Ⓓ
28. Ⓐ Ⓑ Ⓒ Ⓓ
29. Ⓐ Ⓑ Ⓒ Ⓓ
30. Ⓐ Ⓑ Ⓒ Ⓓ
31. Ⓐ Ⓑ Ⓒ Ⓓ
32. Ⓐ Ⓑ Ⓒ Ⓓ
33. Ⓐ Ⓑ Ⓒ Ⓓ
34. Ⓐ Ⓑ Ⓒ Ⓓ
35. Ⓐ Ⓑ Ⓒ Ⓓ
36. Ⓐ Ⓑ Ⓒ Ⓓ
37. Ⓐ Ⓑ Ⓒ Ⓓ
38. Ⓐ Ⓑ Ⓒ Ⓓ
39. Ⓐ Ⓑ Ⓒ Ⓓ
40. Ⓐ Ⓑ Ⓒ Ⓓ
41. Ⓐ Ⓑ Ⓒ Ⓓ
42. Ⓐ Ⓑ Ⓒ Ⓓ
43. Ⓐ Ⓑ Ⓒ Ⓓ
44. Ⓐ Ⓑ Ⓒ Ⓓ
45. Ⓐ Ⓑ Ⓒ Ⓓ
46. Ⓐ Ⓑ Ⓒ Ⓓ
47. Ⓐ Ⓑ Ⓒ Ⓓ
48. Ⓐ Ⓑ Ⓒ Ⓓ
49. Ⓐ Ⓑ Ⓒ Ⓓ
50. Ⓐ Ⓑ Ⓒ Ⓓ

51. Ⓐ Ⓑ Ⓒ Ⓓ
52. Ⓐ Ⓑ Ⓒ Ⓓ
53. Ⓐ Ⓑ Ⓒ Ⓓ
54. Ⓐ Ⓑ Ⓒ Ⓓ
55. Ⓐ Ⓑ Ⓒ Ⓓ
56. Ⓐ Ⓑ Ⓒ Ⓓ
57. Ⓐ Ⓑ Ⓒ Ⓓ
58. Ⓐ Ⓑ Ⓒ Ⓓ
59. Ⓐ Ⓑ Ⓒ Ⓓ
60. Ⓐ Ⓑ Ⓒ Ⓓ
61. Ⓐ Ⓑ Ⓒ Ⓓ
62. Ⓐ Ⓑ Ⓒ Ⓓ
63. Ⓐ Ⓑ Ⓒ Ⓓ
64. Ⓐ Ⓑ Ⓒ Ⓓ
65. Ⓐ Ⓑ Ⓒ Ⓓ
66. Ⓐ Ⓑ Ⓒ Ⓓ
67. Ⓐ Ⓑ Ⓒ Ⓓ
68. Ⓐ Ⓑ Ⓒ Ⓓ
69. Ⓐ Ⓑ Ⓒ Ⓓ
70. Ⓐ Ⓑ Ⓒ Ⓓ
71. Ⓐ Ⓑ Ⓒ Ⓓ
72. Ⓐ Ⓑ Ⓒ Ⓓ
73. Ⓐ Ⓑ Ⓒ Ⓓ
74. Ⓐ Ⓑ Ⓒ Ⓓ
75. Ⓐ Ⓑ Ⓒ Ⓓ

NOTES

NOTES

NOTES

NOTES

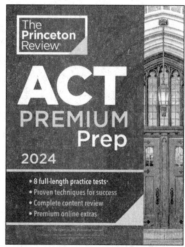